Swept Under the Rug

Swept Under the Rug

A Hidden History of Navajo Weaving

Kathy M'Closkey

PUBLISHED IN COOPERATION WITH
THE UNIVERSITY OF ARIZONA SOUTHWEST CENTER

UNIVERSITY OF NEW MEXICO PRESS
ALBUQUERQUE

A University of Arizona Southwest Center Book
Joseph C. Wilder, Series Editor
© 2002 by the University of New Mexico Press
All rights reserved.
First edition

Library of Congress Cataloging-in-Publication Data

M'Closkey, Kathy, 1943–
Swept under the rug : a hidden history of
Navajo weaving / Kathy M'Closkey.—1st ed.
p. cm.
"Published in cooperation with the
University of Arizona Southwest Center."
Includes bibliographical references and index.
ISBN 0-8263-2831-8 (cloth : alk. paper)
1. Navajo blankets—History. 2. Navajo blankets—Marketing.
3. Navajo textile fabrics—Collectors and collecting. 4. Navajo
weavers—Interviews. 5. Art as an investment—United States.
6. Hubbell, Lorenzo, d. 1942—Archives. 7. Hubbell Trading Post
National Historic Site (Ganado, Ariz.)—History—Sources.
I. University of Arizona. Southwest Center. II. Title
E99.N3 M315 2002
381'.45746'089972—dc21
2002009369

All tables are by Kathy M'Closkey.
DESIGN: MELISSA TANDYSH

Contents

List of Figures

Tables

Figures

Maps

Preface

The blankets and rugs woven by thousands of Navajo women living in the southwestern United States are highly desired "collectibles," as pre-1950 textiles typically sell for thousands of dollars at international auctions and galleries. The investment potential of *historic* weaving coupled with the production of copy weaving or knockoffs imported from Mexico and abroad have diminished the demand for contemporary textiles, which are woven by an estimated thirty thousand Reservation weavers. The recent popularity of the "Southwest look" created a demand for Navajo-like patterns. Entrepreneurs appropriated the designs pictured in lavishly illustrated books on historic textiles as models for third-world weavers to copy. Navajo patterns remain unprotected by copyright as the designs have been in the public domain for decades.

In this book I marshal evidence extracted from archival and published sources and interviews to reveal the cultural and economic consequences of multiple appropriations of Navajo weavers' patterns and production over the past century. Although Navajos are among the most studied peoples on earth, an enormous amount of evidence that reveals how the continued appropriation of weavers' production has sustained impoverishment languishes in archives. This book debunks the romanticist stereotyping of Navajo weavers and traders and reveals the magnitude of recent threats to the survival of a culturally vital activity. It also demonstrates the multiple ways in which Navajo women's production was marginalized by various authorities. Historically, weavers' abilities, the quality of their work, their industriousness—all were remarked on by missionaries, anthropologists, traders, and government personnel. Yet these authorities failed to *substantively* acknowledge the importance of weaving to the southwestern economy as it would have directly counteracted the prevailing Western attitudes about what constituted "appropriate behavior" and the proper sphere for women in general.

Researchers labeled the social relations and practices of female Navajo weavers and male ceremonial chanters dualistically. Although the opposition of sacred and profane in ethnographic works appears to balance activities of men and women in the religious and domestic spheres, it has had unfortunate consequences. Because of the assumption that sacred objects are not sold, symbolic anthropologists seldom discuss weaving in relation to Navajo religion. Moreover, anthropologists have drawn boundaries around economics, art, and religion, thereby determining what will be excluded. The categories constructed through language that are used by social scientists and applied to Navajo material culture have fractured our ability to perceive patterns. Adherence to such a research regime informed by an epistemology that splits cultural pattern from commodity has had devastating consequences for Navajo people.

My book is dedicated to the memory of thousands of women whose families survived because of their efforts. The photograph on the cover provides a visual analogue for my project. Popularly known as "The Unknown Weaver," it is actually Lottie Saunders, photographed by Milton Snow in September 1942 for the Navajo Arts and Crafts Guild. By shifting the emphasis from rugs to the weavers, a great deal can be gleaned from archives and oral histories. Indeed, this research has spawned a second project requiring another publication. What I had inadvertently traced in traders' business records were the fingerprints of free trade. The present book links weavers' production to regional business interests. The volume that will follow, tentatively titled *Double Jeopardy: Navajo Weavers, Reservation Traders and the Spectre of Free Trade,* will reposition Navajo weavers within the globalization and free trade literature.

Acknowledgments

Many people supported me throughout a prolonged period of research and writing. I wish first to extend my thanks to faculty who served as members of my doctoral committee at York University, Ontario, Canada: Penny Van Esterik and Peter Harries-Jones of the Department of Anthropology and Jim McDonald, formerly of the Royal Ontario Museum. Margaret Rodman, Liz Graham, Gerry Gold, Malcolm Blincow, and Bonnie Kettel also provided constructive insight into various aspects of my research. Other faculty and staff and students at York made my odyssey all the more enjoyable. Special thanks to Mané Arratia, B. Lynne Milgram, Rae Bridgman, Ann Howatt-Krahn, Virginia Caputo, Terri, David, Molly Aihoshi, and Pam Downe. Other Toronto friends that I wish to acknowledge are Cory Silverstein and Heather Howard-Bobiwash.

Staff and faculty of other universities also offered assistance. At the University of Windsor, I thank Ray Daly, Lynne Phillips, Suzan Ilcan, Max Hedley, Barry Adam, Barrie Ruth Straus, Rosemarie Denunzio, Branka Malesevic, and Suzanne Matheson. Special thanks to Joan Vastokas of Trent University, who served as my external assessor, Valda Blundell of Carleton University, and Sally Cole of Concordia University, Montreal. Members of the staff at the Special Collections Library, University of Arizona, Tucson, facilitated my archival research in numerous ways. Theresa Salazar, Peter Steere, Jan Kathy Davis, and Roger Myers were particularly helpful.

The National Park Service, Canyon de Chelly, provided lodging at reasonable cost during my research on the Navajo Reservation during fall 1992. Other Park Service employees who assisted me are Kathy Tabaha, Nancy Stone, Maralyn Yazzie, Ed Chamberlin, Bill Malone of Hubbell Trading Post National Historic Site, Ganado, Arizona, and Khaleel Saba of Tucson. Karen Ritts Benally and Tim Benally, Joann Kealiinohomoku, Martha Blue, Anita Caldwell, and the Museum of Northern Arizona loaned household goods or provided temporary accommodations during my fieldwork. I am grateful for the assistance of Clarenda Begay, Rosie Taylor, the Anderson Harvey family, Kee Ike, Carol Perry, Pearl Sunrise, Ray Showa, Eunice Kahn, Sarah Paul Begay, Bonnie Benally Yazzie, Wendy Weston, Irene Silentman, Isabel Dischini, Harry Walters, Klara Kelley, and the Sam Teller family of Newcomb. Tillie Begaye of Red Valley served as interpreter for a portion of my reservation fieldwork. More than thirty Navajo weavers gave graciously of their time by responding to my queries.

David Brugge translated several hundred weavers' names from the Hubbell archives. Martha Blue was generous beyond measure, and much useful information emerged after I perused archival material she so willingly shared. Rahim Akbarzadeh surveyed mountains of material searching for elusive but important information housed at Special Collections, Cline Library, Northern Arizona University, and at the Museum of Northern Arizona, Flagstaff. One could not ask for a more perspicacious colleague than Rahim. My thanks to staff at both institutions, especially Karen Underhill and Michael O'Hara. Canadian students Suzanne Friemann, Kevin Manuel, and Denise Williams served as adept research assistants and Julie Cobb of the Newberry Library, Chicago, unearthed crucial material housed at that venerable institution. I appreciate the assistance of librarians at the State Archives of New Mexico, Santa Fe; the Zimmerman Library, University of New Mexico; the Huntington Library, Los Angeles; the Newberry Library, Chicago; The Museum of International Folk Art, Santa Fe; and the Heard Museum, Phoenix.

Christian Schnyder drew the Navajo loom (appendix III).

Anthropologists Molly Mullin and Dorothy Washburn provided challenging insights into important aspects of my research. I am grateful for the editorial assistance provided by Christine Eber, Beth King, Sheila Berg, and Barrie Ruth Straus. Jim Faris, Charlotte Frisbie, Bea Medicine, Helen Tanner, and Alice Kehoe served as venerable mentors. Katina Simmons, Jennifer Denetdale, Mark Bahti, and Adriel Heisey offered support and thoughtful conversation.

The Social Science and Humanities Research Council (SSHRC) of Canada awarded four years of predoctoral support that allowed me the privilege of returning to the university to research and weave a different narrative. Additional financial aid was provided by the Zdenka Volovka Fellowship in Art History (1995), the Graduate Fund for fieldwork (1992), and a three-year operating grant from SSHRC (1997–2001).

I gratefully acknowledge the financial assistance and collegiality of the Southwest Center at the University of Arizona, which provided a subvention for my book as a contribution to their Southwest Series. Kudos to director Joe Wilder, the intrepid David Yetman, and recently retired Adela Hice. I appreciate the perceptive comments by two unnamed reviewers and additional editorial help from

Durwood Ball and my effervescent editor, Ev Schlatter. Thanks also to indexer Nancy Ford and book designer Melissa Tandysh. This book would not exist were it not for the outstanding word-processing abilities of two staff members at the University of Windsor. Dina Labelle, secretary in the Department of Sociology and Anthropology, and Lorraine Cantin, of Document Services, performed miracles with text that had suffered from overexposure to software applications.

These lengthy acknowledgments would be incomplete without an expression of my profound gratitude to my family, who provided invaluable support and encouragement. My husband, Bob, supplied computer expertise as he organized the production of several illustrations. More important, he provided unstinting support, not to mention numberless gourmet meals over the years for a project too long in completion. Our daughter, Karen, put her drafting talents to work and produced figures 3 and 4. My thanks to her and her partner Keith Van der Sys. Our son, Bob, provided encouragement, stimulating conversations, and, recently, our first grandchild, Luca Giovanni, in concert with his dear wife, Raffaella.

1

Introduction

On 9 October 1992, while interviewing weavers on the Navajo Reservation, I heard bell hooks speak on the Quincentenary at Northern Arizona University. She broke into tears while quoting Chickasaw Linda Hogan on the legacy of Christopher Columbus:

> What has been done to the land has been done to the people; we are the same thing. And all of us are injured by the culture that separates us from the natural world and our inner lives, all of us wounded by a system that grew out of such genocide, destruction to the land, and slavery . . . we Native Americans were invisible or we were commodities. (1992:91)

Colonizers not only separated native peoples from the land. They also appropriated much of what anthropologists designated as "material culture." Although it is well documented that colonizers broke or ignored most treaties between nation-states and indigenous peoples, researchers have paid scant attention to the more insidious acquisitions of native peoples' material culture. As the evidence in this book illustrates, the appropriation of aboriginal material culture was closely related to the loss of native homelands and only slightly less devastating.

Today, many of the most valuable textiles created historically by aboriginal peoples are ensconced in museums or owned by wealthy private collectors and dealers. Prominent auction houses located in major cities around the world feature sales of indigenous material culture in the form of "collectibles" that not infrequently reap hundreds of thousands of dollars for connoisseurs (Sotheby's 1989). Meanwhile, the descendants of the original makers remain impoverished producers. Unlike foodstuffs grown by peasants and consumed shortly after harvest, handwoven textiles frequently outlast their makers. The perpetual circulation and recirculation of their ancestors' creations continues to have inimical effects on contemporary producers.

This book unearths evidence exposing the consequences of multiple forms of appropriation of a popular "collectible"—the blankets and rugs woven by Navajo women of the southwestern United States over the past two hundred years. It tracks the complex connections and financial success between the local and regional business empires subject to global market pressures and links the past to the present in a manner not previously attempted. The story that emerges does not concur with the extant literature on the history of Navajo weaving. However, the information I have uncovered is corroborated in various ways by Navajos I have interviewed.

For a portion of the historic section I analyzed information extracted from trading post business records of the Hubbell family housed at the University of Arizona and government documents either untapped or underutilized by other investigators. To examine the economic consequences of the recent volatile investment market, I incorporate information from auction house and gallery catalogs, newspaper and magazine articles, and museum publications and web-sites and juxtapose these to interviews with contemporary Navajo weavers.

During the 1980s, periodic visits to the Southwest confirmed that an increasing number of retail establishments advertised and sold historic Navajo textiles. The old blankets were displayed as prized works in exclusive galleries catering to an elite market. Bookstores increasingly featured publications by dealers, collectors, and museologists highlighting historic textiles. With greater frequency, the early-nineteenth-century "chief's blankets" were described in terms formerly reserved for fine art. I wondered what sort of effect this activity was having on contemporary Navajo weavers. I knew that out of a population of more than two hundred thousand Navajos, there were thousands of women (and a few men) weaving on the reservation. I also became aware that in tandem with the heightened interest in the historic textiles, imported rugs incorporating Navajo patterns woven by "Indian" weavers were selling at the lower end of the retail scale at many tourist outlets adjacent to the reservation.

In 1987 the anthropologist Gary Witherspoon published a monograph that accompanied an exhibition of Navajo weaving at the Museum of Northern Arizona in Flagstaff. He estimated that at least one hundred thousand weavers had woven more than one million blankets and rugs over two centuries. To a weaver like myself, these are astonishing figures. Yet these women are absent from historical records. Although several books exist on how to weave a Navajo rug, most publications today cater to collectors. Most literature on the subject highlights the influence of a handful of traders. But traders cannot obtain textiles without

Figure 1. "Unknown Weaver," by Milton Snow. Courtesy of the Navajo Nation Museum, Window Rock, Arizona.

weavers: emphasizing traders and individual historic textiles has caused thousands of weavers to vanish (fig. 1).

This book is an attempt to initiate writing these women into the historical record. Given the systemic poverty on the reservation and the magnitude of past and present production, clearly Navajos were not the beneficiaries of their prodigious output. I felt that the Hubbell Papers would hold clues to a number of questions worthy of investigation—questions that puzzled me but remained unaddressed in the published literature. I became aware of major discrepancies in the literature concerning rates of returns to weavers, for it contained inflated figures. Yet Hubbell is eulogized as the "ideal" trader. Indeed, he is deemed the czar of Navajo trade and the father of the Navajo rug. If the weavers who traded with him appeared to receive little in exchange, was it much worse for weavers who bartered with traders who lacked the reputation for fairness that Hubbell enjoyed? It seemed as if the more the Navajos wove, the poorer they became. If that was the case, why would these women continue to weave?

As a weaver, I feel it is unconscionable that a handful of entrepreneurs continue to receive credit for the prodigious production of thousands of women. One way to write these women's contributions into the historical record is to examine primary evidence that can shed light on this refractory problem. Recently Kathy Howard (1999) researched the history of Elle of Ganado, one of the handful of Navajo weavers whose names have come down to us through history. To acknowledge a weaver who wove in the public eye for decades, under the auspices of the Fred Harvey Company, is laudable. But it is important to remember that Elle had thousands of sisters (fig. 2).

Although thousands of weavers currently reside on the reservation, it is increasingly difficult to find contemporary Navajo weaving in a number of southwestern cities, even in Albuquerque, New Mexico, located less than two hours from the southeastern border of the Navajo Reservation (Brugge 1996). However, tourists will encounter little difficulty purchasing imported copy weaving (knockoffs) or historic Navajo textiles there. Indeed, immediately on leaving the airport one sees a colorful billboard emblazoned with the name and telephone number of one of the largest historic textile dealers in the region.

Archival Research

My fieldwork had two components. The first portion involved five months of intensive research in 1992, in archives stored at the University of Arizona's Special Collections Library. This library houses the collected papers of the Lorenzo Hubbell family, traders to the Navajo from 1876 to 1967. Although

Figure 2. "Lottie Saunders Weaving," by Milton Snow. Courtesy of the Navajo Nation Museum, Window Rock, Arizona.

the Hubbells owned more than thirty businesses on or adjacent to the reservation over time, the Ganado, Arizona, post was the single most important post in the history of Navajo trade (Blue 2000). Its unbroken history spanned eighty years, and it continues to function as a trading post under the auspices of the United States Park Service. Consequently it is the oldest continuously operated business in all of northern Arizona. Because it remained in one family for decades, business and personal records remained intact. When Dorothy Hubbell turned over the post and contents to the Park Service in 1967, government personnel discovered 250 cubic feet of papers stored in one hundred crates, boxes, and trunks in the warehouse, barn, and a porch behind the house. Robert Utley had previously prepared a special report on the post for the National Survey of Historic Sites and Buildings. He made the following comments about the papers:

> We found them badly disorganized, laden with quantities of Arizona sand, and in some places suffering from the attacks of rodents. We concluded, however, that not only could most of them be salvaged, but that, properly organized and studied they would yield a treasure of

information about Navajo trading. For a study of the pattern of the Navajo trade, in fact, they are probably the most valuable single collection in existence. (1959:97)

After tabulating relevant data from Hubbell's papers, I perused extant literature to search for similar information to use as a point of comparison or contrast in my project. Although helpful in many respects, other sources proved of somewhat limited use as the information was too general or interpretations of annual cumulative figures too ambiguous for my purposes. Unlike Bailey and Bailey (1986) and Weiss (1984), I chose to illustrate how wealth accrued to the regional mercantile houses while the Navajos became impoverished. More detailed information such as Adams's work (1963) covered the 1950s, a period too recent for my purposes. Social security, welfare, and wool subsidies were available to eligible Navajos by then.

This is the first study to extract detailed financial information from records directly related to Navajo trade before 1950. As Aberle (1966:33) notes, "A better picture of Navajo livelihood will depend on future use of traders' records, diaries and letters, and perhaps of the Navajo Agency Letter Books." To my knowledge the only other comparable records in existence that span the same period are the unprocessed Babbitt Papers housed in Special Collections at Northern Arizona University.

Reservation Fieldwork

The second component of my fieldwork involved moving to the reservation in fall 1992 to interview Navajo weavers. This time was chosen as it was after the monsoon season and resumption of school. I interviewed more than thirty weavers, including follow-up visits with several families.[1] I also excerpted information from weavers' interviews conducted by Clarenda Begay, curator at Ganado, during 1985–86. Additional information was drawn from a series of oral histories that Park Service employees collected from elderly Navajos in the early 1970s. I interviewed several other weavers who lived off-reservation. During the personal interviews, my questions were brief and fairly general, and I asked if weavers would share stories related to weaving and their memoirs of trade relations. I brought along a handwoven jacket as a demonstration of my ability to weave. In March 1994 I attended the conference "Navajo Weaving since the Sixties," organized by Ann Hedlund and sponsored by the Heard Museum in Phoenix. More than two dozen weavers ranging from teenagers to women in their eighties spoke about what weaving meant to them. Many weavers attended with their families, and some of the commentary was translated into English or Navajo because of the number of unilingual speakers.

Prelude to Reconceptualizing Navajo Weaving

Most literature on Navajo weaving begins with a short paragraph from the Creation Story describing the mythological origins of the loom and weaving tools (Reichard [1934] 1974; Wheat 1984). With few exceptions, authors then launch into a description of its historical origins. Everything was borrowed: sheep from the Spanish, the upright loom from the Pueblos, dyes from the Anglos, and designs from traders. Because none of the "ingredients" were indigenous, most authors disclaim any symbolism or sacred associations attached to the woven textiles (Amsden [1934] 1975; Kent 1985; Reichard [1936] 1968; Wheat 1984). Given the increased commodification of weaving during this century, it is not coincidental that only the first extensive publication on the topic (James [1914] 1974) locates the importance of weaving in the Navajo Creation Story, discusses symbolism, and provides the names of more than a dozen weavers. Twenty years later, Charles Avery Amsden published *Navajo Weaving: Its Technique and History,* considered the earliest authoritative text on the subject. An anthropologist affiliated with the Southwest Museum, Amsden shifts the focus to tools, techniques, and trader influence. The role of weaving in the Navajo Creation Story is relegated to a footnote, a charming bit of myth. Subsequent publications typically emphasized production for external markets, foreign influences, and materials, thereby submerging any sacred associations that weaving may have had for Navajos (Kent 1985; Reichard 1936; Rodee 1981; Tanner 1968; Underhill [1956] 1983; Wheat 1988).

The paradigms of cultural particularism and acculturation dominated anthropology when much weaving-related research was published by ethnographers: Reichard ([1934] 1974, [1936] 1968, [1939] 1971) and Underhill ([1956] 1983). As a student of Franz Boas, Gladys Reichard's rich and varied body of work was greatly influenced by her mentor. Her research with Navajos spanned the gamut of sociocultural life, material culture and daily activities, social and economic organization, religion and ritual, art and literature, language and symbolism. The collection of objective facts, in conjunction with the perception that Indians selected or rejected individual traits from the dominant culture, shaped the perspectives adopted by these ethnographers. Reichard (1950) perceived symbols as isomorphic elements relevant to the sacred sphere of elaborate Navajo ceremonials. The aesthetics relevant to Navajo weaving lay in the area of decorative design (Reichard [1936] 1968). This perspective of weaving as a functional, secular commodity dominated published literature on the subject for nearly fifty years. Until recently, Vogt's (1961) acculturation model continued to influence most museologists' publications (Hedlund 1983, 1989a, 1989b, 1990; Kent 1985; Rodee 1981; Tanner 1968; Wheat 1977, 1984).

Rather than emphasize the commodity aspects of Navajo weaving, Witherspoon (1987; Witherspoon and Peterson 1995) suggests that weaving has played a major role in perpetuating Navajo lifeways. He argues for an interpretive approach, suggesting that the vigor and endurance of Navajo people is culturally inspired, not materially determined. A linguist, Witherspoon is married to a Navajo weaver. However, his perspective is critiqued as overly structuralist and antiempiricist by several museologists (Hedlund 1988, 1989a; Wheat 1989). The alternative embraced by museologists currently redefines Navajo weaving as "art." However, it is not enough to discard the word "craft" and add weaving to the art sphere. Neither category adequately describes the context of weaving in Navajo society itself, because the basic tenet of the Western concept of art maintains that the essential value of material culture lies outside the context of its meaning and use (M'Closkey 1996b). In support of this reclassification, the description posited for ethnoaesthetics is "how different societies decide what makes a design look good or bad" (Hedlund 1994a:36). This is not a genuine reformulation. It makes use of an old recipe, adding another scrap to the quilt of culture patched together with bits of disparate information.

The museologists' perspective that continues to dominate the subject emphasizes the empirical domain. What is measurable becomes real. What constitutes knowledge depends on an agreed-upon methodology. Pictured in books or hung in exhibits, textiles are displayed isomorphically. Dimensions, types of yarn, dyes, provenance, and so forth are labeled adjacent to the piece. Cut out of its context, a Navajo rug equals the sum of its parts. The isomorphic facts objectively collected according to museological practices confers its own kind of value.[2]

The aesthetics currently embraced in most texts on Navajo weaving are variants familiar to individuals versed in classical art history. They concern the philosophy of taste and standards of beauty, always referred to the individual. Presumed to be disinterested and value-free, grounded in Kantian idealism, classical aesthetics espouses a type of universalized "atomism." Although at first glance, aesthetics appears to be qualitative and value-free, it frequently is translated into quantified form. For example, a historic textile deemed properly balanced according to formalist Western aesthetic notions will command a higher price at the auction or retail outlet. One type of value is perpetually valorized and continually manifested in quantified form—the price (Sotheby's 1989). Thus the cash value of objects becomes their primary value. The most blatant example of this quantification occurred in 1989, when a nineteenth-century Navajo "chief's blanket," appraised by Sotheby's at $150,000, sold for $522,000.

Clues in the literature on the Navajos aid in explicating Navajo aesthetics (Begay 1996; Thomas 1996; Willink and Zolbrod 1996; Witherspoon 1987; Witherspoon and Peterson 1995). But few clues come from publications by museologists (Kent 1985; Rodee 1981; Wheat 1984), in which the only patterns privileged are the empirical designs woven into individual rugs. Most extant history of Navajo textiles reflects the imposition of the dominant society's ideas. Emphasis is placed on the material, the empirical (fig. 3).

A Striking Lesson

An experience during my archival research in 1992 serves as a graphic example of how the construction of Navajo textile history and the textiles' display and preservation reveal the views, values, and assumptions of the caretakers. I met a graduate student from the reservation who was also a weaver. I had obtained slides of a dozen historic Navajo textiles that form part of an extensive collection of a major museum located in the southwestern United States. The textiles I chose for study were very similar to those woven in the Ganado area at the turn of the century. It is quite likely that several of them had been bartered to the Hubbells. I was interested in calculating production time of individual textiles to demonstrate the appropriation of surplus labor by traders (see chapter 4). Detailed information was available on each textile. The dimensions, number of warps and wefts, and types of fleece, yarns, and dyes had been determined. All information was collated on documentation sheets designed for this study. Indeed, the detailed analyses represented the state of the art in textile analysis. Because I also had slides of individual pieces, the weaver-student would be able to assess the technical complexity of the designs observed in the rugs. All this information would help me calculate the number of hours necessary to weave the textile depicted in each slide.

In anticipation of our appointment, I gathered photocopied notes containing all the information the museum had collected on each Navajo textile. We met over dinner and I explained my plan, hoping that she would be willing to help for an agreed-upon fee. Although I am a weaver, I felt it would be more appropriate for a Navajo to take on this task. She spent considerable time scrutinizing the slides, but when she saw the many pages of data, including the accession numbers and other information "quantifying" the weavings, she became

VISIBLE
COMMODITY RELATIONS

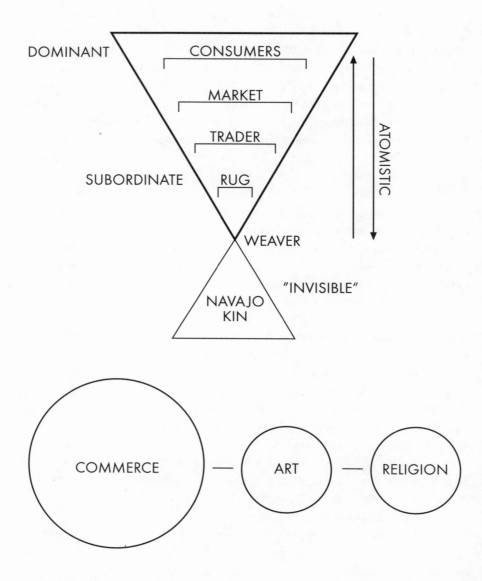

Figure 3. Visible Commodity Relations. Drawn by Karen M'Closkey.

very upset. She swept up the stack of papers and pushed them aside. Raising her voice, she demanded, "What does *this* have to do with Navajo weaving?!" I was quite taken aback, but her strong reaction drove home the realization of how insulting it must be to have objects of great cultural importance reduced to a series of numbers. This experience convinced me that situating Navajo weaving in a typical museum context is destructive. It jams a process-oriented activity dependent on a relational topology, one that perpetuates culture, into the straightjacket of modernism's assumptions.

When I had collected the data sheets and copies of slides from museum personnel the previous week, I remarked to the curator that, as good as the documentation was, there was one piece of information missing—the weight. After spending months with the Hubbell Papers, I knew that each of the textiles, regardless of its current value, had been acquired from the weaver by weight. However, my Navajo dinner companion obviously felt strongly about a deeper issue. What she felt was missing could not be put into words. What she knew had been eradicated by fiat was the proper context. More recently, an active weaver lamented, "All of the emphasis on old textiles leads to neglect of contemporary weavers. They've forgotten about the soul of the weaver; they've forgotten about the soul in the rug." Information from Navajo weavers and family members and selected publications reveals that the Navajo rug is part of a much larger pattern.

Historically, textiles were marginalized in the domains of art, religion, and commerce (Weiner and Schneider 1991). Because of a number of unquestioned assumptions grounded in binary oppositions, textile production by Navajo women has fallen between the paradigmatic cleavages in anthropology. The development of ideas related to gendered spheres of productive and nonproductive labor, art and craft, and sacred and secular spheres were dichotomized and provided the context to justify the absence of thousands of female weavers from the historical record.

Feminist Political Economy

Feminist political economy highlights the centrality of gender relations to the relations of production in both noncapitalist and capitalist economies. Many scholars now recognize that gender relations in many parts of the world have been transformed under the successive impacts of colonization, Westernization, and international capitalism (Albers and Medicine 1983). The study of gender is not just a subdiscipline; it crosscuts economic, political, and cognitive anthropology (Moore 1988:6).

The "domestic/public" dichotomy suggested by Rosaldo and Lamphere

(1974) emerged as an important debate during the 1970s. It is often presented as a description of social reality rather than as a cultural statement masking relations that are highly problematic and ideological. The public/private split was nowhere deeper than in Victorian thought. The Victorian doctrine of separate male and female spheres was quite central to Victorian sociology (Kehoe 1983; Rosaldo 1980:402). Scientists, philosophers, and social scientists "naturalized" the division of labor, which in turn formed the basis of the public/private dichotomy (Sacks 1982:88, 99). Moore summarizes "the prevailing nineteenth-century ideology of the home as refuge":

> [T]he family, the home and the "domestic" are conceptualized as a single unit which is defined in juxtaposition to the "public" sphere of work, business and politics: i.e., the market relations of capitalism. The latter involve relations of competition, negotiation and contract which Western society views as separate from and opposed to the relations of intimacy and nurturance associated with the family and the home. (1988:23)

This axiomatic assumption shaped the perceptions of government agents to the Navajos who for decades routinely charted the escalation in textile production. Thousands of Navajo women were perceived as dark-skinned housewives weaving in their spare time for pin money (Dockstader 1976; Maxwell [1963] 1984). This so-called leisure-time activity produced for external markets was ultimately valued at $1 million annually by 1930 (Amsden [1934] 1975; Luomala 1938).

Since the 1970s Marxist feminists have made major contributions in acknowledging both the importance and the inadequacies of Marxist theory (Bennholdt-Thomsen 1988:46–49). The Marxist notion of productive labor has created the greatest barrier to an understanding of women's work in both capitalist and socialist contexts (Mies 1988). Mies's study (1982) of more than 150,000 Narsapur lace makers highlights the way women's work is defined by a particular set of interconnections between reproductive and productive relations. She provides a detailed analysis of the structure of the crocheted lace industry and the consequences of defining women as nonworking housewives, categorizing their labor as leisure-time activity. Rapid expansion occurred after 1970, and 95 percent of the foreign exchange earnings from the export of handicrafts from the state of Andhra Pradesh came from the lace industry of Narsapur. Yet these women were missing from census records. Mies's study contains interesting parallels with the Navajo story. In both instances, women's household production frequently provided most of the (meager) income or goods. Mies's research demonstrates how women's insertion into capitalist relations of production does not depend on a separation between home and workplace (Moore 1988:85).

However, Navajos provide an interesting exception to Mies's study on several accounts. Gender relations were not significantly altered within Navajo society after merchants began actively trading on the reservation. Navajos are matrilineal and favor matrilocality. The most recent comprehensive studies indicate that gender relations remain quite egalitarian, especially in the remoter areas of the reservation (Lamphere 1977; McCloskey 1999; Witherspoon 1975). Women's status seems not to have decreased. Pastoralism was not imposed on them. Women's ownership and control of animals was not undermined by the traders. Although textile production greatly increased, relations of production remained intact. However, women lost control of marketing of their textiles, as traders had territorial monopolies and bartered perishables and cloth, then shipped bales of rugs to off-reservation markets. Although Navajo textiles became increasingly commodified when marketed by the traders, Navajo social relations continued to emphasize cooperation and reciprocity, especially among close kin (Lamphere 1977; Mitchell and Frisbie 2001; Witherspoon 1975).

Postmodernist Readings of Women's Woven Collectibles

The resurgence of material culture studies reflected in texts by Appadurai (1986) and Miller (1987) has intersected with gender in an intriguing manner. Recent interest in globalization and craft production is reflected in publications by Berlo (1991), Cohen (1990, 1998), Grimes and Milgram (2000), Nash (1993), Stephen (1991a, 1991b, 1993), and Tice (1995). The marked shift in discourse from women as victims of patriarchy and external market factors to women as subjects, as active negotiators demonstrating agency, expresses the importance of textiles as a form of cultural identity. Such texts reflect the response to the asymmetry of women's "power" highlighted in the 1970s feminist literature described above.

Clifford has remarked on the accelerating pace of the postmodern world, signified by increasing eclecticism and stylistic hybridity: "[A]rt collecting and culture collecting now take place within the changing field of counter discourses, syncretisms, and reappropriations, originated both outside and inside 'the West.' (1988:236)"

Commenting on the intersection of this changing field with textile production, Berlo remarks:

American and European textile designers freely take from native sources, proclaiming as their own those designs drawn from Navajo . . . originals. . . . [T]his is part of a long artistic tradition in the West. . . . [T]he contemporary indigenous textile aesthetic is, in many regions, an aesthetic of appropriation and accumulation. (1991:452)

In her research with Zapotec weavers, Stephen (1991a, 1991b, 1993) provides confirmation of the magnitude of appropriation. For more than twenty years, entrepreneurs have copied popular Navajo patterns illustrated in numerous texts and had the designs woven in Mexico and other parts of the world. In an article titled "Weaving in the Fast Lane," Stephen (1993) documents the exponential increase in orders for Navajo-style patterns that kept thousands of Zapotec weavers working overtime during the 1980s. She comments on the alacrity with which Zapotec weavers appropriated the designs provided by entrepreneurs. In 1989, while visiting the Hubbell Trading Post, Stephen (1993:51) spotted a pamphlet informing consumers how to distinguish the genuine Navajo product from imported copies (Bennett 1973). After a discussion with several weavers at the post, she remarked that they "resented the intrusion on their market and the 'stealing' of their designs."

Documentation and confirmation of this appropriation without critique sanctions an activity that threatens Navajo lifeways. It also provides an intellectual rationale for equating the symbols of consumerism with emergent types of communal identity. Stephen's commentary evokes the image of anthropologist as neutral observer-reporter of commodified cultural formation. Such a stance gives intellectual support to this kind of activity. Noting that neoconservatives require free markets on a global scale to permit the spread of consumerism, Harries-Jones provokes reconsideration of this postmodern position:

[T]his gives rise to numerous epistemic problems in anthropology especially where there is a spatial divorce of cultural expression from the intimacies of a defined local space in which cultural forms were hitherto socially reproduced. . . . [T]o continue to treat culture as epistemological object within a defined space . . . and to insist that anthropologists remain neutral observers of this context is, in fact, to take an intellectual position about globalization. Such a position allows little room for critique of the process in which commodified forms of culture are disembedded from active collectivity and marketed through simulations of cultural performance. . . . [W]e need to stand as witnesses, uncovering [such] sets of relations. (1993:9)

The appropriation of popular Navajo patterns is not just a pilfering of pretty designs. It is theft of a way of life. It threatens the destruction of activities vital to Navajo culture. And it is one of the more recent threats that perpetuate processes begun more than a century ago.

Postmodernist readings of cultural reformulations through appropriations demonstrate a deficient understanding of aesthetics. To reconceptualize an alternative interpretation in relation to Navajo weaving, it is necessary to reconfigure the concept of aesthetics that continues to influence Western discourses on forms of material culture. Only by reformulating outmoded concepts of aesthetics can we surmise the threat to Navajo livelihood. Because weaving fell between the paradigmatic cleavages in the discipline (the bifurcation of the political economy and symbolic spheres), it is impossible to adequately acknowledge, much less critique, the multiple appropriations in most of the extant literature on the subject.[3]

Reconceptualizing Navajo Weaving

Scholars working with Navajos in various capacities have recently published significantly different findings on aspects of Navajo culture from former generations of colleagues (Downer 1990; Faris 1990; Griffin-Pierce 1992; Kelley and Francis 1994; Ortiz 1999; Willink and Zolbrod 1996; Witherspoon and Peterson 1995). During his presentation at a Navajo Studies conference, Alan Downer (1990:203), director of the department of historic preservation, noted real concern among Native Americans regarding historic, archaeological, and cultural sites that are the physical manifestations of their cultures. This concern goes beyond recognizing the sites as symbols of a bygone era, because they continue to be part of an ongoing system of beliefs and actions in a way that historic sites normally are not in larger American society. In fact, these sites are frequently viewed as central to cultural self-definition. In their insightful text, *Navajo Sacred Places,* Kelley and Francis (1994:145) enlarge on Downer's theme and critique the demarcation of sacred places on a map. Expunging a sacred place from its context fractures the meaning of that place in the landscape and culture as a whole.

Faris (1993) has critiqued anthropologists' dismissive attitudes regarding Navajo histories and stories juxtaposed to the West's knowledge of the facts. Just as the Bible becomes a code by which Christian believers organize their lives, the Navajo Creation Story continues to serve as an organizing principle for many Navajos. Because weaving is produced for an external market, most scholars perceive it as a secular commodity, an isomorphic item of material culture that is tinged with myth and history (Amsden [1934] 1975; Bailey and

Bailey 1986; Hedlund 1990; Kent 1985; Reichard [1934] 1974, [1936] 1968, [1939] 1971; Rodee 1981; Tanner 1968; Underhill [1956] 1983; Wheat 1976b, 1977, 1984). These assumptions are grounded in a faulty epistemology that unfortunately is currently dominant.

The anthropocentric nature of Euro-American philosophy emphasizes a linear world filled with objects and individuals, in marked contrast to non-Western peoples' perceptions of a more cosmocentric world (Means 1988; Walters 1989, 1992; Wilden 1980; Witherspoon and Peterson 1995). Non-Western societies such as the Navajo have different root metaphors. Because they do not share the Greco-Roman/Renaissance heritage, they "see" the world differently. Not only has an epistemology inappropriate to the subject been adopted, but errors have been compounded by the explicit or implicit insistence on the "truthfulness" of our knowledge of the "objective" world vis-à-vis the interpretations or subjectiveness of the worldviews of non-Western peoples whose cultures were seen as objects of [our] study (Faris 1993; Witherspoon and Peterson 1995). The descriptions we develop reveal properties of the observers because knowledge always bears the mark of its producers. Goody (1977:36) has warned of the pitfalls associated with "objective" thought: "The folk-taxonomy we develop brings order and understanding into a complex universe. But the order is illusory, the meaning superficial. Binary systems and categorizations are often value-laden and ethnocentric."

Anthropologists have produced numerous publications on Navajo religion and art. But the Navajo artist Conrad House says,

> We have no word for art, we have no word for religion. Because there is no need . . . to separate those concepts away from our real life. Because real life has all that. . . . How you live is an art. How you go about is a religion. (Cited in Jones 1994:127)

To perceive patterns, we must be wary of categories and dispense with dualisms. A primary example of a dualism endemic to Western epistemology is represented in the split between substance and form. The path followed by empiricists (including museologists) that continues to be well traveled by social scientists has emphasized the material world of substance:

> In science we have been taught to measure and weigh things. But relationships cannot be weighed and measured—they need to be mapped. And measuring and mapping are two very different approaches. This is the tension between substance and form. The study of substance

begins with the question, "what is it made of?" while the study of form queries "what is its pattern?" (Systems Thinker 1994:6)

The study of form requires attention to context. The etymology of the word is derived from the Latin verb *contexere,* to braid, weave, connect, or unite; and the word "text," from *textus,* web, tissue, texture, or structure. This is a most fitting word for a book on weaving.

An epistemology of pattern and form assumes that people operate within fields of habitual or repetitive activity, expressing customary rules of relationship. Theories of perception and cognition are built on the fundamentals of information and communication—habit and learning modified by experience (Rappaport 1999:410–11). From a communication perspective, a phenomenon can be known only in context. Wholes have properties that parts do not have. Thus it is inappropriate to reduce a Navajo rug to its material components.

A New Formulation for Understanding Navajo Aesthetics

The dualisms supported and manifested in the Western world separating mind from body, sacred from profane, create a barrier that distances us from an understanding of Navajo aesthetics. Differences in language and culture compounded with the inappropriateness of translating from primary unconscious processes to conscious purposiveness of language creates barriers that block a more holistic understanding of Navajo aesthetics and consequently Navajo weaving.

Navajo aesthetics is not concerned with an abstract concept of beauty divorced from process. Navajo weavers' feeling for *hózhǫ́*(beauty, harmony, order) encompasses far more than the Western concept of classical aesthetics that condenses and locates "beauty" or "quality" in the isomorphic object. This is because weavers express, maintain, and perpetuate hózhǫ́ through their weaving, and such activities relate to their cosmology (Witherspoon 1977, 1987; Witherspoon and Peterson 1995). In the Navajo Creation Story, weaving plays a pivotal role in the origin and maintenance of the Navajo people. The Creation Story defines meaningful relationships among members of the community and between the community and the entire cosmos. Such relations are still very real and very important to many Navajos (Faris 1993; Griffin-Pierce 1992). Although kinship functions as the infrastructure, cosmology provides the charter for proper behavior.

To more appropriately integrate Navajo weaving into the Navajo lifeworld from the perspective of communication, it is necessary to review relevant information related to Navajo kinship, language, and cosmology. Such information makes it possible to reconfigure weaving as a cosmological performance (fig. 4).

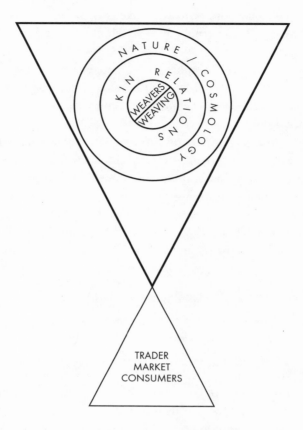

Figure 4. Navajo Relations. Drawn by Karen M'Closkey.

A Weaver's Story

The most detailed and profound statement suggesting weaving as cosmological performance was relayed to me by a woman whose mother was one of the few Navajo weavers of the past whom we know by name. This woman, now a grandmother, wrote the story for a university course. Because her mother worked at a school run by the Bureau of Indian Affairs, which prohibited the children from speaking their native language, she never learned to speak Navajo. Before giving me a copy of her story, she told me that the medicine men know the weaving stories, but they "won't share that information with people. . . . [I]t's sacred." She said that a male relative told her great-grandmother that the warp is like the rainbow; sunlight hit the strings (warp), and it changed into different colors. This is what happens when rain nourishes soil; plants bloom, and so the weaver makes her warp bloom.

To this day . . . a rug placed on the counter for sale at an Indian curio shop is evidence of only a small part of the history of Navajo weaving. Its value and significance as a genuine handmade Navajo rug are diminished by the fact that there are machine-made rugs, more easily accessible to buyers and fewer numbers of people desiring to master Navajo weaving. The Navajo rug, or any type of Navajo weaving, stands between the family of the weaver and starvation. It is money and financial credit to the family. Rugs are not considered by the weaver as personal property that must be kept. It is a thing for giving in exchange for nothing or in exchange for something of value. This is as it should be in Navajo ways, because it is a gift from the Holy People.

The woman goes on to relate a portion of the Creation Story in which the Holy Twins come upon a small opening in the earth. They peer in and see Spider Woman, weaving a beautiful rug. Surrounding her were hung other rugs that had been completed. They descended on a ladder made of pretty yarn. She relates what the loom was made of and continues:

Thus Spider Woman opened to the Twins knowledge of the world of weaving. Years ago, young weavers just learning were taught the sacredness of weaving . . . as a life-giving occupation. From the weaver's hands there are strung out, it is said, cords to the hearts and the essences of wealth, protection and happiness. . . . Through the act of weaving she has control of the world kingdom. Thus at an early age, the weaver is taught the religious and ethical significance as well as the economics of the art of weaving. . . . [W]eaving as work was not just a way of feeding one's family; it meant religion, wealth, and culture. . . . [O]ther writers have explained Navajo weaving in a different manner. . . .
    . . . [T]he religious and mythical concepts of designs were handed down by Spider Woman. . . . [A]t one point during their visit with the "master of weavers" they say that designs and colors in the rugs hanging in her house changed automatically, like watching the colorful glitter of a town at night. Spider Woman instructed that design will come to the Navajo if she truly attempts weaving and that there need not be any plan on the design before she weaves. [That is], the designs evolved from themselves and all that the weaver needed to do was weave them into a

rug. . . . [T]hus, during the rug period, to the Navajo, the wide variation of designs came about as no surprise [this is a quote from her grandfather in 1975]. From the Navajo weavers' hands . . . effortlessly flow the endless designs taught by Spider Woman. Although other literature tells us that Navajo were taught weaving by the Pueblos, the Navajo believe that weaving was taught to them by Holy People who walked Mother Earth at the dawn of mankind. . . . [T]he unwritten folklore and myths perpetuate this belief. Navajo expanded weaving . . . for traders. . . . [They] saw they were going to be annihilated by the U.S. government unless they accepted the American way. . . . [W]eaving became their vehicle and provided money for this new way. . . . [T]o them, weaving was their own. The Navajo brought it with them to this world, they took it with them to Bosque Redondo, they have it with them today. The elements of weaving may have changed in time as the Navajo went through life and encountered other people with different cultures, but the form is not different, it is still Navajo. As long as there are Navajo who cling to their religion, culture and language[,] . . . [s]o long as a Navajo can eloquently express thoughts in Navajo, so also will eloquent expressions flow from Navajo weaving.

This woman's paper offers deep insight into the value of weaving to her people. In her testimony she interleaves cosmology and history, revealing the centrality of weaving as a means of cultural survival.

A Timely Review of Navajo Cosmology

According to Faris (1986:136), Navajos have an extraordinarily rich, extensive, and complex belief system that evolved, according to anthropological orthodoxy, in association with older Athabascan and more recent Pueblo sources. The origin stories collectively embody one of the most exhaustive examples of North American poetry ever recorded (Wyman 1970; Zolbrod 1984). No single text is capable of rendering the rich narrative of *Diné Bahané*, the Navajo Creation Story. The order and character of the world and the place of people, including their relationships with one another and with all living creatures, is defined in the Creation Story. Navajos trace the beginning of their world from a point beneath the present earth surface, before the dawn of time. Stories passed down from generation to generation form the foundation of Navajo life and thought. Navajos believe strongly in the power of thought, which cannot exist without speech. Navajo oral tradition is still living as it is intimately tied to Navajo ritual processes. Ritual and stories are so interdependent that they cannot exist apart. A major portion of Navajo historical stories concern descriptions of origins, incidents, and ceremonial procedures that become archetypes for subsequent performances. Thus Navajo language is indivisible from cosmology. (See appendix I.)

The order inherent in the cosmos serves as a pattern for proper behavior in both general and specific ways (Begay and Maryboy 1996; Griffin-Pierce 1992:87). This harmony epitomizes the pattern of hózhǫ́ manifest everywhere in the Navajo universe. It governs male-female relationships such as earth and sky, night and day, mortals and supernaturals, summer and winter (Zolbrod 1984:11). Major historical figures set examples for the personal growth and maturation of Navajo females and males. Changing Woman, the mother of all Navajos, reminds Father Sun:

[A]s different as we are, you and I, we are of one spirit. As dissimilar as we are, you and I we are of equal worth. . . . [T]here must always be a solidarity between the two of us. . . . [T]here can be no harmony in the universe as long as there is no harmony between us. (Zolbrod 1984:275)

The ideal pattern for the relationship between husband and wife is summed up in the word *k'e*. The pattern for k'e, which translates as "right and respectful relations with others and the nonhuman world," is not an abstract ideal but provides a model for concrete Navajo behaviors encompassing kindness, helpfulness, peace, cooperation, and generosity (McCarty 1983:3; Zolbrod 1984:170).

The Primacy of K'e

The k'e that exists between mother and child provides the foundational concept and form for all relationships in Navajo social life. Motherhood in Navajo culture is identified and defined in terms of life, particularly its source. Mother and child are bound together by the most intense, diffuse, and enduring solidarity found in Navajo culture. The relationship of Changing Woman to her children provides the major conceptual framework for Navajo clans. In Navajo culture, life is created in and sustained by mothers. Changing Woman continues to sustain her children today, for she is symbolized by the earth (Begay and Maryboy 1996; Witherspoon 1975). As Mother Earth provides sustenance for her children, human mothers nurture their children. Navajos define kinship in terms of action or behavior, not in terms of substance. Kinship is discussed in terms of the acts of giving birth and sharing sustenance. Mothers sustain life by providing their children with loving care, assistance, protection, and sustenance.[4]

Navajos assume that there is a potential abundance of goods and that through cooperation the amount of goods will be increased for everyone (Ladd 1957). In other words, Navajos would deny the basic assumption on which much of classical economic theory depends, namely, the scarcity of goods. It is assumed that a neighbor's success will contribute to one's own welfare. The following statement from the Navajo author Steve Darden reflects the reciprocal relationship of k'e and Navajo cosmology:

> [G]ardens are for feeding the family and for giving to others who are hungry. We help everyone because we all come from our earth. . . . [P]lants are one offspring of the Earth Mother and Sky Father. Utilized to perpetuate life, they are symbolic of the essence of life. . . . Father Sky embraces Mother Earth, much as a husband his wife. Water flows throughout the world and embraces the earth, propagating life. . . . [W]ood is rooted in Mother Earth, the womb. She nourishes our wood and cares for it. Our wood and our trees project into Father Sky, and therein they, too, are nourished and strengthened. Wood provides shelter and warmth. . . . Animals are an ancient gift from the Holy People. When born, the animals are as infants. We, the Navajo care for them through the process of herding. When they grow, they provide for us. (Cited in Hooker 1991:n.p.)

Darden links plants, animals, and people to Navajo cosmology. As we shall see, weavers do the same. With few exceptions (Witherspoon 1975, 1987; Roessel 1983a; Roessel 1981, 1983), most studies in which kinship is discussed in relation to cosmology fail to explicitly connect or incorporate weaving. This is the result of the overwhelming perception and treatment of Navajo weaving by anthropologists and others as a commodity. The underlying assumption covertly maintained is, whatever is sacred is never sold.

To attribute the several forms of value to a Navajo rug, to play the symbolic value against the economic quantified value replicates dualisms. For Navajos, weaving as cosmological performance has intrinsic value that is both aesthetic and integrative. Political economists would tend to classify this as use value, related to need, an attenuated interpretation. Adopting the terminology used by political economists maintains dualistic thinking and fails to adequately reflect the multileveled patterns of relationships perpetuated through weaving. Nor is it appropriate to reposition Navajo weaving within the sacred sphere, as it is typically constructed by symbolic anthropologists (Reichard 1950). To perceive the patterns, we must reject the dualisms altogether. Using an approach grounded in communications theory provides an alternative explanation for the continuation of Navajo weaving under adverse economic circumstances.

It is difficult to ferret out information to craft another story, a different history. But recent events in investment and import markets make the telling paramount so as to reveal and critique activities occurring in the art world that contribute to and perpetuate the impoverishment of Navajo people. Although I present a great deal of empirical evidence that demonstrates the importance of women's textile production to the regional economy, my purpose is severalfold: (1) to reveal the extent and continued impoverishment of thousands of Navajos for more than a century; (2) to uncover the correlations between the volatile activity in both the investment and the import markets and their inimical effects on contemporary weavers; and (3) to suggest another way of perceiving weaving based on an epistemology influenced by communications theory (Harries-Jones 1995; Rappaport 1999; Wilden 1980, 1987). To one degree or another all views of the human past are created by those telling the story (Walters 1992). The story related here bears little resemblance to that which exists in the literature. However, it is written from a weaver's perspective, and it corroborates the sad tale of Columbus's legacy.

Trade, Commerce, and Diversification

Navajos are the largest indigenous group north of Mexico. More than 75 percent of the population currently occupies a twenty-million-acre reservation in the southwestern United States. According to their Creation Story, they evolved through at least four underworlds before emerging in the mountains in the region now known as southern Colorado. From there they converged in Dinétah, Old Navajo Land, an area bound by the Continental Divide, the San Juan and La Plata Mountains, and the Carrizo, Lukachukai, and Chuska ranges (see map 1). Their homeland is demarcated by four sacred mountains: Blanca and Hesperus Peaks in Colorado, Mount Taylor in New Mexico, and the San Francisco Peaks in northern Arizona. Ethnologists and archaeologists suggest a different genesis, in which the ancestors of the Navajo crossed the Bering "land bridge," ultimately migrating along the western edge of the great plains (USFTC 1973:63). Archaeologists date the arrival of these Athabaskan speakers to about 1400 B.P. (Hall 1989:38). Navajos had migrated to a region populated by other indigenous groups, including Pueblos, Utes, and Pimas.

Present Navajoland is situated in the south central portion of the Colorado Plateau. To the north and east lie the Middle and Southern Rocky Mountains. The west and south-southeast areas are referred to as Basin and Range country. The region is crosscut by deep canyons, steep escarpments, buttes, and several mountain ranges. Canyonlands are dissected by riparian woodlands. The Colorado and San Juan Rivers form a portion of the northern reservation boundary in Utah. Elevation ranges from 4,500 to over 10,000 feet. Ponderosa pine, Douglas fir, and aspen forests dominate the higher elevations and receive from fifteen to forty inches of precipitation annually. Mean monthly temperatures range from 25° to 64° Fahrenheit. Piñon-juniper and desert scrub dominate the mid- and lower-range elevations (Iverson 1981:6).

The sage-grass ecozone contains perennial shrubs and grasses, and approximately 20 percent is considered ideal farming and grazing land. Desert

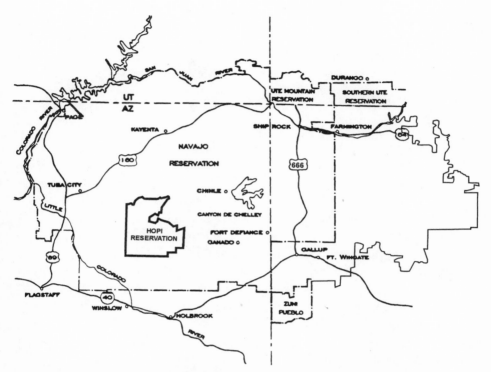

Map 1. The Navajo Reservation. Map by Lorraine Cantin.

comprises more than 75 percent of the reservation. Permanent water sources are too rare for continual transhumance (Kelley and Whiteley 1989:3, 213). Rainfall in this ecozone ranges from six to sixteen inches annually, and monthly temperatures vary from 32° to 77° Fahrenheit.

Intertribal Trade Relations

Although it is impossible to date the origins of trade relations, commerce flourished among the peoples of the Southwest and adjacent areas in prehistoric times (Hill 1948:373). The distribution network and web of exchange relationships were extensive, involving entire regions such as the Pacific Plateau, the Greater Southwest, and the Middle Missouri. Nearly all trade transpired through specially organized expeditions planned in advance. As long-distance travel could be hazardous, ceremonies and ritual behavior were practiced to ensure the personal safety and material success of trading ventures (Adams 1963:149; Hill 1948:393). Exchange as a social aspect of foreign relations made friends of potential enemies:

a kinsman or trade partner was protected and provisioned (White 1983:242). Such was the extensiveness of trade that on the eve of European contact, early Indian-white trade relations should be viewed as "an elaboration of native patterns rather than a European innovation" (Swagerty 1988:353).

Spanish Traders

The Spaniards were the first Europeans to appear in the Southwest in the sixteenth century. They developed an extensive trade network between Santa Fe and rich merchants in Chihuahua, Mexico. In 1680 the normally autonomous Pueblo villages in New Mexico united and expelled the Spanish from the region. By 1692 Spaniards had successfully repressed the revolt. Vicious and sustained retaliation by the victors drove many Pueblo Indians westward into Navajo country. According to archaeologists, during this period Navajos adopted many Pueblo ceremonies and farming practices, as well as weaving (Kluckhohn and Leighton 1974; Underhill [1956] 1983). Kelley and Francis (1994:214) assert that it is more likely that Navajo and Pueblo peoples share common roots in earlier prehistoric peoples.

Caravans from Mexico sought to acquire Indian goods such as hides, jerked meat, salt, horses, and slaves. Unlike intertribal trade, rates were set by the Spaniards to their advantage (Ford 1983:719). Although disease and intertribal warfare took its toll on numerous Indian groups, the Greater Southwest trade network remained relatively intact during the entire Spanish era. The introduction of new goods and livestock by Europeans increased the variety of goods but also altered the worth of trade commodities. Spanish and Mexican traders dominated a large portion of what is now western New Mexico and eastern Arizona for two centuries, playing the marauding Apaches and Navajos against the Pueblos. They sold liquor and guns to both sides, often in exchange for stolen horses or captive slaves (McNitt 1962:227).[1] During the 1750s, Spanish settlers received land grants and began invading Navajo country in northwestern New Mexico (Thompson 1976:3). Although a number of Navajos were baptized, missionaries experienced little success in converting them to Catholicism (Brugge 1985).

The Introduction of Livestock

The introduction of livestock to band people via Spanish colonization was revolutionary (Spicer 1962:546). Lands, fields, and herds became closely identified with women (Underhill [1956] 1983:156). Sheep not only represented a source of food and prestige for the people, they also provided the primary staple for woven wearing blankets (Lamphere 1977). Until 1860 horticulture, animal husbandry, hunting, gathering, raiding, and woven blankets formed the core of Navajo subsistence (Brugge 1983:495). Thus a broad spectrum of subsistence activities augmented by pastoralism acted to cushion the effects of fluctuating environmental factors that could jeopardize crops (Iverson 1981:10).

Textiles and Prereservation Trade

Van Valkenburgh and McPhee (1974:42) referred to the blanket as "the mother from which all external Navajo trade of today developed." Numerous accounts exist that document the importance of the Navajo blanket in early inter- and intratribal trade (Ford 1983; Hill 1948; Matthews 1968:1). And several authors have published long lists of exchange rates that demonstrate a remarkable homogeneity and near-universal knowledge. This suggests that bargaining was quite restricted, although not absent (Ford 1983:720). In table 2, "Equivalent Values of Selected Paired Goods," Ford notes that Navajos would trade a blanket for a buckskin with the Yavapais, Hopis, Havasupais, and Western Apaches. Fourteen of twenty-six items depict blankets as the unit of exchange by which other goods were measured.[2] Most of the items that Navajos traded were finished products, principally blankets. Most of the items they bartered for were raw materials, destined for home consumption and use rather than for manufacture and retrade. The Utes were willing to exchange five buckskins, a good mare, or a dressed buffalo robe for a Navajo chief's blanket, the most popular trade item (Hill 1948:380). If purchased, one small buckskin cost $10, and a large one cost $30. These rates and equivalencies are important to keep in mind when comparing the unequal exchange that developed for goods acquired later from Anglo traders. Although curtailed by the formation of several reservations and the infusion of trading posts beginning in about 1870, intratribal trade continued to some extent among various southwestern societies (Ford 1983:721).

Navajo-Spanish commerce was well developed by the latter part of the seventeenth century (Hill 1948:348). In his classic *Commerce of the Prairies* (1844), Josiah Gregg commented on the high values placed on the "sarape-Navajo," which was woven so densely that it could hold water. Those of fine quality were acquired through barter, then sold by traders among the Mexicans for $50 to $60 each (equivalent to six months' pay for a U.S. Army colonel) (Weiss 1984:35). Each sarape required six months to one year to produce. As the Navajo blanket gained fame, reports from military and government officials commented on the increasing wealth of the Navajo people. On 1 September 1854, D. Merriwether, governor and superintendent of Indian affairs in New Mexico territory, estimated the Navajo population at about eight thousand. He wrote the Commissioner of Indian Affairs:

[T]hey live in a degree of comfort and plenty unknown to the other wild Indians of this section of the Union. They manufacture their own clothes. . . . [I]t is a rare thing to see a Navajo uncomfortably clothed. In the manufacturing of blankets they are believed to surpass any other Indians on this continent, and these blankets will compare favorably with any other manufactured by a civilized people. (RCIA 1854:173)

Sporadic trading with American settlers began early in the nineteenth century; by midcentury it became more formalized as Mormons colonized regions north and west of the Colorado River (Adams 1963:149). Traders often preceded missionaries, administrators, and settlers (Adams 1963:306). After the defeat of Mexico in 1846, the United States became the dominant influence in the region and altered Anglo-Indian relations (Atherton 1982). Rather than promote trade in goods and captives, the United States sought to open up territory to settlement and agriculture. Over the next two decades, many indigenous groups in the region were subdued and confined to reservations.

Bosque Redondo: Subduing the "Wild Tribes"

By the end of the eighteenth century, New Mexicans regarded Navajos as wealthy, settled people. They raised extensive crops of corn and wheat and grazed enormous flocks of sheep as well as cattle and horses. Raiding and warfare increased and disrupted trade networks somewhat as the nonindigenous occupants of the region tried to extend their territory (McNitt 1972). By the 1820s, because of their formidable resistance, Navajos were the most feared Indians in the Southwest (Bailey and Bailey 1986:17–21; Thompson 1976; Underhill [1956] 1983:74).

In 1846 the American army took control of the New Mexico-Arizona region, and the federal government's strategies included military campaigns, treaties, removal of the Indians, and construction of forts to maintain peace (Iverson 1981:8). J. S. Calhoun, governor of New Mexico, divided tribes into two groups: the sedentary (Pueblo) Indians and the wild tribes, the Navajos, Apaches, and Utes. In 1862 property losses to Indian depredations were estimated at $250,000, and settlers lost more than thirty thousand sheep to Navajo raiders (Thompson 1976:10). In 1863, with a scorched earth policy in effect, the government dispatched Kit Carson to kill all Navajo men who resisted arrest, round up the other men, women, and children, and confiscate their animals and destroy their peach orchards and cornfields. More than eight thousand Navajos and Apaches were driven over three hundred miles into eastern New Mexico and placed on a reservation called Bosque Redondo or Hwééldi. General Carleton, military commander of nearby Fort Sumner, anticipated that

> little by little the Navajo would be brought to the reservation and treated with Christian kindness. The children would be taught to read and write. The arts of peace would be instilled in them and the truths of Christianity would be revealed. In time, the Navajos would become a new people. They would acquire new habits, a new lifestyle, and most importantly, new beliefs. Gradually as the old Indians died off, the young Indians would grow up without their ancestors' affection for robbery and murder. (Thompson 1976:21)

Provisioning Hwééldi: A Contractor's Paradise
With the sudden need to feed thousands of Indians, the cost of basic foods including meat skyrocketed in New Mexico, creating real hardship among the poor of that region. The census taken at Hwééldi in December 1864 revealed 8,354 Navajo, or 1,782 families who had a total of 3,038 horses, 6,962 sheep, 2,757 goats and 143 mules (Thompson 1976:71–72). They refused to kill goats and sheep because they needed the milk and wool. Navajo women were reported weaving every day at 630 looms to produce blankets to help combat the cold. Hwééldi (referred to by critics as "a concentration camp") measured forty miles square. It was too large to police effectively. The attempt to turn Navajos into farmers was a miserable failure because of alkaline water, inclement weather, and nearly total destruction by pests of the corn crop (Iverson 1981:9–10). However, there were beneficiaries of this tragic "experiment." Mercantile houses harvested huge financial benefits: contracts ranged in the hundreds of thousands of dollars. Contractors regarded the Bosque as an "enormous plum."

Carleton ran Hwééldi as if he were engaged in a holy crusade, that of civilizing the largest Indian tribe in the United States—and, in the government's view, one of the most unruly. Both Carleton and Hwééldi were targeted by a number of newspapers. Criticism flew because of the enormous expense and reputed corruption and collusion related to lucrative government contracts. But citizens were in agreement that Indians needed rule by law, whether or not they comprehended it. Law was a step toward civilization (Thompson 1976:82). On 31 December 1866 the Indian Bureau assumed responsibility for Hwééldi from the War Department. President Ulysses Grant was convinced that Carleton had presented a blueprint for civilizing the American Indian (Thompson 1976:121, 133). Newspapers hostile to Carleton and the expensive debacle at Hwééldi were against returning Navajos to their country because "whites now needed the region [as there is] much mineral wealth" (Thompson 1976:151).

A Painful Failure

Thousands of Navajos suffered four years in exile, and the entire experiment cost the government in the neighborhood of $10 million. Speculators reaped much of that. Approximately 30 percent of the population died as a result of what became known as the Long Walk disease, or starvation. The people once referred to as proud and wealthy had sunk into a condition of absolute poverty and despair. Comanche raids, crop failures, bad water, unproductive soil, scarcity of wood—all contributed to one of the most devastating experiments ever perpetrated on an indigenous group in North America. By 1868, because the post-Civil War economy was demoralized and interest rates were high, it became imperative that the government divest itself of this financial and political albatross (White 1983:215). Federal authorities created a 3.5-million-acre reservation, about one quarter of the land the Navajos had occupied before their incarceration (Brugge 1993:11; Vogt 1961:315). The reservation was created to help Navajos recover economically and to educate them for assimilation. In the treaty signed on 1 June 1868, the head of each Navajo family was promised seeds and farming tools the following year. The government also allotted $30,000 for initial distribution of sheep.

Federal authorities preferred to settle Navajos as farmers as less land was required and they could be concentrated in villages. Navajos continued to use traditional digging sticks and sometimes traded government-issued farm tools for stock (Bailey and Bailey 1986:46). Most fields were small and after the 1880s farmed for subsistence only (Weiss 1984:33). During the 1880s, over-harvesting of wild animal and plant populations, inclement weather, and encroachment by large herding operations contributed to a decline in hunting and gathering (Bailey and Bailey 1986:49; White 1983:244–45). Thus Navajos lost not only an important source of protein but also their primary source of hides for leather goods as sheep pelts and goatskins were inappropriate substitutes.

Post-Hwééldi Trade

The first traders to the Navajos had been sutlers, itinerant peddlers who supplied the army with food and clothing.[3] When Navajo flocks began to increase after Hwééldi, some sutlers bought the excess Navajo wool. A few sutlers abandoned army trade for the increasingly lucrative Indian commerce. The first license was issued in 1868, at Fort Defiance, but primarily served a white clientele associated with the fort (Utley 1961:15). Gradually the Indian agent encouraged Navajos to sell their excess wool, and by 1889 there were nine posts on the reservation and thirty posts surrounding it, outside government control (McNitt 1962:51; Weiss 1984:50).

Patronage and politics often determined who received a trading license. Competition for licenses, which were obtained from the Commissioner of Indian Affairs (CIA) for an annual fee, was spurred by knowledge of the fortunes made by western entrepreneurs. An Indian agent was not to have direct or indirect interest in the trade carried on by licensed traders at his agency (McNitt 1962:46). Government personnel and traders did not see eye-to-eye on many issues. Many traders felt they were overregulated, whereas agents were wary of the potential for entrepreneurial fraud (Schmedding [1951] 1974:317). Agents often had short terms and could barely begin to cope with numerous problems (McNitt 1962:70). Given the scarcity of government field-workers to address matters of concern to the Indians, traders filled a lacuna and reflected the government's support of "rugged individualism."

Annuity Goods: Link to Survival
From 1869 to 1879 the federal government issued $5 worth of annuity goods to each Navajo, which included rations such as corn, flour, beef, cloth, tow cards (for cleaning fleece before spinning), kitchenware, and yarn (Bailey and Bailey 1986:38, 55; McNitt 1962:128–29; Weiss 1984:47). Between 1863 and 1878, 75,000 pounds of aniline dyed Germantown yarn was issued (Wheat 1981:8). In 1872, $40,000 of the $54,000 annuity distribution was for clothing (Weiss 1984:47). To augment their subsistence, Indian agent Arny shipped 60,000 pounds of Navajo wool in 1875 (Brugge 1993:18). In his 1877 annual report, Agent Irvine states that Navajos had "sold" approximately 200,000 pounds of wool and a large quantity of blankets. These were exchanged for horses in southern Utah, "[which had] no superiors, and [were] to be found in use all over the Southwest" (RCIA 1877:554). Blankets and skins were also traded with indigenous neighbors for food and other goods (Brugge 1993:18).

Blankets continued to be major trade items until the 1880s (Bailey and Bailey 1986:37, 44). In 1879 Agent Eastman reported that Navajo women still wore "woollen cloth . . . of their own manufacture" and that one hundred thousand pounds of wool had been woven into blankets (McNitt 1962:80). Corn, wheat, peaches, and melons were raised in considerable quantities in suitable locations (Roessel 1980:144). In the late 1870s the Navajo economy began to show signs of self-sufficiency. There is evidence that the economy may have returned to its pre-1863 level and, according to one observer, "due to judicious management of their flocks and herds of domestic animals, now attained to a condition virtually independent of government aid" (Bailey and Bailey 1986:50; Van Valkenburgh and McPhee 1974:42).

The wool clip was valued at $80,000 in 1880 (Dockstader 1976). By 1881 the railroad reached the fringes of Navajo country, and 800,000 pounds of wool left the reservation. The 1883 CIA report stated that the size of the herds had increased but a brutal winter destroyed many animals (White 1983:219). The winter of 1886–87 was also severe, and reports indicate that the Navajos butchered approximately 280,000 sheep and goats as "necessary subsistence," bartered 240,000 sheep pelts and 80,000 goatskins (Peterson 1986:107), and shipped more than 1 million pounds of wool (Bailey and Bailey 1986:61). The 1887 CIA report stated that 75 percent of the blankets for intertribal trade were of the "coarse variety" (Bailey and Bailey 1986:60). Apache and Utes were still good customers. As late as 1889 Navajos bartered only $24,000 worth of blankets to traders (Bailey and Bailey 1986:60). By 1890 the reporting agent estimated that their flocks had produced just over 2 million pounds of wool the previous year, and flock owners grazed at least 700,000 sheep (worth $2 each). They "sold" approximately 12,000 sheep and 1.3 million pounds of wool and retained an estimated 700,000 pounds of wool "for home use." During that decade, because of storms decimating their herds, Navajos did not appear to be selling animals in any great numbers. That fact, in conjunction with the steep decline in value of annuity goods after 1878, dramatically affected Navajo well-being.

Cessation of Annuities: Recipe for Impoverishment
When the government stopped its annuity program Navajos received far less per capita in subsistence than other southwestern tribes (Bailey and Bailey 1986; Weiss 1984). For example, in 1880 Navajos received only $0.39 per person, compared to $15.58 at the Southern Ute Agency, $26.82 at the Mescalero Apache Agency, and $34.61 at the San Carlos Apache Agency (Roessel 1980:69). The pleas of Navajo agents fell on deaf ears in Washington. Some agents spent a portion of their salary in a vain attempt to assuage the hunger and cold (Roessel 1980:72).

On 14 August 1883 Agent D. M. Riordan of Fort Defiance tendered his resignation in an angry sixteen-page letter that constituted his annual report to the CIA (Hubbell Papers, Box 43). Riordan's letter reveals the shortcomings in government at arms' length and its attitude of benign neglect because the Navajos had been subdued and confined to the reservation. Apaches continued to resist settlement, and funds were spent on annuities related to pacification. Navajo agents Eastman and Bowman issued similar pleas in their annual reports of 1882 and 1884 respectively, noting the tremendous discrepancy between the minuscule funds allocated to the most populous tribe and their recalcitrant neighbors (Roessel 1980:68–72).

Riordan's report demonstrates that Navajos were under tremendous pressure to augment their subsistence. The cessation of annuity goods left them in a precarious position, exacerbated by the formation of new economic relations. During the 1880s, intratribal trade was drastically curtailed, and entrepreneurial traders filled a void in an effort to civilize and profit from the Navajos. Indian agents and then the traders foresaw the commercial possibilities of sheep, wool, and craftwork (Utley 1961). After Hwééldi the Navajo tribe became a stable and dependent market liable for commercial exploitation by entrepreneurs, unlike the wild profiteering that occurred while the military was still in the region. A thriving wholesale mercantile business emerged, specializing in trading post supply after the arrival of the railroad. Although capital risks were high, because of the size of the confined population, Navajo trading offered impressive, immediate profits from a "virginal consumer market" (USFTC 1973:5).

Diversification: Recipe for Survival

The profit motive is a recurring theme in scholarly works on western entrepreneurs (White 1991). Their highest goals were self-advancement, acquisition of worldly possessions, and success through initiative (Limerick 1987). Their hard work to accumulate personal wealth spawned intense competition. Instead of having a single interest, most pioneer merchants pursued opportunities in many local enterprises (Elder and Weber 1996). If one area languished temporarily as a result of oversupply, inclement weather, or other factors, diversified business interests acted as a buffer (Atherton 1982; White 1991). Throughout the Southwest merchants operated in a barter economy in which the primary source of income was agriculture, ranching, and herding. Terms of credit were geared to a seasonal production cycle in which it was not unusual for settlements on accounts to occur but once a year. Thus the merchant capitalist kept close control over his customers' financial obligations: he often insisted that these obligations be confined solely to him. Wholesale merchants carried producers and traders over long periods of economic hardship. Thus the most successful entrepreneurs were flexible and diversified to protect multiple interests. Three important merchant dynasties, Gross, Kelly and Company, Charles Ilfeld of New Mexico, and the Babbitts of Arizona, exemplify this approach.

Gross, Kelly and Company was one of the oldest mercantile firms in New Mexico. In *The Buffalo Head: A Century of Mercantile Pioneering in the Southwest* (1972), Dan Kelly, son of the company's owner, notes how the pioneer merchant-capitalist was as important to the West as the Yankee trader was to New England. Building and operating a large mercantile company took a special blend of "imagination, stubbornness, and optimism combined with the gambler's flare for mastering a game and playing it ruthlessly, if need be" (Kelly 1972:1). Centered in New Mexico, the mercantile empire of Gross, Kelly and Company extended to seven adjacent western states, California, and major cities in the East (map 2). The company opened its first branch house in 1881, and a dozen more followed between that date and 1929. In 1929 it bought out Lorenzo Hubbell's former business partner, Clinton Cotton of Gallup, New Mexico.

Gross, Kelly and Company was one of the key suppliers to reservation traders for decades. Kelly (1972:106) remarks on the excellent quality of goatskins acquired through the traders from Navajo women who "had the privilege of skinning the goats and sheep, and since they usually owned the family flocks they were allowed to keep the money when these commodities were sold." The skins were sold to East Coast tanners. In 1912 the company handled more than one million pounds of sheepskins alone. Kelly (1972:249) mentions that one year wool, hides, and pelts dropped nearly 50 percent: "we took a big loss though it could have been worse." The company's hide warehouse located in Las Vegas, New Mexico, was piled as high as a man's shoulder with stiff dried hides (Kelly 1972:46). For many years the wholesale price per pound of goatskins and hand-spun, handwoven Navajo saddle blankets was similar (fig. 5).

The Charles Ilfeld Company, which also wholesaled goods to reservation traders, was founded in 1865. Ilfeld maintained diversified interests to protect its profits (Parish 1961). Merchandise sales reached $160,000 in 1889, $188,000 in 1890, and nearly $270,000 in 1892; wool sales alone amounted to nearly $150,000 in 1892 (Parish 1961:121). Between 1895 and 1949 the company's gross profits ranged from a high of 21.8 percent (1897) to a low of 9.3 percent (in 1930) (Parish 1961:table 20). In 1924 Ilfeld absorbed a major competitor, the Gallup Mercantile Company. What is remarkable in the histories of these companies is their continued expansion and high profit margins, even during periods of economic downturns such as the recession of 1923–24. For example, nearly 50 percent of New Mexico's banks failed between 1920 and 1925, yet the Ilfeld Company continued to expand (Parish 1961:251). Keeping a constant eye on diversification paid off in the long run by protecting companies' assets and profits.

Barter accounts were both a necessity and an advantage to mercantile firms. Because of a shortage of cash in the region, this method of trade was encouraged. For decades nearly all transactions, except paying rent on buildings, were bartered (Parish 1961:15, 46). Banking specialists appeared late in the Southwest, soon after the arrival of the railroad and decades after the first merchant capitalists.

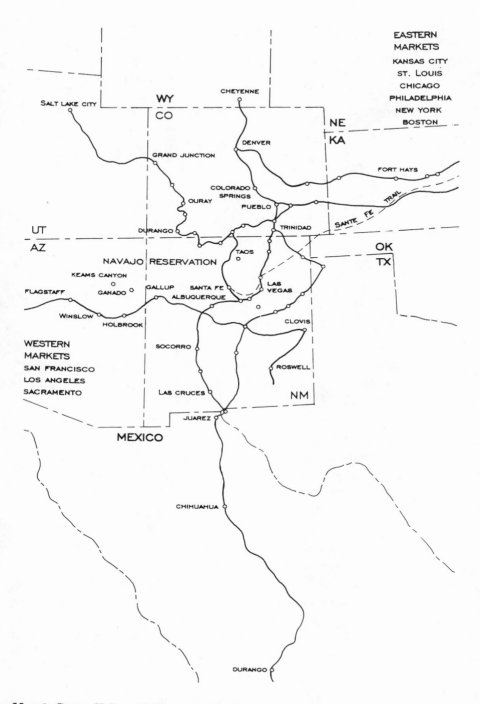

Map 2. Gross, Kelly and Company. Map by Lorraine Cantin.

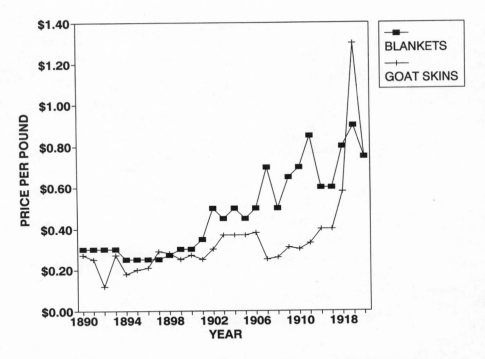

Figure 5. Goatskin/Patterned Saddle Blanket Wholesale Cost, Hubbell Trading Post Records, 1890–1920.

Many petty capitalists gradually had to commit themselves to "production" by contract to the large merchant. Thus the mercantile capitalist sold them supplies on credit, advanced them money, and found markets for their products while demanding a commitment on their production. Sometimes companies retained such a tight grip on the economy of the region that merchants literally became business dictators (Parish 1961:44). One of Kelly's competitors "claimed he knew certain customers better than their mother, since mothers carried them nine months, but he carried them over several years" (Akbarzadeh 1992:296).

The most important entrepreneurs to occupy multiple economic niches in northern Arizona were undoubtedly the Babbitt brothers. The five men sold their grocery business in Cincinnati and migrated to northern Arizona in 1886 to seek their initial fortune in cattle ranching. Within a twenty-year period, the Babbitts completely dominated the economy of the region. Yet traders managed both to compete (the Babbitts ultimately owned a dozen trading posts on or adjacent to the Navajo Reservation) and coexist with this powerful family.

By 1886 only a handful of entrepreneurs were located in Arizona. C. N. Cotton and Lorenzo Hubbell had recently formed a partnership to run the trading post at Ganado in eastern Arizona (called Pueblo Colorado at that time). The Babbitts chose Flagstaff as their base of operations. Many newly arrived entrepreneurs had to start from scratch, but the Babbitts were fortunate in bringing substantial capital with them. Three of the brothers married Verkamp sisters, whose father had made his fortune in Ohio in retailing and manufacturing. Father-in-law Verkamp loaned the brothers more than $100,000 at 5 percent interest between 1885 and 1894 (Akbarzadeh 1992:266). Clearly they were in a unique position to maximize their entrepreneurial abilities in an economically untapped region. After achieving success in cattle ranching, the Babbitts quickly moved into the mercantile field to avoid paying inflated frontier prices for needed goods. Most goods were sold on credit, although the cost of goods was higher on credit than for cash. Although this was a cumbersome form of merchandising, the average western store had more merchandise and served more people than the average specialized eastern store. Carload buying from eastern manufacturers and importers gave the Babbitts a decided advantage over their smaller competitors. Merchants typically maximized profits and minimized costs through bulk purchases (Akbarzadeh 1992:208). The Babbitts quickly expanded, with each brother developing his own area of expertise.

Like Ilfeld and Gross, Kelly and Company, the Babbitts understood that the interdependence of the western frontier economy required diversification. They ultimately controlled "the supply, demand, credit and trade in Northern Arizona in both vertically and horizontally integrated enterprises" (Akbarzadeh 1992:523, 526).[4]

Although ranching brought high profits in good years, adverse weather, fluctuating prices, and economic downturns affected sustained profits. The Babbitts acquired the massive Hashknife outfit in 1901—two million acres in northern Arizona with more than thirty thousand head of cattle (Akbarzadeh 1992:145–46). They had entered the sheep business by 1897, an unusual venture as cattle ranchers and sheep men usually occupied opposite sides of the frontier fence, each blaming the other for woes ranging from environmental degradation to illegal grazing. Sheep ranchers preferred unfenced range; cattlemen preferred fenced range to reduce risk of damage to cows whose hides were marketed for the burgeoning boot and shoe trade. The Arizona Sheep Breeders and Wool Growers Association formed a pressure group in 1886, and in later years the Babbitts and Verkamps served as directors. By building a prosperous mercantile base, the Babbitts acquired many animals in barter, took over assets of defaulting ranchers, and expanded and eventually dominated the regional livestock industry (Akbarzadeh 1992:509).

By 1900 they controlled a local livery stable, slaughterhouse, ice plant (which supplied their grocery stores, meatpacking plant, and funeral parlor), financing firms and warehouses, and retail department stores (Akbarzadeh 1992:507). Thus they became both the clearinghouse and shipping point for other merchants and traders in the region. At the height of their empire before the post-World War I recession, they owned about forty livestock outfits with 157,000 cattle and sheep on 3.5 million acres, a dozen mercantile houses and auto dealerships, more than ten trading posts, a cotton mill, an ice plant, a packing house, lumber yards, and investments in California (ranching and oil), Kansas, Colorado, Montana, and Texas, and numerous other ventures. The firm's net worth rose from $3 million to $5 million between 1915 and 1917. They sold a record-setting $1.5 million worth of beef in 1915 (Smith 1989).

By 1921 the family was doing $5 million worth of business a year. With a capital stock of $25 million divided into 250,000 shares, it was the largest family-owned corporation of its kind in the entire Southwest. In 1922 cattle and sheep markets began to collapse. As the national economy became more sluggish, the postwar recession and several years of drought brought hard times. Unlike Gross, Kelly and Company and Ilfeld, the Babbitts had been accustomed to putting every dollar back into their extensive operations; they had scarce cash reserves (Akbarzadeh 1992:497). The empire went into receivership, threatening the northern Arizona economy. Major efforts at reorganization ensured their survival.

Domestic Wool Production

Chester Wright's *Wool Growing and the Tariff* (1910) makes key points concerning domestic wool production, the wool tariff, the international wool market, and the way in which fluctuations in that market affected all wool growers and buyers, including reservation traders. It provides the context to understand the need for traders to encourage women to weave wool into blankets, as textiles were seen as an alternative means to market a renewable resource subject to volatile price fluctuations (Bailey and Bailey 1986:table 29).

Before the Civil War, wool from the Far West had little effect on eastern markets. But this was the only part of the country that offered any promise for the future of the wool industry. Most sheep in the Far West were in New Mexico and California. The original flocks were kept mainly for mutton rather than wool, which was very coarse. Before 1845 little wool was carried on the Santa Fe Trail. Raising sheep primarily for wool did not begin until about 1852, after the California gold rush. The California clip alone rose from 360,000 pounds in 1855 to 8 million pounds in 1864.

The transfer of the main seat of the industry from east of the Mississippi River to the Far West was the dominating factor in the history of wool growing from 1870 to 1890 (Wright 1910:273). It was the final step of the general westward movement: "Throughout the nineteenth century the process of opening and settling the West had been the most important factor in the country's history" (Wright 1910:274). The last decade of the nineteenth century was a period of transition, marking the close of one era and the opening of a new one. It also marks the increasing control by traders over Navajo livelihood (Bailey and Bailey 1986; Weiss 1984).

Penetration of the railroads changed wool-marketing practices. Stock raising in the West was different from that in other parts of the United States, as it was a range industry divorced from general farming. In 1871 there were nearly 7 million sheep in the Far West (Wright 1910:252); by 1885 the number reached 26 million. The Far West was well adapted to sheep raising. Because of vast arid regions and the type of vegetation, sheep raising did not have competition from dairy farming and crops to any great extent. And because the range was "free," it was five times cheaper to keep a sheep on arid western rangeland than back East. In California droughts occurred during 1863–64, 1871, and 1877, and growers sustained losses in the millions of dollars. In addition, fencing, land enclosure, competition from ranching, and an increase in farming took their toll on wool growers (Wright 1910:255). Owners drove large numbers of sheep to New Mexico.

New Mexico was one of the oldest sheep regions in the country, as Spanish settlers had introduced sheep there (Baxter 1987). But it was not until after 1860 that this region exercised any influence on the sheep industry or the wool market. The Civil War stimulated great demand for wool. Because of the extra needs of the army and the scarcity of cotton, wool rose to $1.00 a pound (Wright 1910:206). By 1867 the annual clip from New Mexico, Oregon, and California totaled more than 11 million pounds (Wright 1910:187). High prices were relatively short lived as cotton again became available and the world's supply of wool increased at an unprecedented rate. The Franco-Prussian War (1870–71) greatly augmented the demand for wool. Prices rose, with the average price of three grades of washed Ohio wool running $0.71 per pound. Eight years later the price of such wool had dropped to $0.56 per pound.

By the mid-1880s commission houses showed a lack of enthusiasm for contracting wool at any price. Sometimes merchants such as Ilfeld had difficulty disposing of their wool except on consignment to eastern buyers. In other words, wool futures became a gamble, and it was buyer beware: buy low and hope to sell at a profit. The small wool grower of this period was in a "somewhat helpless situation" (Parish 1961:137). Once he sheared his animals the wool had to come to market because he had no satisfactory means of storage. In the slow market that existed in most of the years from 1884 to 1897, his opportunity for bargaining was lessened and his logical place of delivery was to the merchant to whom he was indebted. Thus his problem went beyond the local and the national level; it was international as well (White 1991:225). The lack of large textile manufacturers in the West meant growers had to ship their clips to eastern mills, thereby increasing costs.

Partido

Because of the slump in trade, merchant capitalists such as Ilfeld were forced to assume the additional role of sheep husbandmen. The partido contract, an agreement for raising sheep and producing wool, akin to the sharecropping system of the South (Baxter 1987:28–29; White 1991:42–43), was seen as a method of refinancing or funding debt of sheep owners with high balances. Charles Ilfeld's partido holdings peaked at 33,000 in 1897 (Parish 1961:154). The average number of sheep per partido ranged from 799 to 1,021 between 1896 and 1912 (Parish 1961:155). Between 1898 and 1902 Ilfeld handled about 1 million pounds of wool annually, increasing to nearly 1.7 million pounds in 1903 (Parish 1961:147).

Even large off-reservation growers became indebted to merchant capitalists and had to surrender absolute ownership of their herds to survive financially, thus highlighting the tenuous nature of entrepreneurial activities of all types in the latter part of the nineteenth century. Petty capitalists began to realize that "they who produced with their hands were under the control of those who sold by their wits" (Parish 1961:45). For many ranchers, wool growers, and merchants the 1884–97 period was a sobering contrast to the 1860–80 period. Extension of credit to those already indebted served to closely bind the producer-herder to merchants such as Ilfeld, who "never made the mistake of permitting himself to be placed at the mercy of a single dominating risk" (Parish 1961:45).[5]

The Wool Tariff

Although western flocks greatly increased in size relative to the rest of the country, the price of wool changed little between the periods 1840–59 and 1872–89. In the latter period, the huge increase in the world's production caused wool market prices to decline. High tariffs gave added encouragement to domestic growers, who sought to maximize economic returns on both mutton and wool (Wright 1910:271). The tariff of 1867 lasted until July 1883 and became the model for all but one of the succeeding tariffs until 1912 (Wright 1910:213). Anglo-American growers not only held their own but also made substantial gains in their control over the domestic market from 1868 to 1890 (Wright 1910:225). American wools supplied a much larger proportion of domestic consumption than before the tariff. Before the Civil War, all forms of wool imports were 100 to 150 percent over the domestic clip. After the Civil War, imports made up only 75 to 84 percent of the domestic clip. By 1890 the per capita consumption of American manufactures of wool was more than twice that in 1860 (Wright 1910:228).

Growers hoped that the McKinley tariff of 1890 would restore the prosperity of the earlier years, when high tariffs protected domestic wools (Wright 1910:280). But prices plummeted in 1894, when Democrats came to power and put all wool on the free list after Grover Cleveland's election. The importation of Class I wool, which most closely resembled the domestic clip, increased by three and a half times on average, and Class II wool quadrupled. More than 141 million pounds of Class I wool were imported annually into the United States when wool was on the free list (between 1894 and 1897). As wool buyers and partido contractors, merchant capitalists such as Charles Ilfeld and reservation traders fought removal of the tariff. Most sheep and wool men were Republicans (Parish 1961:144). Ilfeld was an active member of the New Mexico Wool Growers Association, which was founded to spark the tariff issue. In 1895 he requested via proxy that a six-cent duty be placed on all classes of imported wool (Parish 1961:145). The industrial depression during the 1890s coincided with the removal of the wool tariff—exacerbating the already depressed prices for domestic wool: "[T]he action . . . must have discouraged many flock owners who appear to have been engaged for years in a desperate and losing struggle with fate" (Wright 1910:314).[6]

From 1890 to 1907 the industry failed to progress, even though the average domestic fleece weighed nearly seven pounds due to improved breeding practices (Wright 1910:312). The entire industry lost ground, chiefly because the general level of prices in the world market was abnormally low. There was a rapid increase in the world's wool supply, with a falling off of its consumption, partly due to the removal of the tariff on cotton. It appears that cotton prices dropped more than wool prices during the 1890s; thus the use of cotton not only increased but also made inroads in manufactured products formerly the province of wool, such as certain kinds of hosiery.

The industrial depression and trade slump affected wool, cattle, and sheep markets. The prices of goods that merchants purchased, indicated by the general wholesale price index, fell from 100 percent in 1880 to 70 percent in 1896. The value of wool declined to less than 40 percent of that before free trade. In two critical periods, 1880–88 and 1893–96, the price of medium and coarse wool fell three and then two and a half times as much as wholesale prices of all goods. In dollar amounts the dramatic decline in prices as a result of changes in the international tariff is illustrated in the following figures: in 1892 non-Indian Arizona growers received $840,000 for their wool, compared to $280,000 the following year (Akbarzadeh 1992:155). By 1894 Arizona growers owned one million fine-wooled sheep, whereas Navajo flocks consisted of coarse-wooled *churros* (Baxter 1983). Thus reservation traders experienced a more drastic decline in the value of the Navajo clip, and an asymmetric relationship developed between herders and traders on the Navajo Reservation.

Terms of Trade

According to White and Cronon (1983:425), sheep alone stood between Navajos and famine after the reservation was established. Limited water resources prevented them from engaging in extensive farming (Bailey and Bailey 1986:140; Kelley and Francis 1994). Arizona was the last of the western regions to open up to commercial sheepherding. It was an ideal time for traders to become involved in marketing products produced by people recently confined to a reservation. Arizona was prime territory for an activity that had brought large fortunes to several generations of southwestern residents. Navajos had already demonstrated their past success as herders. Because the formation of the reservation had reduced their former land base, Navajos had lost access to both prime grazing lands and watering holes. Commercial ranchers increased the size of their herds adjacent to reservation boundaries, thus benefiting from the Navajos' loss (White 1983:231).

Trading posts, more than any other institution, made possible more frequent contact between Navajos and Anglos.[7] They predated other Anglo agencies such as schools and hospitals (Adams 1968:134). By 1890 there were at least forty posts on or adjacent to the Navajo Reservation (Bailey and Bailey 1986; Weiss 1984:151). The government controlled the number, locations, and licensing of posts on the reservation. Off-reservation posts were unregulated, but government regulations prohibited off-reservation buyers from purchasing wool directly from reservation Navajos. Traders frequently consigned their wool to eastern brokers through regional mercantile firms (Hubbell Papers [HP]). In January 1898, more than two million pounds of Arizona wool sold in Boston (Akbarzadeh 1992:151), much of it Navajo wool. Although there are considerable discrepancies in government statistics, herds may have increased from thirty thousand in 1869 to nearly one million by 1890 (Aberle 1966:32). During the annuity period, Navajos received additional stock and withheld butchering to increase their herds. By 1900 drought and storms reduced that estimated number by half (Bailey and Bailey 1986:124; White 1983:219). Cattle never made up more than 10 percent of Navajo stock holdings. The subsistence value of Navajo herds far outweighed the market value until World War I (Bailey and Bailey 1986:136; White 1983:236).

The sheep initially procured from the Spanish were hardy range animals that needed little care. Their wool was long, straight, and nearly greaseless, ideal for hand spinning in arid country (Baxter 1987:20; Underhill [1956] 1983:38). Churros were lightweights in both fleece and meat relative to other breeds. After 1904 Indian agents sporadically introduced new breeds such as the Rambouillet with limited success. Crossbreeding increased the weight of the animals and their fleeces but proved inimical to weavers, as the crimpy, oily wool attracted dirt (Bailey and Bailey 1986:129; Colton 1932; Weiss 1984:80). Navajos also herded goats, primarily for milk and meat. When the demand for mohair increased, Navajos were encouraged to replace the little Spanish milk goat with Angoras, thereby sacrificing subsistence value to commercial value (Bailey and Bailey 1986:132).

The Reservation Traders

"What is the use of having so much if nothing can be given away?"
Elderly Navajo, cited in Utley 1959:14

The trader occupies an ambivalent place in Navajo history. Numerous authors (Adams 1963; Reichard [1936] 1968; Utley 1961; Underhill [1956] 1983) see him as an individual who aided the Navajos' transition into the "modern world." Others (Lamphere 1976; Ruffing 1979; Weiss 1984; USFTC 1973) picture him as often unscrupulous and profit oriented. In fact, some traders befriended the Navajo, acting as interpreters, doctors, lawyers, bankers, and sometimes morticians (Blue 2000; Underhill [1956] 1983), and others casually justified a number of inimical trading practices. Navajos killed more than twenty traders (including Lorenzo Hubbell's brother, Charles) between 1901 and 1934 (Blue 2000:235; McNitt 1962:322). Underhill ([1956] 1983:177) referred to the trader as "the Navajos' Shogun," and noted that trading was doubly profitable: there was a markup on staples sold, and there was a handsome profit made by selling

Navajo products. As the reservation was enlarged government officials had little contact with most Navajos.

The reservation economy gradually shifted to specialized production for the American market, accompanied by debt peonage (Aberle 1983:657). With the expansion of trading posts, the intertribal trading network declined significantly (Bailey and Bailey 1986:147). Traders retained their hold on customers by providing credit to absorb future income from livestock and wage work and by physical control of welfare and social security. Traders held a monopoly on consumer credit (Adams 1963). Thus Navajo trading came to have a stability and continuity unexcelled by trading on other reservations. As recently as the 1960s, it was largely controlled by Anglo families whose ancestors initiated trading in the 1880s. Youngblood's 1935 survey states that gross sales probably differed little from general stores for that period, but because the trader paid no rent, had a low salary and wage account, and paid no taxes, he realized a higher net profit than his urban competitors. Even during the depression, far fewer trading posts went bankrupt relative to other off-reservation businesses. Faunce ([1928] 1981) and Hegemann (1963) state that a post was expected to pay its way within five years.[8] By 1943 there were 146 posts on or near the reservation.

Roberts (1987:xviii) describes an Indian trader as an individual who "exchanges manufactured goods with Navajos for raw materials and crafts, usually on the latter's home ground." The trader carried flour, coffee, sugar, and baking powder, along with canned peaches and tomatoes. Tobacco, flannel, velveteen, calico, and trade blankets were bartered in large quantities (Blue 2000:45; McNitt 1962:78; Reinhart 1999).

Reservation posts were generally constructed of stone, wood, or adobe, with a corrugated roof. Windows were often protected by iron bars. Interiors were similar: the "bull-pen" usually had an iron stove and woodbox and high, wide wooden counters that discouraged shoplifting from shelves that lined the walls. Doors were double locked or equipped with stout drop bars (McNitt 1962:73; Schmedding [1951] 1974:327). Traders owned their own buildings but rarely owned the land. Some posts had a guest hogan on the grounds to accommodate Navajo families who traveled long distances to trade (Blue 2000; McNitt 1962:78). Few Navajos owned trading posts on the reservation, as business ran counter to community values. An Anglo trader could refuse credit to a Navajo, but his Navajo counterpart could not (Roberts 1987:120).

Initially no cash changed hands, as it was always in short supply. Exchange via barter dominated, and because of the instability of the population, it was impossible to extend credit. According to an elderly Navajo, his cohorts were not dependent on traders during the early reservation years (Dyk [1938] 1967).

The transformation from a barter to a commodity credit economy began in about 1885, within a few years of the cancellation of annuities. The first traders sought quick riches in the commodities market, especially in wool. As these opportunities diminished, traders were forced to settle for long-range profit. Adams (1963:279) quotes a trader who had been in the business forty years: "[I]n the old days the Government minded its own business and left traders alone. As long as wool prices held, all you had to do to make a profit was to open the doors. . . . [I]t was not necessary to keep any books." Traders sought to retain and protect their consumer market by performing many ancillary functions (translator, postmaster, recruiter for railroad work, claims agent, etc.). Posts were generally open long hours six days a week. Territorial monopoly rather than price collusion tended to minimize competition (Adams 1963:169). Posts were frequently twenty to fifty miles apart. High freight rates coupled with low volume purchasing and long-term credit contributed to higher prices at trading posts compared to off-reservation retail outlets.

The zeal of the Indian Department to "civilize" the Indians and the role the trader fulfilled in realizing this goal is clear in the following statement by Commissioner Leupp in his treatise, *The Indian and His Problem*:

> He lived in an ell of the store building, and used to leave the door of his living quarters ajar, so that the Indians could peep in and see what uses he made of his simple appliances of toilet and table. After he had sufficiently piqued them to emulation, he refused to sell them a set of cups and saucers unless they would buy a table to set them on. He kept bright mattresses and comforters for sale, but he would not sell one to an Indian who did not buy also a cot to hold them. Thus by degrees he lifted his customers off the ground and got them into an approach, at least, to decent household habits. Pretty soon he set up a sewing machine; and any squaw who would buy sensible goods for her own clothing and that of her children, he would teach how to use the machine. (1925:190–91)[9]

The trader in particular induced, sustained, and expanded native desire for and later dependence on items of white manufacture:

> [P]robably the greatest service to the Indian stemmed from the change in material culture. . . . [He] played the dominant part in replacing the aboriginal economy, which the reservation had destroyed, with an economy linked to the white world and adjusted to the realities of reservation life. Perhaps it was not the best solution, but it worked. (Utley 1959:38–39)

Since the beginning of the reservation period, the Navajo economy has become integrated into the national market via wool production, weaving, lamb production, and wage work (O'Neill 1999). Traders have selectively promoted new subsistence activities to their benefit to perpetuate the seasonal, uncapitalized cycle, with its dependence on post credit (Adams 1963:293). Adams posed as a trader in the 1950s during his doctoral fieldwork. From the traders' perspective, the American ideal was to promote material welfare without disturbing moral and spiritual values (Adams 1963:283–84). Traders saw themselves as best equipped to bridge the gap between the Anglo and Navajo worlds. They alleged that it was better to be a good Navajo than a poor white man. The different forms of credit that developed via trading initiated the economic subordination of Navajo people.

Credit and Credit Saturation

Adams (1963) provides the most detailed explanation of the different forms of credit extended to Navajos by reservation traders. Although his descriptions derive from his experience as a reservation trader during the 1950s, they tend to agree with information culled from earlier traders' memoirs and record books (HP; Richardson 1986; Roberts 1987; Schmedding [1951] 1974). As will be seen, the development of credit and pawn practices fostered a bondagelike dependence of the producers on the traders. Lax enforcement of government regulations concerning inimical trading practices resulted in traders having de facto monopoly control over Navajos, especially since the historical and regional indigenous markets were severed or curtailed (Weiss 1984:152).

Direct, across-the-counter exchange of consumer goods for commodities was initially the backbone of the Navajo trade. Although the commodity trade is referred to as barter in many publications, there was no haggling over prices. Traders acquired all items by quality or quantity according to fixed, preannounced unit prices. Exchanges were based on cash valuation, not on valuation in equivalent goods. Such a policy allowed for free price adjustments, which was much to the trader's benefit (Adams 1963:199). Although it was legally impossible for an Indian trader to demand payment of old debts, traders had ways of "settling" accounts (Adams 1963; Faunce [1928] 1981; Hegemann 1963; HP; McNitt 1962; Schmedding [1951] 1974).

The seasonal nature of Navajo subsistence, for example, their dependence on the annual spring wool clip, made it necessary for traders to extend credit. Different types of trade and credit included (1) cash sales, which were very rare as cash was always in short supply; (2) "book" (unsecured) credit granted against future wool clips, livestock, (in earlier years) textiles, and, more recently, against future wages or unemployment or relief checks; (3) pawn, or secured credit; and (4) direct commodity exchange, for weaving and other crafts, pelts, skins, and piñon nuts (Adams 1963:186).

Any moneys received by check were subject to "credit saturation." Navajos who held wage jobs off-reservation sent their paychecks to the post to pay down accounts. As the trader was usually the postmaster and had acted as labor recruiter, he was well aware of paycheck amounts and allowed or even encouraged family members to spend most of the anticipated income before it was received. This practice was perpetuated when welfare and social security became available to reservation residents. In this way very little cash circulated in the region, preventing residents from trading elsewhere (Adams 1963:186–92). Thus credit saturation allowed the capture and retention of the consumer market. Many traders discouraged off-reservation farm labor as entire families could be absent from the region for months, whereas with railroad work, male breadwinners worked seasonally and had their paychecks sent to the posts (Adams 1963:280–81). Thus the Navajo consumer was in a continual state of "economic indenture[,] . . . tied to the post in a treadmill of payments and future extension of credit" (USFTC 1973:16). The threat of withholding future credit acted as an effective sanction against default. Navajos lived on credit to such an extent that the trader was in effect budget director and finance manager for his "community" (Adams 1963:191).[10]

Seco or "Chips"

During the eighteenth century, next to officials of the provincial government in Santa Fe, traders were the most affluent group in the northern regions of New Spain. Because cash was in such short supply in the region for generations, traders "invented a system of imaginary currency, including four kinds of dollars. . . . [T]he beauty of this system was that the traders always bought for the cheap pesos and sold for the dearer kinds, all being "dollars" to the Indians[,] . . . a trader by two or three barters in a year often getting $64 for a piece of cloth which cost him six" (McNitt 1962:9).

Indians distrusted paper money, so most traders substituted "seco," tin money in various denominations stamped with the post's name on the back (Blue 1988; McNitt 1962:84). In earlier years, traders had issued "due bills," or credit slips. If the customer lost the due bill, the trader could deny its existence (USFTC 1973:21). Traders turned to using seco because some Navajos learned how to counterfeit due bills (Adams 1963:152). Although Indian agents discouraged the practice, traders issued seco to Navajos who had credit balances. They thus ensured their customers would return to trade with them in the future rather than trade at a competitor's post. Acquiring seco benefited Navajos who did not wish to trade out all their credit at one time. Posts only extended credit in the form of merchandise and only "paid" for articles produced by the Navajos with merchandise (Adams 1963:108).[11]

Pawn

Another practice generally discouraged by the Indian Office and subject to abuse was the widespread practice of accepting pawn as a secured form of temporary credit for an individual Navajo. The pawn system developed during the 1880s (Bailey and Bailey 1986:54; HP). Pawning originated from the shortage of money and the Navajo skill in making jewelry (McNitt 1962:55). Pawn was usually held for a minimum of six months, at 10 percent interest per month (HP; Roberts 1987:181). Generally credit was allowed up to 25 percent of the value of the pawned goods. Allowing too much credit made it difficult for the owner to redeem the goods. Pawn credit, like book credit, requires intimate knowledge of both the individual and his past record (Adams 1963:196–97).

Most sources on the subject acknowledge that it was impossible to carry on trading without handling pawns (Adams 1963; HP; McNitt 1962; Richardson 1986; Roberts 1987; Schmedding [1951] 1974). When Navajos brought in their wool or lambs during buying season, they had to redeem their pawn before receiving credit. Sometimes the reclaimed goods were immediately repawned, even after the owner had just "sold" all of his or her wool (Schmedding [1951] 1974:327).

Elizabeth Hegemann, who with her husband traded at Shonto after 1929, remarks:

> [E]verything was barter trade at the outlying posts, a trader automatically took heed of what a Navvy wore or carried on himself or on his horse. A Navvy wearing a new shirt or hat that the trader had not sold him meant that [he] had ridden over to another post to trade. If he did not owe anything, all right let him go, but if he had heavy pawn in, this was a warning signal not to be ignored. He had probably sold some wool or a rug or pawned a piece of jewelry at a competitor's post where he did not owe anything. (1963:271)

Trader abuse of pawn was criticized for decades before the imposition of stricter government regulations (USFTC 1973:22). Because pawn was always valued at much less than its true worth, an unscrupulous trader could sell it at considerable gain. The market value as agreed on by trader and owner was to be marked on the pawn ticket. Sometimes it was left blank, showing only the amount borrowed. If the item was lost, misplaced, or stolen, the owner was out of luck, as the trader was responsible only for the amount displayed on the ticket. If the owner lost the ticket, she or he had no proof of the transaction. If the owner needed cash, exorbitant interest rates were often charged (USFTC 1973:22). Curiously, several sources refer to pawned items as a form of "bank account"—a strange type of account, as, instead of earning interest, the owner was liable for interest fees of up to 120 percent annually (Roberts 1987:48).

Juan Lorenzo Hubbell, Dean of Navajo Traders and Father of the Navajo Rug

The most famous trader to the Navajo was "Don" Juan Lorenzo Hubbell, whose trading activities, especially related to the marketing of textiles, make up a significant portion of this book. His trading post and home at Ganado, Arizona, are now a National Historic Site managed by the Southwest Parks and Monuments Association. The family's papers (1865–1965), including correspondence and business records, are housed at the Special Collections Library at the University of Arizona. (See appendix II.)

Hubbell was born in Pajarito, New Mexico Territory, in 1853, to a Connecticut Yankee father who had been a soldier and sutler and a Spanish mother whose family reputedly had been given one of the original land grants by the king of Spain (Underhill [1956] 1983:183).[12] Señora Julianita Gutierrez Hubbell's paternal grandfather was one of the first governors of New Mexico under Mexican rule (Blue 2000:8; Brugge 1993:21). Hubbell's uncle Charles was a member of Kit Carson's campaign and commanded an escort for the Navajos who were driven to Fort Sumner. Santiago Hubbell owned a bridge on the Rio Puerco (south of Albuquerque) and charged a toll for each Navajo and his or her animals who crossed when Hwééldi was disbanded (Peterson 1986:124). Hubbell's brother Frank was a successful stockman who owned ranches of several hundred thousand acres in New Mexico.

Lorenzo Hubbell has been profiled in numerous popular and anthropological publications. Blue's (2000) "ethnobiography" contains the most detailed study of Hubbell's life to date. I draw from Blue and a number of other sources, including Peterson (1986).[13] Peterson (1993:274) sheds light on Hubbell's early life as well as his trading style, his flair for politics, and the particular advantages that accrued to him throughout his life as a result of his charisma and business acumen. Peterson (1986:185) lists a number of popular references he used and admits: "All of these sources more or less mythologize Hubbell and no doubt I have fallen victim to the same influences." It is difficult not to be impressed (Blue 2000:201). Most sources provide a litany of accolades:

"Lorenzo the Magnificent" (Coolidge and Coolidge 1924); "King of northern Arizona" (Laut 1915:126); "the last and greatest of the Patriarchs and Princes of the Frontier" (Lummis 1925:182). Observers of Navajo history agree that Don Lorenzo had few peers among traders. Utley (1959:84) says that "he was the first and greatest[;] . . . his position was almost baronial." Blue (2000:278) refers to the family as "the Brahmins of southwest trading." Mitchell and Frisbie (2001:50–51) emphasize his laudable reputation among Navajos.

If one were to focus on just the correspondence and memoirs of people who knew Hubbell and ignore his business records, the profile that has emerged would remain intact. But his business records are central to understanding how he supported, managed, and increased the size of his empire. They provide a subterranean text that reveals the often precarious and increasingly competitive entrepreneurial activity that dominated the region.

Hubbell arrived in Navajo country during the early 1870s. He worked in a post office, clerked for a period, and became a Spanish interpreter. His fluency in Spanish and English and eventually Navajo served him well. Hubbell's upbringing, infused with Hispanic values, stamped the development of the "oasis of civilization" he built over time at Ganado: "[T]here was a quality of paternalistic fondness for the people with whom he dealt that was as real as the image of a picturesque influential figure that he enjoyed" (Peterson 1986:127). He began trading in the Ganado area in about 1878 (Dary 1986; Utley 1959:48). By 1900 an extended family group was associated with his trading-freighting-farming domain: several nephews, two brothers, a son-in-law, and eventually his sons and grandchildren. In 1901 he constructed "the Big House," a seven-bedroom home of nearly 4,500 square feet (Blue 2000:91, 286–87). His two daughters managed the household staff, and he entertained visiting artists, politicians, writers, and scientists (Blue 2000:195). His hospitality was legendary. As McNitt (1962:208, 216–20) remarks, "He lived and entertained on an opulent scale."

Hubbell's freighting operation fielded as many as ten teams of fifty to sixty-five mules and horses, driven primarily by Mexicans. Some Navajos worked at the post and seasonally on the farm. For decades they averaged $1 per day in "pay," discharged in goods, not in cash. The Hubbells' horse team drivers and herders were compensated in the same manner (Blue 2000:140). The entire complex also included a blacksmith shop, a bakery, and a one-room school. Books and paintings filled the family library and art gallery. Utley (1959:57) describes the trader's home as a sharp contrast to "the desert wastes. [It was] comfortably furnished[,] picturesquely decorated with Navajo crafts."[14]

Hubbell served a controversial term as sheriff of Apache County from 1884 to 1886 (Blue 2000:72). He became postmaster at Ganado in 1895. That year his business partner, C. N. Cotton, opened a large wholesale firm in Gallup. He was elected to the Council of the Arizona Territorial Legislature in 1893 and served as chairman of the Republican Central Committee (Blue 2000:172–73). Politics in the West generated intense debate, and merchant participation could be strongly partisan. With clerks and family members available and silent partnerships widely practiced, entrepreneurs such as Hubbell could manage business and politics simultaneously. Hubbell was a delegate to the Constitutional Convention in November 1906, and in 1912 he became senator in the first state legislature. He was instrumental in Arizona's achieving statehood that year (HP Box 545 #1; Blue 2000:178). He was away from Ganado for most of the period 1912–14. In 1914 he ran as the Republican candidate in the national Senate race and lost. It appears he never recuperated financially from the defeat (Blue 2000; Peterson 1986:153). Although relations between reservation traders and government officials were frequently strained, the Hubbells were held in high regard by agents and federal authorities locally and nationally (Blue 2000; Hall 1994; Schrader 1983).

Although he may stand head and shoulders above other traders in the history of the Southwest, Hubbell's business creed embraced that of his contemporaries:

> The first duty of an Indian trader, in my belief, is to look after the material welfare of his neighbors; to advise them to produce that which their natural inclinations and talent best adapts them; to treat them honestly and insist upon getting the same treatment from them[;] . . . to find a market for their products and vigilantly watch that they keep improving in the production of same, and advise them which commands the best price. This does not mean that the trader should forget that he is to see that he makes a fair profit for himself, for whatever would injure him would naturally injure those with whom he comes in contact. (Cited in Brugge 1993:47)

Utley may provide a more apt description of Hubbell's nature, one that reflects much of the information revealed in his papers:

> That he was motivated by an ambition for even greater profits also seems evident from the rapid and successful expansion of his trade network. Robert E. Karigan, one of his associates, pictured him as brilliant, shrewd, and ambitious to control the Navajo trade. Cozy McSparron added that the ambition stemmed from a desire to have enough money to give things away, to make people happy, and, above all, to take care of the Indians who depended upon him. (1961:32)

In the history of Gross, Kelly and Company, Kelly mentions that it was not unusual for the Hubbells to owe them $30,000 on an open account, to be paid when their wool came in. His final comment speaks volumes about "the businessman's creed": "Perhaps it was fortunate that he [Hubbell] died between the wool and the lamb seasons when he didn't owe us any money" (1972:216).

In his memoirs (Hogg 1930) Lorenzo Hubbell states that for many years his Ganado post had sold more than a quarter of a million dollars in wool and hides alone. This figure may also reflect the value of stock sold. He says:

> An Indian buck drives up with his wagon in front of the post. He may have several hundred pounds of wool, a bale of goatskins, several rugs that his squaws have made, and a number of articles of Indian silver jewelry. All such goods have a very definite market value, and the trader who is honest will allow the Indian equal value in other staple commodities or manufactured products, according to the market quotations of the day. (Hogg 1930:28)

According to Hubbell, the trader places a stack of silver on the counter, and the Indian "trades out" and acquires goods equal in value to the silver. No mention is made of Navajo blankets, other than the statement that the buck trades for his [mute] squaws. It will become evident that this story conflicts with Hubbell's own business records. As Brugge remarks:

> He wanted the facts to be those he chose to reveal. Like all of us, he tended to omit his sins and mistakes. If his memory was not perfect, the magazine article that J. E. Hogg was to write was even less so. (1993:5)

The fascinating memoirs of the trader Joseph Schmedding provide a revealing portrait of his mentor, Richard Wetherill (who with his brothers "discovered" Mesa Verde), one of Hubbell's contemporaries:

> [Wetherill was] a keen bargainer, a typical "Yankee horse trader" but always and painstakingly fair. He knew every trick of the trade, besides several others of his own invention. No use trying to hoodwink him, he knew the answers before the questions were put. Of course he possessed intimate knowledge of values, but over and above that he was a master psychologist. That, perhaps more than the actual trading knowledge and experience, was the reason for his success. . . . Mr. or Mrs. Navajo might get the better of the green trader in one or two

deals, but after that they would probably find that the master had taken the neophyte in hand and imparted to him special knowledge to offset their wiles and cunning. Every . . . transaction was a battle of wits. ([1951] 1974:306)

Wetherill traded in a remote area of northwestern New Mexico near Chaco Canyon at the turn of the century. He was killed by a Navajo in 1910, and his widow was forced to sell off a portion of their historic textile collection to Herman Schweizer of the Fred Harvey Company (see appendix IVc, n. 2).

Government Regulations and Trading

After 1890, with rare exceptions, the government declared it illegal for an Indian trader to demand payment of old debts. Bob Evans of the Fred Harvey Company remarked:

> Indian traders found a Navajo was a better risk than a white man—once they had judged the Indian's ability to pay it is doubtful if a Navajo ever took advantage of the government's new ruling. (McNitt 1962:57)

This is corroborated many hundreds of times in Hubbell's ledger books. Navajos' concern about products owed to Hubbell to settle accounts persistently recurs in Indian correspondence to the Hubbells between 1902 and 1964 (HP Box 124). New and more stringent regulations on stock purchases and trading practices were mandated in 1914, and traders were threatened with revocation of their licenses if they failed to comply. A letter dated 8 February 1915 from Harry Wetzel, trader at the Hubbells' Cornfields Post, reveals methods he used to maximize returns (HP Box 100). Wetzel described how he convinced the trader at the neighboring Sunrise Post to raise and hold prices on low- and high-grade flour in twenty-five- and fifty-pound bags. He suggested that Hubbell invoice everything to him wholesale.

> [I will] make you more money than has ever been made here before. . . . [Y]ou have to first make it worth his while to trade with you—the chance will eventually come to soak him. . . . [A]s far as credit is concerned I have cut it out, but they haven't stopped trading here as you predicted. . . . [A] lot of my accounts are protected with pawn—good pawn average percent . . . about 66 percent profit, this includes cost—5 percent and freight. . . . [T]here are very few men who can handle the whole job with success [bookkeeping plus trading]. [I have] come up against the

hardest kind of competition possible and have had a bunch of Indians to contend with that were educated to all the twists and turns of the trading game before I was born. . . . During the time the permits allowed me to buy sheep I bought 1726 head and they cost me $3664.20. The total cash received from Ganado to buy sheep with was $640.00. Total amount of cash I turned in to Ganado during this time was $529.30. So you can see that most of the sheep I bought was in trade.

Wetzel's trading practices were clearly in violation of government policy. Traders were reminded that they were to pay Indians cash for all products in letters from Peter Paquette (HP Box 43, 7/07/10) and Superintendent Leo Crane. In the latter correspondence, Crane requested that traders help "stamp out the use of tin money" (HP Box 44, 3/31/16). Don Lorenzo had written a letter to Commissioner Cato Sells the previous month that revealed his trading practices:

The great trouble is that men on this res will agree to pay cash for all I. [Indian] products and then surreptitiously use means to practically force the I. to take out the amt. pd for this product sold in trade. I am going to be very frank with and tell you exactly the way I have been doing business with these I. for forty years. . . . [W]hatever price they may be quoted in the mkt, cash can be realized for them. I pay cash [for] wool, pelts, cattle, sheep. The following I pay cash when they ask for it [and] adhere strictly to it. The traders off the res. do not pay cash, have no freight to pay on same. . . . [T]here is not an I trader now on this reser. that came here when I did [who] pay[s] cash when asked for blankets and baskets, but is seldom asked for. I carry the I. on my books for large amts as they are stockmen. . . . [T]hey require money and provisions to carry them thru from Nov. to shearing time in May. My custom has been that instead of an itemized acct, as they buy the goods, I hand them trade checks to the amt. of goods that they desire and they use them the same as cash either at Ganado or keep them for future use. . . . [W]e all work to keep the I. sober and industrious, and store I. that I come in contact with are the most prosperous and progressive. (HP Box 101, #1, 2/12/16)

The letters of Wetzel and Hubbell reveal a more realistic view of the nature of reservation trade. Although traders were to pay cash to Navajos who requested it, the exigencies of trading on the reservation precluded much cash from changing hands. Cash was frequently in short supply, as is evident from inter- and intrapost correspondence and letters from various wholesalers such as the Babbitts and Cotton.[15] When cash was available, it was used to pay down wholesalers' accounts. As Hubbell admits, it was seldom given to the Navajos; instead trade checks (or seco) were issued. Thus the dollar "income" figures used here should not be mistaken for cash payments.

Superintendent Daniel sent a sharply worded letter dated 10 May 1920 concerning the price of wool (HP Box 44). He quoted Boston prices and informed the Hubbells that under no circumstances were traders to allow wholesalers such as Cotton to dictate the value of wool. Daniel quoted a letter from Cotton that stated he would pay $.20 for white wool and $.15 for black, whereas three classes of wool on the Boston market were valued between $.23 and $.60 per pound. He wrote:

> We are trying to help the trader as well as the Indian and under no circumstances do we propose to allow the wholesale merchant or speculator to dictate wool prices on this reservation. That means that your first obligation is to yourself and the Government by whose permission you are permitted to trade upon the reservation.

Periodically the Hubbells received letters from the government concerning collections of Indian accounts. Edgar Miller, superintendent at Keams Canyon, wrote "Friend Lorenzo":

> I am attaching two copies of the balance owed the Government on wagons, wire and stock. . . . [I] do not ask you to make any collections, but you have devious ways and methods of assisting us in helping the Indians to realize that these balances should be paid. . . . I am using every endeavor to give the Indians all the freighting . . . that I can possibly give them in order to help them pay their debts and become self-supporting. . . . Surely the Government should spend every cent it can among these Indians for they badly need it. (HP Box 44, 11/23/23)

Miller's three-page list contained eighty names of Navajos and Hopis who owed the government a total of $2,631.53 for wagons, wire, and livestock, with balances ranging from $1.70 to $145.00. Some of these accounts dated back to 1915.

For more than a century, traders on the Navajo Reservation have exerted a profound psychological and social influence over their customers, an influence that transcends their economic importance (Adams 1963). Traders represent dominant Anglo society. After receiving complaints for decades concerning inimical trading practices, the Federal Trade Commission (USFTC) held hearings to investigate abuses. It found that traders' monopoly rested on ignorance and poverty (USFTC 1973:15, 49). As recently as 1972, many Navajos were still preliterate and unsophisticated in commercial transactions. More than half of Navajo adults over the age of twenty-five did not read or write English, and one-third could not speak it. Examination of bookkeeping procedures at selected posts revealed numerous opportunities for abuse and concealment through lack of prescribed standards (USFTC 1973:41). Traders' long-term sustained profit was ensured by perpetuating Navajo dependence. In more recent years, post owners actively discouraged mobility of their clientele (who could shop more cheaply in off-reservation border towns) by criticizing truck ownership as too expensive and burdensome and by always demanding cash for gasoline. Adams (1963:273) relates that at the Shonto post, the trader removed mail order catalogs listing cheaper prices and refused to play the Navajo radio station, which featured advertisements of (cheaper) goods in town.

Until the 1960s the modern Navajo market economy was underwritten by wholesale houses such as Ilfeld, Gross, Kelly and Company, and the Babbitts who carried traders on long-term credit. Interest rates on credit were high, and these costs were passed on to Navajo consumers. Since the 1960s wool, lambs, and skins are no longer taken in trade by the wholesale houses to pay down post accounts (Adams 1963:167).

Diversification Denied

Navajos were disadvantaged in many ways. As small growers living in remote regions, they lacked bargaining power. The fleeces from their herds were unimproved, and shearing practices were initially quite crude. The federal government banned outside wool and lamb buyers from coming onto the reservation; therefore, traders enjoyed a monopoly (Weiss 1984). When used for commercial purposes, Navajo wool was most suitable for carpets; it was too coarse for clothing. However, weavers disliked the wool from the "improved" breeds, as it was more difficult to spin (Colton 1932; Reichard [1936] 1968; Roberts 1987:55, White 1983:233).

It was impossible for Navajos to diversify. They were caught in an economic web spun by entrepreneurs; and as the most populous primary producers in a vast region, they suffered the brunt of American capitalism. To make matters worse, because they were so dependent on their flocks for their main staple, mutton, Navajos were unable to sell a maximum number of animals to traders as off-reservation sheep growers could. The government prohibited certain classes of Navajo stock from being sold even to traders, because it was the primary food for the people (White 1983:216). Had Navajos seriously depleted their flocks, the government would have to provide foodstuffs. Periodically droughts, floods, blizzards, or disease took their toll on Navajo herds. Reservation traders were not heavily involved in buying sheep until shortly before World War I (HP Box 349; Kelley and Whiteley 1989). Thus the subsistence value of herds far outweighed their market value. The market for feeder lambs developed during the mid-1920s (Bailey and Bailey 1986:137, 139). Navajos were not to sell breeding stock until 1926. The exception occurred during the war when, with the government's blessing, Navajos sold many animals because of demand.

Because of price fluctuations in the volatile wool market, it was difficult for traders to depend on making a killing on the wool market. Traders had to maximize profits by another means if they were to survive the competitive economic climate that dominated Southwest trade after 1890. Recall that wool was placed on the free list from 1894 to 1897, during the industrial depression. This coincides with the period in which the number of trading posts was increasing on the reservation and traders were acquiring as much Navajo wool as possible. Thus the product that most traders hoped would provide them with greatest profits was continually at the mercy of the fluctuating international markets. Several authors state that the tribe was on the verge of economic recovery around 1900 (Johnston 1966; Utley 1961). One of the primary reasons that recovery failed to materialize was the low price for wool. One way that traders could maximize financial return was through an alternate way to market wool—one that meant little extra effort for them but placed an enormous burden on Navajo women. However, to properly contextualize the way newly imposed trading relations affected the Navajos, it is necessary to review Navajo domestic relations that prevailed until the 1960s.

Kinship, Social Organization, and Residence Patterns

The importance of land to Navajos cannot be overestimated. As farmers and pastoralists, Navajos "grow themselves from the land" (Kelley 1986:1). The flexibility of Navajo social organization has been widely noted in the literature. Livestock is individually owned and jointly managed and fields are jointly used. Women tended to own sheep and goats; men favored horses (Weiss 1984:33). Goats supply milk, cheese, and meat and have twins more frequently. Sheep supply raw materials for trade items and produce wool for weaving. Cattle were of little economic importance for decades. Ownership and control of animals has remained relatively unchanged. However, political policies affecting access to land and size of stock holdings have altered subsistence patterns in many areas. Home consumption of livestock continues to make an important contribution to the diet of some Navajo families, especially when cash is unavailable or in short supply (Bailey and Bailey 1986; Kelley and Whiteley 1989).

The residence group is the fundamental land-using unit, and households are its building blocks. A household is defined as a group of people who share a dwelling (Kelley and Whiteley 1989:51). Occupants of a household tend to be a nuclear family of one or two parents and juvenile children, with possibly a relative or two unable to live alone. A residence group is a collection of people who share a homesite, that is, one or more households. Two or more residence groups make up an "outfit," or coresidential kin group (Witherspoon 1975:101). These groups tend to merge in the winter and disperse in the summer. Rights to use the land on which the residence group is located are controlled by those living in the residence group, particularly the older couple.

The largest kin grouping is the clan, a named group of people who consider themselves the descendants of a common mythological ancestress. Kin relations in Navajo society favor female autonomy (Aberle 1962; Begay and Maryboy 1996; Lamphere 1977; McCloskey 1999; Witherspoon 1975). Navajo society is matrilineal, and clans are exogamous, favoring matrilocal postmarital residence. Residence patterns have shifted to more diverse patterns in recent history. However, even in more recent studies such as those by Witherspoon (1975) and Lamphere (1977), matrilocality continues to dominate, especially in the remoter parts of the reservation. Postmarital residence choices in 1940 resembled those of 1915. As long as a woman has living kin organized into an "extended outfit," she is assured access to land, even if she never marries or is divorced or widowed.

Marriage is normally a gradual process by which an in-marrying affine is separated from his natal unit and incorporated into the unit of his spouse. The initial bond is very tenuous. The new husband usually brings only a small number of his sheep. In the past marriages were arranged. The sexual division of labor is described in the Navajo Creation Story. Men clear and till fields, hunt game, and help women with their work. Women till the soil, carry water, make fire, and weave the blankets. Tools (including weaving tools) are mentioned in the Creation Story. The major role for women is reproducing and sustaining life. Men are leaders in political and religious affairs. As recently as 1970 approximately one-fourth of all marriages were arranged with the couple's approval (Witherspoon 1975:112). Divorce is common. If in-law problems emerge, the couple may choose to live with the husband's relatives. In more recent times, married women's duties were much the same. Women continue to do much of the herding and milking, and they butcher small livestock and process the skins. Men performed heavier tasks such as building and repairing homes, hauling water, chopping wood, and constructing corrals and fences. Many of these tasks are specifically mentioned during the wedding ceremony. Men cook while their wives are away, or women may perform more arduous tasks if their husbands are absent (Kluckhohn and Leighton 1974:94–95; Lamphere 1977).

Navajo notions of cooperation entail diffuse obligations whereby the exact nature and timing of requests and counterrequests need not be equivalent. Navajo ideology of kinship cooperation can be viewed as an instance of a widespread method of interpreting and regulating the exchange of goods and services and the organization of tasks among kinsmen. Kindness, respect, hard work, generosity, and helpfulness are all important values related to behavior for both men and women. These values are inculcated into children at an early age through example and explicitly taught to young Navajo women during the Kinaaldá, or puberty ceremony for girls (Frisbie 1967; Lamphere 1977:43).[16]

Livestock remained the center of Navajo livelihood for more than a century (Downs 1964). The subsistence residential unit is organized around a sheep herd, a customary land use area, a head mother, and sometimes agricultural fields, all of which are called *shimá*, or mother. Thus the head mother is identified with the land, the herd, and fields, and all residence rights can be traced back to her. Mies (1988:73) has described this form as matristic, where femaleness is interpreted "as the social paradigm of all productivity, as the main active principle in the production of life. All women are defined as mothers, but the term had another meaning than it does today [in nonmatrilineal societies]."

During the 1880s, herds increased exponentially. Most families continued to plant small fields, but pastoralism dominated Navajo livelihood. Corn, a few melons, alfalfa, and, where possible, peaches were grown by Navajo families. Because of limited water resources, farming was often confined to washes (Bailey and Bailey 1986:95, 143). Frequently harvests did not meet domestic needs, much less yield a surplus. By 1900 inclement weather conditions had reduced the ratio of Navajos to their sheep to 1:19, less than half that considered necessary for basic subsistence. With the exception of Hwééldi, the seasonal schedule of herding and farming tasks probably remained the same from 1840 to 1940 (Kelley and Whiteley 1989:90; Mitchell and Frisbie 2001).

The Navajo hogan, the round or polygonal home typically constructed of pine logs and earth, has increased in size over the past two centuries. In her ethnoarchaeological study of Navajo land use, Kelley (1986:80) notes that this facilitated activities associated with weaving, especially in the wintertime. Although herd size varied a great deal, poorer Navajos were aided by wealthier outfits that had large stock holdings (Kelley 1986:34; Weiss 1984:32). Although many Navajos continue to live in hogans, small bungalow-style homes clustered in mini-subdivisions now dot the reservation. Often these homes are built adjacent to a hogan as it remains the most appropriate place for ceremonies. Although sheep numbers declined greatly relative to the population, sheep retain an important role in contemporary Navajo life (O'Neill 1999:399).

Kelley (1976:246) notes the unfeasibility of several potential income alternatives to stock raising: (1) less than 1 percent of the region is capable of producing a regular crop even with development of water resources; (2) seasonal wage work requires costly travel over long distances for nearly all Navajos; (3) railroad labor was a minor source of income until World War II; (4) wage work in border towns is difficult to acquire because of language differences and racism. In addition, the influx of settlers in border towns produced an overabundant labor pool.

Collier's analysis of Plains Indian tribes during the nineteenth century places domestic relationships at the core of the political and economic processes of their societies. This is central to an understanding of Navajo society as it was affected by changes in the economy in the postreservation period. For decades, more than 90 percent of the Navajo economy was dependent on production that occurred in the domestic sphere. Although Navajos attempted to maintain a degree of diversification to offset inclement weather and other unpredictable events, per capita income has remained at 20 percent of the national average for more than a century. Russell (1999) reviews the causes and consequences of a persistently anemic reservation economy.

Extant literature asserted that traders "saved" weavers by developing off-reservation markets. In the history of Navajo trade, most if not all well-known traders whose names are household words to aficionados of western history and Navajo textile lovers acquired their fame because of their association with the Navajo blanket. Meanwhile, the names of only a handful of weavers have come down to us in history (James [1914] 1974; Moore [1911] 1987; Reichard [1934] 1974, [1936] 1968, [1939] 1971). Archival research using the Hubbell family's business records and reassessment of published literature both reveal that traders pressured weavers to produce to keep traders' profits higher. Thus a more insidious reason for lack of economic recovery by Navajos is the likelihood that the price of weaving was actually pegged to the price of wool (HP; Reichard [1936] 1968:192). Returns to weavers never increased substantially, except for an extremely brief period following World War I when wool prices peaked along with prices for other basic goods.[17] Analysis of Lorenzo Hubbell's business records revealed that after 1897 his blanket profits were far higher than his wool profits.

In his text on the wool tariff, Wright (1910:348–89) incorporates a table depicting the prices of washed Ohio fleeces (clean raw wool) from 1855 to 1907. For many of the years between 1883 (Hubbell's earliest business records) and 1907, the value in kind received by a Navajo weaver for her hand-spun, hand-woven saddle blanket was pound for pound, almost identical to the value of washed Ohio fleeces. Chapters 3 and 4 illuminate the devastating consequences of this strategy for Navajo weavers and their families. Situating Hubbell and his business contemporaries in the economic history of the Southwest that incorporates price oscillations of the international wool market illuminates an important problem that has not yet been investigated. To do so requires a review of published discourses associated with traders, weavers, and textiles and an analysis of Hubbell family business records.

3

Discourses on
Traders, Weavers,
and Trade Blankets

[Weaving is] no business-like nine-to-five procedure, but a now-and-
then method. She weaves between housekeeping and shepherding
chores, and the preparations to weave are even more tedious, and arduous than is the actual work of weaving itself.

Weiss 1984:105

The more desperate people were, the more they brought in rugs to
acquire goods.

Roberts 1987:128

Navajo women are hard workers. . . . [T]hey work all the time[,] . . .
cooking, weaving, herding[,] . . . all the time.

Coolidge and Coolidge 1930:37

[T]he trader is regulated, the Indian is not. Many persons have lost their
eyeteeth in rug deals with the Navajo. Besides, you have no guaranty,
yet the trader would guarantee the rug.

Admonition to "dudes" by Indian agent Leo Crane, [1925] 1972

The sentiments expressed above occur frequently in literature devoted to
Navajo weaving. Most publications on the topic also focus on technology,
materials, and "external" influences on the development of various regional
rug styles. Extant texts continue to emphasize the traders' influences on designs
and neglect the importance of textile production to traders' profits (Amsden
[1934] 1975; Blomberg 1988; Boles 1977, 1981; James [1976] 1988; Kent
1976, 1981, 1985; McNitt 1962; Rodee 1981; 1987; Underhill [1956] 1983;
Wheat 1977, 1984).

In the prolific literature on Navajo textiles, a cluster of generalizations has emerged on weaver-trader relations that dominate the field: (1) traders saved weaving by developing new off-reservation markets (Amsden [1934] 1975:179; Dedera [1975] 1990:36; Kent 1985:85); (2) "pound" blankets were a short-lived phenomenon at the end of the nineteenth century (Boyd 1979:20; Kent 1985:83; Rodee 1981:9); (3) weavers benefited financially by trading their own blankets for machine-made trade blankets (Amsden [1934] 1975; James [1914] 1974; Kapoun 1992:35; Kaufman and Selser 1985:73; Maxwell [1963] 1984:60; Weiss 1984:54; Wheat 1984:19); (4) rug weaving always decreased when wool prices were high and increased when wool prices dropped (Amsden [1934] 1975:235; Bailey and Bailey 1986:152); (5) traders' greatest profits were in wool (Adams 1963:175, 1968:135; McNitt 1962); (6) traders were responsible for design changes in Navajo weaving (Amsden [1934] 1975; Boles 1977; James [1976] 1988; Kent 1985; Rodee 1981, 1987). My research challenges all these ideas.

Government records reveal that an extraordinary amount of weaving was done and that it became increasingly important to Navajo livelihood in the postreservation period. Weaving was the only product exchanged for trade goods or credit that did not depend on the seasonal cycle. Weaving was also the only fully finished product exchanged for manufactured goods and food-stuffs. Cumulative evidence on the importance of weaving to traders' profits in comparison to other commodities does not exist in any published litera-ture. However, as this chapter demonstrates, enough evidence exists that such information could be collated and analyzed from government documents (e.g., Navajo letter books, CIA annual reports, and Bureau of Indian Affairs reports) and "classic" works (Amsden [1934] 1975; James [1914] 1974; McNitt 1962).

Authors neglected the importance of textile production for several reasons. First, weaving was not considered work but leisure-time activity (Luomala 1938:72). Second, only reservation traders were required to submit annual reports, yet many of them failed to keep adequate records. Third, according to Kelley and Whiteley (1989:209), 40 percent of the population lived outside reservation boundaries at the turn of the century. Fourth, acquisition of tex-tiles by off-reservation traders was undocumented in government reports. Fifth, evidence easily extrapolated from several published sources demonstrates the accelerated production of weaving, but it continues to remain unanalyzed in texts devoted to Navajo political economy because weaving was viewed as a by-product of wool production.

With weaving, these [favorable] circumstances are spare time and cheap wool. Traders long ago noticed that most of their rug purchases are made in the spring because most weaving is done during the long idle days of winter. . . . [T]he Navajo woman weaves when she has nothing better to do, or when the family wool crop cannot be sold to better advantage in the raw. . . . [W]ool in rug form brings a little more money. (Weiss 1984:105, quoting from Amsden [1934] 1975:235)

Demographic Background: The Reservation Period

It is impossible to comprehend the escalating importance of textile production to Navajo livelihood without knowledge of population growth after the reservation was established. One of the most useful studies available is Johnston's *An Analysis of Sources of Information on the Population of the Navajo* (1966). Johnston (1966:14) indicates the difficulty enumerators had acquiring adequate statistics: the transhumant nature of herding, the severely limited road network, errors associated with attributing patrilineal descent to a matrilineal society and other forms of artificial classification, errors in recording names, and cultural differences. He provides a comparative investigation of the two key sources of information on Navajos: the Bureau of Indian Affairs and the Bureau of the Census. Johnston's table 27 (pp. 136–37), drawn primarily from Bureau of Indian Affairs statistics, provides estimates of the Navajo population that aid in assessing the number of weavers in the entire population:

1875	11,767
1900	21,826
1905	28,544
1910	22,455
1915	30,871
1920	30,473
1925	31,985
1930	39,064
1935	43,555
1940	48,722

Johnston (1966:33) notes that before Bosque Redondo, Navajos had "long enjoyed a reputation for relative wealth and prosperity." During the thirty years after their return to the newly formed reservation, Navajos demonstrated remarkable vigor in recovering from the cultural shock of incarceration (Johnston 1966:31). However, the anticipated economic recovery failed to materialize after 1900.

Textile Production Registered in Government Documents

According to the second special census of the Indians (1910), Navajos ranked eighth of forty-four tribes in the proportion of males aged ten years and over, and among all tribes polled whose members had "gainful occupations," the Navajos ranked first in having more than 50 percent of its female population working as weavers (Johnston 1966:35). Cato Sells's annual report to the Commissioner of Indian Affairs, dated 1 July 1912 to 30 June 1913, does not mention weavers in its section, "Employment of Indians." Instead, Sells emphasizes procuring Indian boys for various agricultural and irrigation projects. He devotes several pages to the importance of handicraft production to various Indian tribes. Under a short section titled "Indian Art" (p. 40), he notes that the blanket industry among the Navajos is probably "the most profitable of the native industries." Although the actual number of Navajo weavers is unknown, he estimates the valuation of blankets produced that year at between $600,000 and $700,000. He mentions the initiation of fairs and exhibits with prizes to "discourage inferior work and the making of smaller sizes." Prizes were offered on blankets exceeding $4^{1}/_{2}$ by $6^{1}/_{2}$ feet and woven of hand-spun wool. Sells also mentions that twelve hundred Pima Indians made about nine thousand baskets with a cash valuation of $14,500. This figure represents the next highest amount relative to Navajo weaving.

Sells provides summaries of the number of Indians engaged in industries other than farming and stock raising and the value of products created (Johnston 1966:table 17). Although the number of weavers is unknown, the evaluation of textiles produced by Navajo weavers comprises by far the largest amount in any category. Navajo weaving ranks highest as an income source in all categories, except for a handful of tribes that receive land lease royalties or moneys from timber sales (Johnston 1966:table 6). In fact, "income" from textile production by an estimated seven thousand Navajo weavers in 1913–14 is nearly ten times that acquired by crop sales or wages. However, the value of stock sold by Navajos during that year is unknown. Kelley and Whiteley (1989:76) note that farming never returned to prereservation levels. From 1890 to 1930, crop production stagnated or decreased.

In the section "Native Industries" (pp. 36–38), Sells comments that the Navajo blanket industry "continues to be the most important and remunerative. . . . [T]he work is done by the women usually during their spare time," for which they received about $700,000. He then introduces the plan to tag all blankets valued at $8 or more to "guard against imitations[,] satisfy the public regarding the genuineness[,] . . . and avoid the production of large quantities of low-grade blankets." The evaluation of other handcrafts produced by all other Indian tribes in the United States was estimated at approximately $100,000. Sells (1913:38) notes the drawbacks Indians encounter when trying to sell their work. He attributes the problems primarily to the fact that the markets are "distant" and producers "usually want their money as soon as they bring in their articles." He urges that quality be improved so that better markets could be found and "they might realize the true value of their work."

Although textile production brought a far greater return to Navajos during this period than wage labor, it was realized at great effort. Most adult women wove, and for a large percentage of the population, young girls began their apprenticeship at the loom well before puberty. Thus a far higher percentage of the population was involved in textile production than in wage labor. Kelley (1976:236) estimates that real wages constituted less than 4 percent of Navajo "income" until 1920.

Off-reservation traders were not bound by government regulations to submit annual reports to the CIA. Because many Navajos traded at their posts, government reports that contain figures related only to on-reservation trade lack important information relevant to Navajo livelihood, especially in the realm of textile production. This point alone creates problems concerning the interpretation of annual government reports. Charles Amsden's historical study serves as an example of a discrepancy that should have triggered a response from scholars writing on Navajo livelihood.

Discourse I: Calculating Increased Production

Amsden's classic work on the history and technical aspects of Navajo weaving, published in 1934, draws on information from published government sources to calculate the increase in annual textile production. He notes that annual sales were first assessed in 1890 at $25,000 (~sixteen thousand Navajos; Johnston 1966:136). In 1930 the Navajo population was estimated at forty thousand, and annual textile production amounted to an estimated $1 million, reflecting a fortyfold increase in forty-one years (Amsden [1934] 1975:182). Since the population more than doubled and the evaluation of blankets increased fortyfold, even taking inflation into account, visible benefits should have accrued to the Navajo. In this calculation, therefore, lies a key to understanding that the tremendous increase in production by Navajo weavers was not to their material benefit. Had the population actually received the material benefits forty times over, there is no doubt Navajo living standards would have been visibly improved.

Many scholars frequently quote Amsden's work but fail to question the correlation between the increase in poverty and the [hidden] decreasing returns to weavers (table 1). Even with social security and welfare available (beginning in the 1930s), per capita income on the Navajo Reservation has remained at 20 percent of the national average for decades (Downer 1990:201; Russell 1999). The values reported in various government documents may reflect the amounts realized by traders and other wholesalers. Such information, summarized from licensed traders' annual reports and continually replicated in extant studies on the Navajo, is not sufficiently fine-grained to reveal the growing importance of textile production to the regional economy and the way in which production coincided with the continued impoverishment of Navajo weavers. Had such information been adequate to the task, researchers might have realized the gaps in extant analyses of the Navajo economy and addressed such shortcomings. For these reasons it is important to estimate the rise in the cost of living for Navajos (see tables 2, 3). Bailey and Bailey (1986:306–8) provide figures that demonstrate that the Consumer Price Index (CPI) doubled between 1890 and 1930. Evidence extracted from trading post inventories compared with credit received for their commodities reveals the cost of living increased far more for Navajos than for the rest of the American population. Bailey and Bailey's use of the CPI in a text devoted to Navajo livelihood is somewhat misleading, as it underestimates the rise in their cost of living (1986:appendix B). For purposes of comparison, the figures used for wool and stock are national averages taken from government records that document the market value of those commodities. The first column in table 1 lists the dollar amounts per pound received by Navajos for their wool or the amounts the Hubbells received for Navajo wool. The second column uses information taken from Bailey and Bailey (1986:appendix B).

There is another way to calculate the dramatic increase in textile production over a thirty-year period relative to the rise in population: evidence in government documents cited by various writers since 1914 (Amsden [1934] 1975; James [1914] 1974; Johnston 1966; Kelley and Whiteley 1989; Weiss 1984).

According to Amsden ([1934] 1975:180), the Navajo population was estimated at 14,000 in 1880. Navajo flocks produced 900,000 pounds of wool, with 100,000 pounds woven into blankets (about 12 percent of the clip). Navajos were still weaving for themselves and for intertribal trade to some extent. In 1888, with an estimated population of 16,000, Navajo weavers retained 400,000 pounds of wool, or 33 percent of the clip, for weaving.

Between 1880 and 1890 the wool clip more than doubled, totaling more than 2 million pounds. During that period, the wool retained for weaving increased seven times. At the same time the population increased, from 14,000

Table 1. Annual Wholesale Averages, Primary Navajo Products.

	WOOL (lbs.)		SHEEP		BLANKETS (lbs.)			HIDES (lbs.)	
Year	Navajo White Wool	National Average	National Average	Navajo	Saddle	Bed & Common	Rugs	#1 Sheep Pelts	#1 Goat Skins
1884	.085				.20-.30	.37		.04	
1885	.085	.145	2.19						
1886	.08	.163	1.95		.20-.30	.37			
1887	.08	.18	2.05		.35				
1888		.171	2.06			.40		.07	
1889		.18	2.14		.30	.35			
1890	.12	.171	2.29		.30	.35		.09	.17-.28
1891	.10-.13	.163	2.51		.30	.35		.09	.25-.28
1892	.08	.163	2.60		.30			.05-.09	.12
1893	.08-.12	.145	2.64		.30			.097	.25
1894	.07	.11	1.97		.25	.20-.24		.04	.18
1895	.095	.103	1.57		.25	.25-.30		.03	.20
1896	.055	.103	1.71	1.26	.25			.04	.21
1897	.087	.11	1.84	1.35-2.57	.25			.067	.29
1898	.07-.09	.137	2.51	2.35	.27			.08	.25
1899	.07	.145	2.80	2.25	.30			.08	.25
1900	.097	.137	2.97	2.33	.30	.30	.48	.09	.27
1901	.08	.137	2.96	2.00	.35-.40	.30-.50	.80-1.00	.06	.24
1902	.08	.137	2.62	1.75-2.15	.50	.50-.65	.65	.074	.31
1903	.12	.154	2.62	2.10	.45	.52-.65	.75	.087	.37
1904	.10-.12	.163	2.55	2.20	.35-.50	.41-.70		.08	.25
1905	.16	.222	2.77	2.25	.45		.70	.10-.13	.37
1906	.125	.231	3.51	2.25	.50	.65-1.10	1.09-1.53	.14-.17	.38
1907	.11	.205	3.81	2.25	.70-.80	.65-.90	.85-1.50		.25
1908		.163	3.87	2.25	.50-.65	.70	1.00	.10	.21-.26
1909	.10-.14	.222	3.42	2.25	.65-1.00	.75	.75-1.40	.12	.315
1910	.12	.217	4.06	2.25	.65-.75	>.75	.85-1.50		.25+
1911	.11	.158	3.83	2.25	.85	>.85	.85-1.25		.33
1912	.135	.173	3.42	2-2.25	.60-.75	.70-.90	.90-1.25	.12	.40
1913	.12	.167	3.87	2.25	.60-.75	.85-1.10	.85-1.50		
1914	.14-.17	.166	3.91	2.25	.60-.85	.08-1.25	.75	.08-.10	.40?
1915	.17-.19	.221	4.39	3.00	.50-.65	.65-1.00	1-1.25	.13	.27
1916	.18-.26	.261	5.10	3.00	.75-.85	.85-1.00	.85-2.00	.16-.22	.25-.49
1917	.43-.45	.416	7.06	>5.40	.70-.85	1-1.50	1-1.75	.36?	.40
1918	.45	.577	11.76	3-4.55	.60-.80		1-1.25	.38	.58
1919	.175	.495	11.49	3-5.00	.75-.90	1.10-1.25	1.10-1.75	.38-.43	1-1.30
1920	.25-.29	.455	10.59	3-4.00L	.60-.75	1.00+	1-2.25	.25	.65
1921	.10	.173	6.34	4.62L	.75-1.25	1.50	1.50-2.00	.10	.25
1922	.20-.27	.271	4.79	2.50-6.00	>.50	1.40	1.15-1.25		
1923	.25-.35	.394	7.50	5.00		.90-1.25	1-2.00	.18-.21	.25-.41
1924	.28	.366	7.94	4-5.40L	.50-.90	.90-1.25	1-2.00	.18-.25	.28-.33
1925	.25-.29	.395	9.63	5.00L	.75-1.00	.90-1.25	1.00		.33
1926	.20-.25	.34	10.53	3.33-5.00	.65-1.00		1.40	.20-.26	.36-.40
1927	.25-.32	.303	9.79	5.25+L	.75			.20-.26	.45-.50
1928	.31-.37	.362	10.36	3.74-5.00					
1929	.33	.302	10.71	6.50	.80-1.50	1-1.33	1.50	.20	.25
1930		.195	9.00	2-2.50L	.70-.80				
1931	.11	.136	5.40	2-3.00	.40-.68	.50-.80	.50-1.25	.03-.05	.22-.31
1932	.08	.086	3.44	2-2.15	.50-.65				
1933	.15-.18	.206	2.91	1.75L	.30-.45	.60-.75	.75-1.00	.03	.14
1934	.11-.18	.219	3.77	1-2.00					
1935	.12-.17	.193	4.33	2.20-3.00	.85-1.00	>.79	>.79	.06	.12
1936	.22-.24	.269	6.35	4.00L	.65-.85			.15-.17	.25
1937	.28	.32	6.02	4.50-5.00L	.65-.85			.10-.20	.12-.35
1938	.10-.15	.191	6.13		.65-.75	>3.99	6.80each	.09-.12	.20-.23
1939	.16-.18	.223	5.74	3-4.50	.75-.90		>6.50	.12	.20
1940	.22?	.284	6.35	2.50-2.75	.75-.90	3x5@$6-10	4x6@$10-15	.10	.10

Table 2. Cost per Pound of Foodstuffs Extracted from Hubbell Trading Post Inventories and Wholesalers' Invoices.

Year	Flour or Bread	Sugar	Coffee	Candy or Tobacco	Bacon or Lard	Dairy	Canned Fruit & Vegetables
1881	.06	.17	.25	.65 t	.21 b		
1883	.06	.25	.25	.50	.25 b		
1886-7	.05.5	.10 w	.30		.10 b		
1890-1	.03 w	.06 w		.45-.57 t	.12 b	.18 milk	
1894		.12					
1896			.14	.46			
1900	.04		.16				
1901					.15 L	.15 m	.20
1902					.13 b		.09 raisins
1903	.045	.08	.15 w	.40 chocolate	.20 b	.15 m	.15 tomato
1905-6	$4/100#	.10		.20 c			
1907	.10 bread	.135	.20		.20 b		.25 pears
1908		.20		.25 peanuts	.16 b	.25 cheese	.15 tomato
1909	$4/100#	.09	.30		.16 b		
1910	.04					.35 butter	.25 pears
1911		.07	.30				
1913	.05			.28 c w		.54 eggs	.14 t w
1914		.09				.20 b w	
1915	.04						
1916		.10	.32	.72 cocoa	.20 b	.15 milk	.25 pears
					.23 sausage	.35 butter	
1917	.045 w	.09 w		.15 soda pop	.40 b	.40 b	.35 peach
1918	.065 w	.08 w	.22 w	.21 candy		.70 b	.20 tom w
1919	.09		.40 w	.25 c	.65 b	.20 milk w	.30 peach
						.42 cheese	.20 tom w
1920	.07	.14	.45-.57	.73 t	.25 b w	.70 b	.25 tom
1921	.07-.09	.20	.30 w	.25-.32 c w		.20 milk w	.20 pears
1922	.10 bread				.25 tuna	.50 cheese	
1923	.04-.08 w			.25 peanuts	.44 b	.60 b	.20 pears
1924	.035 w		.34 w	.23 c w	.19 b w	.75 eggs	.24 peach w
1925	.05 w	.075 w		.74 t	.24 crisco		.20 tom w
1927	.03 w	.15	.50	1.40 t	.185 L w	.25 m	.25 tom
1928			.38 w			.50 b w	.13 tom w
1930	.05		.29	1.56 ctn cig w	.34 L		.30 pears
1931			.22 w	.74 t	.13 L w	.35 b w	.12 tom w
				.22 c	.32 b w	.19 m w	.09 pear w
1932			.26 w		.11 L w		.12 tom w
1933	.045	.10	.25				.22 tom
1934	.05	.10	.25				.23
1935	.15 bx cereal	.10 w	.20 w	.15 pkg cig w	.25 crisco w	.25 milk w	.25 tom w
1936		.15 w			.30 corn beef	.25 cheese	
1937	.16 bx cereal		.15 w	.28 c w	.42 butter w	.32 eggs w	.30 dz lem
1938	.12 cracker w	.06 w	.20-.35	1.50 ctn cigs	.24 bacon w	.06 m w	.30 pears
		.15 cookies w		.08 pop w			.30 peach
1939	.08	.09	.65		.25 pork		
1941		.10	.40		.25 peanut bu		
1942					.13 corn beef	.41 butter	
1943	.23 oats w	.07 w	.40			.50 b	.14 tom w

W = wholesale

Table 3. Cost of Consumer Goods and Stock Supplies Extracted from Hubbell Trading Post Inventories and Wholesalers' Invoices.

Year	Wool Sacks Hay/Alfalfa	Yarn/# Tow cards	Trade Blkt Shawl/Robe	Shoes/ Boots	Fabric/yd Calico Velveteen	Clothing Pants Shirts	Misc.
1881	.60 ws	.88	1.55 shawl	4.00 b	.08 c		
1883	.32 ws w		1.65-2.55 w		.75 v .10 c		
1886-7	.25-.50	.86	3.40-5.30 w		.07 c	1.20 p w	.75 overall w
1888-9		.78 w	4.50-5.00 w		.07 c	1.13 coat	.63 vest
1890-1	.34 ws	.35 tow	4.00 w		.27 & .45 v	1.65 p	6.00 suit
1894	.32 ws w	.69 w	2.50 shawl w		.09 c .55 v		.60 indigo
1896		.85 & .93			.10 flannel	.48-1.00 p	1.25-2.quilts
1900	.30 ws	.95	1.20-4.50		.45 v		8.00 stove
1901	.35 ws	.91	3.25-4.25 robe		$7/4yd bayeta		
1902	.35	.86-.97 w		1.00 boys	1.25 "plush"	.75 shirts	.50 underwear
1903	1.42/81# hay			1.50 oversh.	.15 sateen	1.25 pants	.30 fry pan
1905-6	.37 ws	.78	4.50-5.25 w	$17-30/ saddles	.10 c .43 v	4.50 vest & pants	2.50 sheep shears
1907	1.30/120# alfa		5.00-6.50	2.50 boys	.60 v w	2.50-3 pant	3.00 comforts
1908	.45 ws		7.00	2.25-5 mens		3.50-8.coat	.75-2.00gloves
1909		.50 tow	6.00 w		1.40 silk v	2.75 mens	
1910	.35 ws	.79	5.00-12.50	8.00 boots			125.00buggy
1911		.85	12.50	2.50 m w	1.00 v	1.90-2.35 p	20.00buckskn
1913		.10 pkg dy	3.00-9.00 w	3.00		15.overcoat	30.00 gun
1914	.50 ws	.50 tow	5-10.00	7.00 boots	.75 v	1.50 s	4.00 quilt
1915		.81	3.75-6.25 w	3.50-5.00 w		.75 boys p	2-3.sweatr w
1916	.27 ws	.90-1.05 w	3.90-6.00 w	1.45-4.50	.06-.09 c	.36-1.25 s	.45/gal gas
			10.00	6.25 boots		1.35-2.00 p	10.75 rifle
1917	1.75 hay	.30 warp	4.50-8.50 w	4.00 ms	.14 sateen	1.50 boys p	11.00 tent
	.60 ws w		12.50	6.00 boot w	.28-.45 v w		2.00 hat w
1918	1.25 ws	1.40	3.50-13.00 w	5.00oxfords	1.50 plush	3.00 pants	2.00 sweater
1919	.75-1.25 ws	.73 tow	11-17.50	2.70 boys	.25 sateen	.75-1.65 shirt	4.50 quilt
1920		1.50	6.60-16.50 w	7.50 boots	.30 c	3-5.00 p w	2.75 sheep
				4.00 boys w	1.40 v	1.50 s w	shears
1921	1.50 ws		13.50 robe	3-9.50shoes	1.00ea towel	5-6.50 coats	80.00saddle
1922	1.85 hay	1.00 w	13.50-15.00	.50 pr sox	.11 c w	1.25 shirt w	8-20.buckskn
1923	1.20 hay w	.90 tow	8.50-11.00 w	2.60 s w	.12 c w	2.0flannel s	11.50 bed
1924	1.50 alfal;	1.50 tow	14.00 shawl	5.50 b w	.17 sateen w	3.50 coat w	100-175.00/
			13.00 robe	2.50 s w		1.88 m p w	wagon
1925	2.50 hay		3.25-12.00 w	20.00 boots	.62 v w		.30 fry pan
1926	1.50 alfal	1.50 tow	14-15.00	4.00 s	.62 v w		65.00saddle
1927	1.40 hay			2.45girl w	.27 c	4.men coat	>5.men hat
1928	1.75 hay		10-11.00 w	1.85 child		3.50 pants	4.00 comfort
1929	1.50 alfal		15-22.50	6.00 women		54-.70 s w	6.50 trunk
1930	1.00 alfal			2.50 w	.10-.14 ginham	2.25-3.00 p	3.71 bed blkt w
1931	1.28 alfal			2.50 oversh	.55 v w .13 s		9.leathr coat w
1932			5.00 lite s w	2. women w	.09 plaid w	.60overall w	.10 baby food
1933			14.45	2.93 men	1.50 plush	1.50 men p	3.00 hat w
1934			5-10.50 w	6.00 b w	.22 c w	.75-2.00 s w	
1935	1.25 alfal	1.50 tow	17.50	7.50 boots	1.75 plush w	2.00 men p	4-5.00 hats
1936	1.25 alfal		10-11.25 w		.50 v w	2.75 jackt w	
1937	.75 ws	2.33 tow	14-15.50 s	12-17.00 b	.20-.25 plaid	.96 jeans	
1938				1.75-4.00 w	1.00corduroy	6.00sweatr	
1941		1.35 tow	16-17.00				
1942					2.00plush	1.25 s	
1943	.84 w s w			1.60-2.50 w	.25 flannel	5.00dress p	1.25 shirt
				3.75 retail	.35 prints		5.00comfort

W=wholesale

to 17,000, primarily due to enlargement of the reservation in 1880. Navajo wool sold for $0.12 per pound in 1890, and the CPI was 27 (Bailey and Bailey 1986). In 1911 the CPI held at 28 and Navajo wool sold for $.11 per pound. Based on figures reported in government documents, the population rose approximately 50 percent over thirty years (from 14,000 to 22,000 between 1880 and 1911). The total wool clip quintupled (from 900,000 pounds in 1880 to 4,512,213 pounds in 1911). In 1911 approximately 20 percent of the clip, or 843,750 pounds of wool, was used for weaving. Assuming there would be 50 percent more weavers given the increase in population, one would anticipate a concomitant rise in textile production. Yet weavers' output increased by 843 percent, even though wool and the cost of living index were nearly the same for both years. According to Bailey and Bailey, the CPI fluctuated very little (from 27 to 29) over the thirty-year period. These figures could have been calculated without difficulty by other investigators. To further understand the increased burden borne by thousands of weavers, the following calculations were extrapolated from additional published statistics taken from the same sources.

According to Kelley and Whiteley (1989:79), textile production brought the Navajo $711,000 in income in 1911. Approximately 843,750 pounds of fleece (20 percent of the clip) were woven up by an estimated seven thousand weavers. Based on the estimated value of wool that year, I calculated that weavers used $107,156 of their own wool to make textiles, for which they did not receive extra compensation. The cash valuation of their textiles when trading included the fleece used to make them. Calculating twice the amount of wool needed to produce a pound of hand-spun yarn, weavers produced approximately 421,875 pounds of yarn that were woven into blankets and rugs. This averages to 60 pounds of yarn woven by each weaver annually. With saddle blankets ranging from 3 to 7 pounds each and rugs averaging from 4 to 15 pounds apiece, depending on size, a weaver could produce 15 to 18 single saddle blankets, or 8 to 10 double saddle blankets, or 4 to 10 rugs per year, or a combination thereof. Mitchell and Frisbie (2001:47–48) describe continual textile production by Mitchell family members for decades. Given other household tasks, including preparation of goat- and sheepskins, cooking, herding, and child-rearing, one could argue the increasing burden borne by thousands of Navajo women is the North American equivalent of the lace makers of Narsapur (Mies 1982).

Discourse II: Ethnohistorical Perspectives

Here I track the economics of Navajo weaving as reflected in two key publications: Bailey and Bailey's ethnohistorical work (1986) and Larry Weiss's Marxian analysis of the development of capitalism on the Navajo Reservation (1984). These texts, supplemented by other works, provide a backdrop to assess and survey how textiles have been treated by authors working from various perspectives.

Bailey and Bailey (1986:51) state that of the five major types of craft production, weaving was most important to the Navajos. Even after Hwééldi, textiles were the major trade items until the mid-1880s (Bailey and Bailey 1986:37). During the 1880s, Navajos had little reason to seek wage labor (although very little was available) (Bailey and Bailey 1986:155). Adequate rainfall contributed to the maintenance of large herds and high crop yields, and the continuation of intertribal trade in skins, blankets, baskets, and pottery meant the people prospered (Bailey and Bailey 1986:96).

Navajos acquired metal goods and some foodstuffs from traders and bartered their wool clip for credit. Herds increased (per capita) 300 to 400 percent above prereservation estimates (Bailey and Bailey 1986:96) A trader named Leonard purchased a quarter of a million pounds of Navajo wool in 1880 and may have cleared between $5,000 and $10,000 on wool alone that year (McNitt 1962:80). Estimates indicate that as late as 1887 weavers produced one textile for every two women. More than 60 percent of the textiles were traded with Apaches, Utes, and other tribes. The tremendous increase in quantities of raw wool provided the impetus for women to "weave wool into blankets" (Adams 1963:152). Fine-quality Saxony yarns, imported from Germany, had comprised a portion of annuities and inspired weavers to "fabricate a yarn of quality never since equalled in the history of Navajo weaving" (Weiss 1984:34).

This rosy picture was drastically altered during the last decade of the nineteenth century, when global economic and regional environmental factors initiated a collapse of the Navajo economy. The removal of the wool tariff in 1893 allowed duty-free foreign wools to compete with all classes of domestic wools and coincided with the silver market crash. Several massive winter storms in conjunction with excessively dry summers decimated Navajo herds. By 1900 extended drought had decreased Navajo herds by 75 percent. The people had to slaughter stock for subsistence as crops failed, and some surviving stock died of thirst (White 1983:219). (Weiss [1984:43], citing Kelley, does not depict such a drastic drop in stock.) The decline in wool is reflected in Hubbell's wool shipments (fig. 6).

According to the extant literature, the economic collapse of the 1890s made weavers open to suggestions. Traders guided weavers into the production of marketable items, resulting in the shift from blankets to rugs (Kent 1976). Bailey and Bailey (1986:96, 152) note that "rug weaving developed as an alternative means of marketing wool. . . . [R]ug production decreased when wool prices were high, and increased when prices were relatively low. . . . [B]lankets . . .

brought a much higher price per pound than wool." Traders' influences were perceived as "commercializing the industry." Weavers adopted commercial yarns and dyes, which eliminated the arduous processing of raw fleece and the collection of plants for natural dyes. However, Bailey and Bailey do not discuss the cost of these commodities. The railroad provided both increased access to Navajo markets through traders and the means by which indigenous products, including blankets, left the Southwest. According to Bailey and Bailey, changes in material culture, as a result of the invasion of trading posts, "did not reflect acculturation or acceptance of Anglo-American technology, however, because the Navajos traded for manufactured goods functionally equivalent to items they already used, and rejected items that forced them to adopt new methods of production" (1986:96–97). They also mention that Navajos did not relinquish their economic self-sufficiency until the depression (1986:181; see also White 1983:248). However, this is clearly not the case, as Navajos could no longer organize for the market themselves. Weiss's text (1984) also illustrates the loss of economic independence before that time.

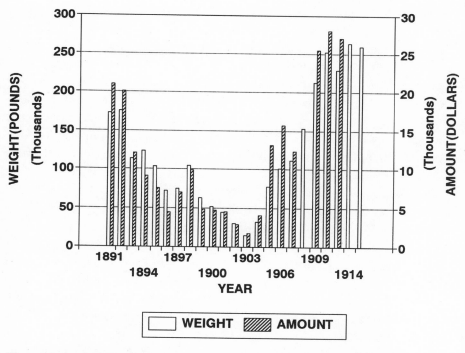

Figure 6. Annual Wool Shipments, 1891–1914, Ganado Trading Post, collated from Hubbell Papers.

In a section titled "The Commercialization of Crafts," Bailey and Bailey (1986:150–55) discuss the increase in the valuation of textile production after 1890. Using information also accessed by Amsden, they claim that Navajos "sold" about $24,000 worth of blankets in 1890 and $50,000 worth in 1899. Within four years the total "income" from weaving reported to the CIA rose to between $280,000 and $350,000, a five- to sevenfold increase. Again, these numbers are published as official figures representing income to Navajo weavers. Weavers, however, received goods in kind, not cash, for their textiles, thus use of the term "income" gives an erroneous impression of the actual transactions. Traders may have reported income "paid" to weavers in their annual summaries because official government policy forbade the use of trade tokens.

A similar problem concerns the total weight of textiles annually shipped off the reservation. These figures are absent in published CIA reports after 1900. Other than information culled from the Hubbell Papers and tables compiled by Fryer in 1939, I have not located any published tables, graphs, or other data that would allow researchers to calculate more realistically the increasingly unequal exchange that developed as the cash valuations of textiles plummeted relative to the cost of traded goods. Information published in border town newspapers during the early part of the century illustrates the amount weavers received per pound for their textiles (Bailey and Bailey 1986:152). By 1907 weavers in the Farmington, New Mexico, area were reported to receive between $0.75 and $3.50 per pound for their weaving. Yet archival records show that reservation traders wholesaled hundreds of pounds of saddle blankets at $0.80 per pound, native wool blankets for $0.65 to $1.00 per pound, and rugs from $1.00 to $1.44 per pound (see chapter 4). Textiles woven entirely of Germantown wool averaged $2.50 per pound wholesale; however, Germantowns made up only a small percentage of textile production (HP; Fred Harvey Company Rug Ledgers). These published prices lead one to believe that weavers received more than they actually did.

By 1910 weaving income had reportedly increased to $700,000 (Bailey and Bailey 1986:fig. 14). Because official government reports do not define how "income" is determined, it is difficult to decipher what these figures really represent. They may reflect the dollar amount calculated by traders of woven goods leaving the reservation annually. Such figures would represent credit traders received from wholesalers and not the credit received by weavers on their accounts. However, McNitt's papers (Box 8) contain information extrapolated from Traders' Reports to Assistant Commissioner F. H. Abbott (Classified Files 71406/11.910). During August 1911, traders reported the cash valuation of textiles acquired from weavers between 1 July 1910 and 30 June 1911. Careful scrutiny and analysis of unpublished reservation traders' annual reports and agents' narratives and statistical reports to the CIA will be necessary to clarify discrepancies.

Between 1910 and 1921 the value of weaving peaked at $700,000 in eight of eleven years. Income received by Navajos for wage labor (railroad and road construction) did not reach that amount until 1926 and held for two more years before dropping to less than $400,000 in 1932. In fact, the "commercialization" of weaving (the shift from blankets woven for indigenous use to rugs woven for an external market) generated most of the economic growth between 1890 and the depression (Bailey and Bailey 1986:164).

The term "commercialization" in association with the Navajo blanket or rug is misleading. Weavers continued to weave on the upright loom and use the large spindle, and some weavers used dyes acquired from traders. But the most time-consuming components of textile production remain unchanged—spinning and weaving. Had weavers been given or had they bartered large amounts of wool or yarn from the traders, it would have defeated the purpose of their acquiring a greater return on their blankets and rugs through using wool from their flocks. Because of the escalation in production, it may appear that textiles were becoming commercialized on a large scale. But production remained as labor intensive as before (Mitchell and Frisbie 2001). This subject is dealt with below.

Another factor that dramatically affected Navajo livelihood was the doubling of the Consumer Price Index after World War I. Although the cash valuation of textiles was maintained at record levels for a short period, their "purchasing power" realized approximately half the cash valuation received by weavers before the war. Thus the postwar rise in inflation led to a resurgence in textile production and an intensified search for wage labor (Bailey and Bailey 1986:118–19). The CPI stood at 30 in 1914 and rose to 60 in 1920 (Bailey and Bailey 1986:307). Sales of feeder lambs did not become an important component of the Navajo economy until the late 1920s; therefore, high rug production was imperative if Navajos were to survive. Although Bailey and Bailey (1986:152) report that "rug weaving always decreased when wool prices were high and increased when wool prices dropped," women trading with the Hubbells continued to increase their production of textiles, regardless of the price of wool (fig. 7). The exception, noted in government reports, occurred for a short time during World War I.

Discourse III: A Marxist Model of the Navajo Economy

Using Lenin's *The Development of Capitalism in Russia* as a model for examining the development of capitalism on the Navajo Reservation, Weiss provides

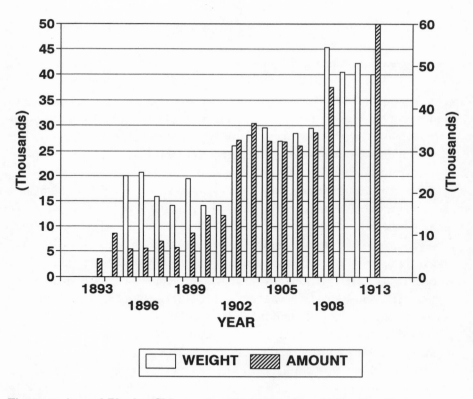

Figure 7. Annual Blanket Shipments, 1893–1913, Ganado Trading Post, collated from Hubbell Papers.

a far gloomier picture of the destruction of the Navajo economy than the ethnohistorians Bailey and Bailey. Weiss (1984:34) remarks on the use of imported dyes, yarns, and bayeta (imported trade cloth) by Navajo weavers before Bosque Redondo. Quoting sources used by the Baileys and others, he notes the importance of textile production to southwestern trade before the formation of the reservation. When the U.S. government incarcerated the Navajos at Bosque Redondo, it destroyed their subsistence base. After their release, traders as merchant capitalists appropriated the markets formerly provisioned by Navajos themselves. By 1889 there were nine licensed posts, with thirty posts outside reservation boundaries (Weiss 1984:50). The use of seco, the restrictions placed on off-reservation sheep buyers' access to Navajo herds and wool, government regulations that restricted grades of stock the Navajo were allowed to sell—all these factors and others gave traders a monopoly that functioned in their interests to the detriment of Navajo livestock owners.

Although Weiss provides one of the most comprehensive analyses of the Navajo economy to date, he relies heavily on official government documents before 1900 and supplements them by quoting from many classic sources published after 1900. He uses several texts written by or for textile dealers and collectors that frequently neglect to identify sources (Berlant and Kahlenberg 1977; Dedera [1975] 1990).[1] No new analyses by extrapolation from published statistics in annual government reports are presented. Although he cites Amsden, he does not extrapolate from Amsden's information quoted previously.

However, Weiss (1984:65) acknowledges that the increasing prosperity of the traders was "inextricably linked with the continued domestic production of the Navajo herder and weaver." Had large Anglo herders gained control of Navajo territory, traders would have lost their customers. It was in the traders' best interests that the reservation be enlarged and the Navajo continue as herders and weavers. Weiss notes that in 1887 a government agent reported that one-third of the adult population lacked stock. Approximately 350 Navajos worked for the railroads by 1898, earning $1.00 to $1.10 per day (Weiss 1984:69). (Hubbell had close to that many women bartering their blankets with him in the Ganado area alone.) Based on population estimates, there may have been more than 4,000 weavers.

Weiss attributes far greater importance to the increase in wage labor, which was a fraction of that provided by textile production between 1900 and 1925 (Bailey and Bailey 1986:153, 159). For example, in 1930 rug production was estimated to bring $1 million in income (Luomala 1938:64; Roessel 1983), whereas wage labor averaged $200,000. The calculated value of cultivated acreage amounted to $140,742 that year (Kelley and Whiteley 1989:211). There was little demand for Navajo seasonal railroad work until World War II (Adams 1963:51).

Weiss highlights the many ways traders (sanctioned by the U.S. government) were able to dominate the Navajo economy rapidly. Implementing credit saturation allowed traders to control Navajo production before commodities were produced. With increasing emphasis on herding as the primary form of subsistence (at the expense of agriculture), many Navajos became increasingly dependent on traders for most foodstuffs, except mutton and some vegetables (Reinhart 1999:102). Unlike the years before Hwééldi, Navajos were compelled to barter unprocessed resources, such as wool, for finished goods, such as clothing, processed foods, and tools. With the exception of their woven textiles, nearly all products that left the reservation remained unprocessed. Sometimes when traders purchased corn and wool from Navajos compelled to reduce their debits, traders held the commodities rather than ship them back East, then resold them to the people at a later date (HP; Parman 1976:127, footnote 60; Weiss 1984:45, 80).

Ample evidence can be extracted from extant literature to challenge assumptions that women wove part time for pin money. Amsden ([1934] 1975:iv), James ([1914] 1974:58), McNitt (1962:223), and Reichard ([1936] 1968) acknowledge the economic importance of textile production. For example, the trader Gladwell Richardson (1986) mentions that while running the post at Sunrise, he acquired an average of ten rugs per day, and in 1932, when boarding school ended and parents picked up their children, four hundred blankets were bartered in one day. Before World War II, rug sales drastically decreased, with fuzzy saddle blankets selling for less per pound than the fleece. Even the trader could get only about $1.25 apiece for a "fuzzy"—about the price of a twenty-five-pound sack of flour (Richardson 1986:180). During that time, he claims that more than 60 percent of the local economy was based on weaving. This type of commentary appears in traders' memoirs with some frequency (Newcomb 1966). However, scholars have neglected to investigate microlevel relations revealed in archival business records or traders' memoirs. Reinhart's (1999) study is an exception, but it focuses on the types of trade goods Navajos acquired from Lorenzo Hubbell without discussing their costs.

Because Weiss's text is the most comprehensive analysis of the Navajo political economy, it is necessary to survey further how he has used sources relevant to textile production in his analysis. Traders' control over the production of Navajo textiles is overemphasized by Weiss. In his glossary, he describes "domestic commodity production" as follows:

> The partial or total working up of a commodity in the home or on the laborer's land to the order of a merchant or industrial capital. For example, at certain periods in history Navajo weavers and silversmiths fabricated commodities at their homes with their own means of production (tools), but specifically to the order of a trader (merchant capital). (1984:176)

Evidence exists in archives and other publications to substantiate the case for smithing (Adair 1944; Bedinger 1973; Volk 1988). Smiths were often supplied with all the materials to fabricate jewelry. In contrast, weavers made their own tools and purchased tow cards, and they were seldom supplied with fleece, as this defeated the purpose of using their own wool to achieve a "greater" return.

Because Weiss does not know how these textiles were actually created, he attributes far more influence to traders than is warranted. Had weavers actually woven to order, traders such as Hubbell would not have had portions of large shipments returned to him by the Fred Harvey Company and other retailers. Evidence collated from correspondence and business records in Hubbell's papers reveals that a very small percentage of weaving was created for specific orders (Bauer 1987; Boles 1977, 1981).

Before the reservation era Navajos had bartered blankets for horses with the Utes, yet their cash evaluation was registered at $.25 per pound at Lee's Ferry trading post, near the Utah border, in the 1870s (Weiss 1984:53). Statements on the continued "cheapening of the product" are not balanced by concomitant critique of the tremendous "devaluation" of Navajo weaving. Weiss neglects to discuss how the treatment of these fully finished products as renewable resources placed an intolerable burden on Navajo weavers. Instead, textiles become just one more expropriated commodity. He quotes without critique Amsden's classic comment on how traders thrice benefited while bartering blankets: on the markup on goods bartered to the weaver for her blanket, on the sale of the blanket to the off-reservation buyer, and on the markup of materials used in the processes of weaving such as commercial dyes and yarn: "three transactions, three separate profits" (Weiss 1984:54).

He claims that between 1900 and 1930, petty commodity production declined in importance as wage labor increased (1984:chapter 4). For example, he quotes from a government report that states nine thousand Indians (from several tribes in Arizona and New Mexico) earned at least $260,000 as wage laborers in 1911 (86). Weiss references James's text periodically, yet he neglects to incorporate relevant evidence that demonstrates the importance of textile production to Navajo livelihood. James ([1914] 1974:57) uses government reports that reveal that in 1911, 25 percent of the annual wool clip was woven into blankets and evaluated at $675,000. The rest of the wool sold for approximately $320,000, and less than 10 percent of it was "improved." James also mentions that a single wholesaler, C. C. Manning of Gallup, sold $40,000 worth of blankets in 1912.

The graphs in Bailey and Bailey (1986:153, 159), also developed from data extrapolated from government documents, provide a more realistic assessment of the importance of textile production than the information provided by Weiss. Yet Weiss draws on disparate sources that continually demonstrate the escalation in textile production alongside the estimated "earnings" per hour of a typical weaver.

For example, Weiss (1984:106) estimated that weaving brought an income of approximately five cents per hour. This amount is based on the results of a well-known experiment during the 1930s "in the economics of weaving" in which two traders from Shiprock furnished an experienced weaver with yarns to weave a 2$\frac{1}{2}$-x-5-foot rug "of a simple pattern." It was appraised at a fair market value of $12.00, yet they paid her $40.80 to weave it (20 cents per hour). Weiss then contrasts the amount a weaver may average (2.5 to 5 cents per hour) with the $2.00 per day paid male Navajo laborers during the same period. In the next sentence he quotes Amsden ([1934] 1975): "the entire Navajo rug industry during the same period, was estimated to be valued in the magnitude of a million dollars a year!" He then sympathizes with the position of independent traders who had to find outlets for the additional tens of thousands of pounds of rugs woven during the 1930s to compensate for depressed wool prices. He makes further comments on the continued debasement of textile quality exacerbated by the poor market, necessitating a revival to improve the quality of textile production. The U.S. government initiated a sheep-breeding program at Fort Wingate in 1936 (Parman 1976:128).

Weiss's sole critique of the above statements concerns traders selecting and retaining the superior wool (from the churro) to sell to weavers in the future. The "improved" strains, such as Rambouillet and Merino, provided a superior fleece for commercial purposes and higher weight yields, but the wool was detrimental to the hand-spinner, who was able to achieve better results with the older straight, hairlike churro wool. Yet Weiss (1984:142) is well aware that preparation of wool is at least as time consuming as the actual weaving process, because he cites an experiment in which a 3-x-5-foot rug required 388 hours to produce. He notes that carding, or cleaning, the wool and spinning took 130 hours; this time estimate did not include shearing or dyeing the wool.

In chapter 6, Weiss acknowledges how women's roles continued to be undermined by the destruction of their herd- and craft-based incomes. He comments on the way weavers receive far less than formally employed Navajos and continues, "[T]he woven commodity is often a cheapened version to compete with the returns of wage labor. . . . [A] substantial amount of weaving is done in large part by unemployed women." He provides a number of tables that designate the existence and importance of wage labor on the reservation. However, only two tables incorporate data related to weaving. No weaving-related figures are reported in tables before 1926.[2] Approaching the end of his analysis, Weiss (1984:122) comments on how craft production nearly stopped during World War II. This may be true for the reservation as a whole, but records from the warehouse in Winslow, Arizona, operated by the Hubbells reveals the continued importance of textile production. Dozens of pages of rug inventories exist that note the weight, measurements, and wholesale price of each textile. This warehouse handled tens of thousands of Navajo textiles until 1954. Although

Youngblood (1935) and Fryer (1939) provide ample evidence to substantiate the importance of weaving over smithing, Weiss overlooks their studies. Weiss neither mentions the cultural importance of weaving for Navajo women nor considers the possible explanations of why women would continue to weave under such arduous conditions.[3] Instead, he trivializes their endeavors by remarking that once transfer payments such as welfare and social security became available, women could "weave on a whim or not at all if they desire" (1984:144).

One of the most distressing aspects of his analysis concerns the inordinate attention he devotes to the importance of silversmithing to the Navajo economy. Careful analysis of government sources used by Bailey and Bailey (1986) and information provided by McNitt (1962), Youngblood (1935), and Fryer (1939) reveal how weaving is short-changed. Before 1940 there were fewer than six hundred smiths on the entire reservation, but the Hubbells alone probably bartered with that many weavers by 1905, if their other posts are included. Weiss's text comprises 158 pages, excluding notes and bibliography. He devotes 23 pages to silversmithing and 28 pages to weaving. This inordinate emphasis on smithing (accompanied by tables and statistics) magnifies its importance to the detriment of textile production. Table 4 draws on information taken from footnotes in McNitt (1962:250–52), which clearly illustrates the dollar amounts of bartered goods received by weavers and silversmiths from nine traders during 1910–11.[4] Although Weiss frequently quotes from McNitt, he neglects to incorporate this information in his analysis. Kluckhohn and Leighton (1974) reported that smithing represented less than 2 percent of total Navajo "income" in 1940.

It is possible that Weiss overemphasizes the importance of smithing because of a competent analysis provided by Adair (1944), to which he frequently refers. We lack an equivalent analysis on the economics of weaving. A fair portion of smithing was carried out by wage laborers making jewelry in established workshops that bordered the eastern portion of the reservation (Adair 1944; Bedinger 1973; Volk 1988; Weiss 1984:97, 111–12, 152). Thus records may be available to calculate wages, use of materials, and control of production processes in extant business and government archives. However, enough evidence is provided in numerous sources to more than hint at the tremendous exploitation of Navajo weavers over the past century. Yet a conceptual framework that cannot factor in nonwaged labor is seriously handicapped in demonstrating the magnitude and extent of production and the subsequent pauperization of thousands of women. Indeed, weavers appear to vanish, even though Weiss (1984:92) acknowledges "almost all [women are]

Table 4. Goods Bartered by Selected Traders, 1910–1911. Extrapolated from McNitt 1962.

TRADERS	BLANKETS [$]	SILVER [$]
WALKER	3570	250
SAMPSON	4000	550
NOEL	6000	350
REITZ/DAVIES	6855	125
WALKER	10,417	397
FOUTZ/BLACK	5420	500
ALDRICH/DODGE	6510	582
BABBITT/PRESTON	2384	2814
BABBITT [RED LAKE]	3912	150
TOTAL	**49,068**	**5718**

engaged in the weaving of rugs for sale or trade to traders. While this produced income, the activity is not included in this analysis since it was not a formal wage in the sense of industrial labor." That he quotes without critique from classic sources demonstrates how an extensive analysis of the Navajo economy constitutes an (unanalyzed) recapitulation of much descriptive information that has been available in some cases for nearly a century.[5]

In his conclusion, Weiss (1984:152) notes how the total dominance by merchant capital over domestic commodity production by the Navajo put it merely "a step away" from a formal wage-labor relationship with direct producers. I suggest that accelerated pauperization has been masked to a far greater extent in the current system on the reservation than direct wage labor. The gross exploitation of weavers would have become far more apparent at a much earlier date had these women been paid wages equal to the credit they received from traders. He acknowledges this point when he comments, "Rug weaving generally gave very low returns to the weavers, with merchant capital skimming everything off the top. The returns to the direct producer were so low that it was not worth it to potential (merchant capital) investors to set up workshops" (1984:154).

This comment raises some disturbing questions. During the depression, the Federal Emergency Relief Administration (FERA) became very concerned about the increase in "sweated labor." The Department of Labor monitored companies reverting from factory to home industries as entrepreneurs sought ways to decrease production costs. Immigrant families and the poor, whether in urban or rural areas, were lured into working long hours at home making "crafts" (Fairbank 1934). National Recovery Act (NRA) codes practically forbade all home industries. Although Navajo weavers owned the means of production, one could argue that their textile production was essentially a variant of sweated labor. Weavers as young as ten were censused under "gainful occupations" (Johnston 1966:35), but they did not fall under U.S. labor codes. For many years Indian agents had documented in their annual reports to the CIA that teenaged girls comprised a significant proportion of weavers (Moore 1910). Government officials perceived traders as the most competent individuals to handle the marketing of textiles. For decades the Hubbells maintained influential political contacts in the nation's capital. In 1931 Lorenzo Hubbell Jr. served as one of the founding members of the Indian Arts and Crafts Board. In light of the evidence revealed in the family's business records, this conceptual blind spot deserves more careful scrutiny.

The lip service paid by Weiss and a handful of others to the exploitation borne by countless women cannot be grasped without analysis of primary documents. Although Witherspoon (1987) estimated that one hundred thousand women have woven one million blankets and rugs over two centuries, a detailed analysis of the Navajo economy has failed to adequately assess the extent of weavers' contributions—both to Navajo livelihood and to the southwestern economy.

Discourse IV: Weaving Time and the Navajo Rug

Over the years several classic experiments similar to the one previously described were conducted to document the amount of time it takes a Navajo weaver to produce a saddle blanket or rug. The processes described below were undertaken by tens of thousands of women since the advent of weaving by Navajos. These processes help to explain the need to transform the Navajo blanket into a rug.

Traders' Experiments

In *Navajo Rugs, Past, Present and Future* (1963), the longtime trader Gilbert Maxwell describes weaving tools and materials and highlights the development of weaving as influenced by various traders. He provides an example of an "experiment" to determine the length of time it takes to weave a saddle blanket and a rug. In 1955 a dealer paid a weaver $1.00 an hour and provided the yarn for her to weave a double saddle blanket in a twill weave (appendix III) and a 3-x-5-foot quality rug. The weaver completed the saddle blanket in 140 hours and the rug in 238 hours. The dealer estimated the entire process likely required another 200 hours if the weaver had to shear, wash, card, spin, and dye the yarn. The typical retail price for a saddle blanket of this type in 1955 was $35.00; for a rug, $65.00. Using the figures Maxwell has provided, one can calculate that the amount per hour at the retail level for the saddle blanket totals $0.14 per hour, while for the rug, it increases to $0.17 per hour. Had she prepared all the yarn, she would have received $0.10 per hour for the saddle blanket and $0.15 for the rug. Recall that the weaver received groceries in exchange for her textiles and that the retail price includes the traders' markup. Maxwell himself provides a table (discussed below) on average prices for rugs. In 1955 his cash valuation averaged $20.20 per rug. Maxwell then makes a classic comment, reiterated in various forms by other sources:

> Weaving a rug can be a lot of work. From time to time we hear reports that a Navajo weaver is poorly paid, maybe an average of five cents or so an hour, for her labor. Unfortunately there is much truth to this, but it should be pointed out that rug weaving is a spare-time avocation. . . . Which brings up a very important point. Although weaving is an essential part of the reservation economy it is not exercised as a full-time occupation. Hence there can be no wage scale. A Navajo woman will do most of her weaving in her spare time, as some of our non-Indian ladies will knit a wool dress in their spare time. (1963:19–20)

These comments epitomize the attitude toward Navajo weaving that many authors shared (Dockstader 1976; Luomala 1938:72). Any part-time activity, regardless of its importance to the economy, is not considered work. Maxwell also speculates on "the future" of weaving and incorporates tables with revealing information concerning the average price he paid for rugs (not saddle blankets) from 1948 to 1962. His prices ranged from a low of $17.60 in 1953 to a "high" of $39.70 in 1962. He provides two photographs of his "rug room": in 1951 the textiles are stacked nearly to the windowtops, whereas in 1961 the piles reach only to the top of a chair seat (Maxwell 1963:62). During this period, day laborers earned on average $1.50 per day. Based on the experiment described above, if a woman wove eight hours per day on her textile, it would require thirty days to hand-spin and weave a double saddle blanket and forty-two days to produce the rug. A single saddle blanket in plain weave ranges from 32 to 36 inches square and weighs from 3 to 4 pounds. Based on these calculations, a weaver would receive less than $2.00 in trade goods for a textile that may take her more than sixty hours to produce, depending on the complexity of pattern. Thus she would supply all materials and receive approximately three cents an hour in credit for her textile.

Museum Experiments

The Museum of Northern Arizona published a six-page article with photographs titled "The Weaver and the Wool: The Process of Navajo Weaving" by its curator, Marsha Gallagher (1981:22–27). The museum chose to highlight the production of a Navajo rug in an issue of its journal, *Plateau*, devoted to Navajo weaving. Many books, articles, and exhibits are devoted to aspects of the subject; however, Gallagher's article is the first to document in photographs and text the creation of a particular rug from beginning to end. On the last page of the article, there is a color photograph of the completed rug still on the loom, which appears to measure approximately 3 x 5 feet (it probably weighs 5 to 6 pounds). The estimate of total hours expended is as follows:

Shearing and cleaning	15
Carding and spinning	368 (~67 hr/lb.)
Dyeing	19
Weaving	158 (~29 hr/lb.)
Total	560

Because the loom and weaving tools have remained unchanged, Navajos weaving centuries ago would have spent the same amount of time creating equivalent textiles. Recall that if shortcuts were taken, it was in relation to using aniline dyes. A few hours would be saved using packaged dyes rather than collecting plants for dyeing. Margaret Grieve, the woman who wove the experiment rug, respun her wool on a Navajo drop spindle three times. She produced approximately three thousand yards of yarn to weave the rug. It is necessary to spin the wool at least twice, up to five times to achieve a fine yarn, or four times for warp yarn (Lipps 1906:22; Bennett and Bighorse 1997:31). Thus preparation of materials may take up 70 percent of the total time expended to produce a completed textile.

Discourse V: Why the Navajo Blanket Became a Rug

If Navajo weaving were to survive (the economic success of the traders was far more dependent on its survival than acknowledged in extant literature), the blanket had to be transformed into a product attractive to American consumers. That is exactly what happened. The quotations below reveal the basis of triple profits for the traders, which translated into a double loss for Navajos.

Pendleton blankets were cheaper than native blankets, and the technical skill and energy consumed by blanket-making could now be utilized more profitably by weaving for trade. (Weiss 1984:54)

Colorful, light, warm, and reasonably affordable shawls and blankets cost between $8 [to] $15 each (according to Pendleton's 1918 price list) [and] were natural substitutes for Navajo wearing blankets, as . . . weavers preferred to spend their time weaving rugs to sell to Anglos. (Kaufman and Selser 1985:73)

[When the weaver] found she could sell her blanket for enough to purchase a dozen American blankets she promptly did so, for the reason before stated, viz., that most of her own blankets are too stiff to give warmth and comfort when wrapped around her. . . . [N]one familiar with Navajo blankets ever buys them for bed-covers or wraps. As soon as this fact dawned clearly upon Messrs. Hubbell and Cotton . . . they immediately began to negotiate with the [trade] blanket manufacturers, for the manufacture of blankets especially designed for the Navajo trade, containing designs and colors which they knew would be pleasing to their Indian customers. They themselves provided the designs—these men, be it especially noted and remembered, whose greatest income is from the sale of genuine Navajo blankets, and whose business would suffer materially if the notion ever became broadcast that the real Navajo could be successfully imitated. They now purchase these [trade] blankets by the carload, and there is not a trader on or off the whole reservation who does not carry a quantity of them in stock. (James [1914] 1974:160–61)

Thus the merchant was inserted into the heart of Navajo trade and in one stroke co-opted both the indigenous and the Anglo markets for Navajo blankets. Traders are perceived as having saved Navajo weaving by developing new off-reservation markets as the old markets were destroyed (Amsden [1934] 1975:179; Dedera [1975] 1990:36; Kent 1985:85). James and others perpetuated the myth by stating that Navajos preferred trade blankets, because they are lighter and because a weaver could sell a good handwoven blanket and obtain the machine-made product and earn additional credit. This opinion, quoted as gospel by writers of various persuasions, is easily refuted by volumes of evidence extant in archival sources (see table 3, fig. 5). Amsden ([1934] 1975:179) valorized the business activities of Hubbell and Cotton and their ingenious plan for sharing some of the so-called advantages of the American methods, in reference to the three transactions-three profits scenario:

> If one man thought of all that, his portrait, crowned with laurel, should be over every trader's doorway. . . . [O]bviously the traders advantage lay in selling the materials of weaving rather than encourage the Navajo to provide their own. (Amsden [1934] 1975:186)

Had Navajo weavers continued to supply both the indigenous and Anglo markets with textiles, even through middlemen, their livelihood may have remained strong. However, from the time traders began operating on and adjacent to the reservation, weavers faced formidable competition from trade blanket manufacturers. Commercial producers began manufacturing double-faced fabrics during the 1880s on Jacquard adapter looms. Although hundreds of woolen mills were in operation during the latter part of the nineteenth century, only a handful targeted the Indian trade. The five major mills and their dates of origins are as follows: Capps Woollen Mills (1864), Oregon City (1864), Buell Manufacturing Company (1860, under another name), Racine Wool Mills (1877), and the giant Pendleton (1895). Kapoun (1992) documents how these major blanket manufacturers usurped the Native American market and also appropriated a large portion of the Anglo market.

Other indigenous textile markets were affected as well. Kapoun (1992:22) reprints a photograph of a potlatch held at Port Rupert, British Columbia, depicting stacks of Hudson Bay blankets. He estimates their worth at $50,000 by 1992 standards. At the time writers failed to recognize the cultural importance of the blanket to Indians, but "its commercial importance was never questioned. In fact[,] . . . it became acknowledged as a standard of trade," replacing its indigenous predecessors, especially Navajo blankets. Until the early 1880s, Navajo weavers were still weaving for home use and trading wearing blankets to some extent. Traders were getting very few finer blankets (McNitt Papers, Box 1, from James [1914] 1974).

Appropriating the Patterns: Commercial Manufacturers' Success

Financial success came early to the commercial blanket manufacturers. By the 1880s the Capps Indian Blanket Company earned annual revenues of more than $200,000 from sales of clothing, cloth, and blankets (Kapoun 1992:75). The "golden age" of the American Indian trade blanket, from 1880 to 1930, parallels the precipitous decline in value of Navajo textiles. Firms had no compunction about appropriating Indian patterns to varying degrees, yet each company guarded its designs carefully. They aggressively marketed their blankets to Indian agents, trading post operators, and other retailers catering to the Indian trade. With the coming of the railroad, wholesale houses brought in manufactured blankets by the carload. According to Williams (1989:33), Clinton Cotton held the regional rights as representative for the Pendleton Company for years and made a dollar on every blanket he wholesaled to traders. His secretary reminisced that he ordered more than one thousand at a time.

Kapoun (1992:chapter 6) defines six general categories of design: the striped, banded, center point, framed, overall, and nine element, with its variant, the six element. Four of these six basic design categories were wholesale derivations of Navajo blanket patterns. Companies sought to fit the preferences of individual tribes. As competition increased, manufacturers produced more colorful blankets in a great variety of patterns (Lipps 1906:19). Capps produced twenty-two distinct designs in more than two hundred color combinations (Kapoun 1992:75). Pendleton carried twenty to fifty styles in each line with a wide range of patterns and colors. Every blanket measured 5 x 6 feet and weighed 3 pounds. Shawls weighed from $1\frac{1}{2}$ to 2 pounds each and averaged between $1.50 and $1.67 per pound, wholesale cost to traders in 1910 (HP Box 66, 8/24/10). By 1918 Pendleton blankets had increased in price, with robes and shawls wholesaling for $10.50 and $11.50 apiece. Although Pendletons were never sold by the pound, their weights are listed on shipping manifests and invoices contained in the Hubbell Papers (Box 66). A commercially manufactured blanket cost Navajos more than $4.00 per pound in 1918—three times the amount a weaver averaged that year for a fancy blanket and more than six times the amount she received in cash valuation for a saddle blanket. Each blanket was distinguished by the name of a North American Indian tribe and associated with the romantic images of the Indian and the American West. Names were assigned for poetic impact rather than concern for accuracy (Kapoun 1992:78).

Because copyright was nonexistent for native designs, the trade blanket manufacturers capitalized on "the Indian's instinct" and turned it into "the white man's reasoning choice" (Kapoun 1992:111). Kapoun writes:

> With European contact and the introduction of trade goods, suddenly the need for these traditional forms of protective clothing was altered. The trade blanket replaced the hide robes and hand-woven blankets previously worn by native people. . . . The development of a market for these blankets parallels the evolution of the Indian people's cultural existence. (1992:x)

Kapoun neglects to discuss a provocative subtext that runs throughout his book. Both in text and photographs, he documents the complete appropriation in form, proportion, style, and patterns of indigenous blankets and discusses the growth, development, and financial success of these companies. He does not discuss why the need for traditional clothing was altered, but the owner of the Racine Mill states in a 1915 interview: "The Indian's love for gaudy colors and loose garments despite all the civilization that the white man has forced upon him, retains for the Racine Woollen Mill a very valuable source of income" (Kapoun 1992:111). At the time of the interview, his company supplied forty Indian tribes with blankets.

Factory representatives visited reservations and "worked side by side with the Indian and come [sic] into possession of his favorite designs and colorings" to produce "the blanket of 1000 uses." And the multiple ways in which they could be used directly competed with the Navajo blanket as early as 1884. The myriad uses for Navajo blankets described by Cotton (HP Box 92) bear remarkable similarity to those mentioned by the trade blanket manufacturers in their glossy high-profile advertising campaigns. Sometimes the advertisements distorted information. The Racine Woollen Mill ad of 1915 reads:

Indians [formerly] made their own [blankets], but being handicapped by the lack of machinery and proper raw materials, they were unable to produce the kind of article they desired. The Indian woman with her crude machinery could not spin the yarn very fine, hence her product was coarse and heavy, more suitable for rugs than for a blanket to be worn. (Cited in Kapoun 1992:113)

Kapoun makes no effort to challenge this statement, which ignores evidence of high-quality blanket production that was the norm before the trading post era. He fails to acknowledge who initiated the decimation of the market for the handwoven articles. He elaborates on the massive intrusion of commercially produced blankets without hinting at the dire economic consequences for Navajos. A number of statements in his text require critique, in particular, remarks related to the salvaging (appropriation) of these designs as tantamount to saving the entire tradition (1992:111). One could ask the hypothetical question: Just how financially successful would these companies have become had copyright been available and enforced for native blanket patterns? Ample evidence appears in Hubbell's papers as to the invidious effect such sales had on the market for Navajo blankets. By 1889 Cotton was ordering trade blankets in large numbers from several manufacturers. Brown Brothers of San Francisco, representatives of the Oregon City Woollen Mills, shipped 877 robes to Ganado that wholesaled for between $3.25 and $6.00 each (HP Boxes 12, 143). On 7 October 1891 the company wrote: "We now have in stock the largest variety of Indian robes that we ever carried, and shall be pleased to receive your order."

The Beckman Company, an affiliate of Northern Ohio Blanket Mills of Cleveland, wrote: "[W]e have seen a Navajo blanket and they are a grand thing, but there is no sale for them here." The following month the company shipped 500 pounds of trade blankets to Ganado (HP Box 8, 327, 5/20/1890, 5/31/1890). That same year finds former Navajo agent D. M. Riordan doing a "booming [mercantile] business" in Flagstaff (HP Box 70). He wrote Ganado saying he was obliged to take Navajo blankets from traders on the west side of the reservation and that it would take months to dispose of the surplus. But, he continued, "[we] think we can handle all that you can get hold of, or care to send us if the prices are right." Between April and August Cotton shipped more than 1,283 pounds of blankets, which paid for much of the merchandise ordered from Riordan. The former Indian agent informed Cotton that he would only pay $0.35 per pound for common blankets: "[T]his is all we're paying other traders. . . . [W]ould rather accept cold cash than blankets anytime." Invoices on six styles of wool trade robes list their weight at just over three pounds (HP Box 70). In 1889 Oregon City Woollen Mills wholesaled robes at from $3.25 to $6.00 (HP Box 12). Manufactured blankets wholesaled from $1.00 to $2.00 per pound, in contrast to weavers receiving $0.20 to $0.30 per pound in credit for their handwoven blankets. Thus before the turn of the century, commercially manufactured trade blankets were three to ten times more expensive per pound than their handwoven counterparts.

Other reservation traders also carried trade blankets in their inventories. Indian agent Bowman received a report from trader Donovan in 1886 noting that he had purchased twelve pairs of wearing blankets ($5.60/pair) and six lap robes (at $4.00 each) in January 1886. The previous November, Sam Reeder, trader at Fort Defiance, had purchased fifteen pairs of black blankets at $5.60 a pair (McNitt Papers, Box 8: "Traders/Letter Received" I-1885).

During the 1930s, Racine advertised that they dealt in blankets, Navajo rugs, and other Indian goods (Kapoun 1992:113). They made no distinction between the indigenous Navajo blanket or rug and their commercial blankets, thus capitalizing on the confusion in the minds of consumers, who for the most part would not know the difference. Oregon City's ads noted how their designs were "conceived by the Indians in the early days" and "used exclusively by Navajo Indians[,] . . . a fine tribute to their authentic designs, beautiful colors and high quality" (Kapoun 1992:92). This company won awards at major national and international exhibitions as early as 1876. In 1919 the company published full-page color illustrations in the *Saturday Evening Post* and operated seven retail outlets in the United States (Kapoun 1992:93).

The Capps ad depicted in Kapoun (1992:76) is the most blatant form of false advertising because it highlights a Capps trade blanket as a "genuine Indian blanket." It also states that "the Indians sold them for fabulous prices." The ad then contrasts the blankets for retail trade with Navajo blankets sent to Indian agencies: the former are "clean, sanitary and sweet." This commentary carried a double meaning. It implied agencies were shipped secondhand goods and that any hand-loomed indigenous blanket was "smelly" and "dirty." The ad appeared in a 1910 issue of the *Delineator*. It raised the ire of J. F. Huckel of the Fred Harvey Company. On 22 November 1910 he fired off a letter marked "Confidential and Private" to Lorenzo Hubbell stating that traders must counteract this false advertising: "[D]o not bring our name into the matter in any way. We prefer to be unknown in the matter. It seems to me it is doing more harm to the Indians and traders than it would to us" (HP Box 37). Obviously the profits garnered by the Fred Harvey Company on the sales of thousands of Navajo textiles annually would be severely threatened had trade blanket manufacturers succeeded in convincing unwitting consumers via such advertisements.

Parish (1961:330) describes the Rio Grande Woollen Mill of Albuquerque, circa 1905, run by Johney Bearrup. Although a small operation compared to its competitors, the mill had two sets of sixty-inch cards for cleaning and straightening wool fibers, 1,588 spindles, and 10 looms. This cooperatively owned mill produced blankets, dress goods, and men's wear fabrics. Mechanized equipment ensured accelerated production.

The Pendleton Woollen Mills: Merchandising Success

In 1895, its first year of operation, Pendleton scoured four million pounds of wool, and not one ounce was Navajo wool. At the time about three hundred thousand Indians lived in the United States. About half that number lived in Indian Territory and the Navajo country of Arizona and New Mexico. The company claims to have originated "the true Indian blanket." Their goal was to weave "the correct designs and color demanded by the Indians of the different tribes" (Kapoun 1992:121, 122, 127).

Pendleton acknowledged the origins of their product in their 1910 catalog (Kapoun 1992:69): "To him [the weaver] is all the credit due for the beautiful patterns and the unique color combinations of the famous Pendleton Line." The company ignores the prior importance of Navajo blankets by commenting in another ad, "The Indian has never found a blanket comparable to Pendletons in quality, serviceability, or with colorings or marking so genuinely expressive of his own inherent art" (Kapoun 1992:132) and "high quality manufacturing standards and an understanding interpretation of the Indians needs has [sic] provided Pendleton with the unique position of being identified in the minds of both Indian and White man as the exclusive manufacturer of Indian design blankets, robes and shawls" (Kapoun 1992:155).

The last comment erases Navajo weaving completely, conveniently so, since by this time the Navajo blanket had become a rug. Yes, skillful designers and weavers using power looms transformed the original designs and colorings into a more refined form and in the process of appropriation, accelerated the destruction of a viable livelihood. A trade blanket was expensive, conferring prestige on its wearer. Adopting the clothing of the white man was seen as "civilizing the savage." Kapoun (1992:16) reprints a photograph of several dozen Indians at the Ouray Agency in 1898, draped only in commercial trade blankets. Many of the trade-blanket-wearing Indians portrayed in Kapoun's texts have Anglicized names, whereas tens of thousands of Navajo women who created handwoven originals remain unnamed and unknown.

The Pendleton catalog published in 1915 and reissued in 1992 states that the new owners who acquired the company in 1909 were graduates of the highly acclaimed Philadelphia Textile School. By the late 1920s Pendleton was well established, with an extensive product line that included all kinds of clothing for the Anglo and Indian markets. Pendleton employed five hundred workers and had an annual revenue in the millions before the depression. Several letters from this period reveal that the company tentatively discussed purchasing improved Navajo wool from the Hubbells. It annually processed about three million pounds of wool from Oregon and surrounding states. Amsden ([1934] 1975:196) notes that a superintendent for the company sold carded and dyed wool to traders in the Shiprock area that competed with the local indigenous wool market.

During World War I, the navy contracted Pendleton to produce wool yardage. Prices increased and the company was unable to fill numerous orders for blankets from traders, leaving the Indians literally out in the cold. Kapoun frequently mentions that trade blanket manufacturers enjoyed a captive market in wholesaling blankets to traders. Companies did not have to invest heavily in advertising to attract and retain this market. During the 1940s, production for the indigenous market slackened again to service the war effort. After the war, because all their competitors had gone out of business, Pendleton slashed production of patterns by 90 percent (Kapoun 1992:129). For fifty years the company enjoyed a monopoly and supplied the entire contemporary American Indian trade blanket market. This monopoly is substantiated in the Hubbell Papers. Reinhart (1999:101) found that twenty-six trade blanket brand names were mentioned in 1895 and only one by 1925—a direct contrast to the proliferation of brand names for clothing and canned goods offered Navajo consumers after 1900. Within the last decade a handful of small companies have produced commercial trade blankets as mementos of historic events.

Kapoun documents a number of clever advertising ploys on the part of blanket manufacturers. All of them acknowledged that their patterns were taken directly from or were inspired by native designs. Sometimes advertisements subtly derided the handwoven creation. In their 1927 catalog, Pendleton reiterated deceptive information:

> These Indian blankets were originated for the Indian—not by him. . . . [W]ith his own crude methods of weaving the Indian could not reproduce the intricate designs and elaborate color combinations sufficiently to interpret his inherent art in a blanket of first quality.

Kapoun (1992:70–71) counters but does not critique Pendleton's claims. He notes that Navajo weavers are able to incorporate more colors on a single horizontal line while working on their vertical looms than the commercial manufacturing companies can add to a trade blanket. The Hamley Company of Pendleton, Oregon, sold saddles and horse tack and marketed Pendleton blankets to cowboys. Lorenzo Hubbell shipped thousands of pounds of saddle blankets to Hamley's and other saddle companies for decades in exchange for leather goods (HP Boxes 35, 180). Even when blankets were used to pay for goods, they still faced competition from manufacturers of trade blankets. Not content with just appropriating patterns, for years the Pendleton logo featured an Indian clothed in buckskin seated in front of an upright loom.

Kapoun (1992:14) relates that Indians from many tribes continued to wear trade blankets or robes as a statement of "individual and tribal identity," a fascinating concept, as identical mechanized designs were reproduced by the thousands and sold to hundreds of thousands of Native Americans for more than a century. Although blanket manufacturers usurped indigenous patterns, particularly Navajo patterns, the reverse did not occur. Amsden ([1934] 1975:62) notes the limited influence of the commercial product on Navajo weavers. They developed a double-sided twill, a challenging weaving technique, possibly inspired by reverse patterning on the trade blankets. How ironic that Kapoun differentiates commercially produced trade blankets by weight and by measurements, the two primary notations that Hubbells and other traders used to distinguish each hand-woven blanket entry in their ledger books. Kapoun concludes by stating that the trade blanket alone makes more of a visual statement of "Indianness" than any other item.

Conclusion

My analysis of information that has been available to researchers for decades reveals the tremendous escalation in textile production relative to population growth. Factors impinging on a fairer return to weavers were revealed, such as the appropriation of the niche for the Navajo blanket by trade blanket manufacturers and the stagnation in the wool market that led to pressures applied by traders to weavers to turn wool into rugs. The gaps in theoretical frameworks used by other investigators have resulted in the neglect of a realistic assessment of the exponential growth of textile production by indigenous "housewives" in tandem with increasing pauperization. Johnston (1966:31) noted that Navajos' vigor almost brought them to ruin after 1900. To counter diminishing returns on both textiles and unprocessed commodities traded for commercial goods, Navajos increased their stock holdings, exacerbating overgrazing and thereby affecting wildlife habitat (White 1983:245). By 1915, 85 percent of all households censused were categorized as "destitute, moderately poor or average" (Weiss 1984:83; White 1983:241). Kelley notes that low prices paid to producers generate increased production in the absence of alternative income sources. Increased production depletes resources, "inducing still greater production, which lowers prices further, the whole process constituting a deviation-amplifying feedback loop" (1976:247).

4

Blankets by Weight
The Hidden Narrative

[Navajo women] were always busy cooking, herding, killing, and dressing mutton, milking goats, shearing sheep, lambing, spinning, dyeing, weaving or looking after children.

Youngblood 1935:4

Remember, blankets are our good business.

Don Lorenzo Hubbell to family members in interpost correspondence, 1905–25

Weavers should get every dime they can, but . . . can't price rugs out of the market."

Leighton 1958:n.p.

In American morality, integrity and intellectual clarity are constantly stifled by a refusal to acknowledge the colonial nature of American nations, followed by the refusal to acknowledge the predicaments and rights of colonized peoples. Is it really possible to take over someone's house, murder most of the family, lock the remaining victims in the closet, and then pretend that it is your own little house on the prairie in the suburbs?

Durham 1992:56

For decades writers have reiterated that traders' greatest profits lay in wool (Adams 1963:135; McNitt 1962). In the earliest days of Navajo trade that may have been the case, but after 1895 archival business records reveal a far different story. Most researchers continue to rely on data contained in annual reports published by the Commissioner of Indian Affairs. Such information is not fine grained enough to explicate how diversification reaped multiple benefits for traders to the detriment of Navajo weavers. Although the importance of textile production has been acknowledged, the extent of impoverishment and increasing workload of thousands of weavers cannot be grasped without analysis of primary documents. Information drawn from the Hubbell Papers corroborates the impoverishment of weavers locally, and unpublished government documents verify the long-term impoverishment of weavers regionally.

Given the need to increase diversification to maintain profit margins, reservation traders encouraged weavers to weave wool into blankets (Bailey and Bailey 1986; Weiss 1984). But, as we shall see, the primary producers were not the principal beneficiaries of their extensive production. The wealth accrued to the traders, dealers, merchant capitalists, and consumers. Traders' business records, unpublished government reports, and other sources substantiate weavers' contributions to Navajo livelihood and the southwestern economy.

Gambling on Wool

High wool prices during the early 1880s fueled the demand for Arizona wool (Kelley and Whiteley 1989:65). The boom was short-lived, however. In the next decade, fluctuations in the market value of wool caused by tariff removal and a recession threatened to jeopardize traders' profits (Wright 1910). Textiles were not as susceptible to fluctuations in the international wool market, nor were they directly affected by weather. For example, inclement weather in the fall could jeopardize driving animals to the railheads. Severe spring weather threatened the lamb crop.

Periodically the wool market became "demoralized," as Hubbell put it in his correspondence. When this happened, wholesalers such as Cotton urged traders to ship blankets, pelts, and skins; otherwise goods remained on shelves of trading posts and wholesale houses bordering the Navajo Reservation. When wool failed to move, traders paid dearly. McPherson relates how two traders lost their shirts on the wool market:

> In 1922, raw Navajo wool, characterized as "coarse in quality and light in quantity" sold for forty cents per pound with a three to six cent margin on market prices. By the time it was transported to the buyer's bin and cleaned, some clips were reduced to 50 percent of their original weight. Two traders reported that between dirty wool and fluctuations in market prices, they suffered disastrous financial problems. They had purchased the wool in 1920 at thirty-five cents per pound, stored it for a year and a half because of poor market conditions, freighted it at one-and-a-half cents per pound then sold it at nine cents per pound for an

estimated loss of $38,000. The accuracy of these figures is difficult to determine, but they do dramatize a very real problem. (1922a:36)

Based on information from archival and ethnohistorical sources (Bailey and Bailey 1986:appendix B; table 1), these figures accurately reflect the fluctuating value of wool just after World War I. Normally merchants bordering the reservation contracted for wool in spring and shipped it by rail to Massachusetts in summer. Yet by late October 1919, Cotton had not sold one pound of wool. Navajo wool had sold for $.45 per pound in 1918, dropping to $.17 in 1919. Cotton no doubt held his wool hoping for a price increase. Wool rose, then plummeted. McPherson (1992a:36) offers a glimpse of the primary importance of textiles relative to other products during this period: "In 1922 in the [Navajo] Western Agency, 23,080 pounds of rugs sold for $41,000; raw wool for $22,000, comprising 78 percent of all the commerce for that year to include the sale of sheep, cattle, pelts, silver and miscellaneous items." In 1926 Cotton again held six thousand bags of scoured wool waiting for a price increase.[1] Clearly the wool market was a gamble.

Table 5. Profit and Loss by Category, Hubbell Trading Post Records, 1891–1909.

YEAR	WOOL	BLANKETS	PELTS	SKINS
1891			486.40	625.94
1892	1559.93	384.67	740.17	514.82
1893	-524.93	1241.90	399.05	388.28
1894	1087.61	2269.00	296.20	287.89
1895	301.17	25.17	125.48	414.03
1896	62.17	64.89	57.53	99.81
1897	537.26	401.70	196.51	333.63
1898	-547.67	2.27	268.37	-374.54
1899	-138.81	176.23	393.36	324.45
1900	147.76	1701.97	212.82	297.16
1901	182.76	7160.95	6.00	129.72
1902	219.00	5135.69	173.11	578.26
1903	-30.25	6541.02	193.54	364.61
1904	8.08	8643.45	173.88	478.90
1905	993.37	7043.27	426.58	439.59
1906	1384.86	5096.98	639.03	233.63
1907	-207.75	9223.60	N/A	767.76
1908	1208.11	20,120.86	1136.15	1036.09
1909	1945.37	27,558.42	791.46	890.90
TOTAL	8188.04	102,791.12	6715.64	7830.93

Traders including the Hubbells seldom risked putting all their entrepreneurial eggs in one basket. Had Hubbell continued to market only wool, he would have lost his shirt (and his empire; see table 5). Instead his empire expanded significantly after the turn of the century. And it was marketing Indian "curios" (especially the Navajo blanket) that enhanced his fame, expanded his influence, and augmented his bank balance.

Evidence Demonstrating Increased Textile Production

When information is presumed to be unavailable or inaccessible, critical aspects of an economy may receive scant attention. Analyzing the Hubbells' business records unearths crucial information about the economic importance of weavers' production.

Although the number of trading posts increased from seventeen to thirty-six in Navajo country, in the eastern part of the reservation no new trading posts were established until after 1896 (Kelley and Whiteley 1989:65). This means that Ganado, Hubbell's original post, was strategically located to capture much of the Indian trade in that region. Hubbell opened several branch posts (Cornfields, Mud Springs, and Cedar Springs) between 1896 and 1905. Ganado was sixty miles from the railroad. The earliest Hubbell records contain evidence substantiating the importance of weaving (HP Boxes 321, 327; Cotton Letter Books, Box 92). The trader's office and the blanket room (fig. 8) were built in 1883, six years before the permanent store and warehouse, and the blanket room was half the size of the "bull pen" (Bauer 1987:44; Blue 2000:287).

The increase in blanket sales occurs early in Hubbell's business records, as he sought to extend the market for Navajo weaving (see fig. 7). Before 1900, 94 percent or 180 of 192 business accounts were primarily for textiles (HP Box 337). Several tables and figures compiled from his business records and incorporated here demonstrate both the importance of women's textile production relative to other commodities and the escalation in production by weavers that benefited Hubbell's entrepreneurial success (tables 5, 6; figs. 6, 7). In 1891, 10 percent of the trader's gross sales (including wool, pelts, and skins) were for textiles, increasing to 49 percent by 1897 (HP Box 331, p. 245).

In Hubbell's pre-1900 ledger books, bed and saddle blankets were whole-saled for $0.30 to $0.40 per pound. Cotton advertised "first grade" small blankets between $4.00 and $10.00, the larger blankets from $20.00 to $60.00. However, I found little evidence that weavers received more than $0.25 to $0.30 per pound for their textiles, regardless of quality. Some record books may be missing, but on the inside cover of the 1886–87 ledger (HP Box 321 #7) from

Figure 8. J. L. Hubbell's office, summer 1906. Photo by Virgil Huff White. HUTR #8702, courtesy of Hubbell Trading Post National Historic Site, Ganado, Arizona.

Chinle, I found several pages of English words translated into Navajo including terms for "money" up to $0.90. Thirty percent of the words dealt directly with weaving and the first four words were as follows:

blanket . . .	bell cladà
good . . .	ya ta
bad . . .	Ta yos shon ne
to much . . .	to ha yoc

How is one to interpret this information in one of the earliest ledger books? Given the tremendous devaluation of weaving, it appears that regardless of quality, the weaver wanted "to [sic] much." And what other choice did she have but to "sell" it to the trader at the "price" he would give her? In 1887, Cotton sold 4-x-6-foot textiles for $10 each: "[The latter is made] of their own wool [and] are much finer woven. . . . It takes months for a squaw to make one as each thread has to be put through the loom by hand" (HP Box 92, p. 682). This remark indicates that weavers were receiving far less than $10 in bartered goods for a textile that required several months to produce.

Table 6. Blanket Shipments, 1901, Ganado Day Book (Box 333, HP).

DATE & PAGE	SDLE BLKTWT	BED/COMMON WEIGHT	INDIAN DYE/WEIGHT	INDIAN DYE PIECE	GERMAN-TOWN	OLD STYLE PIECE	HANOOLCHADI	"FANCY" PORTIERS	GENERIC	SADDLE BLKT/PIECE
JAN.14		100#@.50#			1 old@$100		7@$168			
FEB.12	69#@.39/				1@$50	19@$487.50		2@$110		
p.130	cost/.30/#			10@$88	5@$26.50	8@$142.50		1@$60		
p.136	96#@.35/#	9#@.40 & 66#@.30 & 34#@.37	8#@.50	1@$7 16@$88	1@$9	1@$100 (cost $46.)			1@$15 15@$52.5 1@$10	4@$14
MAR.20					5@$34 4@$9	5@$77				
MAR.29 p.152		41#@$.50		2@$11.50 4@$85	2@$35 o.s.g.y	8@$175 2@$30n.w.		3@$42.50 1@$65		1@$4 7@$22.50
MAR.30 p.153	119#@.40	144#@.30				5@$77		1@$12.50		
APRIL 5										
p.162	76#@.40 10#@.30					5@$80.20			7@ ??	
APR.18 p.171	84#@.40	52#@.50		12@$65. 2@$47.50 9@$53.75	2@$40	8@$197.50 11@$240 5@$75.50 2@$33.50				
p.177										2@$9.75
MAY 1						1@$25				
MAY 2 p.186			202#@.80		4@$100 o.s.	1@$17.50 5@$73.50	1@$19.50 1@$13.50		5@$5	3@$10 o.s.
JUNE 3 p.190		44#@$.50 62#@.50		6@$75 n.w.		11@$197.50				4@$12"light" 2@$25 o.s. 1@$4
JUNE 10 p.194	21#@.40			10@$71.		6@$112	4@$135			
JUN 25 p.201	19#@.40 4#@.30			15@$39		12@$192				3@$12
JULY 3 p.204		40#@$.45		8@$69.50		5@$61.10 12@$365	1@$25 3@$57 o.s.	2@$325 (cost$135) 5@$62.50 "special"	1@$60 (grey)	
JULY 10 p.208	22#@.30 55#@.40	23#@.30		15@$121 3@$36		6@$147 7@$121.50		31#"moqui"	10@$70.70 32@$596.	3@$12
p.221	115#@.40			10@$61.		16@$233				
AUG 12 p.244	25#@.30 61#@.40			16@$85.		6@$88.50				

Table 6. continued

Date / Page										
AUG 29	25#@.40									
SEPT 18	16#@.40				1@$32					
p.236-7	49#@.50 50#@.50	5@$100			35#.12@ $87.50	2@$50	9@$66 n.w. "fancy" (mod.style)	2@$35 dress & shawl	2@$75 "greys"	6@$20
SEPT 18						7@$100 1@$150 (indigo)	4@$90		1@$30	
p.238			26@$232.70		2@$100 2@$17.50	10@$220 5@$62.50		10@$89.50 dress & shawl	7@$122 14@$310 "blue"	
SEPT 28				16@$135.50	2@$60	12@$250.50		2@$425 "blue"		
p.244				4@$60.50 1@$17.50	1@$6.50	5@$110		3@$47.50 1@$17.50 dress		6@$58 o.s.
OCT 5										
p.248				1@$15		1@$50		1@$150	25@$283	
p.255				3@$9 12@$78		14@$141			?@$269	
NOV 2				3@$48.50	1@$25	5@$125		3@$24 Moqui dress	2@$42	
NOV 18						4@$115		2@$35 shawls	greys	
p.265									4@$110	
NOV 20						4@$100		12@$8 (pillow tops)		
p.266										
NOV 25				6@$59 2@$33		18@$291 5@$107.50 2@$37.50	1@$10	1@$25 "blue"	3@$75	
DEC 21				9@$71.10	1@$10	2@$50	1@$25	1@$50		
p.278				$12 o.s.i.d. 5@$35.50 43@$807.00	21@$296	9@$180 21@$481	2@$47.50 2@$35	7@$122.50 (dresses/ shawls)		2@$20
DEC 21						15@$317.50				
p.280								2@$40 Moqui'		
p.281					2@$50 1@$20			2@$40	4@$75	80@$240
283 &								2@$325	1@$75	
284								1@$78	1@$11.50 7@$254.20 12@$254.	
p.295					2@$150	14@$175 5@$15.50		3@$22.50 1@$75 3@$17 squaw dre	3@$3	25@$12.50
p.296					1@$8	25@$575 16@$333			1@$20 "grey"	19@$81 17@$42.50
TOTAL	817#@ 315.90 or .39/#	713.5 # for $302.83+5-5@$100 or .39/#	210# for $165.60 or .79/#	270 for $2607.30	74 for $1266.00 [$17.10 ea]	347 for $6929.30 [19.97 ea]	56 for $1119.50 [$20 ea]	74 for $2304.05	144 for $2744.00*	185 for $603.25

n.w. = Navajo wool
o.s. = old style
o.s.g.y. = old style, Germantown yarn
o.s.i.d. = old style Indian dye
* information missing on large shipment to Albuquerque Blanket acct.

Although government policy mandated that traders give cash in return for goods, the realities of reservation life precluded carrying out transactions in this manner.[2] Because many Navajos were continually in debt, the promised blanket was sufficient to secure a credit advance, while a finished blanket paid down the debt.

By 1895 Hubbell's former partner, Clinton Cotton, moved to Gallup and constructed a large warehouse and store (fifty thousand square feet); he became one of the leading wholesalers in the region. Photographs of his "rug rooms" show hundreds of textiles stacked on floors and shelves. Cotton states that before 1892 few blankets were available and "the demand in the neighborhood of their manufacture was sufficient to exhaust the supply. Since the low price of wool, however, the Navajos, realizing that they could get a much better price for their blankets than for the crude wool, have become extensive manufacturers of rugs and blankets. . . . [O]ne Navajo blanket will outlast half a dozen machine-made blankets" (1896:5).

During the 1890s, when Hubbell shipped blanket stock, he grouped them in bundles: bed blankets, saddle blankets (single and double), fancy blankets (probably Germantowns), and Indian dye blankets (HP Box 332). By the turn of the century, blanket shipments increased in complexity. Much of the demand for handmade articles was fueled by the burgeoning Arts and Crafts Movement. Aficionados rebelled against stuffy Victorian interiors and sought to embrace a simpler lifestyle surrounded by handmade goods both functional and beautiful (Batkin 1999; Goin 1994; Lears 1981; Wilkins 1999).

Hubbell increased the wholesale price of bed and saddle blankets to $0.50 per pound, yet weavers received about $0.30 per pound in book credit (HP Box 333, Ganado Day Books). However, he continued to wholesale some bed and half-saddle blankets to Cotton in Gallup for $0.30 per pound and regular saddle blankets for $0.40 per pound. Many pages from the Ganado Day Book contain blanket entries that comprise 80 percent of the information per page. Old bayeta blankets were sold to collectors for $50.00 each. Some blankets were coded; some noted only the price or the weight. Care was taken not to accidentally duplicate entries. After totaling all categories (and noting that some information was missing), I found that weavers wove more than $7,904.56 in textiles during 1900. More than 478 blankets were entered individually, and another 7,450 pounds were noted only by weight. Two hundred sixty-five entries in this ledger use the CASH [1234] PROFIT [567890] code. Table 7 lists the jobbers, the value weavers received in book credit, and the amount Hubbell charged the dealers for coded textiles. Note that the markups are nearly 100 percent. Figure 9 illustrates the frequency distribution of coded

Table 7. Coded Textiles, Ganado Trading Post, 1900–1901 (Box 333, HP).

Page entry #	Credit Received by Weavers ($)	Jobber	Wholesale Cost ($)
36	$11.25 [4]	W.H. Clark	24.00
104	109.00 [5]	Babbitt Brothers	194.50
131	145.40 [14]	Glasscock & Vroman	229.00
131	437.80 [25]	Albuquerque Blkt Acct	708.30
152	43.00 [4]	Abe Gold	62.00
152	121.00 [8]	Fred Harvey Co.*	207.50
190	186.50 [21]	C.P. Chandler	300.75
237	313.50 [31]	A.B. McGaffy**	651.00
244	151.10 [40]	H.G. Walz	217.50
245	363.00 [10]	H.G. Walz	771.50
295-7	633.31 [N/A]	Albuquerque Blkt Acct	1508.00
Total	2514.86 [265]		$4,874.05

*Uncoded Blankets only
**On Consignment
[ ] # in brackets = # of rugs

rugs reported in table 7, which were sold in six wholesale price categories during 1901.

As table 6 above shows, a great number of rugs and blankets were shipped in ten categories (this includes textiles identified only by weight). The large number of categories counters the often-quoted assumption that textile styles decreased with the advent of trader-controlled weaving. Comparing Hubbell's prices printed in his 1902 catalog with coded entries reveals, for example, that a weaver received $12.50 in credit for weaving an "old style red ground" blanket, which Hubbell in turn sold to Marshall Field Department Store in Chicago for $25.00 to $30.00.

Between August and December 1901 Hubbell purchased $4,000 in goods from Cotton. Of this amount, $1,529 was paid down with blankets (HP Box 337, p. 186). On 17 May 1902 Hubbell bought the trading post at Keams Canyon for his nineteen-year-old son, Lorenzo Jr. (HP Box 94). Exactly one month later Cotton wrote to Hubbell:

Lorencito buying blankets cheap and that is the only way I know of to

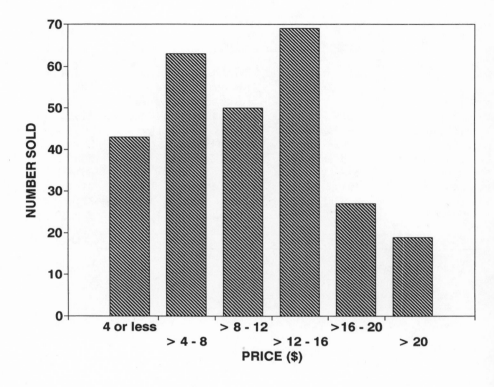

Figure 9. Frequency Distribution of Coded Rugs, Ganado Trading Post, 1900–1901 (Box 333, HP).

handle them, as if a good price is paid, you will be unable to sell at such a profit as you should have. I think that Lorencito will do well, as he has a good head on him, and is not going to allow the indians any [sic] the best of it. (HP Box 19, 6/17/02)

Hubbell admits to another retailer that large blankets take six months to weave (HP Box 94, 2/15/02) and that he sold $27,000 worth of textiles in 1901 and half were old-style patterns.[3] He comments on how few of the large Indian dye blankets were produced because "[the low price] has not justified them making them" (HP Box 94, 3/24/02). Hubbell wholesaled Indian dye blankets for $.75 per pound. Weavers received $.45 per pound in credit for this type of textile and Hubbell received $.08 a pound for Navajo wool. Mrs. Frank Churchill, wife of a government Indian inspector, kept a charming "diary" in which she highlights the weaver's vulnerable position in bartering her textiles. After describing a delightful dinner at Ganado and the interesting company at the table, she wrote:

> [T]here are several hogans near the store and one woman came to the store while we were there with a blanket. Mr. Hubbell was not willing to pay the price she asked. She said she could get much more at Gallup (60 miles distant). She told him he had three partners in his business, he asked who they were and she replied "cold, rain and mud." If it wasn't for them she could get her price. (HP Box 16 #6, 12/28/04)

Textile production dramatically increased after publication of Hubbell's 1902 pamphlet with photographs and descriptions of Indian "curios." Shortly after he began distributing his catalog he responded to an inquiry on 17 October 1902:

> [I have] a large assortment of grey grounds, Navy Blue & Black stripes, white grounds lg / black & red figures. Native wool, well made all wool sell in 1000–5000 lb lots at 65 c also 75c–$1.00. (HP Box 94)

His textile shipments doubled (from fourteen thousand to twenty-eight thousand pounds) within the year, and for several decades more than 90 percent of his annual shipments of "curios" by weight were composed of textiles (see fig. 7). During the first decade, textile sales and shipments continued to escalate while prices for Navajo wool fluctuated 100 percent (see table 1).

It appears that by 1906 some of the materials used for weaving were valued more than the cash valuation of saddle blankets per pound: Hubbell charged $.65 per pound for fuzzy roving yarn. Rough yarn, wool warp, and spun wool were retailed to weavers for $.50 per pound. Given the pressure to increase production, sometimes weavers engaged in forms of resistance. Comments about sand in blankets and wool appear throughout correspondence with C. N. Cotton and other wholesalers. In attempting to receive a greater return for their efforts, some weavers either spun the wool fewer times or more loosely or packed it lightly (rather than firmly) during the weaving process. Any blanket or rug that was loosely woven would probably suffer from uneven edges. Such a textile would be classified as a "poor [quality] blanket." Several sources claim that traders paid for weaving by weight for just a short period before the turn of the century. For example, Rodee (1981:9) states that weavers "outsmarted the traders by weaving loose, coarse rugs from poorly cleaned and carded wool, and then pounding more dirt and sand into the finished product. This increased the weight of the rug, but did nothing to enhance the quality." The information in Hubbell's records soundly refutes such an assumption. Experienced traders were always wise to such tricks and penalized weavers and wool growers accordingly.

Although Hubbell's catalog illustrated several styles priced by the piece, buyers insisted on purchasing blankets by weight. H. L. Dixon of Durango, Colorado, complained in a letter to Hubbell that although the portieres he shipped were "very pretty, they figure out over $3.00 per pound" (HP Box 24, 9/7/06). For many decades, curio shops absorbed a large percentage of blankets and rugs acquired by the Hubbells (Batkin 1999). The most famous relationship of course was that sustained with the Fred Harvey Company (M'Closkey 1994; Weigle and Babcock 1996; appendix IVa, b). However, the Hubbell Papers contain letters and invoices from hundreds of curio shops nationwide. Many letters reveal how dealers were accustomed to purchasing by weight, were very general in their requests concerning size and colors, and frequently dealt in large quantities. The G. M. Harris Curio Co. of Denver wholesaled and retailed Navajo blankets and Indian, Mexican, and Japanese curios. The initial inquiry noted that the company required three thousand pounds of Navajo weaving from May to December 1907 (HP Box 36, 3/30/07). On 15 April 1907 the owner wrote to Don Lorenzo at Ganado, requesting a general assortment of rugs up to 6 x 10 feet:

> [A]ll we ask is to give us good saleable colors at reasonable figures. Competition is keen, and we try to sell close. We want your very lowest legitimate figures and will throw our entire trade to you—if you treat us well. . . . [W]e have a large local following—which indicates that we must be right as the local trade naturally look around before buying. We cannot handle a thick heavy blanket. . . . [S]hip 300 pounds by express from Gallup. (HP Box 36)

Ganado shipped as requested, and Harris responded that he chose sixteen blankets for $224. However:

> the balance are too high priced for us at this time. . . . [T]rouble with this lot is that there are no small cheap blankets—that is what we expected. The grays are pretty but sell slower than the reds and we never carry more than six at a time. We are buying good blankets, not the very coarse grade, at $0.65 and $0.90 per pound, a good clipped

grade at $1.00 per pound. . . . [D]o you not sell by the pound? We prefer to buy that way.[4]

Hubbell advertised a large selection of handwoven blankets from 6 x 7 to 10½ x 11 feet. He wrote Cris Miller of Madison, Wisconsin, that various types of native wool blankets were "much finer than they were made before" (HP Box 96, 7/14/09). He admitted to correspondents that he was making more money on saddle blankets than on any other commodity acquired from the Navajos (Bauer 1987:88). On 11 February 1909 (HP Box 95), he wrote a retailer: ". . . sell $6,000 this month compared to $1300 [this time] last year [at] $1.00 per pound to $2 depends upon the quality of weave and beauty of design." Two weeks later he noted that it was "a good year in selling rugs." On 26 February he wrote to Lorencito: "Our Bkt business is the very best and we must keep up its standards." February's sales peaked at $7,000. On 9 May 1909 he wrote to his brother Charlie at Cedar Springs:

> There was a demand for a cheap saddle blanket. Not desiring to spoil my indians by having them make that kind of goods. . . . [P]rices: saddle, common, 70–75 cents, saddle, best kind, 85-$1.10; white w/red [rugs], .75–1.25, white w/black & red, .75–1.25; grey, 85–1.50; grey w/white & black, 1.00–2.00; red w/black & white, 1.00–2.00; blue & black stripe, 1.00–1.50; sm. rugs, 1.00–2.50; Germantown yarn pillow case 1.25; and my motto is when once my customer I make his interest mine and seldom lose one. (HP Box 96)

That same week, Hubbell responded to a request from Tillman Brothers in LaCrosse, Wisconsin (HP Box 96), and quoted the prices listed above. He also noted that he carried a wide variety of blankets weighing from three to fifty pounds:

> [I]t is difficult to give prices on Blankets as each blanket is different from the other both in quality and design. Now in regard to the high priced blankets, that are quoted from 1.25 to 2.00. At first sight these would look as the highest prices but they are really the cheapest and in which there is the most money.

He also wrote to Lorencito on 3 May:

> we need all the good blankets we can get, particularly bkts 6 feet wide and from 7½ to 8½ and nine feet long. . . . I have orders this morning

for about 1500.00 of Bkts. one order for 1000.00 of good Bkts and the others for Bkts at 75 cts. But I cannot fill that order for we buy very few Bkts that are poor ones here and yours cost at least that if not more. . . . [T]he people in Gallup are getting that trade now. They buy there poor Bkts. much cheaper, for they are out of good ones all the time, so they do not get many. (HP Box 96)

Ten days later he wrote to B. A. Whalen, a Los Angeles dealer, that he hoped his company would push the $1.50 rugs, as Hubbell had more than four hundred in stock, and that he "bought" between $3,000 and $4,000 worth of Navajo blankets a month (HP Box 96). On 12 May 1909 he corresponded with Lorencito again, noting that the best blankets would be made within the next three months, as well as some poor ones. He continued: "We want to buy the poor ones cheap, and the good ones attract them to you the very best way that you can and as cheap as you can, or as high as you have to."

Cotton notified Hubbell that he would take any bales of rugs that the Fred Harvey Company returned. In June 1909 (HP Box 20), Cotton commented that although the wool market appeared weak, the blanket situation "has been very good, in fact twice as good as it was last year at this time." Hubbell wrote the Bank of Commerce in Albuquerque:

[B]usiness has never been better with us since we have been in business. We have bought twice as much wool as we did last year, we have nearly double the number of Bkts. that we did last year and have nearly doubled our sale of merchandise. . . . [W]e retail between 1000.00 per day between us all, and sometimes 1500. But the latter . . . only during the sheep shearing season. (HP Box 96)

Don Lorenzo (HP Box 96, 6/14/09) reported that the Indians in his vicinity had never been so prosperous. Their herds had increased 25 to 50 percent, their wool sold for a good price, and weavers had increased their sales of blankets by 50 percent compared to previous years. Hubbell's admission counters the common assertion that weaving increased only when wool prices were depressed. Evidence in the Hubbell Papers from previous years also counters this refrain. For example, figures 6 and 7 and table 1 show that although wool increased 50 percent in value between 1902 and 1903, textile production rose from 28,000 to 30,000 pounds. During the following two years, wool rose from $0.10 to $0.12 to $0.16 per pound, and rug production increased by 7 percent. Wool fluctuated between $0.11 and $0.12^{1}/$_{2}$ per pound between 1906 and 1908, yet textile production by weavers trading with the Hubbells escalated from 29,000 to more than 40,000 pounds (see fig. 7). His 1907 rug profits were $9,223.60. Hubbell suffered a net loss of $207.75 on the wool market that year. Such discrepancies demonstrate how weavers' production provided a very comfortable cushion to offset losses in the volatile wool market.

The blanket profits totaled from information contained in Hubbell's shipping and profit and loss records that year are corroborated by statements made in his business correspondence. He reaped record profits of $27,000 for "curios" (mostly textiles) in 1909 (see table 5).[5] Based on evidence in his papers, he would have had to sell at least 1.35 million pounds of wool (at two cents per pound net profit) to make equivalent profits. According to my survey of his wool shipments, the Hubbells do not appear to sell more than 400,000 pounds of wool in a record year. Few traders ran freighting operations the size of the Hubbells'. Most traders not only lacked adequate storage and shipping facilities for enormous amounts of wool but also the economic security to hold wool for an extended period because of debts owing to wholesalers.

By July 1910 the wool market appeared "thoroughly demoralized." With the wool market down, Hubbell shipped a massive number of rugs to Cotton on 28 October: 6,500 pounds to his Gallup warehouse to pay down his accounts and 2,583 pounds to other clients (HP Box 348). Earlier that year, Hubbell had shipped nineteen bales, or 3,333 pounds, of textiles to the Fred Harvey Company over an eight-week period (HP Box 348).

One of the most important long-term arrangements the Hubbells sustained with merchants other than off-reservation wholesale houses involved trading Navajo blankets and rugs for horse tack and saddles. For decades the Hubbells exchanged thousands of textiles with more than a dozen saddlery firms, including Schoellkopf of Dallas, Texas (HP Box 74, 1905–15), Furstnow of Miles City, Montana (HP Box 31, 3/10/20), Gallup Saddlery of Pueblo, Colorado (HP Box 31, 4/4/02), Heiser of Denver (Box 39 #10; 182, 1925–37), Atkins-Boothman (formerly Edelbrock) of Fort Worth, Texas (Box 10, 1937–47), and Hamley of Pendleton, Oregon (Box 35 and 180 1928–49).

Don Lorenzo initially dealt with Schoellkopf in 1905, a company that described itself as "very large jobbers of Navajo saddle blankets." Their elaborate letterhead illustrates an impressive four-story building "established 1872 and incorporated 1902." The company wrote Ganado requesting the "very best wholesale price in lots from 1000 to 5000 pounds" (HP Box 74, 5/31/05). Schoellkopf rejected the initial quote as far too high, because they were accustomed to paying $.40 per pound. Ganado immediately shipped samples that

Schoellkopf agreed were worth $.45 per pound. By 1909 the firm had outgrown its headquarters and relocated to a six-story building that occupied an entire city block, claiming to be the "largest exclusive saddlery establishment in the world" (HP Box 74, 6/22/09). The firm requested a large quantity of "Navajo Blue Blankets" measuring 3 x 5 feet, not to weigh more than seven pounds: "if you are in position to quote us some very low prices, we will be glad to send you an order." Before World War I the Dallas company requested a large quantity of saddle blankets with "fancy colors with plenty of red and a wool warp. . . . [W]e have some interesting quotations from some other houses." At the bottom of this request, Forrest Parker wrote to Hubbell that he had not replied because he needed to know what such blankets were selling for in Gallup. Don Lorenzo responded by quoting Gallup prices at $.60 to $.65 per pound (HP Box 74, 2/2/15). At the time Navajo wool was averaging about $.18 per pound. Weavers needed nearly $.35 worth of wool per pound of saddle blanket, and they typically received $.50 per pound in credit for this type of textile.

Hubbell's prowess in wholesaling wool in the form of blankets is amply documented. Table 5 and figures 6 and 7 show that Hubbell's wool shipments in 1891 were worth ten times his blanket shipments. By 1900 blanket shipments were valued at 260 percent more than his wool shipments. By 1909 Hubbell's profits in blankets were nearly fourteen times higher than his wool profits. In fact, his blanket profits that year were greater than the total amount of wool sold. For every pound of weaving Hubbell shipped from 1891 to 1909, he netted $.27 per pound in profits (table 5). Over a twenty-year period, his blanket profits averaged twelve and a half times his wool profits. Between 1906 and 1909 his sales and shipments of wool doubled. Over the same period his curio profits increased twentyfold over wool profits. These calculations provide irrefutable evidence that Hubbell's greatest profits lay in wool woven into textiles.

Post-World War I Rug Production and Sales

Trading post records containing information related to cumulative shipments of all commodities are somewhat deficient for the 1911–13 period, when Hubbell served in the territorial legislature. Don Lorenzo left his younger son, Roman, barely out of his teens, and other family members in charge of Ganado. Bookkeeping rapidly deteriorated and Hubbell periodically returned to Ganado to organize accounts. By 1 March 1913 Roman held a $30,000 inventory in blankets (HP Box 99), and Cotton pressed for payment on the post's account while complaining about the quality of saddle blankets shipped by Roman. Don Lorenzo returned during the summer and on 25 and 27 August 1913 shipped his disgruntled former business partner 20,597 pounds of weaving to pay down his long overdue accounts (HP Box 352 #4, pp. 234–35).[6] Roman left Ganado on his father's return as relations between them were strained. Lorenzo penned a revealing letter to his younger son on 28 August:

> [B]usiness has been extremely good and collections [on accounts] are first class so far. . . . I sold all the blankets. . . . [I] have about two thousand Dollars left and Lorenzo about three thousand, and Charley must have quite a few. . . . Blankets are going to be very much cheaper. (HP Box 99)

In 1914 he returned to Ganado after losing his bid for the U.S. senatorial race on the Republican ticket (Blue 2000:184–88).

Space constraints preclude a review of business correspondence from 1914 to 1920. However, a series of letters written by Lorenzo Jr. from Oraibi reveal some interesting developments relative to the fluctuations in the volatile wool market just after World War I. They counter the generalization that weavers always increased production when wool prices dropped and reveal traders' dependence on Navajo weavers. They also counter the notion that massive shipments of textiles from the reservation "standardized" Navajo weaving. Had traders continually insisted on specific sizes, colors, and patterns, many trade goods would have remained on post shelves.

Lorenzo Jr. wrote to Superintendent Daniel at Keams Canyon that he had purchased far less wool at $.24 per pound in 1920, as Navajos were holding wool to weave into blankets (HP Box 102 #2, 8/12/20). He commented that since he had known them, blankets were their main revenue and continued:

> [M]ore Navajo blankets have been made by the Navajo tribe in general, than ever before, or I can safely say in the last four or five years . . . the Navajo fared better by making blankets, than to have sold . . . wool at the prices offered. . . . [A]t the beginning of season #1 grade wool was 50c/pound and #2 grade wool was 40c/pound, both were 20c/pound at seasons end; common hairy wool was 30c/pound and 10c/pound at seasons end.

In 1920 the Hubbells were receiving approximately $.25 to $.29 per pound on Navajo wool. In 1921 the market plummeted, with wool bringing a scant $.10 per pound (McPherson 1992a:36). Yet women were not weaving. In a 4 September 1921 letter to a relative, marked "personal" (HP Box 102), Lorenzo Jr. was obviously feeling the postwar economic pinch. All commodities were depressed, as was his stock of goods: "Trade is very dull. . . . I'm not getting a third of the rugs I usually get. They are not making them. . . . [G]ood rugs are as scarce as hens teeth." Without rugs, Hubbell was unable to pay down his accounts with his creditors. Therefore, he could not order in any goods. Without goods, weavers will not weave for trade. It was a vicious circle. He mentioned having a Hopi get one thousand pieces of pottery. Although he claimed he was low on rugs, Hubbell planned to ship 1,500 pounds to his brother-in-law, Forrest Parker, who was managing their new store in Long Beach, California.[7] On 12 September he wrote again, mentioning that he could not encourage weavers right now, since he did not have the goods: "[W]e are out of cash and goods both. . . . I still believe rugs are going to be scarce. . . . Babbitt Brothers only have about 7000 pounds." On 7 October 1921 Lorenzo Jr. confided to Parker:

> I was counting on the wool, and rugs, and particularly on rugs, and I have enough of these at present that with our sales this fall, we should be able to reduce our indebtedness ten thousand dollars by the first of the year. . . . [I] sold wool at 9c/pound so as not to have to borrow more [money]. (HP Box 102)[8]

In 1924 Lorenzo Jr. purchased a large warehouse in Winslow, which ultimately stocked ten thousand Navajo blankets and rugs (HP Boxes 465, 482, 483). On 24 May 1926 he submitted a confidential report to the CIA as to the value of goods he acquired from Navajos on the reservation and those living on the Hopi Reservation (a joint-use area). Of seven categories, including sheep, the only commodity valued higher than blankets was wool. Since it is difficult to interpret the wording and decipher the numbers, I have not replicated the information here. However, rugs from both reservations outrank all other commodities except wool (HP Box 527).

Like most reservation traders, the Hubbells typically wholesaled rugs directly from their trading posts to mercantile establishments to pay down their accounts. There were several exceptions in which they opened up off-reservation stores to sell curios. Lorenzo Jr. had short-term locations in Phoenix and two stores in Los Angeles during the 1920s. The Arizona Navajo Indian Rug Company, managed by Parker, opened in Long Beach on 2 May 1921. Two days later Lorenzo Jr. wrote to his father: "I sent down the finest collection of rugs I ever saw [to California]. I don't think anyone has ever had such a collection. We had hundreds and hundreds of rugs of the very finest kind. I have been putting them away for nearly a year. The store measures 25 by 140 feet with a basement" (HP Box 102, 5/04/21). As the postwar recession deepened, the store was forced to close on 26 January 1922. Four years later Lorenzo Jr. opened another retail store on Hollywood Boulevard that featured baskets, plaques, jewelry, moccasins, pottery, kachinas, bows and arrows, "novelties," and Navajo rugs (Blue 2000:248). The shop typically maintained $20,000 worth of rugs (HP Box 102, 10/14/26).[9]

The wool market suffered its usual jitters in 1925. That spring Louis Ilfeld of Albuquerque wrote to Lorenzo Hubbell at Oraibi, "[N]o one seems to know what wool is worth" (HP Box 42, 4/28/25). On 9 May he noted, "[W]ool is still going down." Within the week Ilfeld notified Oraibi that he could pay only $.22 to $.23 per pound (HP Box 42, 5/15/25). By 18 May the market continued to decline, prompting Lorenzo to instruct Piñon to pay $.17 per pound for coarse wool, $.22 for improved, and $.15 for black wool (HP Box 104). On 10 June Lorenzo noted the need for cash to purchase skins, wool, and sheep but remarked, "[I]f we can sell the rugs we can forget the rest of the business" (HP Box 104).[10]

During 1928 Lorenzo Jr. purchased $97,123.04 worth of wool and $38,149.03 worth of weaving; the latter comprised 28 percent of the $135,272.07 total for both products (HP Box 527). In retrospect, these figures were the highest the trader was to achieve for many years. Yet the ratio of blankets to wool was lower than that reported by traders to Superintendent Duclos (see below). Lorenzo received a letter from Gallup Mercantile before the stock market crash alerting him that the company would no longer take blankets from traders in payment of accounts or in trade for merchandise as prices were too high and they were grossly overstocked (HP Box 31, 6/26/29). Other wholesalers had also issued similar directives in the past (Babbitt Brothers: HP Box 6, 9/30/18; Kirk: Box 21, 3/13/19; C. N. Cotton: Box 21, 3/19/25). This policy worked a severe hardship on traders who in turn decreased credit allowed to weavers. However, Kirk in Gallup accepted thirty-one bales of blankets from Oraibi that weighed 3,893 pounds (Box 523 #4, 4/28/31).

Evidence for an Increase in Weavers' Workload

The amount of labor extended by traders to market blankets was minuscule relative to the extreme effort expended by thousands of women transforming a devalued resource into a marketable product. Data analyzed from archival sources demonstrates that weavers' workloads tripled after 1890. Not only were women compelled to accelerate weaving, they had to barter for cloth (by the yard) and sew much of their families' clothing. Evidence from the Hubbells' business records parallels the increase in reservation-wide production. Additional evidence is provided by a government study during the 1930s.

The Hubbell archives reveal a high volume of rug production as information related to textiles appears everywhere—in inter- and intrapost correspondence, off-reservation general correspondence, day books, journals and ledgers, shipping manifests, and invoices. Textile production rose dramatically after Hubbell published his 1902 pamphlet. Information from the weavers' ledgers in his business records reveals how weavers were squeezed. The shift from blankets to rugs, to offset increased competition from trade blanket manufacturers, pressured weavers in the following manner. Before 1900 bed blankets formed a portion of Navajo textile production (HP, pre-1900 Cotton correspondence). Many of these were more loosely woven and had simpler patterns. When the Navajo blanket became a rug, wool had to be spun one to two more times. It also had to be packed down more tightly while weaving; otherwise the rug would be too soft and would not withstand hard wear.

Recall that most of the experiments described in chapter 3 involved weavers provisioned with yarns. The Hubbells seldom provided weavers with yarns as that defeated the purpose of using weaving as an "alternative means to market wool" (Bailey and Bailey 1986:152). Evidence previously shown demonstrates that preparing materials prior to weaving often takes more time than weaving itself. Information from these experiments helps in calculating the number of hours needed to produce a pound of weaving.[11]

Saddle blankets are fairly standardized according to size, with singles averaging 32 to 36 inches square and weighing 3 to 4 pounds each. Double saddle blankets measure approximately 30 x 50 or 60 inches and weigh from 5 to 7 pounds apiece. Based on published experiments, I calculated that patterned double saddle blankets may take 140 hours to weave (this includes warping the loom), which averages 20 hours per pound of yarn. If the weaver also cleans, cards, spins, and dyes all the wool, the workload per pound of finished weaving will more than double. The time required to turn raw fleece into a textile will vary quite a bit, depending on the number of times the yarn must be spun to achieve the desired diameter and the complexity of the pattern. For example, simple horizontal stripes of coarsely spun wool can be woven more quickly than a complex pattern created with fine hand-spun yarn. If a 3-x-5-foot rug weighs approximately 6 pounds, it may take from 204 hours (simple pattern, coarsely spun wool) to 560 hours (complex pattern, finely spun wool) to spin and weave. Given the escalation in production, weavers may not have been able to afford the extra time necessary to collect plants for dyes. Plants cannot be collected in the winter and frequently are at their peak for short periods during the growing season. Thus weavers resorted to using aniline dyes.

Hubbell's branch post at Cornfields has detailed, readable records for 1906 and 1907. Tracking the movement of commodities shows that for four months per year, weavers' production was exchanged for more than 50 percent of all goods acquired from the trader. The rest of the time, weaving was exchanged for 21 to 44 percent of all goods. In 1906 (HP Box 66), weavers received $0.73 per pound credit for large rugs. Hubbell wholesaled them for $1.22 per pound. Navajos received $0.12½ per pound in credit for their wool at Cornfields. Weavers needed approximately $0.25 worth of wool to produce a pound of yarn. They are netting less than $0.50 per pound in credit for their large rugs, which generally take months to weave (appendix V). Traders needed textiles to augment trading post sales. Thacker wrote from Cornfields, "I am after the I about blankets and they say they are too busy with their corn to weave any yet" (HP Box 95, 10/25/05). Additional evidence from archives demonstrating the importance of women's textile production and subsequent increase in workload is exhibited in this chapter. For example, figure 10 shows the number of blankets bartered by weavers monthly at Ganado in 1906. Table 8 reveals the breakdown by month of all goods bartered by Navajos trading at Ganado in 1906.[12]

To summarize the escalation in production by weavers from 1892 to 1909: Hubbell shipped more than four hundred thousand pounds, or more than two hundred tons, of textiles from Ganado over an eighteen-year period (see fig. 7). This rise in textile production corroborates the reservation-wide increase shown by Amsden ([1934] 1975). Such an escalation in production over less than a generation provides direct evidence of the increased workload for many Navajo women.

Government-Trader Relations

Periodically the Hubbells received letters from government officials concerned with the transformation of wool into rugs. On 25 October 1912 Charles Dawes, supervisor of farming, wrote traders, "Navajo blanket industry needs proper and efficient promotion of a higher degree of art and mechanical skill. . . . [T]oo great a sameness of price for various classes of work . . . [generates] mediocrity" (HP Box 44).

Government bureaucrats were concerned that wholesale merchants such as Cotton not "dictate" wool prices to reservation traders. Superintendent Daniel made the following comment:

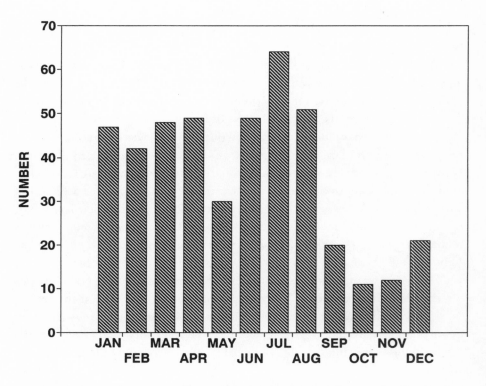

Figure 10. Number of Blankets Bartered by Weavers, 1906, Ganado Day Book #3 (Box 332, HP).

It is the desire of this office that the Indians be especially encouraged to use as much of the low grade or "cow tail" wool as possible in the making of blankets. The fact that this wool on the market will bring only 23 to 28 cents per pound and $2.00 to $3.00 per pound in a blanket leaves no room for argument. (HP Box 44, 5/10/20)

The Hubbell Papers reveal that Daniel's assumption with regard to blanket prices is extremely generous. In 1920 wholesalers paid the Hubbells $0.60 to $0.75 a pound for saddle blankets (HP Clinton Cotton, Box 21). Furstnow paid $1.25 for "nice double saddles." Cotton paid $1.00 per pound for native wool rugs and $2.00 per pound for "excellent" ones. The Fred Harvey Company, who never handled the "cheaper grade" textiles, paid between $1.45 and $2.30 per pound that year. Had weavers used "cow tail yarn," they were likely to receive far less than $1.00 per pound in credit for their textiles. They usually chose the best parts of the fleece for spinning, as it yielded the most ideal yarn for weaving. Such statements from the superintendent reveal how little he knew about the exigencies of weaving, whether technical or economic.

Significant information related to the magnitude and value of Navajo textile production resides in unpublished portions of Indian agents' reports to the Commissioner of Indian Affairs. In his 1915 narrative report (Section IV-Industries), from the Leupp Agency located in northwestern Arizona, Superintendent Stephen Janus commented favorably on the government policy of upgrading Navajo flocks, although many animals died as newly introduced breeds faced the rigors of climate and elevation.[13] Janus voiced his feelings regarding the conundrum Navajos faced when their flocks were bred up:

> Blanket weaving is the only other industry besides stock and agriculture that concerns the Navajo. A good deal of talk has been made about the breeding up of the Navajo sheep making it impossible on account of the change in the wool for them to make blankets. If the

Table 8. Cash Valuation of Bartered Goods, Hubbell Trading Post Records, Ganado, 1906.

Month	Wool	Skins	Pelts	Blankets	Mdse	Pawn
Jan	17.45	37.65	17.00	317.75	265.15	107.60
Feb	87.95	40.30	13.05	276.45	92.10	85.30
Mar	137.60	50.70	27.50	415.35	160.30	163.80
Apr	410.60	49.00	10.95	320.50	153.80	157.15
May	2498.65	47.50	15.62	163.00	104.25	211.30
Jun	866.36	47.15	12.80	330.10	346.10	151.85
Jul	158.45	55.55	24.10	405.25	192.00	166.85
Aug	365.65	57.95	24.14	388.60	198.55	164.30
Sep	275.30	51.70	17.45	88.10	229.45	139.40
Oct	195.90	35.35	10.15	64.25	1004.00	251.95
Nov	64.40	39.95	14.15	104.00	2084.60	317.90
Dec	3.90	54.45	8.15	184.50	864.10	153.65
Total	5082.21	567.25	195.06	3057.85	5694.45	2071.05

Navajos had half as many well bred sheep as they now have poor sheep and destructive goats, and it entirely destroyed the blanket business it would be a blessing. The weaving of a blanket by a Navajo woman is a long, tedious, and profitless job. It not only takes days and days, but weeks and weeks during which the woman is a perfect slave and does nothing else but weave and weave, and weave, and weave, and weave, while the children are neglected, the hogan dirty, and her lord and master riding the country from one "sing" to another. Better sheep and less blanket weaving would give the Navajo woman a chance to clean up and attend more to her neglected domestic duties.

In his 1916 report, Janus reiterated his comments about the dilemma faced by Navajo women:

The Indians weave blankets and this is the only industry outside of their stock. It is rather a slavery for the women and they cannot do the domestic work constantly urged by the Office and weave but no one has apparently sensed this inconsistency. A better wool that would produce more revenue per animal and free the women from this exacting toil might be better.

Thus Janus acknowledged how the low quality of wool made weaving necessary. Navajo women failed to become accomplished *housewives* because they were constantly at their looms (fig. 11; Jensen 1994).

Information about weaving extracted from the statistical section of Janus's report from the Leupp Agency reveals that an estimated four hundred weavers produced eight thousand rugs totaling $80,000, or $10 each. Out of a population of 622 women and girls, 275 adult women and 125 girls under the age of seventeen were weaving: 65 percent of the entire female population. Annual weaving income averaged $200 per weaver. Janus estimated that one hundred silversmiths in the Leupp jurisdiction produced $4,500 worth of jewelry, or an average of $45 per smith per year. Therefore, four times as many weavers produced eighteen times the income of smithing. Navajos sold only 2 percent of their sheep and goats that year. The total value of all stock sold, including horses and cattle, amounted to $20,800, or 25 percent of the value of weaving. However, the value of wool sales was not incorporated in Janus's report. The superintendent's reports and accompanying statistics demonstrate great industry, especially in the realm of textile production. However, in his 1917 report

Figure 11. Two Views of Hahs-e-ba, Canyon de Chelly, circa 1914. Photo by
Carl Moon. Carl Moon Photographs MS 285 Box 1 folder 2 #11,
courtesy of Special Collections Library, University of Arizona.

to the Board of Indian Commissioners, board member Edward A. Ayer of Chicago adamantly stated his support of mass hiring of Indians as cotton pickers to alleviate the labor shortages: "[W]hat our Indians need most is to be taught to work. There are nearly 50,000 Indians in Arizona and a very small percentage of them do any useful work" (quoted in Lockwood 1929:222). Only nonsubsistence farming and waged labor performed outside the home counted as work. Although thousands of Navajo women and girls were weaving at this time, with few exceptions textile production within the household remained absent from the published record. Participation in the informal economy translated into invisibility.

W. O. Roberts, who had replaced Janus as superintendent at Leupp by 1926, also remarked on the importance of the blanket weaving industry:

> There is a particular demand for the Navajo product at the present time, particularly if the standard of the product is good. The work is suffering to some extent by the influence of outsiders who try to influence the I to make various designs which, of course, are not the native Ind. Patterns. Also due to the fact that the length of time required to weave a rug makes the economic value of weaving questionable. All the traders appear to be doing a heavy business in the N rug and this industry will doubtless continue for some years.

The economic importance of textile production was not confined to the Leupp jurisdiction. In 1925, in response to his request, eighteen licensed traders reported to Superintendent A. F. Duclos of Fort Defiance on acquisitions of pelts, skins, blankets, and wool from Navajos. Traders acquired $64,928 worth of wool valued from $0.21 to $0.28 per pound from growers.[14] Weavers earned $69,172 in credit or goods for their textiles. Six traders reported purchasing 16,378 pounds of weaving for $21,825 (~$1.34 per pound). Twelve traders acquired more than 4,022 textiles, averaging from $7.30 to $14.78 apiece. However, weavers trading with Newcombs at Crystal earned $24.86 per rug. The value of rug purchases relative to wool purchases ranged from 20 percent to 71 percent, with over 60 percent of the posts exhibiting higher rug rates relative to wool (fig. 12).

Evidence for Sustained Appropriation of Weavers' Surplus Labor

Except for mutton, wool, and some vegetable crops, Navajos became increasingly dependent on provisioning themselves through "barter" with traders.

Figure 12a.
Pound blanket/rug,
circa 1905, photo
by Kathy M'Closkey.

Figure 12b.
Saddle blanket,
circa 1950, photo
by Kathy M'Closkey.

Analysis of archival records demonstrates the overwhelming necessity of textile production to the maintenance of a livelihood damaged by direct competition engendered by appropriation of indigenous designs. As trade blanket manufacturers usurped the markets formerly served by Navajo weavers, textile production escalated dramatically (see fig. 7).

Evidence of a market saturated by Navajo weaving occurs early in Hubbell's records. Don Lorenzo held between $10,000 and $12,000 stock in blankets (HP Box 94, 12/05/03). Although Hubbell's financial assets continued to grow, trader Charles S. Day wrote about his concern over the glut of Navajo blankets on the market creating depressed returns to weavers:

> Trade is fair here but no sale for blankets. Cotton wrote me that if blankets came in for the next 30 days as they had been coming for the last 30 he could not take any more. I do not know what we will do if there is no sale for blkts, as that is about all the Indians have to sell. (HP Box 23, 7/22/03)

A plea to the commissioner to visit and assuage the problem was to no avail.[15] The "glut" exemplifies the impoverishment of weavers in conjunction with the relentless usurpation of the market by trade blanket manufacturers. Coincidentally, the average retail cost of trade blankets to Navajos increased 800 percent, from $1.55 to $12.50, between 1880 and 1911, paralleling the escalation in production of Navajo weaving relative to the 50 percent increase in population. Wool moved from $.13^1/$_2$ to $.18 a pound between 1912 and 1915. Although textile production had increased and Navajos were selling more stock because of the war, Weiss (1984:83) reported that 85 percent of the Navajo population was "destitute, moderately poor or average" in 1915.

Reports by Youngblood (1935) and Fryer (1939) in the Hubbell archives (HP Box 527) together with Hubbell's business records substantiate my claim that the more Navajos wove, the poorer they became. Youngblood's study provides a more realistic assessment of the proportionately higher cost of living for Navajos than that reflected in the CPI used by Bailey and Bailey (1986). Fryer's survey demonstrates the magnitude and importance of textile production to the regional economy. Although the reports, produced by government personnel during the 1930s, contain data compiled years after most of the information I analyzed in archival records (see tables and figures in chaps. 3, 4), they corroborate information in the Hubbells' business records. References to these government reports by a handful of authors (Bailey and Bailey 1986; Kelley 1976; Kelley and Whiteley 1989), appear sporadically rather than as independent publications. Amalgamating the published and archival information allows us to estimate the appropriation of surplus labor by merchant capital for decades. Before focusing on textile production, it is useful to look at trading.

Youngblood's Survey, 1929–1934

Bonney Youngblood, an agricultural economist with the U.S. Department of Agriculture (HP Box 527 #4), surveyed more than one hundred posts on and adjacent to the Navajo Reservation. Traders were generally cooperative; some kept adequate account books, others almost none. Youngblood found the bulk of Navajo trade was with licensed on-reservation traders. On average the trading posts remained solvent throughout the depression. Three of eighty posts failed during his study. Figures contained in Youngblood's report (1935:23) demonstrate that posts in Navajo country probably weathered the depression better than the average American business. Reservation-wide there was great variation in retail prices that bore no relation to wholesale prices. This is quite remarkable as one would expect lowered retail prices as an aid to assist Navajos in overcoming the collapse of the wool, mohair, and lamb markets in the depression years. A government directive published in 1924 had stipulated that retail prices at trading posts were to be no greater than 25 to 35 percent over wholesale costs. Edgar Miller, superintendent of the Hopi Agency, admonished traders for overpricing goods during the depression (HP Box 44, 4/28/32). Retailers nationwide had reduced prices on commodities, and traders should do likewise.

In tables 95 and 96 of his published report, Youngblood compares operating costs of chain stores and trading posts. He found the net operating profit for posts was 276 percent *higher* than chain stores because the margin of profit on goods was (slightly) higher but operating expenses were considerably lower.[16] Table 16 from Youngblood (1935) illustrates the average undelivered wholesale cost of twelve key items of merchandise at forty-five trading posts on the Navajo Reservation in 1933 and 1934. All the items are represented in tables 2 and 3, compiled from Hubbell's post inventories and wholesalers' invoices. Because Youngblood's figures are very similar to the figures in the Hubbells' 1933 and 1934 inventories, I have used his information to demonstrate the average percentage of markups on goods represented in my tables. Youngblood's table 58, "Average mark-ups for six months period January–June 1933, is compiled from information gathered at from 24 to 44 trading posts on the reservation. With the exception of coffee and alfalfa, markups are far greater than the ceiling mandated by the government in 1924:

Consumer Item	Markup
Flour	43%
Sugar	57%
Coffee	37%
Fats	69%
Canned milk	84%
Canned pears	58%
Canned peaches	86%
Canned tomatoes	81%
Alfalfa	30%
Trade blankets	53%
Women's shoes	69%
Men's work shoes	74%
Velveteen	94%
Sateen	96%
Cotton yardage	102%
Thread	139%
Overalls	77%
Men's cotton shirts	83%
Men's hats	64%

According to Kelley and Whiteley (1989:229), Navajo families surveyed in 1936–37 spent an average of $233.56 annually on food and clothing. Sixty percent was spent for food, 40 percent for clothing. Of the latter amount, 35 percent was for trade blankets and 20 percent for yardage.[17] A postdepression publication by Boyce (1942) demonstrates how traders reaped far greater returns in net profits relative to off-reservation stores. For every $35,000 in sales, reservation traders earned $4,600 in net profits (13 percent). During 1930–31, general stores averaged $3,400 per $95,000 in sales, or 3.5 percent; and in 1928 chain stores in the mountain states netted $3,200 (3.8 percent) for every $85,000 in sales. Although traders' profits were three and a half times higher in comparison to other retail establishments, they shouldered greater risks as they bought and sold wool and sheep in unprotected markets.

The Navajo Agency Report, 1939–1940
E. R. Fryer's government report incorporates information relevant to textile production. As general superintendent with the Navajo Service, Fryer requested information from all traders on the Navajo Reservation about the amount of wool retained for weaving. He also requested information on "cost price" of

rugs acquired from weavers. Although traders were not required to report this information, they appear to have complied with his request. Fryer noted that "the great majority of rugs . . . are sold to the wholesale houses in Gallup, Winslow, and elsewhere."

[A wholesaler] must maintain connections through which he can dispose of wool, lambs, rugs and other Indian products in volume. In the late 1930s, rugs sold in various ways[,] . . . either locally, by mail order, or delivered to the wholesaler on account. Wholesalers advance no cash for the purchase of rugs. The wholesaler must find markets for rugs he accepts on account. Wholesalers average 10% markup [on goods sold to traders]: 8% on staples, 10% on dry goods (including shawls & robes), and 15% on canned goods, and possibly 5% on flour. (1939:101–2)

He found that markups on goods were higher because cash sales were rare. Traders granted Navajos "unsecured credit" for at least six months per year. Several religious organizations also advertised Navajo weaving. The Franciscan friars of St. Michaels, Arizona, printed a brochure depicting nicely patterned 3-x-4-foot rugs for $5 to $7 (Franciscan Missionary Fathers 1935:13). In the late 1930s it was reported that traders paid down their accounts with wholesalers with Indian products (80 percent) and cash (20 percent). Cash payments had increased because of Indian Emergency Conservation and Soil Erosion Service programs initiated during the depression. Additional cash was generated through the stock reduction program mandated by Commissioner of Indian Affairs John Collier. Between 1934 and 1937 Navajos were forced to sell many of their animals. Stock was slaughtered on site if railcars were unavailable to transport them (Parman 1976; Schoepfle et al. 1988; White 1983:chapter 12). By 1939 the percentage of weaving applied to pay down traders' accounts with wholesalers ranged from 8 percent to 55 percent. It had been far higher before the depression and the Civilian Conservation Corps (CCC) programs.

According to Fryer (1939:table 1), textiles made up 19 percent, or $333,056, of the commercial revenue in 1939, with 303,325 pounds acquired from weavers (table 9). Thus there was a sharp decline over the decade, reflecting the drastic effects of the stock reduction program that decreased the amount of wool available to weavers. By 1939, 29 percent of tribal income was from sheep and 20 percent from wool, which sold for $0.17 per pound that year. Navajos working for traders earned 3 percent of reservation-generated income. Youngblood's detailed study noted:

[R]ug income is of greater economic significance to the Navajo than the values involved would indicate. It is practically the only income they can normally depend upon between wool and lamb marketing seasons. . . . There are no silversmiths in the vicinity of 50 percent of posts. (1935:9, copy in HP Box 527)

This revealing statement demonstrates the continued importance of textile production despite its recent sharp decline. Fryer's comment also corroborates the voluminous evidence in the Hubbells' business records.

Fryer's report confirms the sustained appropriation of weavers' labor for decades. The figures in his table 8 represent the actual cash valuation of textiles woven by Navajo women in 1939. In other words, they reflect the actual amount of credit weavers received. There is no ambiguity about whether the reported figures reflect the value of rugs wholesaled off the reservation or credit allotted to weavers. Calculations based on information from this report demonstrate the extent of impoverishment of Navajo weavers and corroborate much of the evidence compiled from earlier archived business records. According to table 1 in the Navajo Agency report, wages earned working for traders amounted to $57,873 in 1939. If they worked an "average" eight-hour day for $0.25 an hour, the dollar figure approximates 231,492 hours of labor. Using the amount of wool woven into rugs during that year (303,000 pounds) and incorporating information from the weaving experiments, I calculated that each pound of wool required at least forty hours' preparation and weaving time. In 1939 the labor expended by thousands of Navajo weavers totals at least 12 million hours and earned them $333,056 in credit. However, weavers supplied all the wool valued at $103,713 (Fryer 1939:table 8, col. 6). The value of the wool must be subtracted from the total, as Navajos could sell the wool to traders instead of weaving it into rugs and saddle blankets. Thus weavers netted $229,343 in credit for producing 303,325 pounds of textiles (table 9). Weavers also supplied all their own tools and paid for dyes and tow cards used for cleaning and straightening the wool fibers.

Fryer's table suggests that weavers earned only four times the value of the fleece in weaving a saddle blanket or rug—received in credit, not cash. Figure 13, below, shows the amount of credit per pound extended by the trader ($1.06 computed mean value) and the revised amount ($0.71 computed mean value), after deducting the value of the wool ($0.17 per pound). Weavers averaged $0.01 to $0.02 per hour for their labor, or $0.08 to $0.16 per "weaving day." Using dependable information for this year reveals an astounding amount of "hidden" labor. In previous years with higher volume output (in 1911, weavers used 843,750 pounds of wool and produced more than 420,000 pounds of finished

Table 9. Rug Schedule from Traders' Purchases, Navajo Reservation, 1939. From Fryer 1939.

RUGS($)	WEIGHT (LBS)	AVERAGE (PER LB)	WOOL USED			LABOR REVENUE FROM WEAVING	DISTRICT	NUMBER OF POSTS	%RUGS/ DISTRICT
			LBS	PRICE	TOTAL				
10,802	13,939	.775	27,878	.17	4,739	6,002	1	4	3.26
3,057	4,170	.733	8,340	.166	1,390	1,651	2	3	.91
9,774	10,564	.925	21,128	.159	3,359	6,351	3	5	2.94
8,000	8,421	.95	16,842	.18	3,031	4,919	4	2	2.4
10,485	10,265	1.02	20,530	.164	3,358	7,056	5-6	6	3.15
30,573	33,459	.914	66,918	.167	11,155	19,224	7	7	9.18
6,936	6,380	1.087	12,760	.151	1,927	4,959	8	6	2.08
15,729	12,096	1.30	24,192	.158	3,825	11,785	9	5	4.73
33,237	27,748	1.20	55,496	.166	9,212	23,784	10	7	9.98
11,573	9,395	1.23	18,790	.158	2,973	8,514	11	3	3.48
45,121	31,027	1.45	62,054	.158	9,805	34,963	12	16	13.5
8,696	8,259	1.05	16,518	.173	2,868	5,770	13	4	2.62
12,172	10,974	1.11	21,948	.161	3,540	8,545	14	5	3.65
17,166	18,840	.91	37,680	.178	6,707	10,354	15	9	5.16
22,799	24,547	.93	49,094	.183	8,960	13,701	16	13	6.84
34,522	24,742	1.39	49,484	.185	9,174	25,114	17	10	10.37
29,064	25,471	1.14	50,942	.18	9,170	19,695	18	20	8.74
23,360	23,028	1.01	46,056	.185	8,520	14,682	19	12	7.01
333,056	303,325	1.09	606,650	.17	103,713	227,069		137	100

textiles), fewer weavers had to work even harder.[18] But regardless of how hard they worked, it appears weavers received less than $0.03 per hour in book credit, even when they supplied all the inputs. Despite covering an earlier period, the Hubbell data corroborates much of Fryer's information. The estimate of $0.01 to $0.02 per hour was corroborated in a recent conversation with a Navajo weaver in her forties. Further, both her mother and grandmother wove for decades and received approximately $15.00 in credit for their 4-x-6-foot rugs. My correspondent has been weaving for decades and had calculated the hourly return based on her own experience.

Fryer's comprehensive report also provides a breakdown by each of the nineteen districts of the Navajo Reservation, incorporating 137 trading posts (the total number of posts on the reservation). Ganado, the Hubbell family's key post, is located in District 17, and Lorenzo Jr.'s post at Oraibi is located in

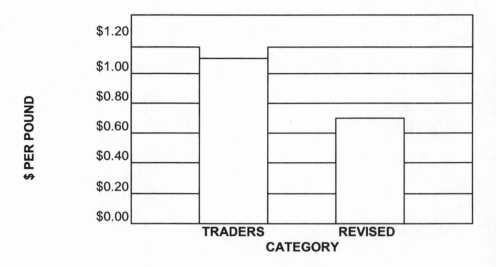

Figure 13. Credit Received by Weavers. From Fryer 1939.

District 5–6. Although a major portion of the Hubbells' business enterprises centered on Navajo textiles, the output from these two districts does not exceed that of the others. The six posts located in District 5–6 represent just over 3 percent of all textiles acquired from weavers on the reservation in 1939. The ten posts located in District 17, including several small Hubbell posts, handled 10 percent of all textiles obtained from weavers that year. Weavers in District 5–6 received an average of $.70 in credit per pound of weaving, compared to an average of $1.02 in District 17. Although the volume of the Hubbells' "rug business" was high compared to that reported by traders from other districts, weavers trading with the Hubbells did not receive greater compensation.[19]

The Perpetual Need for Pawning

Pawning continued to be an important source of credit for Navajos trading with the Hubbells (HP Box 350). It appears that Navajos pawned on a daily basis. In descending order, pawn was exchanged for food, clothing, hay or alfalfa, and cash (5 percent). Nearly all names in the pawn records are in Navajo. Bracelets, beads (coral and silver), and other jewelry, moccasins, saddle blankets, and buckskins were pawned. Regardless of when an article was pawned during the month, Hubbell charged 10 percent interest. Most accounts appeared to be "paid up" by the end of the month. During May 1905, 156 Navajos pawned $297.30 worth of goods, an average of five a day or $1.90 per person. In June, 203 Navajos pawned $360.00 worth of goods, which were redeemed for a total of $407.85. Twenty-one accounts remained unredeemed. From May through November, there were 857 pawn transactions for $1,613.30, an average of $1.88 per transaction. As the year passed, the average amount of each transaction tended to increase from a low of $1.77 in June to a high of $2.34 in November. The account totaled $2,352.55, which probably reflects the total value of articles plus interest pawned throughout the year. The need to pawn goods would temporarily decrease in the spring when the annual wool clip was brought in to the post. The similarity between total amounts for 227 weavers' accounts ($2,603.17; Box 523 #6) and pawn for 1905 is deceptive because weavers' accounts represent only those women who had a blanket owing on 1 January, the day the annual "inventory" was taken. In 1906 there were 1,135 pawn transactions totaling $2,336.35. Each transaction averaged a low of $1.11, in February 1906, and a high of $3.31, in December (HP Box 344).

The number and amounts of pawn transactions continued to increase over the years, even though craft production had risen significantly since 1900 (see

Table 10. Navajo Pawn Records, compiled from HP Boxes 350, 496, and 523(6).

Year	Annual Totals ($)	Number of Transactions
1905	2352.55	Incomplete
1906	2336.35	1135
1907	3210.75	1263
1908	3455.00	1507
1910	3753.00	Unknown
1912	5411.30	"
1915	5774.90	"
1916	4450.21	"
1921	5618.87	"
1929	8429.00	"
1932	16,756.00	"
1934	11,000.00	"

Compiled from Boxes 350, 496, and 523(6)

fig. 7). For Navajos trading with the Hubbells, pawn continued as an important source of credit during the depression. It rose from $8,429 in 1929 to a high of $16,756 in 1932, dropping to just under $11,000 in 1934 (table 10).

Elizabeth Hegemann reminisced about trading at Shonto:

> Due to drop in wool prices during the Depression, weaving became very important. [More rugs were woven because] they did bring in slightly more credit at the post per pound than the raw wool. . . . [A particular Navajo man's] pawn, consisting of several turquoise and silver bracelets, went in and out when redeemed by his wife's rugs. She was an excellent weaver, but often she was forced to weave quickies, or "bread and coffee rugs" which of course we had to buy. (1963:298)

Other reservation traders' records indicate that Navajos pawned their sheep (Sam Day Papers).

Tremulous Times: Navajo Trade during the Depression

In a letter to Superintendent Miller on 11 June 1931, Lorenzo Hubbell Jr. wrote that traders seldom realized more than two cents per pound on the sale of Navajo wool. Table 5, above, reveals how the Hubbells' cumulative profits in blankets were far greater than their wool profits for two decades. In fact, their profits in pelts and skins were nearly double their wool profits for that period. The depression and then the stock reduction program had devastating consequences for Navajo families (Parman 1976; Roessel 1974).

Although rug purchases from weavers declined to less than $14,000 annually in 1932 and 1933, Lorenzo's inventories increased from $32,993.70 in 1930 to $37,936.22 the following year. A new threat emerged when mass-produced rugs bearing Navajo patterns flooded eastern markets. Traders were forced to stop acquiring rugs from weavers because consumers now purchased a "crude substitute" (HP Box 4, 2/5/32).[20] Rug inventories were typically twelve to fourteen times higher than inventories of pottery, jewelry, and baskets.

The deepening depression increasingly threatened the reservation economy. A massive snowstorm on 16 January 1932 killed thousands of sheep and reduced the lamb crop by 50 percent. Hubbell's lamb sales declined dramatically between 1929 ($56,782.40) and 1933 ($7,142.30). That year 3,367 lambs were purchased at Oraibi, averaging $2.22 apiece. One hundred thirty-two perished on the journey to the railroad, and after tallying his receipts, Lorenzo Jr. wrote "Damn" as he noted his $1,123.63 loss (HP Box 527, p. 49). Interpost correspondence shows that the price of wool dropped to $0.08 per pound by May 20 (HP Box 107, 5/20/32). The mohair market collapsed, prompting Gallup Mercantile to instruct traders to pay growers a paltry $0.03 per pound (HP Box 31, 3/30/32). In his letter to Lorenzo at Oraibi, C. H. Baird detailed the 80 percent decline in the value of mohair since 1928, noting that 5 million pounds of Texas mohair had recently sold to a major carpet manufacturer for $0.06 per pound, and the manufacturer was likely to purchase another 5 million pounds of the 23-million-pound surplus:

> It is evident from this, that at least one of the manufacturers has nerve enough to go ahead and install the proper machinery for the manufacture of carpets from mohair. . . . [I]t will give the American public a better class of merchandise than can possibly be made from carpet wools. (HP Box 31, 3/30/32)

For more than two decades, reservation traders had encouraged stock owners to shift from herding milk goats along with their sheep to raising Angoras for their mohair as that fiber typically brought far higher returns to growers than Navajo wool.

To offset such miserable returns, Roman extended credit to more than fifty women to spin from thirty-five to seventy pounds of mohair to be woven into large sand painting blankets between July 1932 and June 1934 (HP Box 107, 5/29/32; Box 401 #4). From weavers' records for this period, it appears that women needed from eight months to one year to complete a 9-x-9-or 12-x-12-foot textile. On completing the larger blanket, the maximum amount a weaver was able to discharge from her account was $300 (HP Boxes 401, 403). "Chis chili Beg #2 wife" was issued thirty pounds of mohair to spin and weave two 6-x-7-foot "blankets." She received $30 in credit for her efforts. The amount of credit received by weavers of these special blankets is confirmed in McNitt's papers (Box 10). In his interview with Franc Newcomb on 5 September 1957, she noted that a 6-x-6-foot sand painting weaving retailed for $250 during the depression. Saddle blankets were graded and wholesaled for between $0.70 and $1.25 per pound, comparable to 1902 prices (HP Box 106). Hall (1994:143) confirms these low prices.

Within a week of receiving Baird's letter, Lorenzo Jr. instructed George Hubbell at Piñon that rugs should be 75 percent of one color, with well-washed wool. He continues:

> We have paid more than the market warrants but it cannot be helped,

and could not have been avoided, I just cannot see how wool is so cheap, I am ashamed to buy it, knowing that in reality they are not getting paid what is just, and at the same time we are helpless to do anything about it. (HP Box 107, 5/31/32)

Yet he had cautioned Herman Peterson: "I want to take care of the Indians, but to be able to do so we also have to take good care of our business; we must not let them make fools of us" (HP Box 106, 7/2/30). Two years earlier Lorenzo Jr. had wholesaled common saddle blankets for $.80 per pound (HP Box 106, 2/11/30). During spring 1931, the trader instructed his employees to "buy rugs cheap" as they were so difficult to sell in Gallup and elsewhere.

By late summer Lorenzo paid only $0.50 to $0.80 per pound for rugs and $0.40 per pound for saddle blankets. Weavers were to receive $1.40 per pound for only the *very best* rugs (HP Box 106, 8/20/31). On 15 December 1932 Fletcher Corrigan wrote a potential buyer that the "modern" 3-x-5-foot Navajo rugs that were "firm and lasting" cost from $7.50 to $12.50 apiece (HP Box 107).[21]

Although Lorenzo Hubbell Jr. was headquartered at Oraibi, on the Hopi Reservation, most of his customers were Navajos. Oraibi served six hundred Indian families and fifteen white families and handled 100 percent of the wool clip in the area and 90 percent of the rug output. In his report to the Navajo Agency, Hubbell remarked, "Competition regulates the price paid the Indian for his products. All transactions on a barter basis" (Box 527, 1933, p. 56). He maintained extensive rug inventories at both his Piñon post and his Winslow warehouse. Lorenzo Jr. also owned Greasewood, Black Mountain, Nakai Tso or Na-ah Tee, and Tenebito, and he held an interest in Ganado with his three siblings. Lorenzo acquired Cow Springs, located forty miles northwest of Tuba City, from L. D. Smyth by debt default in summer 1935 (HP Box 109, 6/30/35). Although women averaged less than $4.00 for a rug, weaving remained an important means to obtain credit. Bright Roddy, the trader at Cow Springs, detailed the weekly sales at the post. During July 1935, Roddy reported $97.20 worth of wool purchases and $195.50 in blankets. He took in $312.40 in pawn and registered $253.56 in cash sales. He bought 839 sheep for $1.79 each, an indication of the "success" of the stock reduction program (HP Box 496 #2). Lorenzo tried to sell the post that summer (HP Box 109, 7/15/35). The sale was successfully completed in the fall, and the post sold for $8,000 (including the inventory) to Babbitt Brothers (HP Box 6, 10/23/35). Throughout the 1930s weavers trading at Black Mountain bartered vegetal dyed rugs (HP Box 321). Hubbell advertised them at $6.00 to $10.00 for 2½ x 4 feet and $8.00 to $15.00 for 3 x 5 feet (HP Box 107, 12/15/32). The Fred Harvey Company purchased them (HP Box

108, 10/8/34) and curio buyer Herman Schweizer reduced Hubbell's wholesale price by 10 to 20 percent on nearly 70 percent of one shipment (HP Box 38, 7/22/36).

A detailed analysis of Lorenzo's activities in the volatile wool market of the 1930s reveals a scenario that would make any but the most stalwart individual suffer heart failure. Although Bailey and Bailey (1986:182) state that wool dropped from $.25 to $.17 per pound by 1931, these figures do not reflect the significant costs associated with marketing the Navajo wool clip. The following data are extrapolated from several of Lorenzo's wool contracts (HP Boxes 523, 527).

Date	Weight (lb)	Number of Bags	Gross	Net	Ratio/Cost of Processing*
1931	291,411	1,125	$54,256.09 (.186/LB)	$33,230.31** (.114/LB)	38%
1933	~350,000	1,414	$62,897.41 (.179/lb)	$44,908.36 (.128/lb)	29%
1935	206,995***	800	$51,440.01 (.248/lb)	$36,295.32 (.175/lb)	29%

*Processing costs include freighting, shipping, sorting, scouring, storage, insurance, commission, and interest on advance.

**Hubbell noted net sales of $42,075.87 in his detailed report to the government (Box 527). The information reported here is taken directly from his 1931 wool contract with Gallup Mercantile. He likely contracted additional wool with another vendor.

***This figure reflects only the Gallup Mercantile sale. Lorenzo Jr. also sold 80,431 pounds through the Arizona Wool Growers Association, netting $8,973.48.

Gross, Kelly and Company's and Gallup Mercantile's breakdowns on Hubbell wools resemble rug shipments in that there are dozens of entries demonstrating the unstandardized nature of both commodities. Just as Lorenzo typically shipped textiles, each with differing measurements and weights, his wool was sorted into a dozen grades and types, thereby increasing handling costs (HP Boxes 75, 221, 523).[22] In a detailed report covering his assets and liabilities during the depression, Lorenzo admits that although he encouraged Navajos to breed up their flocks, he had not purchased ewes for ten years or interfered with the quality of carpet wool for weavers (HP Box 527, 8/27/34, p. 55).

By 1935 only 20 percent of Lorenzo's wool purchases graded #1, as revealed in a Gross, Kelly and Company invoice detailing the breakdown of 199 sacks of wool sold (HP Box 34, 6/19/35). By 1937 the ratio had dropped to 16 percent, likely because the Navajos were selling off more churro sheep under the pressure of stock reduction (HP Boxes 34, 178). During 1937 and 1938, the Gallup company continued to handle Lorenzo Hubbell's wool. Although wool was quoted at $0.28 per pound in April 1937, by September 15 the company warned Lorenzo to hold wool as nothing was selling, including skins (HP Boxes 34, 177, 178). Wool prices continued to fluctuate, with Hubbell paying growers an average of $0.28 at Oraibi and Piñon during 1937, but values dropped to $0.10 in 1938 and partially recovered at $0.16 to $0.18 in 1939 (HP Box 523). Gross, Kelly and Company purchased 253,849 pounds of wool from Hubbell, allowing an advance of $0.10 per pound in 1938 (HP Box 34, 11/25/38). The wool scoured out at 155,977 pounds (including some mohair) and Hubbell grossed $56,789.73. However, processing costs, commissions, and interest on advances amounted to $18,175.79, thereby reducing his net return by 32 percent (HP Boxes 34, 178).

Although weaving was affected by devaluation, stock reduction, and "copy" weaving during the depression, it still constituted 20 percent of the reservation economy, second only to livestock sales (39 percent). Indeed, it tied with wool sales (Fryer 1939:table 1; HP Box 527). Although the Hubbells' rug inventories remained high during the 1930s, weaving continued to remain crucial to sustaining their economic viability. For example, in his Business Summary for 30 June 1937 (HP Box 509), Lorenzo's rug inventories from all posts were twice the value of his merchandise ($41,899.50 to $20,249.48). And his rug profits ($3,047.17) equaled his gross sales profits, yet gross sales ($130,000) were eight times the value of his rug sales. Rug profits made up 40 percent of total profits in all categories, including pottery, furs, goatskins, and sheep pelts. His gross profits were 34.1 percent of all sales, adjusted downward to 26 percent due to "shortages." His volume of Oraibi sales during the first half of 1937 shows a typical pattern, with Navajo purchases peaking in May due to wool sales. The 2,494 rugs inventoried at Oraibi totaled $13,349.05 (an average of $5.35 each; HP Box 509). Although the government mandated that traders pay Navajos in cash, his summary records reveal that only 13 percent of May purchases (total $12,949.92) were cash sales. Lorenzo Jr. had purchased more than $95,000 worth of wool from growers, but he sustained a $6,562.36 loss on the wool market that year (HP Box 509).

Hubbell's interpost correspondence reveals how the depression affected the reservation economy. Government make-work projects temporarily mitigated the deteriorating economy as hundreds of Navajo men found work on road and irrigation projects and earned $1.60 a day (HP Box 108, 6/15/34). But Emergency Conservation Works and Soil Erosion projects were relatively short lived given the financial ruin faced by many Navajo families threatened with the loss of their livestock. Traders tightened access to credit. Interpost correspondence during the depression reveals policies instigated by the Hubbells to cope with economic collapse. Trading posts cut down their acceptance of pawn (HP Box 107, 1/9/33, 3/5/33). Lorenzo issued a notice to extend credit only to Indians who were working (HP Box 108, 12/17/34; Box 109, 7/22/35). By April 1935 Lorenzo warned that he could not order any goods from wholesalers because of his debt load. He was uncertain that he could survive (HP Box 108, 4/6/35 and 4/17/35). Cash only was accepted for dry goods, but food could be charged (HP Box 108, 4/20/35). Lorenzo allowed $0.12 per pound for white wool and $0.08 per pound for black wool. In September Roman noted that he might lose the Farmington ranch (HP Box 109, 9/4/35). Lorenzo's commercial ratings dropped that year. A series of letters from Sheldon and Company, wool brokers to Hubbell during the depression, reveal that the Boston firm went to court in July 1942 to collect $1,909.98 owing, the balance of overpayment on his 1935 wools (HP Box 75). During spring 1936, the trading posts were instructed to use new tin money for purchases and wool, and old tin for pawn (HP Box 109, 3/2/36, 5/17/36). The family tried to divest itself of several properties and rent eighty acres of the Pajarito property south of Albuquerque (HP Box 109, 2/25/36). Reduced access to credit was sustained into the 1940s. For example, neither credit nor pawn was allowed at Big Mountain (HP Box 111, 10/23/39) or Na-ah Tee (HP Box 112, 1/22/40).

Sometimes manufacturers and distributors took rugs in trade for Pepsi (Clark 1993) and candy (HP Box 23, 8/24/48; Box 70, 1/25/27), in addition to horse tack. Youngblood (1935:102) has some interesting statistics on payments. Some wholesalers who typically dealt with reservation traders allowed 80 percent in trade and 20 percent in cash. The ratio changed with the advent of Emergency Conservation work on the reservation in 1934 (Sheridan 1994). In Youngblood's survey, five wholesalers accepted payments in rugs, from a low of 7.5 percent to a high of 55 percent. Rugs and hides were shipped to jobbers on a weekly basis. All other products such as wool, lambs, and piñon nuts were seasonal. During the depression, merchants other than reservation wholesalers became more desperate to obtain goods without cash. When wool dropped to $.08 per pound, Roman traded rugs for potatoes (HP Box 107, 4/30/32). A week later, Lorenzo paid a seed company with rugs (HP Box 108, 5/3/32). And in spring 1933 Lorenzo paid 75 percent of his overdue account with the Janesville Clothing Company with rugs (HP Box 73, 4/3/32). Rugs were also used to pay down J. L. Hubbell Trading Post debts (HP Box 107, 12/24/32; Box 108, 5/3/34), as Don Lorenzo Sr. had passed away on November 12, 1930.

During 1932, Lorenzo Jr. fell into arrears with Heiser Saddlery. In a series of exchanges, the firm repeatedly requested payment of his overdue account with cash or rugs. In late September it thanked Lorenzo for a rug shipment to clear the account and promised to send him some saddles. They placed an order to be shipped in the near future, commenting that they typically paid $2.50 apiece for four-pound fancy weave double saddle blankets (HP Box 39, 9/24/32). Even during the depression, such dismal prices reflect the formidable competition encountered by nearly 150 reservation traders trying to divest themselves of thousands of pounds of weaving.

Salvaging Sales

As wool prices plummeted in 1938, thousands of blankets and rugs were shipped from Oraibi and Piñon. More than 205 bales containing at least fifteen textiles each were shipped from Oraibi alone. Saddle blankets were priced at $.74 per pound and rugs at $.84 per pound. Most shipments contained textiles acquired from weavers for $3.90 to $4.79 in credit (HP Box 110, 2/28/38; National Park Service [NPS] Group VIII, Box 65). Interpost correspondence reveals that the current stock of blankets at Winslow was the best in several years (3/16/38) and prices ranged from $5 to $30 a piece (HP Box 110, 3/31/38). In April 1938 rug sales increased, and receipts indicate that nearly $5,000 worth of rugs were shipped from Piñon and Oraibi (NPS Group VIII, Box 65). The Denver Dry Goods Stockmen's Catalogue featured rug-patterned saddle blankets retailing for $1.65 per pound (HP Box 570). Lorenzo arranged promotions with JC Penney's Department Store (10/17/38) and contacted Montgomery Ward (HP Box 111, 11/7/38). He offered Penney's 100 runners with cotton warp at $1.89 each, to retail for $2.00 to $3.50 elsewhere. Penney's in Hollywood sold nearly 125 rugs of 400 on consignment, with a Navajo weaver to highlight the event (HP Box 111, 10/21/38).

Although sales increased, Lorenzo's fall inventory summary shows 2,335 rugs at Oraibi valued at $16,122.00 and an astonishing $30,830.52 at Piñon (HP Box 509, 11/30/38). He had consigned nearly $7,000 worth of rugs to department stores and curio shops in the greater Los Angeles area (Hollywood, Santa Monica, Pasadena, and Westwood); Reno, Nevada; and Flagstaff, Arizona (Box 509). By mid-December sales were "exceedingly good," and in early January 1939 the greatly relieved trader commented, "[I] had success in selling rugs in 1938. I feel that the human touch in dealing with the I gives me an opportunity to be very happy to be in this line . . . where so many fingers are at work even to the little girls" (HP Box 111, 1/9/39). And ten days later he commented: "Everything points to a very good year, we have been very fortunate in doing a nice business, a happy feeling as the rug is such an important economic help to the Navajo."

During the 1940s, prices for weaving remained extremely depressed. In fall 1940 wholesale prices ranged from $3 to $6 for a 2-x-3- or 4-foot rug; $6.00 to $10.00 for a 3-x-5-foot rug; $10.00 to $15.00 for a 4-x-6-foot rug; and $16.00 to $25.00 for a 5-x-6- or 5-x-7-foot rug. Double saddle blankets wholesaled for $4.50 each, and singles were $2.25. Rugs at these prices contained "nice designs," whereas many of the saddle blankets had stripes (HP Box 112, 10/03/40). These prices are lower than those in Hubbell's 1902 catalog. In 1940 Lorenzo Jr. responded to an inquiry:

[W]e pride ourselves in the quality, quantity, and assortment of sizes and designs of Navajo Rugs; at no time do we wish to make the impression that we sell the Indians material at bargain prices. . . . [O]ur interest is to keep on creating an income to these people. (HP Box 112, 12/24/40)

And two days later:

It is such a help to us and these primitive people in obtaining an income from these hand made rugs, the only small permanent income they have, the Lord knows its not much, as they come not less than 15 miles to sell them, and they utilize wool to make them which in itself is a cash commodity. (HP Box 112, 12/26/40)

Although the price of wool continued to fluctuate, rug prices during World War II remained abysmally low. In interpost correspondence, Lorenzo and later Roman remarked on the shortage of textiles because women were working in munitions factories. Navajos working on government projects averaged $1 an hour in pay. Rug inventories shrank, but credit extended to weavers rose infrequently. Perhaps prices *had* to remain low, because once the war ended and production increased, prices would inevitably drop. However, Lorenzo anticipated sustained demand for weaving, for he ordered six thousand "certificates of genuineness" for "Navajo handspun and woven wool fabrics not woven in factory conditions" in July 1940 and reordered again the following summer (HP Box 185, 7/12/41).

Hamley and Company typically paid $1.25 to $9.00 for saddle blankets and

$4.50 to $6.38 for rugs (HP Box 180, 8/30/41, 3/17/43). In exchange, the firm wholesaled saddles to Lorenzo for $60.00 apiece. On 5 July 1941, with wool valued at $0.30 per pound, Hamley's responded to a letter from Lorenzo: "We can understand why the Indians may want a little more money for blankets. We have faith enough in you to know that the prices you charge us will be the lowest possible considering your cost, so if you have to charge $3.00 and $3.50 each for the singles, that is all right." Lorenzo had issued a directive to an employee that single saddle blankets "should be made nice and with design in the corners, a showy rug, heavy with a good edge, pay 65c per pound for those 30 x 30 rugs that are showy, but no more than $2.00 each for them" (HP Box 113, 3/20/41). It is important to note that since these blankets typically weighed over three pounds, nearly $2.00 worth of wool would be needed to weave one. Between February 1942 and April 1943, the Winslow warehouse shipped Hamley's 353 rugs and 106 saddle blankets, or 459 textiles averaging $5.41 each. The statement totaled $2,571.75, equivalent to the wholesale value of forty-two saddles. Although the traders had back orders on saddle blankets during the war, Roman instructed another employee not to allow weavers over $3.00 in credit per saddle blanket (HP Box 115, 3/03/44). On 8 April 1941 Lorenzo inventoried 56 large rugs held at Oraibi. They ranged in size from 4 x 10 to $11^{1}/_{2}$ x 16 feet; the latter weighed 79 pounds and was priced at $150.00. Deciphering the rug values coded using cash profit reveals the price per pound ranged from $1.00 to $3.75, with three over $5.00 a pound (HP Box 521).[23]

Returns to weavers stagnated as the cost of living continued to rise. A postwar consignment of eighty rugs to Charles Jacobs, proprietor of Indian Village in Chambers, Arizona, reveals a $2^{1}/_{2}$-x-5-foot vegetal dye rug wholesaling for $15.00 (HP Box 185, Invoice B-270, 5/20/47). A comparison of more than a dozen similar rugs in this shipment with textiles advertised in the 1902 catalog reveals price overlaps of 80 percent. In response to a query, Roman noted that weavers "averaged $.60 day for their rugs which we do not think is enough, but probably we will keep blankets in this range for a long time to come" (HP Box 117, 5/20/46). Roman's estimate included the value of wool used in weaving the rug. The rate that he states is a gross overestimate of what a weaver actually received. It includes the value of the wool and dyes that the weaver supplied, and it is apparent from hundreds of trading post receipts that weavers, irrespective of the fluctuating value of the wool, were more likely to "earn" $0.12 per day in credit. For example, in a series of receipts from Oraibi dated 15 July 1941, weavers averaged $1.18 per pound for their rugs. Growers were receiving $0.30 a pound for wool. Weavers needed about $0.55 worth of wool to produce one pound of hand-spun yarn, thereby netting $0.63 per pound for their labor. Five 4-x-7-foot rugs were priced at $13.00 and weighed about 12 pounds apiece. Each rug required at least 20 pounds, or $6.00, of wool, netting the weaver $7.00 for her efforts (NPS Group VIII, Box 65, 7/15/41). It is highly unlikely that a weaver could shear, spin, dye, warp, and weave a 4-x-7-foot rug in eleven days, which is exactly what she would need to do to "earn" the amount reported by Roman.

The Winslow warehouse claimed to have ten thousand rugs in stock at all times (HP Box 117, 5/18/47). By 1948 Winslow raised the wholesale price of good double saddle blankets to $12.50. Although wool values had increased (HP Box 180, 9/3/48), the Navajos were in deep trouble. Per capita income in 1944 rose to $200 per year (Sheridan 1994:265), but two years later it dropped to $80, less than the retail cost of a Hamley saddle or three Pendleton blankets (HP Box 564). Secretary of the Interior Krug (1948) noted in his report that of sixty-one thousand Navajos, only one-third of the population of twenty-four thousand children attended school. And even though one-fourth of the adult population had served the war effort in some way, 80 percent of the population could not speak English. Stock reduction had not only decreased access to good rug wool, it reduced the size of the average family's flock to well below subsistence. Before Christmas 1948, Roman wrote, "I know hundreds and hundreds of needy Indians. . . . Navajo as much in need this year as last (HP Box 119, 11/18/48).

Weaving continued to remain an important means to market Navajo wool. In 1956 the Indian Arts and Crafts Board published the pamphlet "Navajo Indian Rugs." Approximately 750,000 pounds of wool were woven into rugs, about 25 percent of the clip. Curio shop sales continued, and Ganado shipped saddle blankets for $4.50 and $5.00 and "good typical Navajo design measuring 33 x 54 inches for $20" (HP Box 121, 11/19/57). In 1957 Brate's Indian Arts and Crafts, Okara Lakes, Old Forge, New York, sold 3-x-5-foot rugs for $14.00 (HP Box 12). Prices for Navajo weaving remained depressed until the early 1970s (see chapter 6). Bailey and Bailey (1986:appendix B) report the CPI at 26 in 1902, 42 in 1940, and 116.3 in 1970.

Conclusion

The archival information provided here refutes most of the generalizations that continue to dominate anthropological and popular literature on Navajo weaving. It shows the tremendous increase in (hidden) labor endured by Navajo women in tandem with growing impoverishment. Aligning relevant information from published literature with archival evidence reveals that for more than eighty years weavers received an average of two cents per hour *in credit* for the prolific production that was so necessary for their families' survival. Thus the constant refrain throughout the Hubbell family's interpost correspondence for decades, "remember, blankets [rugs] are our good business," acquires deeper significance.

The archival evidence also dispels the myth that Navajo weavers preferred to weave for "barter" as they could acquire, for example, a Pendleton blanket and additional credit by trading their handwoven textiles (Amsden [1934] 1975; James [1914] 1974; Dedera, in Kapoun 1992:35; Maxwell 1963:60; Weiss 1984:54; Wheat 1984:19). Invoices issued by Pendleton and other trade blanket manufacturers, which include the weights of shawls and blankets for shipping purposes, reveals that the commercial textiles wholesaled on average for more than $1.50 per pound. Unlike their handwoven counterparts, however, commercially manufactured trade blankets were never *sold* by weight. For decades, the price of a Pendleton trade blanket averaged six times per pound the cash valuation of a saddle blanket and three times the amount a rug would bring.

Witherspoon (1987:41) estimates conservatively that at least one hundred thousand Navajos have woven more than one million blankets and rugs over two centuries. With the escalation in production that began around 1890, it is quite probable that 90 percent of these textiles were wholesaled off the reservation as "pound blankets." Several of my informants recall their mothers' rugs placed on wool scales in trading posts as recently as 1967 (field notes 1992). The treatment of Navajo weaving as an alternative means to market wool accelerated pauperization on the reservation more than any other factor. Thus subsistence insecurity initiated by increasingly unequal exchange began the day a weaver first bartered her blanket to a reservation trader well over a century ago.

Blankets by Design
Assessing Traders' Influence

When it comes to effectiveness of design, harmoniousness of color-schemes, strength of warp, cleanliness of wool, care in dyeing, fineness in weft, skill in weaving, closeness and neatness of weave, there are scores of Navajo women today who can equal any of the fine weavers of the past.

James 1917:79

[T]he implements and the weaving process look simple, but the setting-up and stringing of the loom and technique required to make a fine, smooth, firm rug are, in fact, intricate, demanding a skill only learned in childhood and with years of practice by a person of superior craft intelligence.

Coolidge and Coolidge 1930:94

The Navajo rug weaver develops her design as she weaves; she is an artist in her own right; emphasizing all wool, Navajo made, outwear any rug, no two rugs are alike.

Roman Hubbell, HP Box 115, 3/28/44

I don't think you can tell a weaver how to weave a rug anymore than you can tell a painter how to paint a picture.

Leighton 1958:n.p.

Traders introduced manufactured yarns and commercially manufactured aniline dyes, pressed for technical quality, and controlled marketing weavers' products, but it is doubtful they controlled the production of Navajo patterns to the extent that is claimed. With few exceptions (Willink and Zolbrod 1996; Witherspoon 1987), however, most literature on Navajo weaving insists that traders influenced rug designs. For example:

Traders became the catalyst that caused Navajo weaving to change radically[,] . . . quite possibly saving it from extinction. . . . In order to raise the quality of the rugs and sell them as genuinely handmade, traders paid weavers higher prices for textiles that were of a superior technical quality, woven from the wool of the Navajo sheep. . . . [The] Modern [rug] Period [was] dominated by what were originally trader-influenced rug designs for the Anglo-American market. (Nestor 1987:57)

Several traders have left memoirs describing the unrelenting winter solitude of the posts. Days and weeks could pass without another soul appearing. Some posts were "fifty to two hundred miles from nowhere" (McNitt 1962:78; Richardson 1986:78), with "reservation roads . . . little more than bridle paths" (Moore 1909:31). Given the isolation of the reservation and the fact that textile production was consistently high in the winter, it would have been difficult for traders to exert a great deal of influence on Navajo weavers (Richardson 1986:42–43).

Traders and Weavers in the Published Record

According to Weiss (1984:73), there were 79 posts on the Navajo Reservation in 1900 and 154 by 1930. All sources on trader influence, however, document the importance of only a handful of traders. For example, James ([1976] 1988) highlights the history of a dozen traders, including Hubbell and J. B. Moore. Hubbell owned more than 15 posts for various periods during this era (Bauer 1987:appendix 6; Blue 2000:284). Evidence from Hubbell's personal papers calls into question his influence on weaving patterns at Ganado, his key post. In fact, traders' correspondence, their advertising brochures, and the magnitude of production provide convincing evidence for their limited influence on patterns. Paradoxes emerge in the published literature about the extent of traders' influence on Navajo weavers.

Synthetic, or aniline, dyes manufactured from coal-tar derivatives were introduced around Fort Defiance, Arizona Territory, in about 1884. Shades were violent, unfixed, and unpredictable. However, the dyes were improved and saved women time. Traders purchased selected colors, weeding out the more obnoxious shades (Coolidge and Coolidge 1930:97; Moore [1911] 1987; McNitt 1962). Women began to weave with commercial yarns too; however, the yarns cost as much or more per pound as the woven textiles (Coolidge and Coolidge 1930:97; HP tables 1 and 3). James ([1914] 1974), Amsden ([1934] 1975), and Utley (1959), among others, perceived traders' influence on weaving as having positive economic effects but negative artistic effects, because in the rush to weave wool into blankets, many traders began to barter string and aniline dyes, which cheapened the product. It was traders such as Hubbell and J. B. Moore who put a stop to this.

Because water was usually in short supply on the reservation, weavers could not always wash the fleece before spinning. Dirty wool streaks when taking up the dye, and the woven result is not always pleasing. Cotton string is not an appropriate substitute for hand-spun wool warp. Wool provides a much stronger, longer-wearing foundation for a floor rug. As weavers were under so much pressure, some used cotton and were subsequently penalized when they brought the textile into the post. Cotton string is an acceptable substitute in a pillow cover woven of commercial Germantown yarn, as it is quite lightweight. But no rug, regardless of how well the weft yarn is spun, can withstand the wear and tear of many feet if the warp is made of cotton string. Only the wool-warped genuine product will do.

George Wharton James, the Earliest "Classic"

Curio dealer, collector, and popular writer George Wharton James wrote the first "classic" publication on the Navajo blanket ([1914] 1974:203), in which he designated Cotton and Hubbell "the fathers of the rug business among the white race."[1] James's description encapsulates attitudes toward Hubbell that continually reappear in numerous texts:

Mr. Hubbell saw the art deteriorate, and set himself to work to stem the tide of ignorance and carelessness which bid fair speedily to wreck what his far-seeing vision knew might be a means of great wealth to an industrious and struggling people. He spoke the Navajo language fluently, lived in the very heart of the reservation and was in daily contact with some of the most progressive men and women of the tribe. He took them into his office and talked with them, one by one. As rapidly as was possible, he eliminated the use of cotton warp, . . . certain dyes [and] discouraged the use of Germantown yarns. . . . [He] urged thorough cleaning and scouring, carding, spinning and dyeing of their own wool. During all this time he was urging the weavers to higher endeavor, and giving special privileges and favors to those who showed not only skill and originality of design, but general acquiescence in his endeavors to improve the art. The final result[,] . . . now he has gathered around him by far the finest set of weavers on the whole reservation. . . . [H]e has learned from practical experience what designs of pure Navajo origin please the most exacting patrons. . . . [T]hese [are] copied in oil or water-colors and they line the walls of his office by the score. . . . When a certain type of blanket is needed, he can point to the design, or . . . loan the painting to the weaver[,] [and] he can supply wool. . . . [T]hus he gains the best kind of work. . . . That his name is synonymous with honorable and upright dealing goes without saying, for no man can stand as he does with the Navahoes. ([1914] 1974:204–5)

James was an antimodernist, and his book was published for commercial purposes. Hubbell and several other traders were charged $150 each for the privilege of being included in the book as "reliable dealers." James requested payment in blankets; Hubbell complied and shipped a fifty-six-pound bale of blankets to Pasadena on 4 February 1916 (HP Box 353, p. 3).

At the time James published his text, only J. B. Moore and Lorenzo Hubbell had become intimately involved with "improving" the Navajo blanket. Along with the improvement came the genesis of new styles. Consequently, James has not categorized weaving according to regional styles, as these were in the process of "development."[2]

The Influence of J. B. Moore, 1897–1911

If the Navajos make it, I can supply it. Not the cheapest, may be but the very best they can make it.

Moore [1911] 1987, catalog inscription

J. B. Moore operated the post at Crystal from 1897 to 1911. He issued two catalogs of Navajo textiles, the first in 1903 and the second in 1911. Designs in the earlier catalog were based on "traditional" weaving patterns common in the last quarter of the nineteenth century. In his foreword, Moore, like Hubbell, returned "to the old time weaves, colors and patterns . . . to perpetuate the noblest of all Indian Arts." He discouraged the use of Germantown yarns, as it was not a "Navajo product," and he never carried textiles woven with cotton warp. He also described the differences between handwoven rugs and their machine-made counterparts. Moore graded his rugs, as did Cotton in his 1896 publication. Portions of Moore's text reveal his tenacity in pursuing the marketing of Navajo weaving.

In the beginning I had stubborn and conservative workers in these Navajo women, and a discredited product to contend with on one hand; and on the other, a prejudice and lack of knowledge that has proved harder to break down and overcome than I had anticipated. . . . Resistance, stubborn, hurtful, and senseless opposition on the part of the weavers, has given place to cheerful co-operation, good natured rivalry and friendly strife for excellence in their work. . . . [G]reatly increased prosperity and better conditions of life . . . come to the people. But I am no philanthropist and must disclaim any philanthropic motives for my part in it. I saw . . . in their dormant skill and patience a business opportunity, provided they could be aroused, encouraged and led on to do their best if they prospered, that I would come in for a share with them at least. ([1911] 1987:3)

In his informative catalog, Moore refers to an earlier period when all blankets were "coarse, heavy and unclean" and "woven on cotton warps . . . with abominable colors." Traders purchased by weight, but with the return to good weaving "it has become impossible to make weight a basis of value." However, he admits that 75 percent of his stock is cheaper blankets, and he advertises the lower-grade rugs to retail by the pound. Because "no two textiles are alike," pricing is difficult. His blankets, he says, are higher priced than his competitors' blankets because they are superior. Thus Moore and Hubbell shared similar views on marketing Navajo weaving, although it is doubtful that Moore wholesaled as many rugs as he had only one trading post and bartered with fewer weavers.

Most of the rugs in Moore's 1911 catalog are advertised at between $0.90 and $1.00 per square foot. However, Moore takes pains to translate these prices into pounds, as "there are still those who insist on pound quotations." In his 1911 catalog he refers to the Navajos as "Bedouins of the great Southwestern Desert" and reiterates his business philosophy:

Our first thought of course is to get them to weave for us and for us only, all the fine rugs they possibly can, and then find a buyer for these. But it is also our mission here to buy any and everything the Navajo has to sell; his wool and pelts, his farm produce when he has any, the surplus of his flocks, herds of cattle and horses—any and everything that he has which he wants to turn into cash; and then it is up to us to find a market for it in turn. And, it is also our purpose to sell him in turn, all his supplies, groceries, dry goods, clothing, wagons, harness and saddles, everything in fact that he has need for and the money to buy with; or as much of it as we possibly can. Nor, is there room for failure in any of these many things for the man who would make a success of Indian trading. He must be onto his job all the time, and see to it that he is not overmatched by as clever a people as ever worked their way up from savagery.

Moore's text reflects the monopoly mentality of traders and reveals that for him the cornerstone of civilization is hard work leading to self-improvement. His final sentence reflects an attitude that persists in historic documents, especially those penned by traders.

In the years between the publication of his two catalogs, Moore issued individual color plates with descriptions to introduce new patterns to potential clients. His second catalog exhibits a marked departure from its predecessor and shows influences reputedly of Oriental origins. Moore also includes black-and-white photographs of several of the weavers, and he credits one in particular with designing four of the patterns in the catalog. Because unfamiliar, Oriental-like motifs appear in these rugs, Rodee (1981) asserts that Moore probably showed his most talented designers new patterns and they then used "their skill and good taste" to weave them. Yet in his catalog, Moore himself lists the names of individual weavers underneath each color reproduction, crediting them as the designers. Moore credits Bi-leen al pai hi zha ahd as the designer of the most "Oriental" of all patterns, yet he claims "she will never weave after another" (Moore [1911] 1987:23). The foregoing is an excellent example of the paradoxes associated with the genesis of Navajo weaving patterns after the formation of the reservation. Although we lack empirical evidence tracing the Oriental influence, Rodee (1981:21) claims proofs of the influence are those of "logic and visual similarity." She states that Amsden was the first to discuss this influence, yet he does not link Moore to this development but does note that some traders "preferred" Oriental rugs.[3] Jett (1993) and others have written on the subject, and in 1975 the Maxwell Museum of the University of New Mexico mounted a display of Navajo textiles and Oriental floor rugs titled "East Meets West."

In 1911 Moore suddenly left the reservation under unsettling conditions having to do with a scandal. The trader who succeeded him found a lot of scoured wool and about two thousand blanket catalogs (McNitt 1962:255). As Moore's plates were large and reproduced in color, he was obviously serious about this endeavor. Of all the traders who supposedly "fathered" new patterns, Moore probably had the most influence, as he continually collaborated with fewer than twenty weavers whose textiles are featured in his catalogs. Yet, he writes, "each blanket is a matter of individual taste and skill on the part of its weaver, they are made in all sizes, all weights, and the variations of designs and color combinations are . . . numerous" (Moore 1910:103). Although standardization may be desirable, it was virtually impossible to achieve.

In an infrequently cited article, Moore (1910) provides insight into weavers' industry, commenting on the great number of excellent weavers under twenty years of age. As a result of trachoma and other eye problems, many older women were unable to weave fine rugs. He also admitted that "there is no more dismal wage proposition than her [the weaver's] remuneration for her part in the industry. Given any other paying outlet for her labor, there would very soon be no such thing as a blanket industry. . . . [I]t is her one and only way of earning money" (Moore 1910:101–2). Moore's wife, Marion, wrote to Hubbell on 13 August 1908, saying she thought the quality of their rugs was surpassed only by his (Boles 1977:129).[4]

James's Critique of Traders' Influence

James ([1914] 1974) condemned the deleterious effects that cotton warp, garish dyes, and sloppy weaving had on the Navajo blanket. He blames the traders and notes that they were forced to stop these practices as no one would purchase woven monstrosities. But in describing the degradation and noting the turnaround, James inadvertently provides evidence for the increasing pressures on Navajo weavers in the ensuing years as their textiles improved. He attributes their improvement to the efforts of Hubbell, Cotton, Moore, and the Fred Harvey Company. He ([1914] 1974) comments positively on Moore's providing commercially scoured wool that ensured "odorless, perfect cleanliness, [and] uniformity of quality." He notes that even Moore had problems getting weavers to copy designs exactly, and he comments:

> [T]he constant surprise of the careful observer is the great variety of color and design. Every collection is sure to contain specimens utterly unlike those gathered by other collectors of many years' experience, and the variety is the ever-increasing wonder of the student. ([1914] 1974:38)

Although Moore was one of the few exceptions in having special designs made to order, the natural impulse of the weavers was to never copy and to never repeat their designs (James [1914] 1974:120). James notes that all traders claim that "the Navajo is a shrewd business man, and the women are as keen, intelligent, and self-reliant as the men" ([1914] 1974:54). He sees this as one of the key reasons for the improvement in the blanket. Traders also needed education, because poor quality would not be tolerated by an increasingly educated public (James [1914] 1974:55). Thus "the quality of blankets will continue to improve, even though the output increases and becomes four times what it now is." He lists the steps by which improvement occurred, including the elimination of cotton warps and (supposedly) higher reimbursement to weavers ([1914] 1974:55–56). Germantown yarn was seldom used, because the weavers realized that "if they would preserve their profitable industry, they must themselves make a yarn that is equal to Germantown." The annual fairs enjoyed great success, with large exhibits of "the best" weavings (James [1914] 1974:58–59). The first San Juan Agency fair, held at Shiprock in 1909, displayed 230 native wool blankets and 25 Germantowns. Four years later more than 700 blankets were exhibited. These events placed great pressure on weavers, who labored to improve their textiles continually. Weavers residing in regions where textile production was more competitive were likely placed under the greatest pressure (Moore 1910).

James ([1914] 1974:72–102) includes a chapter on Navajo blanket designs. He notes that generally Indians are conservative, and so a design may become "permanent" even when "its meaning is not recognized." He cites Father Berard who claimed that there are no "stories" in their weavings; rather the blanket demonstrates "untiring patience and diligence, the exquisite taste and deftness, of semi-barbaric people, and the high art and quality of their work, wrought with simple tools and materials" ([1914] 1974:72). According to James, the modern blanket is now designed in accordance with the known wishes of the trader and is a purely commercial proposition. Yet he remarks paradoxically:

> [T]o the real good Navajos, the genuine artists, every trader knows he dares offer no chart. They are not to be perverted from the religious ideas of their ancestors, who taught them that the creative and artistic gift was of the gods, to be prized and used, and that only by so doing could it be retained. Hence every design is new, every new blanket must have its original design which the active brain of its weaver creates out of suggestions gained from a life-time of careful observation of Nature. The stars, clouds, lightning, falling rain, electric phenomena, springs, rivers[,] . . . trees, flowers,—everything is grist to the mill of the Navajo artist's creative mind. (James 1917:78)

He claims it is important to understand the attitudes and lives of Navajos to comprehend the origins of their designs. Others have attributed their origins to the Pueblos, the Mexicans, and even "nature" (Franciscan Missionary Fathers 1935; Indian Print Shop 1907). James ([1914] 1974:112–13) cites Matthews ([1884] 1968) on the development of the "double or two-ply weave." The ethnologist noted that American Indians were "generally believed to be neither imitative nor inventive"; thus the development of this unusual, difficult weave was all the more puzzling. This was a rare weave, first encountered in about 1890. Amsden claims weavers developed it in imitation of the trade blankets. The weaver uses double the number of warps and heddles; thus two completely different patterns can be woven at the same time. Various explanations were offered for how the two-faced weave was accomplished, many of them incorrect. In his chapter, "Designs on Modern Navajo Blankets," James ([1914] 1974:120–29) provides the names of several well-known weavers, including Bi-leen al pi bi zha ahd, of "artistic temperament" or "creative instinct" who wove only her own patterns for J. B. Moore. James ([1914] 1974:154) notes this woman's "natural aptitude" and says she admitted she would never duplicate a pattern because "the voices of Those Above will no longer inspire her to make new designs. . . . [S]he must trust the gods to supply her artistic needs and ever be in the receptive condition to take in what they send." Yet he neglects to acknowledge that she is the designer of the most Oriental-looking pattern (Moore [1911] 1987:23).

James is one of the few authors until recently to highlight a handful of Navajo weavers (see Howard 1999). He describes several weavers who demonstrated for the Fred Harvey Company, including Elle of Ganado and another young girl, Tuli (appendix IVb). He provides a charming description of a weaver inspired by trains speeding across the landscape near her hogan. She wove railroad cars filled with people, cattle, and goods, and birds filled the sky. He praises weavers' designing ability:

> [T]he Navajo have proven themselves possessed of inventive genius in this department of art. There are no "stock" designs as far as they are concerned. Repetition of design comes from the desire of the white race for duplication[,] . . . never from the unperverted, natural instincts of the weaver. Multiply the designs reproduced herein by ten thousand and still new and striking designs will continually be found. ([1914] 1974:146)

James ([1914] 1974:147) notes the difficulty of classifying Navajo blankets in ways similar to the classifications and descriptions attributed to machine-made textiles: "The colors are dissimilar, the weave is different, the designs are individualistic. . . . [E]very blanket must be examined for itself." However, he provides photographs and descriptions of blankets typical of particular categories, such as "saddle blankets," "standard," "native wools, undyed," "extras" (the class of blanket of which the Harvey Company made a specialty, as they never sold the cheaper grades), "native wool, fancy," and "Germantowns." James also notes that it was unusual for a weaver to create a design in sand before weaving; weavers "design from their heads." Much of his commentary undermines the reputed influence of traders on weavers' patterns. Overall, James's remarks underscore the autonomy of Navajo weavers in developing patterns. Thus his statement that the modern blanket is designed "in accordance with the known wishes of the trader" is perplexing.

Charles Avery Amsden, the Earliest "Orthodox" Source on Designs

Charles Avery Amsden wrote and published the second "classic" text on Navajo weaving in 1934. His comprehensive work provides the foundation of Navajo textile studies and is usually referred to more than James's. According to Amsden ([1934] 1975:31), the size and pattern of blankets are influenced by the preferences and prejudices of the buying public and by the fine artistic sense of the Indian trader who acts as middleman. Amsden's ([1934] 1975:67) description of native peoples paints an unflattering portrait: "Inordinate love of color is popularly considered an outstanding trait of primitive people the world over. . . . [P]rimitive peoples revel in the possession of colored objects because they are color-starved."

Both Amsden and James described the bayeta period as the high point or golden age of Navajo weaving. This harkens to a romanticized past and belies the deteriorating economic conditions associated with weaving. Amsden also develops the scenario of the dependence of the weaver on the trader and romanticizes the weaver "after the conquest":

> It set an alien master . . . beside every loom in the land, to tell a sensitive, talented, and artistic weaver how to make a blanket that would have a proper barbaric appeal to an intruding white man; to impose the dictates of a selfish instinct of gain upon an artist immensely superior to her instructor except in her simplicity and helplessness. . . . [T]he conquest of the Navajo commercialized that article for all time to come[,] . . . bought from her for a pittance by an unresponsive trader whose sole interest was in making a profitable sale. The conquest . . . made the blanket a rug, made a journeyman weaver of the Navajo artist in wool. Is it any wonder that the blanket of pre-Bosque times is an utterly different thing from the rug of today? ([1934] 1975:170)

The ghost of the high-quality "pre-Bosque" chief's blankets haunted weavers nearly a century ago. Amsden ([1934] 1975:186) notes that the demand for Navajo textiles increased during the transition period that followed the Navajos' return from Hwééldi. This demand was "fostered by many shrewd and zealous minds . . . [but] the Navajo was lucky. . . . [T]he white man coveted his weavings, not his land." With regard to the tremendous number of rug sales in recent years,

Amsden ([1934] 1975:189) says they were not "attained without striving and struggle. Commercial demand was an intoxicating stimulus[, creating an] aesthetic debauch." He chronicles the important influence wielded by the Fred Harvey Company in keeping the Navajo product "genuine" and of "high quality." Amsden follows this comment with a discussion of regional styles. Navajo weaving had always been in part an alien craft—borrowing the Pueblo loom and tools, Spanish sheep, English baize, and commercial yarns. According to Amsden, Hubbell was the "leading innovator" of the early days of the Navajo rug business. And he comments on the influences of traders such as Moore and the Hyde Exploring Expedition.[5]

Large rugs, financed through special arrangements, could take six months to produce and were a Hubbell specialty (Amsden [1934] 1975:193). Amsden ([1934] 1975:196) mentions that the Pendleton Woollen Mills sold the Shiprock Trading Company a long-stapled commercially carded wool that was dyed with expensive Swiss dyes. Although he has mixed emotions about this, as a coals-to-Newcastle situation, he maintains such interventions helped to "set, maintain, and compensate a high technical standard where without them the trend has been fairly constantly downward to the detriment of all concerned" ([1934] 1975:197). Although the standards were "set and maintained," there was little evidence of requisite compensation to weavers in either the Hubbell Papers or government documents (see chapter 4).

Amsden ([1934] 1975:205) demarcates four dominant pattern styles, each preeminent at a given period of time: the striped, to 1800; the terraced, to 1863; the diamond, 1863–1900; and the bordered, from blanket to rug, 1890 to the present. There was some blending of types as weavers were continually borrowing and adapting. He constructs a rosy scenario:

> The white man is demanding blankets—big ones, little ones. The trader pays handsomely for everything brought in. Smart weavers are buying the new yarn, ready-spun, ready-dyed, and of such brilliant colorings! . . . Everything is made easy for the weaver. It is her millennium. The white man's ways are best, after all. ([1934] 1975:214)

Yet Amsden makes some curiously relevant remarks concerning the incubation of Navajo weaving patterns:

> All [the styles] are linked by an increasing complexity upon the basic foundation of the horizontal line in repetitious rhythm. They are allied too by the common factor of pure design expressed in rectilinear geometric form.

We feel strongly that these styles do truly and worthily express the Navajo artist in wool, just as they expressed her artistic Southwestern forebears in their basketry, their simple finger weaving, and their ceramic decoration. How the transition came . . . will never be exactly known. . . . [Patterns encountered] on old baskets, or clay vessels may have given a gifted weaver her formula. . . . The supposition is not preposterous when we consider that all the outstanding modern forms of aesthetic expression are credited to a handful of men of genius who wrought virtually the whole fabric. The individual genius fills a large segment of the entire human horizon, and especially is this true in the arts. ([1934] 1975:217)

Amsden's statement not only reflects attitudes toward "art" that are typical for the period, but it contains the seeds of the aesthetics of weaving (see chapter 8).

In the last chapter of his book, Amsden discusses "the revival" in Navajo weaving from 1920 to 1934, the year his book was published. He discusses the influence of Mary Cabot Wheelwright and her collaboration with trader Cozy McSparron at Chinle concerning the resurgence in vegetal dyes. Concurrently, both Diamond Dyes and DuPont Chemical began to market dyes that produced softer colors. He also mentions the interests developed by the Eastern Association on Indian Affairs in improving Navajo weaving by returning to the old patterns and colors (Amsden 1932). In its 1932 report, the association noted that although more than $1 million worth of rugs were sold from the reservation, because the quality was "poor" the price per rug received by the weaver, considering the work involved, was "ridiculously low." The problem would be rectified by distributing large photographs of old, desirable patterns. Rather than have exact copies made, the photographs would stimulate and revive the older patterns.

Amsden ([1934] 1975:232–33) favored the revivalist movement. He felt that although the average trader may balk, because his "approach is commercial from first to last," the aficionados of Indian arts welcomed it. Rather than offer continued support of the bordered rug with garish aniline colors that suited the sunporch or den, Amsden felt the Navajo rug "must be made worthy of the living room and the bedroom; it must harmonize with the French wallpaper, the Colonial furniture. . . . A certain degree of boldness maybe allowed at times[,] . . . but whatever the situation, it must chime in with the prevailing harmony" ([1934] 1975:233). A return to the older patterns and colors would make the textile "more Navajo" as

nature created the colors in the Navajo country and the patterns in which they were displayed bore the authentic tribal stamp. There is the true Navajo expression, not in the later rug which got its colors from a factory and its pattern from a catalogue. . . . [F]ar from dictating his weaving, we would protect it from that dictation which has brought it, in both technic and artistry, already so low. ([1934] 1975:233)

Thus the "revivalist" movement provided the impetus for an "artistic renaissance,"

for a return to the days when weaving was (presumably) done with pride and joy and a complete, self-effacing devotion to the task of producing textiles both useful and beautiful—the miracle may come to pass: we know so little of the Indian and his ultimate artistic potentialities. But we know a great deal of the trader, the tourist, . . . the influence of Government school, the automobile, the movie; and knowing these, how hard it is to believe that the thoroughly industrialized craft of Navajo weaving will throw off its shackles and emerge untrammelled as a joyous art. ([1934] 1975:234)

The importance of the market would ultimately determine the perpetuation of weaving among the Navajos. As the blanket became a rug (1895–1905), the taste and market expectations of the Anglo trader became the dominant influence on Navajo weaving:

Some traders had a taste for Oriental rugs, some for Classic Period nineteenth century blankets, and some for Pueblo/Rio Grande-style striped blankets, and they all made their preferences known to the weavers. Of course the weavers usually had ideas and market expectations of their own. . . . Today's regional rug styles can be traced directly back to the personal design preferences of a few influential traders. Juan Lorenzo Hubbell, who ran the trading post at Ganado, Arizona, wanted his weavers to return to the bold patterns of the Classic Period and he encouraged them to do so by hanging oil paintings of the old blankets on the walls. (Amsden [1934] 1975:234)

Nearly all authors addressing the subject consider Amsden the earliest "orthodox" source. It is from his work that most of the generalizations that dominate the literature today developed. And he firmly believed that Navajo women wove for "primarily economic reasons." A key distinction between the "classic" texts by Amsden and James is the photographs each chose to use. James's text was published twenty years before Amsden's, yet he includes far more photographs of post-1900 rugs. Although Amsden included many more photographs of weavers, none of the weavers are identified, in contrast to James, who names at least a dozen. However, Amsden identifies dozens of individuals: traders, military men, collectors, Indian curio dealers, Indian agents, and "revivalists." In a heavily illustrated text devoted to the *subject* of Navajo weaving, it is remarkable that not one weaver is identified by name. (Elle of Ganado is pictured, but not identified in plate 16.) Thus the emphasis continues to shift from the weaver and her textile to the trader (or revivalist) as "producer."[6]

Additional Sources on Traders' Influence: The Historian Frank McNitt

In his classic text on Indian traders, Southwest historian Frank McNitt (1962:200–213) devotes an entire chapter to Ganado. He comments extensively on Hubbell's positive influence on the development of the Navajo blanket due to his insistence on quality and his preference for generous-sized blankets and mentions that Burbank painted fifty or sixty "rug studies" from patterns that Hubbell preferred. He describes the importance of J. B. Moore of Crystal trading post and his influence on the development of a regional style of weaving, noting that Moore had about sixteen weavers "working for him." Sometimes Moore provided commercially scoured wool to avoid grayish whites.[7] McNitt writes:

> [W]ith only slight variations in design, Moore's weavers departed from the usual practice and turned out the same rug patterns again and again. . . . [I]n 1910–11 he said he paid his weavers $13,000 for their blankets and only $1000 . . . to his silversmiths. (1962:254)

The dollar amount quoted above, contained in a report sent to the Indian Office in 1910–11, is deceiving. Because Moore ran a trading post, he also bartered rugs from other weavers; he mentions that only 25 percent of the rugs produced in his region were made from the specially scoured, dyed, and spun wool. Readers may have inferred that sixteen women averaged over $800 per year each (or $70 per month) weaving for Moore. This is highly unlikely for the simple reason that Moore would have priced himself out of the market.

Alice Kaufman and Christopher Selser

According to Kaufman and Selser (1985), Hubbell's influence on Navajo weaving derived from his insistence on high-quality weaving, oversized textiles, reliance on old patterns depicted in oil paintings, abandonment of cotton warps, and minimum use of aniline dyes with the exception of red. Hubbell is credited with being the father of the first regional style, identifiable by the incorporation of Classic Period design elements (crosses, terraced diamonds, and stripes) in a bordered rug pattern (1985:67–68). A description of the Hubbell-Harvey connection reiterates the old refrain that the Harvey Company purchased all Hubbell's textiles of "good" or "better" quality. Kaufman and Selser note that the Harvey Company's standards were as high as Hubbell's. They mention the emergence of various styles based on traders' influences. For example, the Storm pattern, reputed to have emerged from the western portion of the reservation, is attributed to J. B. Moore, since an example is depicted in his 1911 catalog. According to Kate Peck Kent, Babbitt Brothers used this pattern on their stationery before 1900 (Rodee 1981:93). Moore may have purchased goods from these wholesalers and seen the pattern on their stationery. Jett (1993) provides an exhaustive review of the genesis of Oriental motifs and the Storm pattern. He was unable to arrive at a firm conclusion. A letter from George Bloomfield, former trader at Toadlena, to McNitt (1958 Box 8) sheds light on the mystery. Bloomfield admits to working with Two Grey Hills trader Ed Davies to improve weaving as the first rugs he purchased in 1912 were "just common." They showed weavers old pottery, dug locally, thereby suggesting that designs on pottery led to the genesis of the Two Grey Hills rug. Within a few years the rugs were winning awards at the annual Shiprock fair. They photographed the best rugs, initially purchased by weight but later by size, weave, and pattern.

Larry Weiss

Weiss draws extensively on both government documents and classic sources on trading and weaving. He cites James ([1914] 1974), Amsden ([1934] 1975), and McNitt (1962) regarding the traders' influences on Navajo weaving patterns. For example, Weiss (1984:79) quotes James at length about the hours traders spent with "their weavers" pointing out flaws in their work and encouraging them to produce textiles attractive to the Harvey Company and other buyers. Although Hubbell was reputed to be the "dean" of Navajo textiles and probably *the* most influential figure with the exception of J. B. Moore, overwhelming evidence in his papers soundly refutes the extent of his control (thus calling into question the influence of other, lesser figures). Table 6 contains information extrapolated from the Ganado Day Book (Box 333) and illustrates the various types and amounts of textiles wholesaled off the reservation by Hubbell in 1901, when sizes and designs were initially "standardized." Weiss (1984:79) also quotes James about the "larger pay" that traders such as Hubbell offered to "their" weavers to improve their production. Unfortunately, scant evidence in the Hubbell Papers supports this assumption. However, in his next paragraph, Weiss comments on how "the more intelligent" traders created rivalry among weavers by exhibiting and offering prizes for the best blankets at annual fairs. This happened, of course, with annual fairs initiated in about 1910 featuring prizes for the best blankets in the region (Wade 1985:177–79).

Kate Peck Kent

In her discussion of traders' influences, textile expert and museologist Kate Peck Kent designates from 1895 until 1950 as a period of "directed change" in textile design. Because most rugs woven at that time were marketed through reservation trading posts, weavers were so strongly influenced by local traders that distinct styles emerged in several areas of the reservation. Kent (1985:86) notes Hubbell's instigation of the "revival" pieces based on nineteenth-century Navajo patterns, his insistence on high technical standards, and his penchant for oversized textiles. Because traders "saved" weaving by encouraging weavers to create rugs instead of blankets, they invariably imposed their own aesthetic and that of Anglo-American buyers on the weavers. Kent (1985:107–15) devotes an entire chapter to the topic of "the search for a Navajo aesthetic," stipulating that a distinctly Navajo aesthetic vanished with the onset of the rug period. Recently published texts incorporating weavers' statements provide a critique of Kent's position (see chapter 7).

Terms of Trade: Issues Related to Standardization

Adams describes a typical trader's reaction when a weaver appeared at the post with her rug:

> [He will] look it over in silence for a minute or more, without touching it . . . or measuring it. The trader can then come out in a firm voice with the first figure that enters his head and stick resolutely to it. The trader who examines a proffered rug closely weakens the authority of his judgement since he is supposed to be able to spot . . . defects at a glance. . . . [T]rading is a white man's game. (1963:200–201)

This statement from an anthropologist who posed as a trader while doing fieldwork for his Ph.D. lends credence to the generalization that traders wielded great influence over weavers. However, given the escalation in textile production, much of the information already covered in this chapter tempers that generalization to a great degree. Several other sources also comment on traders' influences.

The historian Edgar Moore (1979:8) credits Hubbell as the individual most responsible for "improving and standardizing" the quality of Navajo weaving. Yet in Hubbell's voluminous records, by the turn of the century there are at least a dozen categories of textiles, with varying sizes in each category, a far cry from "standardization" (see table 6). Had textiles actually become standardized, it is doubtful that Herman Schweizer would have rejected so many. C. N. Cotton often acquired Schweizer's rejects for his own rug warehouse in Gallup, in "payment" for Hubbell's merchandise accounts (HP Box 6). In his landmark study during the depression, Youngblood (HP Box 527) remarked that the reason for traders not advertising Navajo rugs more widely was the lack of standardization of rugs as to "size, quality and design." Traders preferred "clean, straight edged rugs," and there is no question that rug borders were trader induced. The following statement is a familiar refrain in their advertisements: "[T]here's no such thing as two Navajo rugs alike" (HP). Although it appears to be a marketing ploy, it reflects the situation based on both Hubbell and Schweizer's ledger books, as well as traders' advertising pamphlets and their letters to government officials. Tens of thousands of blankets were entered into the Hubbells' business records and Schweizer's ledger books. Weights and measurements continually differed, and patterns and colors were never described, although the background color may be mentioned. Such great variation and volume made that impossible. Hubbell wrote customers that he could ship "rugs of any color, size and design." Standardization was far more likely to occur in the low returns weavers received for their arduous labor.[8]

Traders and Weavers in Unpublished Archives

Hubbell's Influence on Navajo Designs

Although archival information has been available for decades, researchers have neglected to use those sources that reveal the escalation in production and shipment of weaving. Because of the enormous number of blankets shipped off-reservation, traders' influence has been greatly overemphasized. Weavers almost always wove at home, often many miles from the post, and they never worked from full-size drawings (appendix V). Before 1896 Hubbell's business partner, C. N. Cotton, purchased hundreds of pounds of commercial yarn, trade blankets, and robes from A. Grunsfeld of Albuquerque, successor to the Spiegelberg Brothers. On 3 March 1887 Grunsfeld shipped $104.78 worth of yarn in scarlet (87 pounds), yellow (15 pounds), and dark green (25 pounds), at $0.82 per pound. He later remarks, "I have never seen two blankets woven exactly alike" (HP Box 92, 11/2/1887). By 1888 Cotton was purchasing

Perfection Dyes in dark green, yellow, orange, and scarlet, in addition to the commercially dyed yarns. By 1900 Hubbell was primarily interested in reviving the "old-style" classic patterns. He certainly facilitated their production by encouraging women to weave them (see table 6). Discussion of these old patterns appears in some of his correspondence for the period, and they are highlighted in his 1902 curio catalog. Several artists, including E. A. Burbank, painted a number of the classic patterns and Hubbell hung them in his office for weavers to see (fig. 8).[9]

The ledger books for this period reveal that Hubbell periodically lent a woman a blanket or, in rare cases, a little painting "to weave by." For example, "Tom's Niece has blanket to weave by" is written in tiny print adjacent to the ledger entry (HP Box 344 #2, p. 170). With several hundred weavers trading at Ganado, Hubbell noted in his journal when a weaver had "borrowed" a painting or a blanket "to weave by." The latter phrase was found nine times in folder #2, which contains close to one thousand entries. Most of these entries have the word "Settled" or "Paid" scrawled across the original notation. The detailed information contained in the "Weavers' Journals" and incorporated in appendix V challenges Hubbell's much-publicized reputed influence on Ganado area weavers (Boles 1977, 1981; James [1976] 1988; McNitt 1962; Rodee 1981, 1987). The acknowledged "innovator" capitalized on a business opportunity by encouraging women to weave patterns originated by their ancestresses. All of these patterns were created long before traders "influenced" weavers. Boles (1981:88) discovered that all the rug studies Hubbell had made up were from old-style patterns taken from nineteenth-century chief's blankets, bi'ils (women's dresses), mantas, and sarapes, created before Hubbell's trading career. Even the rug studies containing borders surrounded by floating motifs were borrowed from old-style patterns. Contrary to being foreign or new, these patterns were part of weavers' cultural repertoires.

In the only catalog he ever published, Don Lorenzo (1902) noted that the popularity of Navajo weaving had increased in recent years. He says that because demand exceeded supply, quality degenerated and unscrupulous dealers foisted shoddy goods on an unsuspecting public. To counter this activity, Hubbell claims he took the "greatest pains" to perpetuate old patterns, that he had "patiently unravelled" some of the old blankets to show contemporary weavers how they were made.[10] Thus he guaranteed a beautiful reproduction of a genuine old pattern. Because Hubbell never updated his catalog, information related to types of blankets and various color combinations seldom appears in his correspondence until after 1905. Given the dramatic escalation in production after 1900 (see fig. 7) and the increasing value of historic weaving, it is highly unlikely that

Hubbell had either the time or the inclination to unravel many old blankets. The text in Hubbell's 1902 brochure was written by the Chicago artist and advertiser H. G. Maratta.[11] James's ([1914] 1974) text, Moore's report (1911), brochures published by the Babbitts during the 1920s and by Lorenzo Hubbell Jr. in 1933, and the sheer magnitude of production provide ample evidence of the limited influence traders actually had on weavers' patterns. Recent publications incorporating weavers' statements provide corroborating evidence (Bonar 1996; Mitchell and Frisbie 2001; Willink and Zolbrod 1996).

After 1907, when rug shipments had escalated to more than forty thousand pounds per year, close to one-half of Hubbell's stock came from his other posts. It was not unusual for bales of blankets to be shipped unopened to Gallup. If Hubbell never saw these rugs, how could he have influenced the women who wove them? During the period in which he shipped more than four hundred thousand pounds of textiles off the reservation (see fig. 7), Hubbell was active in politics and also oversaw the construction of the Ganado dam and irrigation system, the single largest construction project on the Navajo Reservation until the depression.[12] One wonders, given the thousands of pounds of textiles shipped annually, when he had the time to commiserate with each of several hundred weavers who bartered at Ganado. Without examining his business records, researchers lack information critical to assessing the extent of his influence.

Dissertation Study by Joann Boles

Boles (1977) wrote a dissertation on Hubbell's influence on Navajo weaving patterns, combing all the Hubbell correspondence over a thirty-year period (1890–1920). She researched major collections in American museums, and the only exact copies of rugs found were those that the National Park Service commissioned to replace the originals on the floor at Ganado (1977:87). (Because of increased foot traffic, the Park Service did not want to subject the original rugs to additional abuse.) Boles (1977:114) discovered that requests for patterns were made in very general terms. She found nine sketches accompanying letters, with a total of 243 requests over a thirty-year period for specific colors, averaging out to 8 per year (1977:fig. 4).[13]

During the eighteen-year period in which Hubbell shipped more than two hundred tons of weaving (fig. 7), there were 155 requests for specific colors or color combinations. Hubbell himself made few comments concerning color and design until 1909, seven years after he issued his sales catalog and more than thirty years into his trading career. Hubbell never wrote about the weavers themselves (Bauer 1987). Some customers complained because rugs were inadequately wrapped for shipping and arrived in poor condition, sometimes infested with moths. The most consistent comments in the correspondence dealing with Navajo textiles concern the acquisition of textiles with "the best weave, the best yarn, the best pattern, the best color, and the largest size for the lowest price" (Boles 1981:60). My own research into the correspondence contained in the Hubbell Papers confirms this.[14]

Additional evidence regarding weavers' autonomy is noted by Anderson (1951). Anderson interviewed thirty-one weavers, all of whom maintained that they had a complete mental image of their rug before they wove it and that they wove whatever size they wanted. Anderson noted that nearly all weavers showed remarkable "design sense" in that they limited pattern in their rugs to one to three themes and made variations on these throughout. The only moderator of design was the weaver, who never duplicated a pattern. The Newcombs, traders at Crystal, Naschiti, and Two Grey Hills, admitted to McNitt that they did not suggest designs to weavers (McNitt Papers Box 10, 9/5/57).

Witherspoon (1987) also argues that traders' influence on designs is overrated. In his text explicating the origins of specific motifs, Witherspoon notes that traders may have pressured weavers to improve quality, but they influenced weavers only in the most general way in regard to patterns. Witherspoon's contributions to the "design debate" will be more fully covered in the last chapter.

The Fred Harvey Company-Hubbell Correspondence

The Fred Harvey Company, premier promoters of the Southwest, purchased thousands of Navajo blankets and rugs from the Hubbells for decades (Schweizer Ledger Books; fig. 14). Fred Harvey Sr. founded the company in 1876, to manage the eating houses and later the dining cars for the Santa Fe Railway (Babcock 1990; Jett 1990; Weigle and Babcock 1996; Weigle 1989). A number of letters in the Hubbell-Fred Harvey Company correspondence (HP Boxes 36–38) deal with requests for particular colors or changes in designs. In light of the thousands of pounds of textiles shipped annually by Hubbell (fig. 7), these requests from company employees J. F. Huckel and Herman Schweizer are very general. Other researchers state that these men had extensive influence on changes in Navajo weaving over a long period (Blomberg 1988; Boles 1977; McNitt 1962; Rodee 1981). Such commentary cannot be sustained in light of archival evidence that refutes it.

Periodically, the Harvey Company requested a different background color. On 16 July 1908 Huckel wrote to Hubbell from Los Angeles: "[T]he public getting tired of grey. . . . [W]e have got to get up something new all the time to keep the public interested so they will buy. This is good business for you as well as for us" (HP Box 37). Far more of the Harvey Company correspondence deals with complaints about Hubbell's high prices rather than requests for specific colors or patterns (appendix IVb). However, Schweizer complained if rugs made with cotton warp were shipped. In a letter dated 12 September 1907, he warns of the shortcomings of the cotton warp blanket:

> When we started in the curio business several years ago, we made it a point to keep the general public informed in regard to cotton warp blankets, and succeeded to a great extent in killing the sale of this class of goods. . . . [I]t now appears they are again making them. . . . In the first place an ordinary Navajo blanket can be made in several days less time, by using a cotton string for warp, as the wool warp, properly made and strung, is one of the most difficult parts of making a good blanket.

> When cotton . . . is used, the blanket is not at all durable. . . . [It] can be made in much less time, and much cheaper, and we consider them practically worthless. . . . I believe it is necessary that we must again keep this information before the public at all times, not only to protect

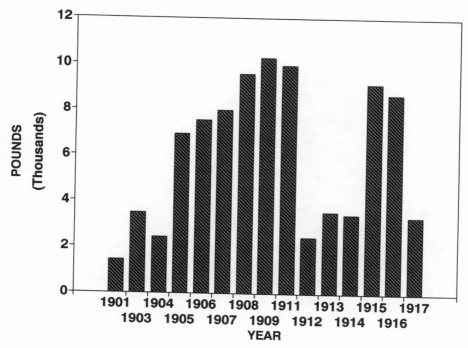

Figure 14. Annual Blanket Shipments to the Fred Harvey Company, 1901–1917, collated from Hubbell Papers.

our own interests, but in an endeavor to again stop as much as possible, the production of cotton warp blankets, and I will be glad if you will keep this letter before you for a little while, so as to keep the matter in mind. (HP Box 37)

Schweizer's insistence on hand-spun, handwoven, all-wool textiles acted to differentiate the "authentic" product from the commercially produced trade blanket woven on a cotton warp—but at great cost to thousands of Navajo spinners and weavers.

The following comments demonstrate how "unstandardized" Indian "curios" were. On 28 May 1909 Hubbell wrote Lorenzo Jr. and enclosed a letter from the Fred Harvey Company:

You will note that he [Schweizer] wants them [rugs] practically all different and if you could get a lot of them made we can sell them. . . . [I]t will make no difference if you can get 100 or 200 of them as we can sell them. Be sure and attend to this. (HP Box 96)

Periodically Schweizer requested articles such as kachinas to be made a certain size. For example, he requested kachinas measuring from five to eight inches and costing between $.25 and $.50 each:

[I]t would seem to me that the Indians could make more money if they would make the things that people want. . . . [A]ny American merchant or manufacturer manufactures the things that he has demand for. (HP Box 38, 11/8/30)

Further evidence that the Hubbells refrained from disseminating "their" blanket patterns is found in the interpost correspondence. The senior Hubbell served in the Arizona Senate in 1912. On 2 April Lorenzo Jr., trading at Keams Canyon, wrote to Roman at Ganado and rejected the possibility of duplicating the oil-painted blanket patterns to distribute to weavers:

[T]he cards we distribute to the Indians will be an advantage to other traders as the Indian will always want to show these cards . . . and traders . . . will . . . bid on all blankets being made. At present we are the only people that have these patterns in oil. . . . I am not going to give my patterns to any squaws that are not regular customers or live near another trader's store. (HP Box 97)

"The Rug Business": Selected Inter- and Intrapost Correspondence, 1909–1940, Related to Standardization

After serving in the Arizona legislature for nearly two years, the senior Hubbell returned to trading. He wrote to several potential customers:

[I now have] as fine an assortment of blankets as we have ever had and are in a position to make these blankets much cheaper to you than ever before. . . . I am now buying blankets in greater quantities and at a much cheaper price and can therefore make you prices on blankets much less than ever before. (HP Box 99, 1/14)

Another letter "to the trade" from Cotton provides a classic example of how blankets were treated as merchandise and of the pressures on weavers.

We note considerable improvement in both weave and design of Navajo Blankets, which no doubt is caused by the traders encouraging the Indian to make them better. . . . By encouraging the Indians to make blankets of good weave and design you are not only helping the Indians out, but yourself as well. (HP Box 21, 4/25/21)

Within the month Forrest wrote to Lorenzo that people were after "size and pattern." He suggested that if Lorenzo could get loosely woven rugs with fair pattern and little white "at cheap prices we will be in the swim" (HP Box 102). By 25 March 1922 Cotton paid $1.15 and $1.25 a pound for blankets (HP Box 21). Lorenzo Jr. wrote to Ed Morris, the trader at Black Mountain, to acquire as many nice small rugs as possible from the weavers: "[T]ell them not to make them so thick, add that they must be clean, and straight" (HP Box 102).

Babbitts wrote to Lorencito on 19 April 1922 (HP Box 6) about a new type of yarn at $1.00 per pound that was selling well to the traders at Crystal: "[W]e thought it would be wise to do this [sell at cost] until the Indians had gotten use to using it." Returns to weavers were very poor during the 1930s and early 1940s. Lorenzo Jr. tried to increase weaving sales, knowing how important they were to Navajo well-being. On 13 November 1931 he wrote to a potential customer that "the variety of patterns, sizes and quality was unlimited." On 6 April 1938 he responded to a query about a commissioned rug:

[T]he Indians idea of color and design is so very different from the white man, and it is very difficult to get anything near like what you want[,]

. . . but if you draw a design and state size and colors [I] will have someone weave it.

On 6 September 1940 he wrote:

> I consider the Navajo Rug the most important in bringing up the Navajo
> people's income, providing the Navajo is made to understand that clean-
> liness, size, finish and design determine its value. . . . [O]ur objective is
> that at all times, that clean wool be used, that the edging is straight and
> strong, [and] well designed. (HP Box 112, 9/6/40)

In February 1945, in response to another query, an employee wrote:

> Mr. Hubbell encourages the weavers to use red in the rugs since the
> average purchaser seems to prefer it, however, the choice of color, design
> and quality of weave is entirely up to the weaver. (HP Box 116, 2/13/45)

Before Christmas that year, Roman wrote to the traders at their Tennebito Post
to pay weavers $4.50 each if they would weave single saddle blankets with
designs and $9.00 each for doubles (HP Box 116, 12/5/45). "Give every squaw
a string with the right measurements so she will be sure to get the right size."
The letters written by the "most influential traders" in the business dispute their
influence in "fathering" Navajo weaving patterns.

Lorenzo Jr. engineered numerous schemes to augment rug sales. Because
the rugs were so unstandardized, it was difficult to satisfy customers reluctant
to purchase rugs sight unseen. An interesting sidelight to all this activity concerns the trials and tribulations of a young relative, Tom Hubbell, who traveled 23,500 miles from the West Coast to Texas over a seven-month period
during 1940 to hawk the ubiquitous Navajo textiles. Although his expenses ate
up 70 percent of the profits, his reports to Lorenzo Jr. make interesting reading. In report #5, dated Wednesday, 19 June 1940, Tom requested "[t]wo large
rugs . . . from 8 feet six inches to 11 feet 6 inches but not larger than 9 x 12
rugs fairly heavy that will lay on the floor . . . straight sides . . . Gray background if possible with red white black and brown . . . NO ORANGE . . .
THESE FOR SPECIAL FRIEND NOT OVER $75" (HP Box 521). Uncle
Lorenzo had guaranteed Tom $350 a month for expenses. He sold just over
$10,000 worth of rugs that cost $7,130 in five and a half months. Young Tom
earned nearly $2,000 of the $2,906.57 profit (HP Box 521, 11/21/40, letter
from El Paso, Texas). But this type of promotion was the exception rather than

the rule. Rug expenses typically were a fraction of the costs associated with handling wool. For example, in 1939 "general and rug room expenses" came to $614.50 on nearly $30,000 worth of rug sales (HP Box 521). In winter 1940 Tom sold forty-four rugs to curio dealer R. B. Creagar of Palm Springs, California, for $1,793.50 (including a $550.00 oversized rug). Lorenzo noted the uniqueness of several of the rugs, including a two-faced double weave for $7.50, a Hopi Indian rug for $17.50, a Storm pattern at $10.50, and a Kachina rug for $32.50 (HP Box 521, 3/1/40).

In Report #8 written from Taos, New Mexico, Tom mentioned that in the previous two weeks he sold 110 rugs out of the car and 100 more had to be shipped: "[P]rofits have been better than 33 percent on the wholesale cost which is pretty good." Lorenzo shipped him 373 pounds of rugs on 28 June and another three bales weighing 312 pounds the following week. On 20 August Tom wrote:

> I NEVER WORKED SO D . . . HARD IN MY LIFE TRYING TO FIND AND OUTLET FOR MY MDSE. . . . THERE IS SOME ONE STORE IN "LOS ANGELES THAT WILL SELL RUGS." . . . BUT TO FIND IT IS ONE JOB. . . . THE CURIO DEALERS ARE DEAD ON THEIR FEET. . . . DEPT STORES WILL CHISEL . . . AND I JUST HAVEN'T BEEN ABLE TO FIND MY MAN. . . . MAYBE YOU THINK THIS IS FUNNY . . . AND I'M LOAFING BUT it surely is a tough baby this Navajo Rug business in Los Angeles. (HP Box 521 #5)

Both the bookstore at Stanford University and the military post exchange handled rugs at one time. Tom approached trading posts, curio shops, large and small department stores, car dealerships, furniture stores, saddle and leather retailers, sporting goods stores, and even hardware stores. Rug prices were appallingly low, as wholesale prices ranged from $3.24 to $6.00 each (HP Box 521 #5). Tom's road trips proved far too expensive. On 28 August 1940, in response to his report, Lorenzo Jr. informed Tom that he could no longer sustain the experiment without more cash sales. In fact, he admitted, "[I'm] in the worse hole I've ever been in" (HP Box 112, 8/15/40) However, Tom continued to travel, and in October he was forced to buy another car for $400. In late October he sold seventy rugs and saddle blankets averaging $3.70 wholesale to C. L. White of White's City, Carlsbad Caverns, New Mexico. Only twenty-seven rugs were eligible for government tags, indicating weavers received a minimum of $0.75 per pound (HP Box 521). Tom quit just before Christmas as sales continued to decline (HP Box 112, 12/21/40). For one of his last sales, Tom sold ten vegetal dye rugs to the Hilton Hotel in Phoenix for $284.50 (HP Box 521 #5, 12/7/40). Lorenzo's health suffered as a result of financial woes and the strain of overwork, and he spent more than two months—December 1939 to February 1940—in a treatment center in Loma Linda, California (HP Box 111). He died on 2 March 1942.

Although Tom had difficulty selling to the May Company and Broadway department stores in Los Angeles, in-store promotions were generally very successful if a weaver was present. Ernest Wesson preceded Tom as a road salesman, and a weaver by the name of Caroline accompanied him on a trip to Denver and was paid $30 for demonstrating over a two-week period at the JC Penney store (HP Box 66, 1/15/40). In 1939 the five promotions held in the greater Los Angeles area, three in central California, and one in Denver resulted in $7,727.57 in rug sales (HP Box 66, 1/15/40). JC Penney in Hollywood received a shipment of 1,162 textiles, including 170 pillow tops priced at $0.65 apiece, 200 runners for $1.30 each, 783 rugs wholesaling between $3.50 and $9.50, and 9 large rugs at $8.00 to $60.00. The store returned unsold stock amounting to 788 textiles (HP Box 66). Another report filed in February included sales in Flagstaff, Arizona; Oklahoma City, Oklahoma; Hemet, California; and New York City (HP Box 66, 2/19/40). Wesson sold more than $2,500 in weaving through Penney's, with returns amounting to $943.75 (HP Box 521 #6). Another Penney's promotion at Colorado Springs, Colorado, netted a weaver $3.00 per day, and $2,500 worth of rugs were featured (HP Box 521). In 1941 Sears Roebuck mounted a similar promotion and requested a shipment with "none to cost more than $7.00." The company commented that the rugs varied greatly in size (HP Box 74, 6/16/41). On 3 July 1941 Hamilton Stores requested 150 blankets and rugs, none more than $15.00, and all rugs were to be tagged (HP Box 35).

Department stores in the eastern United States also mounted rug promotions during the depression. Macy's wished to "introduce Indian products to the public." Nina Collier, John Collier's daughter-in-law, arranged for a big promotion through Macy's in New York City. Nina's father-in-law had founded the American Indian Defence Association (AIDA) in 1922, before becoming Commissioner of Indian Affairs. As her "reward" for arranging the Macy's sales with Lorenzo Hubbell, Nina donated 10 percent of the sales to the AIDA. In fall 1934 Macy's ordered more than 1,000 rugs for a spring sale, to include vegetal dyed, Hopi stripes, and "natural" Navajo rugs. In the meantime, a Christmas promotion proved such a success that the store decided to maintain an "Indian Shop" as part of their rug department indefinitely (HP Box 18, 1/11/35). In February 1936 department manager Otto Black wrote to Oraibi requesting 180 rugs from $3.50

(2 x 4 feet) to $20.00 to $25.00 (5 x 8 feet). He agreed to keep the stock until summer (HP Box 54, 2/26/36). A Macy's ad appeared in the *New York Herald Tribune* on 30 March 1936. Oliver LaFarge, president of the National Association of Indian Affairs, fired off a letter to Collier blasting Macy's for advertising rugs "woven in Indian [*sic*] to Navajo designs at a price with which our Indians cannot compete. The rugs featured are clearly copies of Navajo weavings." Yet it is quite possible that these were the rugs shipped from Oraibi. The prices that Macy's requested in 1936 were more than 50 percent lower than prices listed in Hubbell's 1902 curio catalog. However, LaFarge's closing remarks presage a problem that haunts contemporary weavers:

> It must be recognized in all work for stimulating Indian Arts and Crafts, that excessive popular development will always produce this type of competition. When honest, as in this case, it will not steal the trade of those who want Indian products for sentimental reasons, but will seriously cut into, perhaps destroy, the market among those who buy simply for the attractiveness of the article itself. (Record Group 435, 4/20/36)[15]

Periodically government officials promoted the Hubbells' expertise in curios. Superintendent Miller sent them a copy of his response to a query:

> Mr. Hubbell can furnish you anything you might want from their handicraft. He is absolutely reliable and carries a large stock. His assortment is the finest and largest in this country. Of course, the Navajo blanket is the best thing these Indians on this reservation make. It is an article of utility as well as of interest. Mr. Hubbell can furnish these in any design, size or color made. (HP Box 44, 4/30/29)

Because of Don Lorenzo's political career and contacts in Arizona and Washington, D.C., and Lorenzo Jr.'s service on the Indian Arts and Crafts Board, government officials and federal agencies ordered directly from the traders and bypassed retailers.

At one point a number of reservation traders were polled about ways to improve the quality of Navajo weaving. The government-sponsored First Navajo Rug Project Conference was attended by several dozen weavers, who studied old rugs and heard lectures on wool types and cleaning, carding, and dyeing of wool. The conference was held in Santa Fe, New Mexico, at the height of the depression, when weavers received less per pound for their textiles than their mothers and grandmothers had before the turn of the century.

The absurdity of weavers reviving the quality of the historic wearing blankets was not lost on weaver Sarah Smith:

> It's this way, the Indians weave blankets only for their eats especially, than for their clothing. It will be very hard on those that live far away from the trading stores, they say it takes a year or two to finish one blanket like that. What if they run out of coffee or sugar, and if they get hungry for meat what could they do, get to work and weave a blanket quick so they can sell it and get some coffee and sugar and meat or maybe a sack of flour and something else. (Quoted in Jacobs 1998:208)

Coolidge and Coolidge (1930:103) acknowledged that traders "improved" the product by taking in trade only "well-woven, firm and tasteful rugs. As the women had no other market and no other direct way of making money, they were slowly induced to return to older and better methods." According to Coolidge and Coolidge and others, by 1900 the rug of commerce had become "approximately standardized" as to grades, colors, and weaves (but see table 6). It appeared that the colors used were determined by what the weaver had discovered the traders would pay a good price for in trade. We have seen that weavers paid a high price for the "privilege" of weaving for the most influential traders. Traders' own advertisements and comments in correspondence belie the notion of "standardization." The need to move goods off trading post shelves, particularly outside of wool season, offset the imposition of rigid norms. Rather than reject "unsatisfactory" textiles outright, traders probably allowed a reduced amount in trade or credit (Reichard [1936] 1968:141).

Letters from Navajos

More than one hundred letters from Navajos to the Hubbells span a period from the turn of the century to 1966 (HP Box 124). Many were written by children away at boarding school. As they were lonesome and had no one to correspond with in English, they wrote to the trader and requested that he read the letters to their families. A number of letters from adults requested that the Hubbells extend the period for pawned items. Others expressed concern about overdue accounts. Many letters began with the salutation "Dearest brother," or "Dearest father."

The "Letters from Indians" file contains a handful of letters from weavers. Louise Alcott wrote from Sand Spring, Arizona, requesting flour, coffee, sugar, and baking powder while she was working on a rug for the Hubbells:

> This morning I will asked you to help me out again as when ever I make

a Navajo Rug I always take it to your Store at the Tenabeto, I make pretty Rugs sometimes but the prise is so low. I do not get much out of what I Weved. So I do so much for you in that way I help you out all the time. (HP Box 124, 11/27/35)

Another letter from a weaver who lived in Blue Canyon promised the Hubbells a rug if they would send food for her children (HP Box 124, 12/38). None of the letters in this file contain any questions or sketches related to weaving patterns, dyes, or sizes. This is surprising, given the magnitude and extent of production. However, it demonstrates further the autonomy of weavers who wove miles away from trading posts. They were the experts who seldom needed the guiding hand of the traders except in the most general sense, for example, a piece of string equivalent to the length of a single or double saddle blanket. In the hundreds of pounds of evidence available in the Hubbell Papers, it is remarkable that only a handful of detailed blanket sketches exist. Boles (1981:53) found fewer than a dozen, most of them rough sketches by potential customers.

Rethinking Standardization

The statement by Coolidge and Coolidge (1930) in conjunction with the evidence in the Hubbell Papers provides provocative testimony to the pressures borne by thousands of Navajo women to accelerate production while maintaining quality to meet the traders' demands. Several factors weighed heavily in maintaining this pressure. First, the ever-present commercially produced trade blanket provided an error-free product, unlike a handwoven textile, which could contain mistakes. Second, trade blankets usurped the market for handwoven textiles. Third, commercially spun yarn was fine, smooth, and had no color gradations. Weavers were compelled to duplicate the machine-spun counterpart by laboriously hand-spinning the yarn several times to achieve the desired fineness. Even today, contemporary weavers remark on how traders will criticize their rugs by saying "You're not there yet" or "You can do better." Fourth, there was competition from handwoven imports. By 1910 Navajo weavers were facing stiff competition from Mexico, as the Fred Harvey Company began importing "Mexican greys." On 29 June 1910 Herman Schweizer wrote to Hubbell that such blankets "come in close competition with your fine greys and are much cheaper and very good quality" (HP Box 37).

Traders' statements and records reveal the limited extent of their influence on Navajo patterns. One could argue that standards were imposed concerning quality (i.e., clean wool, straight edges), excepting special orders, and preferences for conservative versus innovative designs. The inducement to place borders around the perimeter of the rug took nearly a generation to effect. There is no question that traders were responsible for this change, as the niche for the Navajo wearing blanket had vanished. For the most part, although Hubbell encouraged the production of oversized textiles, weavers held their own in matters of color, design, and size.

As I argued in chapter 4, given the eightfold increase in textile production and the less than 50 percent increase in population between 1880 and 1910 (Kelley and Whiteley 1989:213), it was impossible for traders to "standardize" the Navajo rug. This lack of standardization has created a serious problem for contemporary weavers. Unlike foodstuffs grown by peasants and consumed shortly after harvest, thousands of unique Navajo textiles have outlived their makers.[16] Chapter 6 explores another pressure encountered by Navajo weavers over the past century—an invidious pressure that they could not foresee but one that has become apparent through analysis of extant records and continues to escalate today: the collectors' market for historic (pre-1950s) Navajo weaving.

6

From Flea Market to Fifth Avenue: Tracking the Investment Market

We owe to the voyagers, colonials, and ethnologists the arrival of these objects in the West. But we owe primarily to the convictions of the pioneer modern artists their promotion from the rank of curiosities and artifacts to that of major art, indeed to the status of art at all.

Rubin, in Foster 1985:47

The relations of power whereby one portion of humanity can select, value and collect the pure products of others need to be criticized and transformed. This is no small task.

Clifford 1988:213

It would be folly for any museum curator or other scholar active in the southwest field to presume to work independently of the Indian arts market. Academic scholarship and commerce have been entwined since before the turn of the century. From purchasing personal garments made of new or recycled ethnic cloth to commissioning pieces for museums' permanent collections, we are all implicated.

Hedlund 1994a:42

Ethnographical museums may collect widely, but they do not dig deeply. The political consequences of doing so would be too serious, or so it is felt.

Hudson 1991:458

Looking at the repercussions associated with the transformation of historic Navajo textiles from craft to art and their subsequent escalation in value reveals the role of textile scholars and museologists as facilitators. It also shows how this metamorphosis has provided a lucrative environment for collectors, investors, and non-Navajo "mainstream" artists, who received a wealth of inspiration for their own work. When such artists lend their blankets to international traveling exhibitions, the market for historic textiles rises along with the price. Navajos, however, remain further deprived as their cultural heritage becomes far beyond the financial reach of their own museum. Navajo weavers see ancestresses' creations in books or are forced to travel to museums far from the reservation to view historic works. Articles and advertisements in arts and antiques magazines lure collectors and dealers to invest in historic textiles.

Today many Navajo weavers struggle to continue weaving but lack buyers. Weavers' own statements document the inimical effects on Navajo livelihood. Intermittent recessions, competition from copies imported from Mexico and overseas, the difficulty of traveling to cities to market their work, and the persistence of dealers, traders, and collectors in retailing historic textiles all negatively affect the sales of contemporary Navajo weaving.

From Woven Craft to High Art

As previous chapters have shown, published statements (Amsden [1934] 1975; James [1914] 1974; Kent 1985; Underhill [1956] 1983) stress that a textile's functional aspect far outweighed any consideration of its overriding aesthetic, although a weaver may have spent hundreds of hours spinning, dyeing, and weaving her blanket or rug. The literature has acknowledged Navajo "dexterity" but until recently has not accorded it the status of art (M'Closkey 1985).[1]

Nineteenth-century Navajo blankets were instrumental in the development of color field painting, an important genre that emerged during the 1960s. Indeed, many aboriginal textiles prefigure major developments in contemporary art, in some cases by centuries. Some specialists note that the "color aesthetics" of Navajo weavers was superior to that of painters inspired by their work.[2] Gallery owner Lee Cohen remarked that early Navajo wearing blankets "were the beginning of the roots of American abstract art, using color and form to create a dynamic and a third dimension" (Pyne 1987:20). Witherspoon (1977:174) lists nearly two dozen famous American artists who have owned Navajo weaving, including Tony Berlant, Jasper Johns, Frank Stella, Tony Smith, Andy Warhol, and Kenneth Noland. A portion of the eighty-one historic Navajo textiles in the first major international exhibition (1972–76) was culled from their collections. When the textiles were exhibited in London, the art critic Ralph Pomeroy wrote:

I am going to forget, in order to really see them, that a group of Navajo blankets are not only that. In order to consider them as I feel they ought to be considered as ART with a capital "A"—I am going to look at them as paintings—created with dye instead of canvas—by several nameless masters of abstract art. (1974:30)

Feminist art critics and historians responded to this aesthetic revisionism:

Several manoeuvres are necessary in order to see these works as art. The geometric becomes abstract, woven blankets become paintings and women weavers become nameless masters. . . . [I]n art history the status of an art work is inextricably tied to the status of the maker. (Parker and Pollock 1981:68)

Lucy Lippard wryly critiqued this newfound notoriety:

They were eulogized as neutral, un-gendered sources for big bold geometric abstractions by male artists like Frank Stella and Kenneth Noland. Had they been presented as exhibitions of women's art, they would not have been seen at all in a fine arts context. When feminists pointed out that their much admired "strong works" were crafts . . . one would expect the women's art to be taken more seriously, yet such borrowings from "below" must still be validated from "above." (1984:102)

Textile curator Mary Hunt Kahlenberg, of the Los Angeles County Museum of Art, and sculptor Tony Berlant co-wrote the catalog that toured with the textile exhibition. In it they wrote:

In visual power and force of statement Navajo blankets represent a high point in the history of American Indian art. . . . [W]ithin the traditional Navajo culture the majority of weavers were able to produce works of art on a level that can only be matched by a handful of professional artists in our own culture. . . . Navajo weavers . . . dealt with many of the same concerns as contemporary American artists. (1972:26–28)

The curators also published articles simultaneously in *ARTnews* and *Art in America* (1972a, 1972b). Berlant began collecting historic Navajo blankets during the 1960s and early 1970s. He owned more than three hundred textiles and required a warehouse to store them (Baer 1989:539). This inaugural exhibition spawned several others. In 1973 New York gallery owner Andre Emmerich mounted "Navajo Blankets from the Private Collections of Contemporary Artists." In the catalog essay, Berlant noted:

> [T]hese [nineteenth-century] blankets are entirely secular objects and without ceremonial significance, neither are they symbolic in any direct sense. . . . [E]ach blanket carries the dynamic expression of a self-image[;] this priority of individual creation . . . carries through the sense of a specific artist and it is as they gain power in contemplation that this sense of the individual is revealed. (1973:n.p.)

With the genesis of color field painting, the cant of modernism and the aesthetics of formalism altered the perception and treatment of historic Navajo weaving within the academy. Suddenly, the aesthetic concerns of nameless weavers and internationally known painters were discussed in the same breath by dealers, modernist critics, and museologists.[3]

Unraveling Academic Scholarship and Commerce

In 1974 the University of Arizona Museum of Art mounted an exhibition of several dozen blankets owned by Berlant. The director, William E. Steadman, acknowledged the museum's indebtedness to the Los Angeles collector and real estate developer Edwin Janss for suggesting an exhibition of a portion of Berlant's collection. In the introduction to the exhibition catalog, he remarked:

> This exhibition . . . brings together thirty masterpieces ranging from 1800 to 1890 in which craftsmanship and color are the keynotes of the composition. . . . [T]he blankets . . . show . . . the spirit in which great painters have treated their craft. . . . [This is] the most splendid collection of Navajo blankets in the world. (1974:n.p.)

The archaeologist Joe Ben Wheat, formerly of the University of Colorado Museum, wrote the catalog essay for the exhibition. Acknowledged as the doyen of Navajo textile studies, Wheat (1976a, 1976b, 1977, 1981, 1984, 1988, 1996) exhaustively studied the history, techniques, and materials of Navajo weaving (Hedlund 1989b). He researched early-nineteenth-century archives for the types and values of imported materials such as bayeta, ultimately incorporated in southwestern textiles. He analyzed, cataloged, and appraised hundreds of historic textiles in private and public collections. He developed a cluster of "diagnostic techniques," including dye analyses, to aid in dating nineteenth-century textiles. Navajo weaving is classified according to design (banded, striped, zoned), function, yarn type, and weaving technique. Chief's blanket styles are generally divided into four subgroups: First, Second, Third, and Fourth Phases (Blomberg 1988). Wheat has reassessed much of Amsden's research, to which curators, textile scholars, gallery owners, collectors, and dealers frequently refer. Wheat's admiration for prereservation pieces can be seen in his catalog essay accompanying Berlant's solo exhibition:

> [F]or purity of color and clarity of design and composition, Navajo blankets of the Classic period have never been excelled . . . and . . . the achievements of the past which produced the magnificent textiles of the 19th century are not likely ever to be repeated. (1974:n.p.)

In 1994 Wheat's contributions to Southwest textiles studies were lauded by dealer-curator Mary Hunt Kahlenberg. In her presentation at the conference Navajo Weaving since the Sixties, hosted by the Heard Museum, Kahlenberg pointed out that Wheat's research aided in establishing the provenance, pedigree, and importance of individual blankets. When a blanket's age could be determined, it was "guaranteed," attracting new collectors because of its potential increase in value.[4] Today nineteenth-century weaving is acknowledged as "art," since the aesthetics of Navajo weavers is seen to parallel that of painters. As the historic weaving has become art, privileging the conceptual, information concerning (manual) technique is no longer considered as important (see n. 1). In a New Age twist, Kahlenberg suggests that Navajo weaving provides a link for Americans searching for spirituality. Acquiring a blanket is like a "fetish in the pocket": we can bring spirituality into our lives by owning "a piece of history."

Tracking the Journey from Collectible to High Camp

In 1968 Berlant acquired a Second Phase chief's blanket for $50. By 1974 *Arizona Highways* noted that chief's blankets currently sold at auction for $15,000 to $20,000 (1974:43). Five years later, Berlant began selling off a portion of his large collection. During the 1980s, the market for historic Navajo blankets became increasingly volatile, with chief's blankets remaining the "most recognizable" of all American Indian works of art (Baer 1989). In 1984 a Navajo saltillo sarape was auctioned by Sotheby's for $115,000, a record-setting amount for a Native American artifact (Johnson 1984:17).[5] In 1989 Sotheby's auctioned a rare First Phase chief's blanket owned by Edwin Janss for $522,000.[6] What is the connection between this spectacular increase in price and several New York gallery exhibits mounted within the previous decade highlighting the "inspired" works of prominent contemporary male artists juxtaposed to Navajo weaving? One exhibition prompted the *New York Times* art critic to query, "How 'primitive' is the folk art of the Navajo?" (Kramer 1972:27). Collecting, exhibiting, and auctioning historic textiles and other artifacts created by indigenous peoples before they were "spoiled" by "modernization" has become big business (Price 1989).[7] Auctions sponsored by Christie's and Sotheby's in major cities around the world represent the most elite sales of Indian artifacts. Such activity can be tracked in the Albuquerque publication *Artlist,* which has been published since 1985. The editor, Laurence Smith, provides year-to-year comparisons of prices realized at major auctions of native art. He also writes the column "Auction Track" for the *Indian Trader.*

Smith's October 1986 column (p. 24) highlights data collated from fifteen recent auctions. Textiles made up 10 percent of all offerings (the fifth of six categories), yet ranked first in value of sales, or 25 percent of the $3,323,896 total. By March 1987 (p. 16), Smith claimed the market was dominated by nineteenth-century Navajo textiles. In July he provided average square inch prices of Germantowns, noting that the aging process gives "an overall visual effect that can hardly be achieved with new yarns" (p. 16). He also highlights antique Navajo weavings in his September 1987 (p. 27) column. Between 1985 and 1987 nearly one thousand textiles sold at thirty-three auctions for $1,538,869. Weavings continued to dominate by dollar volume, especially lots over $5,000. In August 1990 Smith commented on the popularity of his publication, noting that both new and experienced collectors and galleries were using his books (p. 31) (fig. 15).

In June 1990 Smith wrote that "top prices are higher than ever" (p. 31). He analyzed Sotheby's auctions over the previous decade. In 1979 nearly 50 percent of 401 lots were offered for under $500. Ten years later only 3 percent fell below that amount. Between 1979 and 1989 prices for historic Native American articles increased 400 percent, with the shift "being most marked for Navajo weavings." (7/90:31). Ron McCoy (1989:5–6) noted that the market began to peak during the mid-1980s and attributed the rise to dealers and collectors jockeying for the best material, mirroring Wall Street brokers. Smith's June 1991 column (p. 20) was three times its normal length and dealt with the recession and the health of the American Indian antiquities market. Polling nearly three dozen dealers, Smith found some noted a downturn in sales, although "collectible items retain[ed] their popularity." The auction market, however, remained unscathed. Venice, California, gallery owner Philip Garaway provided ten important tips for collectors of Indian

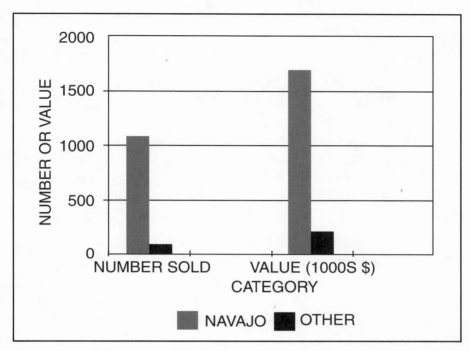

Figure 15. Textiles Sold at International Auctions, collated from Smith 1989.

art, among them, shop around, read scholarly books, review museum collections, work with a reputable dealer, and consider collecting antiquities:

> [An antiquity is] one of a kind, and many pieces aren't any more expensive than contemporary works. . . . [Antiquities] are much easier to resell because of their rarity, and they usually appreciate faster. What's more, there's a certain magical quality[,] . . . a primal link to America's native heritage. (1991:10)

An article in an adjacent column discusses the public's "explosive interest" in American Indian antiquities. In the February 1990 issue, Smith highlights "Records set at Sotheby's."[8]

In November 1991 Sotheby's auctioned a pair of portieres woven of Germantown yarns and attributed to the Ganado area (circa 1910). Appraised at $35,000 to $45,000, they are similar to portieres advertised by Hubbell in his 1902 catalog for $200 to $300. Weavers received from $27 to (rarely) $75 in credit for weaving one pair of portieres (appendix V). Twenty other classic and transitional blankets illustrated in color and conservatively appraised at $250,000 were also auctioned. At the back of the catalog, with five to eight black-and-white illustrations per page, more textiles are depicted along with other items such as kachinas, pottery, and baskets. Rugs are described as "Navajo pictorial" or "Navajo regional," and appraisals range from $1,000 to $9,000 each. All were originally "pound blankets" woven by Navajo women after 1900.

Antique Indian art sales are held in major North American cities monthly. During my archival research in 1992, a university archivist attended an auction at a local hotel. The well-advertised event attracted more than four hundred people. The archivist sat next to a dealer who purchased five rugs for $2,000 each. She admitted each one would sell for two to three times her cost at the annual Santa Fe antiquities sale slated the following week (Steere 1992).

Marketing in a Museum Context

The myth of fine quality old textiles juxtaposed to inferior "modern" weaving frequently pervades the collection and research methods of many museums. "Masterpiece" and "treasure" are terms applied almost exclusively to "traditional" historic textiles categorized as museum quality. During the nineteenth century, many textiles were deemed primitive because they were constructed by a technology inferior to that used in Europe (see chapter 2). By the time the efforts of colonial educators and missionaries were felt, Anglo-Americans began to experience nostalgia for the "untouched primitive lifestyles" and expressed a horror of indigenous creations debauched by Western influences. For example, in describing the changes in weaving after the reservation was established, Kahlenberg and Berlant wrote: "[A]fter traders appropriated the market, weavers began to produce the 'trading post controlled rug,' . . . often following explicit instruction and designs suggested by the trader" (1972:25). Thus the creative, personal edge was dulled as the connection between blanket and individual self-image was lost. Today descendants of weavers once criticized for their primitive technology find their creations discriminated against for being "nontraditional" (Rodee 1981).

Although the recent mania for historic textiles is not a new phenomenon (appendix IVc), the current craze is far better advertised. *Old Navajo Rugs: Their Development from 1900 to 1940* (1981), by Rodee, curator at the University of New Mexico's Maxwell Museum, was supported by the National Endowment for the Arts and has enjoyed ten reprintings. It was recently enlarged and published in hardcover. The text is geared to inform collectors and dealers about properly identifying early-twentieth-century Navajo textiles. Rodee uses wool type and quality as the most accurate markers for dating a particular textile. Dating via the pattern alone is not an accurate indicator, as particular designs are periodically "revived." The following paragraph appears in the preface:

> Old Navajo rugs exert an appeal that is frequently lacking in contemporary weaving. In contrast with many modern rugs that are sold as wall hangings, beautiful but remote from their original function, old Navajo rugs remain engaging, well woven, strong. This book is designed to fill a lacuna in their history—the period from 1890 to World War II. I hope . . . to assist both private and public collectors who are turning to this period as nineteenth-century weaving becomes increasingly expensive. (Rodee 1981:xiii)

Because of the volatility of the market, museums face threats to their collections of historic Navajo weaving. On 27 August 1989, the Amerind Foundation Museum located in Dragoon, Arizona, suffered a theft of a Second Phase chief's blanket (*Indian Trader* 10/89:11). In February 1990 (p. 9), *Indian Trader* reported the Southwest Museum of Los Angeles discovered that more than $2 million worth of Indian artifacts were missing, including several rare Navajo textiles. Years later, their former director was charged with the theft. The Denver Art Museum has disputed the 1970s deaccessioning of a rare Navajo blanket that sold at a New York auction in 1997 for $431,500. The blanket was one of thirty or forty historic Navajo blankets valued at $1.5 million displayed at the sellers' eighteenth-century estate. Concerned about lack of security and threat of fire, they opted to auction the most valuable textiles (*Art-Talk* 1998:13). The money will remain in escrow until the dispute is settled. The Adobe Gallery in Old Town, Albuquerque, reported on its Web site that it was burglarized on 12 May 2000, and twenty-one old Navajo rugs were stolen (http://www.adobegallery.com/stolen/textiles).

Countervoices and the Politics of Representation

The terminology used by art historians, dealers, collectors, and museum curators has altered remarkably over the last thirty years. For example, some of the "wild" or "coarse" pound blankets and rugs of the past are now "eye dazzlers" whose makers are perceived as part of mainstream American art (Arnold 1988:41). The recent interrogation of museum practices and issues of representation emerging from the academy and from First Nations peoples have not yet addressed these altered discourses surrounding Navajo textiles (Ames 1991, 1994; Handler 1992, 1993; Krech 1994; Phillips 1994; Phillips and Steiner

1999). However, some of their commentary speaks to issues relevant to situating this problem in current museum discourse.

Postmodernist trends in recent scholarship have tended to question the isolation of "art" or "science" from cultural narratives that inform a society's values (Mullin 2001; Penney 1988). Museums, responsible for arranging the "facts" of art and science into public narratives, have found that their representations are inherently political; they either reinforce a consensus of values or challenge it. If the latter occurs, they risk censorship or loss of funding. Many museums are reluctant to alienate wealthy patrons whose financial support is crucial to their survival but whose politics seldom embrace the postcolonial antihegemonic Other (Krech 1994:6).

Ames (1991:7) notes how the word "museum" is used in its generic sense to include museums of art and museums of history, science, and technology. The word encompasses both types by papering over profound differences in curatorial perspectives and practices. It is more than a division between "art" and "artifact"—codewords for a range of ideological, social, and political differences. Ideas about aesthetics, the process of making art, and the role of the artist (as it has evolved in Western societies over the past several centuries) form the basis of art museum policies and their definitions of "art." Classical art history defines art as a "heroically personal, subjective, and non-utilitarian expression of creativity" (Ames 1991:7). In contrast, history museums are founded on the Western ideology of science, which views the world "objectively" as a field of potential specimens used as representations of the natural world. Cultural materials are divided and treated separately, as artful creations by named individuals if the works are Western in origin or as anonymous "collective representations" made by unnamed tribal craftspeople if works are non-Western in origin (Price 1989:chapter 4). The "artspeak" currently operating in the field of historic Navajo weaving clearly straddles the two domains. A coterie of experts, many associated with museums, has contributed to the construction of the postreservation narrative that culminated in the often-repeated and erroneous generalizations discussed earlier. This narrative is presumed to describe the context in which the historic weaving was produced. However, we have seen that the economic conditions under which these textiles were produced have not been adequately investigated. Such information is considered unnecessary to either the modernist or the current artspeak climate that dominates current discourse on Navajo textiles. Nor is the cultural context perceived as essential to an aesthetic appreciation:

> [A]n ignorance of cultural context seems almost a precondition for artistic appreciation. In this object system a tribal piece is detached from

one milieu in order to circulate freely in another, a world of art—of museums, markets, and connoisseurship. . . . [T]he "masterpiece" is universally recognizable. (Clifford 1988:200)

The "Primitivism" exhibition mounted by the Museum of Modern Art in New York (MOMA) in 1984 juxtaposed tribal and modern art and sparked critiques by postmodernist art historians and critics (Clifford 1986, 1988; Foster 1985). Clifford provides a critique that encapsulates the hegemony enjoyed by culture brokers in defining and extending the parameters of the art world:

[T]he "discovery" of tribal objects by modernist artists occurred at the moment of high colonialism. . . . [T]he story involves reclassification[,] . . . not redemption or discovery. The fact that rather abruptly, in the space of a few decades, a large class of non-Western artifacts came to be redefined as art is a taxonomic shift that requires critical historical discussion, not celebration. . . . [That] this expansion of the category "art" . . . occurred just as the planet's tribal peoples came massively under European political, economic, and evangelical dominion cannot be irrelevant. . . . [T]he scope and underlying logic of the "discovery" of tribal art reproduces hegemonic Western assumptions rooted in the colonial and neocolonial epoch. (1988:196–97)

Clifford's critique has yet to trigger a reflexive reconsideration by Southwest scholars concerning the radical transformation in the discourse on historic Navajo textiles. However, such a wholesale appropriation and absorption of indigenous expressive forms has spawned a generalized critique from First Nations quarters.

Critique from First Nations Perspectives
According to the Cree artist Alfred Young-Man (Ames 1994:11), First Nations peoples resent having their cultures, which they view holistically, "separated and interpreted according to alien categories of domination." It is also a matter of status and prestige. Artifacts are ranked lower than art, crafts below artifacts. Categorizing an object as art or craft becomes a political act because such categorization shapes its subsequent history (Ames 1991). Many First Nations members perceive the "universalism" enunciated by mainstream institutions as a form of imperialism that denies or devalues the importance of collective difference. The Métis filmmaker Loretta Todd offers this critique:

[T]he missionary zeal with which colonialism sought to make us all

Christians persisted in artistic realms. Our cultural orders, our cultural expressions were not of value until they were washed in the holy waters of western thought[,] . . . until the critics, academics, the artists recognized or discovered the worth of our work. (1990:26)

Native critiques provide a penetrating countervoice to hegemonic Western views as reflected in the reconstitution of the Navajo aesthetic in historic blankets. Ames (1994:13) remarks that First Nations peoples are discomfited by academic institutions and professions such as anthropology, museology, and art history that frequently manifest the values of rationality, linear logic, and depersonalized methodologies and persistently "order, dissect and classify everything in sight." These critiques become increasingly relevant in scrutinizing the evidence related to the recent volatility of the market for historic Navajo textiles. Southwest museologists' willingness to facilitate this market in the face of the decreasing demand for contemporary textiles calls for critique.

The anthropologist Suzanne Baizerman has written about the escalating interest in historic Navajo weaving and the shift in the type of publications on it. She comments on the changing discourses in a 1989 volume honoring the legacy of Kate Peck Kent. Nearly 70 percent of all books, dissertations, and theses on Navajo weaving since the 1880s were published after 1960. Documenting the increasing number of books and catalogs on the topic, Baizerman notes the shift in authorship from academic anthropologists in the earlier periods (e.g., Reichard [1934] 1974, [1936] 1968, [1939] 1971) to art historians and museologists in the last twenty years. For example, ten publications intended for academics were produced between 1960 and 1979, whereas only one was written between 1980 and 1988 (Baizerman 1989:table 2). A concomitant rise occurred in the number of museum-gallery catalogs. In the first period, eleven catalogs were published, jumping to seventeen during the 1980s. We see an increase from one catalog every two years to two catalogs per year. In fact, nearly half of the total number of catalogs on the subject since 1884 were written between 1980 and 1988. Baizerman also notes:

[S]ome museum curators and anthropologists became dealers, and some dealers received training in anthropology. . . . [I]t is evident that the museum is the center of publishing on Navajo textiles [in 1989], and the trend is getting stronger. . . .

Publications are important to establish authority and expertise and to provide the publicity necessary to help sustain the value of the product. . . . [T]he rise in the number of publications on Navajo textiles correlates with the rise in their monetary value. (1989:16, 17)

She notes further that general interest in craft peaked in the 1960s and 1970s and then declined in recent years. This trend, however, is not reflected in publications on historic Navajo weaving. Howard Bahr's (1999) massive Navajo bibliography, containing 6,326 references, indexes more than forty entries under "Catalogs" and "Exhibitions" and four under "Economics."

Artspeak: From Barbarism to Eye Dazzling

The following story is a provocative example of how the shift from craft to art has altered the discourse on a style of historic Navajo weaving. When Navajos wove the bright Germantown yarns into busy serrate patterns, the "eye dazzler" was created, so named because of the pulsating optical effects it created. It was these creations and their aniline-dyed counterparts woven between 1880 to 1900 that early critics such as Amsden and James referred to as "barbaric" and "an aesthetic debauch." Techniques once referred to as "lazy lines" and "bungling" in historic texts are now described as creating "extremely subtle and beautiful effects" (Pomeroy 1974:35). The redemption of the "eye dazzler" was initiated in an exhibition mounted at the University of Iowa Museum of Art in 1976. In the foreword to the catalog, the director, Jan Keene Muhlert, lamented the "disappearance" of indigenous peoples:

> [I]t may be altogether fitting at this time to contemplate the remnants of a native American culture which has been displaced, in some cases destroyed, or perhaps so totally distorted by now as to be beyond recognition of its indigenous forms. . . . We owe the [delayed] appreciation of these "works of art" to the artist, due to his "universalizing aesthetic." (Muhlert 1976:n.p.)

When this statement was made, the "remnant" population comprised more than 150,000 Navajos, with possibly 15,000 weavers. The exhibition curator, J. J. Brody, admits he was blind to these eye dazzlers, even though he worked with them daily as director of the Maxwell Museum of Anthropology until the late 1960s. Brody attributes the "fresh vision" of four artists—Bernard Cohen, Carol and Paul Sarkisian, and Greg LaChapelle—to altering his perception. Kaufman and Selser describe the textiles' reception:

> Many eyedazzlers were outstanding examples of artistic expression, completely different in visual appeal from the blankets that preceded them and the rugs that followed. Today, eyedazzlers have become the

pets of twentieth-century color-field painters, art critics, and collectors of Navajo weaving. They have been favorably compared to Op Art, a style that reached its peak of popularity with "The Responsive Eye," the 1965 exhibit at The Museum of Modern Art in New York City. (1985:65)

Newspapers such as the *New York Times* have also covered the recent mania for historic Navajo weaving. The columnist Rita Reif states in her article, "Navajo Weavings Are Choice Collectors' Items," in the "Antiques View" column:

> Over the past 15 years, ever since artists and other collectors began seriously acquiring "eye dazzlers," these stunning weavings have been studied, written about, exhibited and acquired with mounting enthusiasm. . . . [T]he visually arresting blankets are regarded as the precursors of the Op Art paintings of the 1960s. . . . [They are] explosive in their colors, and dynamic in their designs. . . . [They] project extraordinary passion [and] possess raw intensity. (1983:H35)

Their raw intensity or deep turbulence is contrasted with the quiet control conveyed by the prereservation weavings. Reif suggests that the dramatic contrast may be due to the emotional despair experienced by a once proud and free people who became captives at Bosque Redondo. She mentions two concurrent events: an exhibition in Scottsdale, Arizona, and an auction of eye dazzlers scheduled at Sotheby's in New York City, predicted to set sales records. She concludes:

> Navajo blankets have skyrocketed in price in recent years. . . . Germantown weavings have risen from 10 to 40 percent in less than two years. Over the last decade the Indian blankets have escalated 10 times or more in value. And collectors see no end in sight to rising prices, as the finer examples become scarce and new collectors compete for the few available. (1983:H35)

The journal the *Collector-Investor* also highlighted the explosive growth in demand for historic Navajo weaving (Montgomery 1982). And in 1988 *Oriental Rug Review* devoted an entire issue to Navajo weaving, emphasizing the historic blankets.

Judith Arnold, in "An Investment in Beauty" for *Southwest Profile* (1988), interviewed Lee Cohen, owner of Gallery 10, which has outlets in Scottsdale and Santa Fe. Viewing historic Navajo weaving through the lens of art history,

Cohen comments on why historic Navajo textiles were collected by American modernist painters:

> Navajo women had an intuitive grasp of using color and form to create a third dimension and dynamic . . . without using perspective or representational imagery. This is precisely what the abstract painters were experimenting with, creating a third dimension with color and form. So these Navajo weavings . . . are an important part of the mainstream of American art, not just a regionally interesting craft. (Arnold 1988:41)

The aesthetic importance of the older pieces and the prices they bring at auction—$50,000 to $100,000 and more—have helped to establish the intrinsic worth of post-1900 Navajo weaving (Arnold 1988:41). Three years later, Cohen exhibited blankets in the $200,000 range:

> For a blanket or rug to qualify in this range, it must be historically rare, finely woven, and must have survived a great time with little or no damage. It must also be aesthetically powerful when judged by the standards of integrity for great weaving and great two-dimensional art. These textiles are as artistically satisfying as breathtaking colorist paintings with strong dynamic designs (Indian Trader 6/91:18).

In 1989 the New York gallery Hirschl and Adler Folk mounted "Eye Dazzlers: Navajo Weavings and Contemporary Counterparts." This exhibition "explored the tradition of contemporary artists drawing inspiration from the abstract qualities of Indian art" (Miele 1989:n.p.). In the catalog essay Frank Miele notes:

> American Indian art has been a very integral and vital part of mainstream American art and both, in fact have exerted a profound influence upon the contemporary American art of this century. (1989:n.p.)

The exhibition featured paintings by Donald Judd, Frank Stella, and Kenneth Noland. The terms "affinity" and "inspiration" are used to describe correlations between these artists' work and Navajo weaving. About Noland's *Every Third*, painted in 1963, Miele said, "[I]t is truly startling to find that so many of the descriptions of Noland's work are so apropos in describing an eyedazzler as well."[9]

The Santa Fe dealer-collector Joshua Baer frequently publishes on Navajo weaving. Baer places the best Indian antiquities alongside half-million-dollar paintings by famous American artists and considers classic American Indian material undervalued (*Indian Trader* 9/89:5–6). In the October 1991 issue of *Antiques* magazine's ten-page article, "Garments of Brightness: The Art and History of the Navajo Eye Dazzler," Baer provides a précis of Navajo weaving history, noting that the Navajo language contains no words for "art" or "sacred." He surveys the importance of Navajo textiles in prereservation trade and notes that they were exchanged for gold, buffalo hides, or horses. Stating that after the advent of trading posts weavers were "at the mercy of traders' aesthetic preferences," since the extension of credit bound them to a particular post, he perpetuates the conviction that weavers sold the eye dazzler textiles for enough credit to purchase yarn for three or four more blankets. Only the best weavers could afford large quantities of these expensive machine-spun yarns. As the time-consuming processes of shearing, spinning, and dyeing were dispensed with, they could concentrate on colors and designs. Weavers achieved "a level of design innovation and technical expertise that had not existed in Navajo weaving since the early classic period (1820–1840)" (Baer 1991:586). According to Baer, weavers received more credit if they produced blankets that looked machine-made. Although the bold, complex designs of these eye dazzlers appeared distinct from earlier patterns, they tend to be exaggerated versions of elements influenced by Pueblo and Spanish weaving that had been incorporated in earlier Navajo textiles.

Baer's text exemplifies how dealers, collectors, and curators weave nostalgic scenarios to fan an already volatile market for historic weavings. As described in chapter 4, the eye dazzlers brought weavers $3 to $10 in credit at the trading post when first exchanged for goods. Today they are routinely auctioned or retailed for between $3,000 and $50,000.[10]

Historic Navajo Weaving and the Local and Regional Scene

The last fifteen years have seen a noticeable increase in the appearance of historic alongside contemporary textiles at reservation trading posts and southwestern retail outlets. Many of the historic textiles advertised by dealers and collectors are in the same price range as counterparts woven by contemporary weavers (Reno 1988). Southwestern museums of ethnology now sell historic pieces adjacent to contemporary Navajo weaving in their gift shops. Because nineteenth-century Navajo textiles have become prohibitively expensive, curators, dealers, and collectors have shifted their attention to textiles woven after 1900 (Arnold 1988; Rodee 1981). The director of the gift shop at a New Mexico museum described these rugs as "Affordable. Available. Beautiful." Such textiles are now realized as "perfect examples of the ideal collectible—intrinsic beauty, a history of rising prices, limited and decreasing supply yet still plentiful enough to allow for comparison shopping and a relatively active resale market" (Arnold 1988:38).

One rug, possibly from the Ganado area, was estimated to have increased in value more than fiftyfold, from $25 in 1925 to $1,300 in 1988. The director predicted its worth would more than double by 1995. However, although it is impossible to generalize, a comparison of the technical quality in identically priced historic and contemporary weavings offered in retail establishments shows the latter are generally superior. For example, in comparing two textiles priced at $2,000, the contemporary rug is likely to contain more finely spun and evenly dyed yarn and a more detailed pattern.

Collectors consign old pieces during annual exhibits featuring creations by contemporary artists. At a recent event sponsored by a museum in the Southwest, nearly half of the jewelry for sale was consigned by members wishing to cash in on nostalgia for the Old West. For example, a bracelet circa 1930 that probably sold for fifty cents initially carried a price tag of $180. Approximately 25 percent of the contemporary jewelry on display was priced under $200 and met direct competition from historic goods possibly produced under sweatshop conditions. This museum had several stacks of old blankets and rugs with $1,000 to $5,000 price tags—in direct competition with similarly priced contemporary textiles. Museums generally retain a percentage of the retail value, whether the work is consigned by a First Nations artist or a collector.

In conjunction with escalating auction and gallery activity, a dramatic increase has occurred in the last ten years in advertisements featuring historic Navajo textiles in magazines devoted to Native American art. During the 1970s and early 1980s, advertisements featured rugs by contemporary weavers. A full-page color ad in a 1995 issue of *American Indian Art Magazine* features the new gallery of historic Indian art in a retail establishment that formerly advertised itself as "the largest dealer in contemporary Navajo weaving in the world." Years ago, when one visited this gallery, a small portion of their stock consisted of historic weaving; today they have dozens of old pound blankets for sale.[11]

American Indian Art Magazine, published in Scottsdale, Arizona, caters to individuals interested in the history, aesthetics, and market value of Indian art. It features articles by scholars and dealers and advertisements by dealers and galleries, with an emphasis on historic material. A two-page advertisement with text by Baer (autumn 1992) notes the dramatic increase in prices of antique Indian art: pottery, baskets, and blankets are "all worth multiples of what they were selling for in 1982." Published quarterly, the magazine devotes several pages of every issue to recent sales activity of historic Indian-made goods held in different parts of the country by Sotheby's, Christie's, and regional auction houses. Old Navajo textiles make up a prominent portion of the auctions. Anthropologists, ethnologists, museologists, dealers, collectors, and artists sit on the editorial advisory board of this publication. Articles on contemporary makers are rare, although a few galleries feature their creations in colorful advertisements.

> Dealers continue to push the investment potential of historic Navajo weaving: NASDAQ stocks lost more than $3 trillion in value during 2000. The biggest losses were sustained by investors with the most to lose. Given the extent of their losses, certain wealthy collectors of Navajo blankets may decide to sell. . . . [If you purchase] a great blanket . . . what it says to you while you own it is as much a part of the return on your investment as the profit you realize when you sell it. (Baer 2001:n.p.)

Baer, one of the most active dealers in antique Navajo blankets, advertises continually in *American Indian Art Magazine.* The winter 2000 issue featured a synopsis of the highest prices realized (from $200,500 to $684,500) in post-1988 auction sales of twenty American Indian antique artifacts. Eight historic Navajo textiles constituted 34 percent of the nearly $6.5 million in sales. The international auction market, "though vast, is but a fraction of the business" (Johnson 2000:25).

The *Indian Trader,* a newspaper published in Gallup, New Mexico, by Martin Link, former director of the Navajo Tribal Museum, is a popular monthly that appeals to dealers, collectors, and retailers of Native American goods. In February 1980 the editor reprinted an article first published ten years previously. It noted that given the recent bearish trend in the stock market, Indian and Western art was increasing in value as speculators were entering the market. Groups wishing to diversify their investments were purchasing historic Indian art. This investment activity was noted in the *Wall Street Journal* and *Business Week.* Increasing demand along with a diminishing supply led to price escalations.

A recent issue of *Indian Trader* featured an article on physician-cum-Indian-antiquities-dealer J. Mark Sublette of Tucson, describing his new gallery in Santa Fe and his recent success advertising on the Internet:

> The arts and crafts business has never been better. . . . [W]e are selling a lot on our [Web] site and at our two locations. We sell the higher end

stuff and the demand is huge. Our problem is not selling what we have but getting the stuff people want to buy. (Miller 2001:5)

Sublette markets Native American pottery, baskets, and textiles created between 1850 and 1950. He and his contemporaries cater to a dedicated coterie of collectors who increasingly invest in Indian antiquities as a more reliable and lucrative option than the stock market.

Curators and dealers have noted a change in the type of collector. The recent volatility in the market has attracted "educated, sophisticated and demanding buyers" who formerly invested in "fine art" or expensive Oriental rugs (Arnold 1988). Ralph Lauren, Dick Cavett, James Caan, and Walter Annenberg are among the "sophisticated" collectors. The St. Louis Art Museum recently exhibited an impressive collection owned by Andy Williams. In the introduction to the catalog, an old friend of Williams remarked on the attention garnered by a Third Phase chief's blanket displayed at Williams's home (Pearson 1997). Guests frequently commented on the blanket, slighting the Mark Rothko hung in the same room. Williams immediately sold the blanket because he had paid $300,000 for the painting (which he later sold for $1.7 million). When a Navajo textile woven by "Anonymous" trumps a Rothko, the sky is no longer the limit.

The Dark Side of the Market

Art theft is on the increase, with the multimillion-dollar international market ranking second to narcotics (*Indian Trader* 1/86:6). Looting archaeological sites remains a serious problem, particularly in the Southwest (Parezo 1990:571). Although fines can range up to $100,000 for looting on federal lands, few people are caught (*Indian Trader* 1/85:18). More than fifty thousand cultural sites are located in New Mexico alone (*Indian Trader* 10/89:7). When a mining recession left workers hungry in the Four Corners region, scavengers looted hundreds of Indian burial grounds. Collectors offered huge bounties, and tax laws aided destruction of sites as collectors donated overvalued antiquities to museums and took full tax writeoffs. A dealer in antique Navajo textiles had his multimillion-dollar collection impounded on his arrest by federal Drug Enforcement Administration agents in 1990. He was allegedly involved in a money-laundering scheme to smuggle drugs from Thailand into the United States (Chronis 1990).[12]

Karl Meyer, author of *The Plundered Past* (1973), attributes the escalation of illicit activities to the implementation of the UNESCO Convention in 1970. The convention forbids the illicit import, export, and transfer of ownership of cultural property. It deals primarily with looting archaeological sites, particularly those located in Third World countries. This convention frightened North American dealers in antiquities, as they saw sources for their sales vanish. What better way to salvage one's profitable occupation than to search closer to home for possible sources of goods that did not need to be smuggled into the country? The transformation of the market for historic North American material culture occurred with the 1971 auction of the Green Collection of Native American artifacts, the inaugural auction of a major collection featured by Sotheby's in New York. Meyer also remarks on how Sotheby's kick-starts new fields of collector interest rather than wait for trends to develop. He estimates that 5 to 10 percent of art sales occur at public auctions. Most sales are private transactions.

Popular paperbacks also demonstrate the attraction that "collectibles" hold for investors. In 1988 Dawn Reno published the first edition of *American Indian Collectibles: Official Identification and Price Guide.* It covers a broad spectrum of arts and crafts ranging in price from under $100 to more than $100,000. In the introduction, Reno notes that during the 1980s dealers began putting together investment portfolios that specialize in the acquisition of Amerind artifacts. Traveling throughout the Southwest while researching material for her book, she encountered people taking money out of the stock market to invest in Indian arts: "Indian art is part of the American heritage, and, should you own a piece of work in this category, you have an investment that will continue to grow" (Reno 1988:3). She acknowledges that Navajos continue to weave by hand and that "their work sells for very high prices" (1988:112, 117). In the conclusion of Reno's book, a short section titled "The Modern Artist/Artisan," she comments that some of the work produced by contemporary makers "is highly collectible" (1988:366–68). She suggests that if you are fortunate to purchase directly from the makers,

> make sure you get their signature on the piece you are purchasing because it will make it easier to identify later and will add to its value. . . . [J]ewelry, pottery and other crafts have been identified for many years and have, therefore, increased tremendously in value. . . . [S]ince antique Indian items are among the hottest collectibles in the antiques world right now, some of them might be out of your price range[,] . . . which gives you another reason to patronize the younger and upcoming artists—their work is still easy on the pocketbook! (1988:367–68)

The Conservation of Historic Treasures

Textile conservators have hosted seminars on the history and care of historic Navajo textiles and investing in them. A 1980 conference in Santa Fe attracted

150 devotees. Museum personnel, conservators, anthropologists, and curators chaired sessions devoted to fiber identification, regional styles, dyes, restoration, and imitations. Longtime trader Bill Young related many stories. He informed his audience that during the 1920s rugs were bought by weight, and listeners were astonished to hear that prices ranged from $1.25 to $1.65 per pound. The conference was organized by Noel Bennett, a California native who had learned to weave when her husband served for more than a decade with the U.S. Public Health Service on the reservation (Emmanuel 1980). Bennett opened a textile restoration center to "give back to the Navajo." She has published several books on various aspects of Navajo weaving (1974, 1979, 1987; Bennett and Bighorse 1997), has given numerous workshops and lecture demonstrations, and has taught Navajo weaving at the Gallup Branch of the University of New Mexico (*Indian Trader* 6/80:34). She has said:

> Weaving is boring[,] . . . but the stories are the source of power. They fill your mind with a "life away" to put in the long hours. You focus on the legends—Spider Woman, the Spirit Trail, weaving taboos. (Indian Trader 6/80:34)

Several presenters disagreed about the practice of restoring old weaving. Museum curator Marian Rodee finds stabilizing a textile may be necessary but thinks it ought not to be touched just "to make it more attractive." Artist Tony Berlant disagreed, arguing that restoration may be "an act of generosity to the spirit of the piece [and] may improve market value." A textile conservator remarked that when damaged areas are repaired they are no longer the focal point, and thus "other relationships can speak with their original intensity." Textile conservationists generally earn between $40 and $80 per hour. Many contemporary Navajo weavers argue against the repair of Navajo weaving, because "the thoughts and ideas of the original weaver are in the piece." When queried whether repairing old textiles may bring "bad luck," an Anglo conservationist remarked: "By reweaving the damage, I feel I'm healing the piece, making it complete again" (Hastings 1994:12).

Conundrums associated with conservation and restoration of old textiles have been discussed in several publications but not from Navajo perspectives. Ron McCoy's article, "Guarantees," in *American Indian Art Magazine*'s (1995) "Legal Briefs" column provides a (hypothetical) caveat to collectors paying hundreds of thousands of dollars for a First Phase chief's blanket purchased from a Santa Fe gallery. He comments that "auction prices are related to those of the marketplace." However, if you discover that 10 percent of the piece you paid

$225,000 for is what "you thought it was," but the remaining 90 percent is the work of a contemporary restorer, you are "peeved [as] one could argue that an implied warranty existed" in connection with this transaction. He queries: "After all, who would pay such a sum for a modern weaving?" The dealer's location in a city noted for its exclusive galleries suggests that the textile was an "old piece" even though no one said it was.

Curators generally focus on individual textiles and include information related to political economy in exhibitions and publications as an adjunct (if noted at all). In a recent conversation with a conservator, I mentioned that the Navajo Nation Museum held a small collection of historic textiles in comparison to collections in various museums in the Southwest and elsewhere. The conservator remarked: "Well, if the Navajo don't realize what they have, they don't deserve to keep it!" Centuries of domination are expunged, with collectors and museums viewed as "saviors."[13] Another textile curator remarked in a recent conversation that she was not surprised that nearly all Navajo weaving was acquired from weavers by weight as recently as the late 1960s.

The Contemporary Scene

Autobiographical evidence of the exploitation of weavers is poignantly expressed by the Navajo weaver Nancy Woodman:

> I learned to weave when I was 13 years old, and weaving became my trade. When I learned it, I gained my independence. I got so I could support myself by my work and I kept it up. I made fairly good rugs, and still do—I've made a great many rugs. I just take them to the trading post, where I have always just taken them out in trade.
>
> I get food for my rugs. . . . [I]t is now 49 years since I learned to weave . . . and back there in the days of my innocence I merely took them to the trader accepting whatever he offered for them. . . .
>
> There is not a trader here amongst us who pays cash. I ask for even so little as a nickel in cash, but they won't give it to me. As I now give thought to this matter, I wonder why this is true, why is it? Could there be some law which makes it that way? Maybe there's a regulation. . . . [I]t's for this reason that even when I take a little rug to the trader I feel sort of unhappy at letting it go. I put a great deal of effort into my rugs, and it is this fact which causes me to be a bit unhappy at letting them go to the traders hereabout. ([1954] 1980:81–82)

Woodman's statement provides public corroboration of the mountain of evidence in Hubbell's business records documenting the minuscule returns to weavers. Republished in 1980, her statement has failed to trigger a response by authors who continue to perpetuate "comfortable stories." Yet several writers have noted the minuscule return to weavers even a generation ago (Maxwell 1963:19–20). For example, Dedera (1990:101) comments on how many reservation weavers "earned" about $0.15 an hour during the 1960s. Underhill (1983:264) reported the average annual family income at $200 in 1961. Hall (1994:144) remarked that rugs selling for $1 per pound during the 1930s now sell for five figures.

In 1987 Gloria Duus, director of the Office of Navajo Women and Families in Window Rock, distributed a questionnaire that surveyed the feasibility of organizing weaving cooperatives on the reservation. Four hundred lengthy questionnaires were distributed to weavers in ten areas. Only 4 percent of the weavers surveyed had received more than $2,500 in cash or goods for their weaving the previous year. More than 70 percent of the weavers who responded "earned" $600 or less. Sixty percent of the women used wool from their flocks, and more than 90 percent made their own tools, or family members made them. Nearly two hundred women had been weaving for more than fifteen years, and 65 percent were over thirty-six years of age. Nearly 75 percent of the women still took their rugs to the trading post. A coffee-table book published the same year, *Harmony by Hand: Art of the Southwest Indians,* provides a striking contrast to Duus's unpublished study. Sarah Nestor (1987:58) commented that contemporary Navajo weavers had difficulty meeting the demands of collectors and the prices of their textiles continued to rise in consequence.

Within the last ten years, I have noted a great deal of overlap—as much as 80 percent—in the prices for the historic and contemporary weavings at southwestern retail outlets and trading posts. In 1992 I interviewed thirty weavers on the reservation, some of them quite well known. Several weavers were very candid, noting that collectors and dealers were paying them approximately 40 percent less than they had received five years earlier for the same quality textile. At the Heard Museum's March 1994 conference, "Navajo Weaving since the Sixties," several women were quite outspoken about how the market for their weaving has evaporated. An elderly weaver wondered if the reason was that fewer weavers were spinning their own yarn. Such information was not translated, as the Navajo translators "did not want to offend the conference organizers." (A bilingual Navajo friend told me about the comments.) One of the trader-dealers invited to participate on a panel admitted that "the market for contemporary Navajo weaving is no longer strong."

Tracking the Drop in Demand

The contemporary weaving market was very strong during the late 1970s and early 1980s. In 1981 Lea Lundburg's article "Threads of Tradition" appeared in *Arizona Living*. She interviewed the Garlands, retailers in Sedona, Arizona, who claim to have the largest selection of Navajo rugs in the world. The cost of rugs was increasing at approximately 20 percent annually, and "prices [had] doubled in the last five years." This price increase follows the publication of a special issue of the popular *Arizona Highways* magazine in 1974. Published during the gasoline shortages of the early 1970s, the issue featured contemporary Navajo weaving. Other issues that year featured Indian pottery, baskets, and jewelry. When the fuel shortages eased, tourists flocked to the Southwest, precipitating another "Indian craze." The jewelry craze peaked in the late 1970s, and the rug craze continued for several more years. For the first time in history, demand outstripped supply, and for a short time some weavers received a much fairer return for their textiles (Leafdale 1974:29). Although prices increased, the Garlands admitted that a weaver may need to spend six to eight months creating a rug that would retail for $3,000 or $4,000. This does not take into consideration the time spent cleaning, carding, dyeing, and spinning the wool in preparation for weaving. One woman is described as weaving a 9-x-15-foot Two Grey Hills rug that would retail for $6,000 to $8,000. More than a year's labor was required to complete the rug. According to Lundburg, the Garlands try to keep their markups reasonable to provide a fairer return to the weaver. This article and other publications (Arnold 1988; Montgomery 1982:22) corroborate the escalation in rug prices during the late 1970s and continuing into the early 1980s.

During the 1980s, articles on the healthy markets for both historic and contemporary Navajo weaving appeared with some frequency. A long article appeared in the *Indian Trader* in November 1980. The market for rugs appeared stronger than that for jewelry and pottery. According to the article, it was not expected to "peak for quite some time" and would "stay 'very healthy' for a long time" (1980:3). Prices appeared to have doubled from 1975 to 1980, or in some cases within two years. One longtime reservation trader remarked on the increase in foreign tourists who "appreciate the craft involved in weaving a rug [because] the world is losing our traditional art forms." Several dealers interviewed noted that fewer younger women appeared to be taking up weaving and that inflation has led to increases in rug prices. One dealer remarked that he could sell three to four times as many rugs, if he could find them. Those halcyon days were short-lived.

Prices for contemporary textiles stalled around 1984 and began to drop.

The decrease coincided with the escalation in the investment market for historic textiles. Arnold (1988:41) queried Baer about the market for Navajo weaving. Baer admitted that contemporary textiles fluctuated in value. According to Baer, the market peaked in 1982–83 and dropped 25 to 30 percent after 1984. Another dealer, active since 1972, said he had never seen the historic rugs drop in value while he had been in the business. He remarked that rugs woven between 1900 and 1940 were still available "at good prices . . . between $500 to $1,200" (Arnold 1988:41). The individuals interviewed commented that the general consensus was that it did not matter whether a buyer invests in a new or old rug; the important thing is quality. A dealer who was collaborating on a book with Wheat stated that he personally preferred the old rugs. Another dealer claimed that the current market for classics is a fine art market. The nineteenth-century classics are now available only through auctions or private dealers. Most traders and dealers admitted that it may take from twenty to thirty years for a contemporary rug to appreciate in value. Arnold (1988:41) concludes her article by commenting on her own historic woven treasure, acquired at a garage sale during the 1960s. When she approached the owner to inquire about purchasing it, she recognized a well-known southwestern ethnologist. The ethnologist stalked off after refusing to pay $75, muttering she'd "gotten much better for $30." The drop in demand for contemporary weaving in the late 1980s is borne out in other articles published in the *Indian Trader* and in stories related by Navajo weavers during my 1992 fieldwork.

Continued Appropriation of Patterns

Correspondence during 1910 between Lorenzo Hubbell and Herman Schweizer reveals that the latter was importing "well-woven greys" from Mexico that were much cheaper than Navajo weaving (HP Box 37, 6/29/10). Today copy or "imitation" Navajo weaving is imported from Guatemala, Hong Kong, India, Japan, northern Thailand, Romania, and, in particular, Mexico. Brugge (1971) surveyed six stores on Interstate 40 in New Mexico and five stores in Gallup, a town southeast of the Navajo Reservation. Most stores carried the copy weaving. Some of the copies were mixed in with the genuine rugs. Brugge (1971:3) found that the imitations sold at prices well below the authentic textiles, which gives Navajo weavers "unfair competition and undermines the public's confidence in the craft." The Mexican rugs are also woven of hand-spun wool yarn, with designs that are very similar (Dockstader 1976:475; Dutton 1975:10). Most copies are single and double saddle blanket sizes, up to 4 x 6 feet. Some Mexicans are even weaving variants of the Yei patterns, taken from the Navajo ceremonial sand paintings. There are differences between the techniques used in making the side cords and top and bottom selvages that a knowledgeable individual can spot. Just looking through a pile of rugs without carefully checking, one can be easily "fooled." Noel Bennett (1973) provides information on how to determine if a rug is a genuine Navajo textile or a fake. On 7 March 1972 John Burden, manager of Gouldings Lodge in Monument Valley, wrote Arizona Senator Barry Goldwater and expressed concern over competition posed by "$20 Mexican rugs that would sell for $300 if woven by Navajo" (Record Group 435, Correspondence Concerning Misrepresentation of Native American Arts and Crafts [CMNAAC]).

More recently, far more sophisticated copies, including the earlier "chief's blanket" styles, have been imported from Oaxaca, Mexico. These carefully dyed and woven rugs are created by thousands of Zapotec weavers active in cottage industries. Weaving traditions in this region of Mexico date from pre-Columbian times; historic patterns differ markedly from Navajo designs (Barton 1989). Entrepreneurs who appropriated Navajo patterns to this region import the finished products into the United States and earn profits of 200 to 1,000 percent (Stephen 1993). By law, all woven imports must have a label attached when checked at customs noting country of origin and materials. However, tags sometimes conveniently "fall off" between the customs office and the shops. Retail outlets in the Southwest frequently display large signs advertising "Navajo rugs" or "Indian rugs." Once inside the shop, one discovers that only a portion of the stock is the genuine Navajo product. These rugs provide a real threat to the Navajo textile market, as they are priced well below their Navajo counterparts (Kwok 1989:24). National parks may carry knockoffs in their gift shops. Knockoffs in various sizes may be purchased at the Petrified Forest National Park in Arizona, adjacent to the Navajo Reservation. Old-time trader Don Smouse complained about the damage Mexican knockoffs were doing to his rug business. Importers advertising by mail had offered the Borrego Pass trader imitation rugs for $14 each (*Indian Trader* 3/86:7). Textile dealers suggest purchasing imitation rugs for the floor and hanging the genuine product on the wall (Bowers 1988). The crisis created by the importation of "fakes" flooding the Indian arts and crafts markets was the topic of a front-page article in *USA Today* (Shiffman 1998:1–2A).

The anthropologist Lynn Stephen (1991a, 1991b, 1993) has tracked the development of external markets for Zapotec weaving. In an article published a decade ago, Stephen describes the four levels of production engaged in by Zapotec weavers.

[The third level consists of] mass produced pieces, up to five by seven feet, that feature several popular designs; Navajo designs currently dominate. These pieces are bought by smaller-scale Mexican and US distributors who run their own businesses. This is the largest sector of the market in Teotitlán. The 1980s were marked by a surge of orders for Navajo designs. (1991a:384)

Stephen remarks that because of demand, there is a shortage of weaving labor. Zapotec weavers often have more work than they can handle. The Mexican weavers do not understand American taste, but they want to produce what sells. Thousands of weavers effectively produce a technically high quality product by incorporating elements of foreign design, color, and content into their work. As avid weavers, Zapotecans are able to sustain ritual and kinship obligations within their communities, and many families have enlarged their homes (Barton 1989:23; Jones 1994; Stanton 1999:40). Weaving is now the primary source of income for 90 percent of the families of Teotitlán del Valle (Klein 1997:123; Stephen 1991c:106).

The most recent phenomenon to affect contemporary Navajo weavers is the escalating sales of knockoffs advertised via sophisticated Web sites. Dozens of retail outlets advertise on the Internet. For example, Santa Fe Interiors maintains a colorful Web site featuring Michael Wineland as "The Zapotec Trader." He compares his role to the legendary Juan Lorenzo Hubbell (http://www.inter-art.net/shops/santafe.interiors/default.html). Wineland works closely with dozens of Zapotecans of Teotitlán del Valle who are "reinterpreting long-forgotten nineteenth century Navajo designs." He and other entrepreneurs oversee the details of piecework production. Many of the patterns are appropriated from lavishly illustrated books on historic collections formerly owned by wealthy individuals such as William Randolph Hearst (Blomberg 1988). The finest quality rugs use prespun wool colored with dyes imported from Switzerland. Entrepreneurs frequently exhibit the knockoffs at national home shows in major cities or advertise in interior decorator magazines and *Architectural Digest*.

Recently published texts highlight the effects of globalization on indigenous Central American weavers (Ehlers 1990; Nash 1993; Schevill et al. 1991; Stephen 1991a, 1991b, 1991c, 1993). Within the last few years, Zapotec weavers encountered competition from Dhuri rugs woven in India and imported into North America by retail chains such as Pier One. This development demonstrates how appropriated patterns can be reappropriated by entrepreneurs attempting to fill new market niches and increase their profits (Stephen 1993:48). However, postmodernist readings of the events described above and the inimical effects on Navajo livelihood preclude critique. Clifford (1988:236) reminds us, "[A]rt collecting and culture collecting now take place within a changing field of counterdiscourses, syncretisms, and reappropriations, originating both outside and inside 'the West.'" And Berlo comments:

> American and European textile designers freely take from native sources, proclaiming as their own those designs drawn from Navajo . . . originals. . . . [T]his is part of a long artistic tradition in the West. . . . [T]he contemporary indigenous textile aesthetic is, in many regions, an aesthetic of appropriation and accumulation. (1991:452–53)

As noted above, entrepreneurs have recently appropriated Navajo designs and their Zapotec counterparts and had rugs of all sizes expertly woven in India. A consumer may purchase a 9-x-12-foot rug for less than $1,000, whereas its Navajo counterpart likely would retail for $6,000 to $8,000. These rugs were observed in 1994, at a large trading post in Cameron, Arizona, *within the western boundary of the Navajo Reservation*. The post is near the junction of the highway that leads to the Grand Canyon, which attracts millions of visitors annually. This post began sponsoring semiannual auctions of historic Indian art in 1986. Many of the articles are drawn from the post's collections. The most recent auction netted $500,000.[14] Other traders have capitalized on their connections with Navajos. Al and Frank Packard sold many articles through the Don Bennett Auction House (*Indian Trader* 10/89:31). Walter Kennedy of Dennehotso offered his 912-piece collection for sale in March 1989 (*Indian Trader* 3/89:17–18). For decades he maintained careful records of each article, as most were acquired directly from his Navajo customers in a remote section of the reservation.

Regional Off-Reservation Rug Auctions

Susan Doerfler's (1986) article on contemporary Navajo weaving in the *Arizona Republic* noted how some weavers incorporated pastel colors into their rugs to accommodate market trends. One trader remarked that during the 1970s, at the height of the Indian craze, rugs were seen as a means for entrepreneurs to "make a fast buck." This man has sponsored auctions since 1983 at the Moqui Lodge near the Grand Canyon. No weavers are present. Instead, dealers and traders bring textiles that average between $40 and $1,500, about half the suggested retail price. One of the auctioneers remarked that unless weavers are well known, their rugs do not command high prices (Doerfler 1987). Very few weavers are "well known" relative to the thousands that reside on the reservation. In the final presentation at the Heard Museum conference in 1994, Gloria Emerson remarked on the importance of such events when weavers "speak for themselves." However, she expressed concern about the thousands of weavers on the reservation who had no voice.

During my fieldwork on the Navajo Reservation in 1992, several interviews with weavers corroborated the decline in prices. One woman, whose rugs are depicted in a popular publication, was deeply concerned about the devaluation of her work by an active collector-dealer who generally paid her more than $1,100 per rug. Within the previous five years, he not only purchased her rugs less frequently, he refused to pay her more than $700 for a textile of equivalent quality. This weaver was raising three of her grandchildren, as her daughter and son-in-law had moved to Phoenix to find jobs. This dealer has become increasingly active in the investment market for historic Navajo weaving. He has counterparts in other areas of the Southwest, so that currently many weavers are having a difficult time finding dealers who will purchase their weavings at equitable prices.

Rug Auctions on the Reservation

Periodically, rug auctions are held on the Navajo Reservation at various chapter houses. The best known is the auction at Crownpoint in northwestern New Mexico, formerly held quarterly and now held monthly in a school gymnasium. The event is currently the only nonprofit Navajo-run market for textiles held on a monthly basis. It was begun during the 1960s by the trader at Crownpoint who was discouraged at the $6 to $8 that local weavers averaged for their rugs at that time (Conner 1991:46). For a time the Bureau of Indian Affairs superintendent and the trader supervised the auction.

During the 1970s, as market conditions improved, the auction grew in popularity, which continues today. From three hundred to six hundred rugs may be brought to each auction. Many of the weavers are over fifty years old (Conner 1991:51). Weavers suggest the minimum acceptable bid and receive 85 percent of the proceeds. Depending on weather and time of year, several hundred people crowd into the gym to watch or participate in the bidding. I attended the Crownpoint auction in October 1992. Approximately 200 people attended, and 154 individuals acquired bidding numbers. One hundred ninety-one rugs ranging in price from $40 to $4,000 were entered. Six "large" rugs ranging from 4 x 6 to 6 x 8 feet were priced from $1,100 to $4,000. No one bid on the two most expensive rugs, and the four large rugs that did sell went for $400 above the lowest acceptable bid. More than two dozen rugs were sold at the minimum bid. Only a small percentage of rugs elicited "volatile" bidding. At the end of the evening, the unsold textiles were retrieved by their owners.[15] Ed Chamberlin, curator at Hubbell Trading Post in Ganado, has tracked the monthly sales at Crownpoint for a decade. Sales increased from an average of $225 in 1992 to

$256 in 1998. Clearly, contemporary weavers are not experiencing brisk sales of their work.

The previous year I had attended an auction at Ganado that was organized to coincide with the Sixth Annual Navajo Studies Conference. Participants were bused to the Ganado Chapter House. The only other attendees were teachers and local hospital employees. Many weavers attended the auction, and more than one hundred rugs were "registered." Many of the smaller rugs did not receive minimum bids. Four finely woven large rugs entered at a minimum of $2,000 were purchased by the local trader, who now operates Hubbell Trading Post for the Park Service. Had these rugs been offered through a gallery in a tourist hot spot, the retail prices may have averaged more than $6,000.

Evidence from varying sources reveals the drop in demand from dealers and the public at large for contemporary Navajo weaving. Interviews with weavers, traders, and off-reservation dealers corroborate the downturn in the market for contemporary weaving. One southern Colorado dealer who was on a panel at the Heard Museum conference in 1994 admitted that "the market is no longer there." In the recent past he frequently declined to purchase fine textiles brought to him by excellent weavers, as their previous creations remain in his stockroom. In an interview in 1993, another dealer remarked to me that there was no question the investment market in historic textiles was harming the market for contemporary weaving. Chuck Jackson of Dunning's Auction Service commented that contemporary Indian pieces are more difficult to sell (*Indian Trader* 5/90:33). The ailing arts industry was the topic of discussion at the first Navajo Arts and Crafts Forum held in June 1998 (*Indian Trader* 6/98:8–9). The Navajo Arts and Crafts Enterprise board passed a resolution requesting the Navajo Nation Council to explore the possibility of a Navajo trademark to fight proliferation of fakes and imports. Publications on contemporary weaving frequently mention knockoffs but primarily in the context of "buyer beware," demonstrating concern for authenticity and neglecting to note the threat to weavers' livelihood (Dockstader 1987b:43).

In May 1998 residents of the Chilchinbeto, Arizona, Chapter on the Navajo Reservation sent "Little Sister" to Sotheby's in an attempt to save their medical clinic. The Indian Health Service had reduced funding to the clinic, which serves twelve thousand people. The second largest rug in existence, at 28 x 26 feet, it took a dozen women nearly a year to weave. Because of its size and quality, Navajos hoped it would bring $3.5 million, enough money to provide an endowment to cover the $300,000 annual operating costs. Although the rug had been woven as an insurance policy to protect the clinic, Sotheby's reported no bidders. Spokesperson Ellen Taubman expressed regret that the auction house had been unable to help the Navajos (*Arizona Star* 5/20/98).

Worried Weavers' Voices

An interview with a Navajo woman temporarily residing in Phoenix provides a sobering example of the economic squeeze endured by weavers. This woman comes from a family of relatively well-known weavers and jewelers. In 1991 she accompanied her sister to a large off-reservation dealer of Navajo rugs. Her sister had woven a small fine rug (2 x 3 feet) of her own hand-spun yarn with an intricate pattern. The gallery owner inquired how much she thought her rug was worth. The woman replied, "$600." He answered, "You've got to be kidding—I'll give you $25." Shocked, they turned to leave, and he said, "Well, I'll give you $50."

Unfortunately, such stories are not rare. I documented several other cases in which weavers were offered the equivalent of a nickel an hour for their textiles. Weavers also admitted that traders and dealers compared their rugs to those of other weavers and commented on the continual need for "improvement" to perfect their weaving. The latter comment is corroborated in statements made by weavers interviewed as part of an oral history project in the Ganado area in the 1970s and 1980s. I have heard it from weavers myself. It appears to be a standard refrain used by traders and dealers to pressure women to accept less cash or goods in exchange for their textiles. Although weavers resent traders making derogatory comments about their work in comparison to textiles woven by other Navajos, there is little they can do about it.[16] Dealers also caution buyers about commissioning rugs directly from weavers, relating horror stories about unsuccessful attempts (Montgomery 1982:27; Trevathan 1997:37). Such rhetoric appearing in popular publications perpetuates dealers' control over marketing weavers' creations.

Periodically, weavers' stories surface about the meager return they receive for their textiles. During my field interviews in 1992, I was told on several occasions, either through interpreters or directly by weavers, how they remember their mothers' weavings being put on the wool scale (this happened as recently as 1968). In one incident, a woman currently acknowledged as a master weaver, who raised her eleven children by her weaving, needed cash when her husband required medical attention. She had spent nearly a year spinning wool from her own sheep, then dyeing and weaving a 9-x-12-foot rug. Several traders refused to pay her cash, insisting on trade. In 1967 the trader at Black Hat paid her $250 for the rug. Today a similar rug of superb quality woven of hand-spun wool would sell for more than $20,000 in a gallery. In figure 16, Susie Hosteen is pictured standing in front of her rug that was completed in 1955. She received a wagon and a case of milk from the trader in exchange for the rug. A number of weavers I interviewed over the years said they have told Anglos about "pound blankets and rugs" woven by themselves or their relatives, but people do not believe them.

The fluctuating collectors' market in historic Navajo weaving has affected contemporary weavers for nearly a century. This would not be cause for concern had Navajo weaving ceased. However, an estimated thirty thousand weavers reside on the reservation today (Malone 1997). Current interest in historic weaving focuses on individual textiles and their provenance and pedigree while ignoring the systemic economic problems, both past and present, which are severe. Hundreds of pounds of documents provide evidence of the conditions endured by Navajo weavers to provision their households (Hubbell Papers, Babbitt Brothers Papers, Fred Harvey Company Rug Ledgers). This evidence is ignored, while museologists continue to order, dissect, and classify by determining the kinds of dyes and yarns, the number of warps and wefts, and the types of fleece used in historic textiles. Such information accompanied by art world rhetoric occupies center stage and neglects the political-economic domain. The stories of the makers of these historic blankets that now bring so much money have literally been swept under the rug. Instead, extant literature continues to valorize the quixotic relationship between traders and weavers (James [1976] 1988; Kaufman and Selser 1985; Kent 1985; McNitt 1962; Rodee 1981, 1987; Underhill [1956] 1983). We have just seen how both the investment market and the "copy" weaving have precipitated the downturn in sales of contemporary weaving. Museums and galleries highlight treasures saved from a destructive history, relics from a vanishing world (see Muhlert 1976).[17] That it has not vanished is painfully evident in a poignantly illustrated article in a recent issue in *U.S. News and World Report* on the topic of poverty on Indian reservations (Satchell and Bowermaster 1994:61–64). No doubt there is a correlation between the persistent poverty on the reservation and the consistently inadequate returns to most Navajo weavers.

Many Navajo weavers are out of the loop. Faced with formidable competition from the investment and knockoff markets in tandem with their sophisticated advertisements featured on Web sites, many reservation weavers are increasingly disadvantaged as no infrastructure exists to aid them in marketing their textiles. The sixty-four-page *Southwest Indian Foundation* catalog of Indian-made goods contains many pages featuring jewelry but none featuring Navajo textiles. The Smithsonian Institution hosted an international textile symposium in spring 1999; Navajo weavers were conspicuously absent. Navajo weavers make up less than 3 percent of more than one thousand exhibitors at the Santa Fe Indian Market held in August each year. In contrast, a handful of non-Navajo weavers from New Mexico are profiled in an informative Web site, *The Thread of New Mexico*. It provides vignettes on six tapestry weavers, including two whose large wall hangings were commissioned for public buildings throughout the state. A common thread runs through the artists' narratives as they describe how the landscape and

Figure 16. Susie Hosteen Lee of Tselani Springs, 1955, photo from the collection of Marletha Suzanne Harvey and Anderson Harvey family.

patterns of the region's early residents have influenced their work. Although Navajo weavers' voices are absent, historic Navajo patterns are very much present. Nancy Kozikowski's *Red Chief's Blanket* measures 8 x 30 feet and covers one wall of the Bernalillo County Courthouse in Albuquerque. James Koehler's four-part *Ceremonial Masks* covers a large wall on the first level of the new State Library and Archives building in Santa Fe. Koehler has also produced a separate *Chief Blanket* series. Although thousands of Navajo weavers live in northwestern New Mexico, they remain absent from the roster of artists chosen to create commissioned works (http://www.collectorsguide.com/fa/fao36.shtml).

This is not to say that Navajo weavers are never involved in commissioned work. Several years ago an Anglo friend midwifed the production of thirteen rugs by eight reservation weavers to be featured in a large Southwest hotel undergoing renovation. The interior decorator in charge of the project notified the owners that she had arranged to have attractive but inexpensive Navajo-patterned rugs woven abroad. The owners balked, realizing how inappropriate it would be to feature Navajo knockoffs in the hotel's new wing. My friend volunteered to work with weavers willing to create rugs with a variety of patterns and sizes dyed with vegetal dyes and woven with hand-spun yarns. Although her initial budget was very modest, the owners cut it by 50 percent. The largest rug, measuring 5 x 8 feet, with a finely woven pattern, took two weavers five months to produce. They received less than $1,500 for their efforts. Commissioning the authentic product is a laudable endeavor; however, the hotel owners acquired them at knockoff prices.

During the 1980 seminar on historic Navajo weaving held in Santa Fe for 150 collectors, dealers, and textile experts, Rain Parrish, curator at the Wheelwright Museum and at the time the only Navajo in attendance, reminded her audience,

> We must, when we look at Navajo weaving, think back to the Blessing Way, back to the daughter placed in the cradle beside the mother's loom. We are thinking [here] too much of weaving in terms of money as the end product for the Navajo woman. Rather I would like to see the Anglo supporting the cultural identity of the Navajo and our ritual life cycle. You must be careful not to be pompous in terms of what you think you know of the Navajo lifestyle. You must not impose upon the Navajo what you feel is best for our culture. (Emmanuel 1980:33)

Parrish's eloquent statement provides the theme of the next chapter—the value of weaving for Navajo weavers, a topic relegated to a footnote in the vast literature on Navajo culture.

7

Toward an Understanding of Navajo Aesthetics

Art and beauty are integral to life, [whereas] in the West, art is seen as part of "high culture." No word exists in the hundreds of Native American languages that comes close to our definition of art. What does this mean? Indians did not set out to create art for its own sake. . . . Art, beauty and spirituality are so firmly intertwined in the routine of living that no words are needed to separate them.

Walters 1989:17

In Western aesthetics, emphasis is on the finished product. In Navajo society, one experiences beauty in creating and expressing, not in preserving and possessing. The construction of Navajo culture is learned through interaction[,] . . . through songs, stories and prayers.

Thomas 1994

My mother always wove, and raised her children through her weaving. . . . [I]t makes you a person, it makes you who you are. . . . [T]his is art, this is life. (Roessel 1994)

With few exceptions, prevailing discourses emphasize Navajo textiles as commodities. The Anglo-American concept of the functions of textiles shaped their perceptions of what a blanket or rug "means." The popularity of the Navajo rug as a "collectible" has obscured the importance of weaving to Navajo people and has also diminished our understanding of Navajo aesthetics, including the process of weaving. Most non-Navajos read or write about Navajo weaving, fitting it into their own cognitive frameworks. With few exceptions, they fail to see it as part of a circuit of relationships in which Navajos are themselves embedded. Textile experts and museologists subject individual textiles to detailed, even microscopic analyses (Kent 1985; Spencer 1989; Wheat 1989,

1990). An elaborate typology has been developed as an aid to classification. These methodologies are reported to facilitate the discovery of the "elusive" Navajo aesthetic (Hedlund 1989a; Kent 1985). In a recent publication documenting the struggles of First Nations women, Anna Lee Walters explains why scholars have had difficulty understanding native lifeworlds:

> Modern American society for the most part has passed through a western education system that breaks down lifestyles and the cycles of the cultures and lifestyles exposed to it into the smallest units for study and examination, habitually separating politics from social life, medicine from education. . . . [I]n much the same way academic disciplines or areas of specialization are now separated or viewed in our everyday life, and this fragmentation will prevent anyone from perceiving tribal lifestyles on this continent as they were a century or a millennium ago. In more traditional tribal lifestyles these cultural aspects have been fully integrated with each other. (1993:12)

As the latter portion of this chapter reveals, Navajo weavers' feeling for hózhǫ́ (beauty, harmony, local order) encompasses far more than the Western concept of "classical aesthetics," which condenses and locates "beauty" in an isomorphic object (Witherspoon 1977, 1987; Witherspoon and Peterson 1995). The classical perspective privileges the object in the external world isomorphic to the form or image that current aesthetic taste represents as "beautiful" or containing quality. In contrast, Navajo aesthetics emphasizes patterns of relations. Rather than privilege typology, Navajo aesthetics appears topological, with the patterns of interconnections that emerge through weaving of primary significance. In their own statements, weavers express, maintain, and perpetuate hózhǫ́ through their weaving, and such activities relate to their cosmology.

In the Navajo Creation Story, weaving plays a pivotal role in the origin and maintenance of the Navajo people. Their Creation Story defines meaningful social relationships among members of the community and between the community and the entire cosmos. These relationships are still very real and important to many Navajos (Faris 1993; Griffin-Pierce 1992). Navajo cosmology provides the charter for proper social behavior. Few publications on Navajo weaving acknowledge the links between social relations and cosmology, for the reasons revealed in Walters's statement. Historically, anthropologists categorized weaving as a secular, functional activity vis-à-vis the sacred sphere of Navajo ceremonials.[1] Such bifurcation reflects the larger dualisms discussed earlier.

In the voluminous literature on Navajos, ethnographers such as Reichard repeatedly use terms such as "religion," "sacred," "ceremony," and "ritual" to describe practices engaged in by medicine men. The use of such terms, however, connotes a division between the sacred and secular spheres that is alien to many Navajos (Kelley and Francis 1994:9; Ortiz 1999). Similarly, Navajo weavers do not categorize weaving as secular, but they do express reluctance to discuss matters relating to the sacred. Thus it is important to focus on the differences in perception about the "Navajo aesthetic." Statements of Navajo weavers differ markedly from those of scholars in the literature on Navajo weaving.

The Aesthetics of Navajo Weaving: Anthropologists' Perspectives

The Rug as Functional Commodity

Texts on Navajo weaving frequently begin with a description of the mythological origins of the loom and weaving tools excerpted from the Navajo Creation Story:

> Spider Woman instructed the Navajo women how to weave on a loom which Spider Man told them how to make. The crosspoles were made of sky and earth cords, the warp sticks of sun rays, the healds of rock crystal and sheet lightning. The batten was a sun halo, white shell made the comb. There were four spindles: one a stick of zigzag lightning with a whorl of cannel coal; one a stick of flash lightning with a whorl of turquoise; a third had a stick of sheet lightning with a whorl of abalone; a rain streamer formed the stick of the fourth, and its whorl was white shell. (Reichard [1934] 1974:title page)

As we have seen, most ethnographers sanctioned the categorization of functional objects created by indigenous peoples as "nonsacred" craft commodities produced for an external market. Such a designation is generally acknowledged as reflecting the actual circumstances, as Native Americans sought ways to increase their incomes (Phillips 1998). Because the epistemology that justifies this view still informs many researchers in the field, it is impossible to critique it without adopting a very different perspective.

Like her contemporary Ruth Bunzel, Gladys Reichard was one of the few anthropologists to undertake long-term studies of a craft. She continued her research on social organization and ritual life of the Navajos as a weaver-apprentice through the 1930s. Reichard was a master of poetic description and a keen observer who produced three books during the 1930s specifically on Navajo weaving (Frazier 1993). In these texts she weaves the story of her frustrating apprenticeship into the daily activities, religious ceremonials, excursions, and festivities that make up the annual cycle of Navajo life. The rich detail in her texts appears to provide the reader with a holistic, insightful view into another lifeworld. She comments on the unceasing cooperation and reciprocity among Navajos. When she spoke of weavers' feelings about their work, Reichard couched them in terms of Western aesthetics associated with decorative design. That is, a certain percentage of weavers in the tribe were "real artists . . . who would experiment with colors for hours" (Reichard [1936] 1968:27). Although Reichard ([1934] 1974) excerpts a portion of the Navajo Creation Story, she seldom refers back to Navajo cosmology in her account of the trials and tribulations of learning to spin and weave. One of the striking aspects of her texts on the subject concerns the ease with which weaving is incorporated into Navajo daily domestic life, unlike the sacred time when the hogan is purified and male chanters create the elaborate sand paintings in preparation for a ceremony. Such a perceived demarcation appears to fulfill Mircea Eliade's contrast between mythical time and religion (the sacred past) and the profane, historical present (Kelley and Francis 1994:189–90). Until 1939 Reichard's fieldwork took place in the summer, when Navajos never share stories (Lyon 1989). However, in her texts she refers to activities or taboos related to weaving and incorporates them as bits of folklore.

Noting that weavers and other handworkers never receive enough financial compensation, Reichard ([1936] 1968:186) comments on the inappropriateness of emphasizing the commercial component. She remarks that satisfaction gained creating a beautiful object should be considered equally important. Yet in other portions of her texts, Reichard notes that weaving provides the only income for some Navajo families.[2]

Reichard (1950:xix) perceived traders as businessmen and catalysts for arts and crafts production. While admitting that she could never make her living as a weaver, she approved of traders' insistence on greater technical perfection in weaving ([1934] 1974:32–33; [1936] 1968:141).

The Symbolic World of the Sacred

In her magnum opus, *Navajo Religion*, Reichard (1950) provides a synthesis of Navajo religion by developing an account "which takes up the function of each element in a highly elaborated whole." An extensive dictionary of symbols provides the function and position of implements, names, Holy People, and ritual paraphernalia. She notes how diverse elements are frequently combined in a unit. As Navajo religion is a philosophy of life and preservation, "the scheme may be compared to a language" (1950:147).

In a short text devoted to Navajo prayer, Reichard (1944) provides a moment-by-moment description of a Navajo ceremony, giving remarkable detail about Navajo chants. In its prolific and rhythmic repetition, prayer demonstrates reverence for order and form (1944:14). Prayers also celebrate the beauty of the landscape. Navajo categories are inclusive rather than exclusive, maintaining an essential unity in all things. The most unexpected things are associated, such as lightning, snakes, arrows, wind, and clouds. All these diverse things occupy the same class, associated in function. Such classifications differ sharply from Euro-American thinking, which distinguishes classes based on uniqueness and distinctiveness (1944:4). Navajo religion is perceived as a huge compilation of elements from which each innovator may choose depending on the notion he wishes to emphasize. Prayer is an unending system of symbolic associations that cannot be considered free. They are too orderly and depend on decree. Prayer may exist without words; for example, strewing pollen is a form of prayer. As Reichard comments:

> Prayers are organized in complicated patterns. The chanter must learn it by hearing the whole. If there is repetition it is of the whole, no words are to be spoken out of its setting. . . . [I]t is learned in its entirety or not at all. Although prayer is only a small element of the complex to which it belongs . . . he [the chanter] constantly reiterates in myth, ritual, teaching and practice that its oneness be preserved. (1944:8, 12)

Reichard perceived symbols as cognized isomorphic elements relevant to the sacred sphere of elaborate Navajo ceremonials. She defines a symbol as "a design unit or even an entire composition which has a definite emotional content or meaning, immediately and spontaneously recognized by a group of people" ([1936] 1968:178). Juxtaposed to this definition is a page of symbols including crosses, hourglasses, and arrows.

The Nonsymbolic World of the Secular
Reichard notes that silverwork and weaving were borrowed fairly recently from Mexican and Pueblo sources, adopted for primarily economic reasons. Thus weaving and silversmithing never became thoroughly integrated into the spiritual life of the tribe:

> [There is a] lack of imagination with regard to designs used on things the Navajo sell. . . . They have a well-worked-out symbolism with functions generally understood in their religious life. . . . [Sacred] symbols

represent to the people who believe in them, supernatural power. That power may be mistreated; if it is used too much, it "wears out." Who, understanding this attitude, would expect its owners to give it away? For that is what selling a blanket or a piece of silver with "sacred patterns" means. ([1936] 1968:181–82)

Horses were acquired from the Spaniards recently too, but a Navajo never gave up his horses; they were traded with his own people. Rugs and smithing were different.[3] They were always traded with outsiders: "They never became packed with the emotional content typical of their most important activity, religion" ([1936] 1968:182). Although Navajos lack a word for religion, Reichard categorizes activities associated with rituals as "religious." Both color and motif have meaning or emotional content in the religious act of sand painting. She explains:

The Navajo have kept the symbolic designs of their religion apart, in a separate compartment of their minds, from their ordinary blanket and silverwork patterns. The form occasionally overlaps; the emotions are kept distinct. (Reichard [1936] 1968:183)

With few exceptions, such statements sanction the eventual development of a pragmatic approach to explaining the persistence of Navajo weaving. By the time Reichard wrote her ethnography, *Spider Woman, a Story of Navajo Weavers and Chanters* ([1934] 1974), Navajo textiles had been marketed by weight for more than fifty years.[4] Reichard claims that trader and market influences relegated weaving to the secular domain. Her research is considered definitive in its depth and breadth, and anthropologists currently working in the field continue to quote her. During a personal interview, a noted authority supports Reichard's thesis concerning the secular nature and lack of symbolism in weaving while maintaining that "the activity of weaving and the names for the weaving tools take you right to the heart of Navajo religion" (1991, field notes).

Thus Reichard was convinced that weaving was a "profane" activity, unlike the sacred sand paintings created by the medicine men. Navajo medicine men perpetuate religion and culture in the spiritual realm, while Navajo women provide material sustenance by weaving commodities. Both are functional activities in their respective spheres. Therefore, a balance appears to be created. But Reichard bifurcates Navajo social relations and practices through dualistic labeling. Because of this proposed split, her ethnography provides support for the treatment of Navajo textiles as commodity collectibles by many anthropologists and museologists (Dutton 1975, 1983; Ellis 1974; Hedlund 1983, 1986, 1997; Kent 1976, 1981,

1985; Kluckhohn and Leighton 1974; Lamphere 1977; Tanner 1968; Underhill [1956] 1983; Wheat 1976a, 1976b, 1977, 1981, 1984, 1988).[5] However, several recent publications by Navajos provide more nuanced interpretations (Begay 1994, 1996; Tabaha 1999; Thomas 1996; Willink and Zolbrod 1996).

A Counterinterpretation: Gary Witherspoon and Semiotic Geometry

Witherspoon provides an alternative interpretation of the continuation of Navajo weaving. Rather than emphasize its commodity aspects, he suggests that weaving has played a major role in perpetuating Navajo lifeways (1987). He argues for an interpretive approach, in that the vigor and endurance of Navajo people is culturally inspired, not materially determined. Weaving continues regardless of financial compensation; therefore, economics is not the primary motivation. According to Witherspoon (1981:31), the dominant theme in Navajo aesthetics is creative synthesis, and the Navajo essence of beauty, hózhǫ, is simultaneously moral, physiological, philosophical, and emotional. Order is based on the pairing of contrasting but complementary elements. Hózhǫ encompasses order, harmony, health, peace, and blessing (Faris 1986:138).[6] For Navajos, positive health involves far more than a physiological dimension; it entails proper relationships to everything in one's environment. The goal of Navajo life is to live to maturity in the condition described as hózhǫ and to die of old age. Kluckhohn commented on the difficulty in translating Navajo words into English because the latter lacks terms that simultaneously have moral and aesthetic meanings (cited in Witherspoon 1983a:572).

In contrast to previous interpretations, Witherspoon (1987) claims that Navajo women have woven (and continue to weave) archetypal symbols of Navajo cosmology. The hourglass motif he identifies as "Changing Woman" forms the outline of figures 3 and 4 (I have exaggerated the upper portions of the figures). These symbols are found in petroglyphs, adult hairstyles, and ritual paraphernalia. Forms and patterns have changed over time, but the underlying motifs remain distinctly Navajo. Navajo weaving has not lost its identity or its creative autonomy even though it underwent a period of Pueblo absorption and Spanish influence before the appearance of Anglo traders and markets. Navajos were neither diminished nor destroyed by more numerous, more powerful, and technologically superior societies (Witherspoon 1987:4).

Witherspoon claims the primary metaphysical assumption on which the Navajo worldview is built is the opposition between static and active phases of phenomena. This dualism pervades all Navajo material culture: energy, activity, and motion constantly recur in Navajo sand paintings, ritual music, and weaving. The dualism of the passive male principle and the active female principle is expressed by maintaining hózhǫ through rigid adherence to formulaic ritual and the more fluid productive-reproductive activities. Both ritual activity and weavers' artistic compositions express, accentuate, and celebrate the inherent beauty and magnificence of the universe (Witherspoon 1987:103).

Witherspoon's interpretive analysis reveals far more about the relations of Navajo society and culture that are implicated in textile design and production than all the tabulating, classifying, and dating of Navajo artifacts favored by typologists. Although he has made major contributions to explicating Navajo kinship, social organization, and language, he is soundly criticized for arguing for the existence of meaning in Navajo weaving. In the publication devoted to the legacy of the museologist Kate Peck Kent, Wheat notes that Kent was unable to find a single aesthetic that bound all Navajo weaving together, whereas

> Gary Witherspoon . . . sees every design as having derived from Navajo religion—every terraced or stepped element represents a Navajo religious figure, but the examples he chooses are so far-fetched as to have little credibility. (1989:30)

In the same publication, Hedlund describes Witherspoon's perception of the Navajo aesthetic style as "one of dynamic symmetry based on the idea of similar and complementary but inexact, imperfect and unequal pairing or balancing. Navajo woven designs are said to demonstrate a unity of diversity, a synthesis of differences, a harmony of divergence and a confluence of contrast" (1989a:26) Hedlund (1989a:26) disagrees with Witherspoon, stating that his "poetic interpretation of form makes little contribution to our understanding of ethnoaesthetics." Thus Hedlund and Wheat perceive Witherspoon's research as overly structuralist and antiempiricist.[7]

Counterdiscussions from Navajo Perspectives

Until 1996 only a handful of publications explicitly linked weaving to Navajo cosmology and kinship in a nondualistic manner. That is, there was no split between the secular domestic sphere and the sacred religious sphere as exemplified in Reichard's ethnographies.[8] Two texts, by the Navajo weaver and educator Ruth Roessel (1981) and her husband, Robert Roessel (1983a), demonstrate how the Creation Story provides a charter for behavior, with weaving as an important component. Ruth Roessel writes:

> Navajo women are basic to the understanding of Navajo life and culture.

We women are the heart and center of our society. If there is no teaching of Navajo life to our children there will be no future for the Navajo people. We, the Navajo women, must know the role and traditions of Navajo culture so that we can carry and pass it on. Countless generations ago, when things were out of hand, Changing Woman came and taught the Navajo the right ways. We now need to bring her teachings to our children. (1981:ix)

Changing Woman, the genitrix of the Navajo people, is an exemplary model; she represents all that is good and right. Roessel speaks of Changing Woman and crops as having similar cycles. Women are very important in perpetuating the growth of corn and other plants. Roessel feels that the extensive literature by non-Navajos has not emphasized this enough. Some Navajos say as long as they have corn and Kinaaldá (the female puberty ritual), they have nothing to worry about.[9] Roessel devotes an entire chapter to the Holy People's instructions on child rearing. Women show their daughters how to cook, spin, and weave. These activities and other family responsibilities are learned by observing and doing. The word "teach" is a very recent addition to the Navajos' vocabulary.

Robert Roessel begins his *Navajo Arts and Crafts* by describing how Spider Woman taught Changing Woman to weave. Weaving provided clothing, so that Navajos would not suffer from the cold. The Holy People recognized women who wove and properly respected their tools. Another Navajo value is reflected in weaving: the mother's industriousness. All this refers back to the original lessons Changing Woman learned from Spider Woman. Weaving perpetuates kin relations as directed by the Holy People. Loom weaving expresses the Navajo philosophy of hózhǫ́. Roessel concludes that weaving will never die out because it is a vital and dynamic part of Navajo life and culture. However, many non-Navajo authorities predicted the demise of weaving (Amsden [1934] 1975; Kent 1985; Maxwell [1963] 1984; Tanner 1968; Weiss 1984). Because it is such a labor-intensive activity with little financial return and because more Navajo women are attending school, it is assumed the practice will be abandoned.

The Rug As a Way of Life for Navajos

In my interviews of weavers over a seven-week period in fall 1992, I found that they universally spoke about relationships. They linked cosmology, kinship solidarity, harmony, and process. Weavers' statements support the Roessels' perspective but contrast sharply with most published literature on Navajo textiles.[10]

Indeed, most ethnographies that cover Navajo weaving lack any information that is relevant to interpreting my informants' statements.

Several weavers remarked that weaving is a very emotional skill that is difficult to talk about. Sometimes weavers make direct reference to the landscape. A weaver, looking out from her hogan at the beautiful colors, may see a "rug" of many shades. One weaver said:

> Life grows out of the land, woman grows out of the earth, the Beautyway. . . . Women change the world. [They] rear sheep, shear sheep, and weave all the movements and tensions into a rug.

Another weaver remarked that art provides a chance to experience "hózhǫ́, beauty, harmony," that "there's a song, story, and prayer behind each rug." Another weaver repeated the phrase and added, "And they are all from the spider."

Grace Joe (fig. 17), a weaver in her eighties, told me a story (through a translator) that her mother had told her:

> Long ago a woman named Mary got frustrated with her weaving—just couldn't weave, so she cut up her weaving and threw it toward the east. A few days later she heard singing. . . . She traveled toward the sounds and found her rug singing. She brought it back and started weaving toward all directions. The song came from her weaving, and the loom frame and tools were making the music.

Several other weavers and other Navajos also knew this story, with variations. One woman said that the weaver's tools began to cry when she threw them away. When she picked them up again, they began to sing. Another weaver remarked that the weaver's frustration was "a lesson in itself." In a follow-up interview with a weaver who spoke no English, I told this story and her sister-in-law translated. Suddenly the woman became very excited and began to speak very quickly in Navajo: "There's a song for everything [she picked up her spindle], for spinning, for weaving, and they're all from the spider." She admitted she prays all the time too. She is Christian, but she also goes to the medicine man when necessary. Both women emphasized that it is important for Navajos to keep animals and to weave. One of them said, "We don't know what is going to happen in the future. We must raise animals, grow food, and provide for our families."

One interview took place at the Heard Museum with a woman who was an intern. Her family still lives on the reservation and has been weaving for generations. She spoke about "feeding your weaving tools" with white

Figure 17. Grace Joe, Red Valley, Arizona, fall 1992. Photo by Kathy M'Closkey.

cornmeal (which is also given to the bride in the Navajo wedding ceremony; yellow cornmeal is given to the groom). Pregnant with her first child, she remarked that it is important to leave a rug unfinished just before one's child is born, so one doesn't "close up the opening." Weaving is part of the "normal cycle" of life: "If you don't have a loom set up, you'll lose money, there won't be enough to eat." She will not reveal stories or songs because "it diminishes one's abilities."

A young Navajo woman, an accomplished weaver, who was interviewed while working at a trading post told me that her grandmother warned her it is bad luck to tell stories—especially to whites. Her mother, who died recently, had told her:

> With these hands, you can make money. . . . Your hands will bring you wealth. . . . The more complicated designs a weaver does, the brighter she is. . . . Weavers who don't do complicated designs are dull.

Some weavers express reluctance to teach non-Navajos. Several weavers remarked that they dream their patterns. Others said as young girls they were told, "This is what our creator gave to you to support your family."

The richest interview lasted six hours and involved a mother, her daughter, and her daughter's husband. A weaver in her sixties, Susie raised her eleven children by weaving (figs. 18, 19; see also fig. 16). She was told not to tell the weaving stories that her grandfather related on winter evenings: "If you tell others, it diminishes the value of your work. . . . They take it away from you." Susie told her daughter (who translated) that she cannot talk about this to non-Navajos. "All of it begins at creation with Spider Woman. The rug is sacred—enfolded. . . . There is wealth in it. . . . Our hearts are in it." Susie had a sacred ceremony done for her, so it was easier for her to weave. A wise weaver is chosen to press weaving tools on the young girl during her Kinaaldá: "This will be her life. . . . It will bless her/pray for her." Susie no longer goes to medicine men now because she is a Christian, but "the weaving part is in her heart." (See figs. 20, 21.) She said, "Traders don't care about sacred songs." Her daughter continued:

> When you weave you don't go by the hour, by time. . . . You weave your rug in your mind. . . . Even to feel the touch of the rug is sacred. . . . There's a song to go over the weaving after it's finished, but one cannot talk about it. . . . The thoughts and ideas of the original weaver are in the rug. . . . It must not be touched [i.e., repaired], nor should one copy another's pattern.

Another weaver adamantly opposed repairing old Navajo textiles: "It's best to leave the rug alone. . . . It's like an old man or an old woman—you can't renew them. . . . One must weave an entire [new] piece."

Several weavers mentioned that they prayed and asked for help when first starting a rug. When you want an intricate design, it is difficult to think it through. Few weavers I spoke with sketch their designs. Several weavers mentioned it is not good to think bad thoughts or speak negatively near a loom, especially when a rug is on it. A few others said they feel like they are "selling their minds" when they sell their rugs. I was also told that "any pattern in a Navajo rug is 'Navajo.'" One man married to a weaver told me that when he sees the hourglass pattern, all sorts of things pop into his head. Another Navajo

Figure 18. Susie Hosteen on a horse, 1944, photo from the collection of Marletha Suzanne Harvey and Anderson Harvey family.

man said that his mother told him her weaving made the sheep and goats happy because she is using their wool. And a third man said, "My mom's rugs put food on the table."

Few of the weavers interviewed were comfortable weaving Yeis, or sand painting blankets. Most of the weavers who make them are from the Four Corners—Shiprock area. A number of these women have had "sings," special ceremonies that ensure protection. Almost all other weavers I interviewed said that one's eyesight would suffer if one were to weave those kinds of blankets. Regardless of their age, many of the weavers interviewed through the Park Service interpreter during the 1980s made similar statements.

Another woman in her thirties, with six children, learned to weave from her grandmother when she was six years old. She gave it up while attending school. After her grandmother died in 1984, she began weaving again. Once she was given a rug to copy and had a very difficult time of it. Strong "vibrations" came

Figure 19. Home beneath Tselani Springs, Arizona, 1955, photo from the collection of Marletha Suzanne Harvey and Anderson Harvey family.

off the picture: "The weaver of it didn't want me to do it." She finished the rug and gave it to the client. He paid her so little she was very upset. She never copies at all now. Every three or four months her grandmother comes to her in her dreams and shows her rug designs. Some have blue ribbons. This is how Sarah came up with the design for her "Beyond Native Tradition." This 7-x-10-foot rug incorporates more than twenty Navajo patterns superimposed on a Burntwater pattern given to her by her grandmother in a dream. She will not teach non-Navajo women to weave. However, she has shown all of her daughters. Sarah's grandmother told her, "This is what our Creator gave to you to support your family. I have taught you and you can do what you like, but do not teach others."

The former director of the Office of Navajo Women and Families has woven for decades. During an interview, she told me that if things "aren't right" in a weaver's life, her weaving gets "mixed up." The weaver knows where problems are. "When things are going smoothly, when family relations are right, the weaving is always beautiful." Vangie said that when women weave a "storm pattern," family members know that things are out of kilter, so they talk about it and try to sort things out. "Lately so many things are changing, families [are] splitting up. . . . [The] family network isn't there like it used to be. This is hard on everyone." She made statements similar to other weavers:

> When one is at her weaving, you don't think about time, it just doesn't matter. . . . Because the weaving is beautiful, it will bring the weaver beautiful things. . . . Women develop patterns in their minds.

In the Park Service rug study interviews (1985–86), a well-known weaver related the story of how Changing Woman had difficulty learning how to spin:

> The spindle goes toward you. . . . Your mind and prayers are connected to it. Medicine men have ceremonial doings for it in the happy way. . . . If you want to be a weaver, learn the whole process, [it's] the only way it will work.

Another weaver who is also a medicine woman was interviewed through an interpreter in the same series. She remarked that she always prays and asks for help when she first starts a rug, as it takes lots of time to think through how to weave intricate designs. She loves the art of weaving. It is the first thing in her heart; she does not search for other ways to support herself. "You have to take good care of your tools. You keep them for your grandchildren to use." She

Figure 20. Susie Hosteen Lee, 1996. Photo by Kathy M'Closkey.

Figure 21.
Susie Hosteen Lee surrounded by her family: (back row) Julia, Shirleen with Cody, Susie, Michelle, Elouise, Marletha Suzanne, Charlotte, Dale; (center row) Pam, Nigel, Nathan; (front row) Talia, Charmaine, Toni, Ronda, Cherilyn, Brian Sha'nah, Rodney, Janelle. Photo from the collection of Marletha Suzanne Harvey and Anderson Harvey family.

won't weave Yeis, sand painting rugs, or repair old rugs. During my interview with her in 1992, she admitted to weaving reproductions, but she does not like to do them because "the weaver's thoughts are in that old rug."

If you copy or repair rugs woven by someone who is dead, the medicine men say that you can lose your eyesight or get sick. Leave old rugs the way they are, and notify people who are repairing them that they should not do it.

A Navajo weaver in his thirties offered his version of why Navajos weave:

They said that weaving was for the woman so she could stay home and spin and weave. The men had the job of taking care of the sheep. Both men and women shear the sheep. The lady would be at home weaving while the man was out hunting, hoeing in the field. She would be spinning and weaving and then there will be a blanket. From that there will be food again. That's how I know it and that's what I heard.

Both he and his wife enjoy weaving, but he has not made weaving tools "because you have to be a grandfather before you make those. Just the grandfathers made them. The babies could have a birth defect. . . . Only grandfathers make cradleboards too." He also remarked on why one should not weave Yei rugs:

Don't bother with it, you could lose your eyesight and lose your hearing. It could do anything it wants to you. . . . You would have to have all kinds of sings if you really want to do it. I guess [at] the next Yeibechai dance you should go look through the mask and then see how your Yeibechai rugs—if you put corn pollen out for it [if one is in your home] nothing will happen.

They weave in the spirit line. "You weave in your mind" if you fail to do this. And they do not weave after midnight:

Spider Woman did weave like that. From her everyone started weaving, . . . but you are not supposed to finish a rug at night, or weave after midnight. . . . [You] could lose your eyesight.

The Aesthetics of Navajo Weaving: Museologists' Perspectives

The perspective on Navajo aesthetics adopted by most museologists is derived from Reichard. Based on research spanning three decades, Kent maintained,

Rugs woven in this century will not tell us anything about Navajo personality or values because Anglo traders and markets have influenced Navajo weavers so much that any meanings or aesthetic styles which may have existed in early weavings were extinguished. . . . The search for a distinctive Navajo aesthetic ends with the onset of the Rug period. When weavers ceased to manufacture blankets for their own use and turned to the production of rugs for sale to whites, they accepted Anglo American standards of taste. (1985:111)

Kent (1985:105) acknowledged that most Navajos "value weaving as a distinct cultural attribute." She gained an understanding of the technological processes associated with weaving by replicating portions of specific archaeological or historic textiles (Spencer 1989). Kent's work was based on empirical descriptions of textiles in various public and private collections, in conjunction with analyses of archival and published documents on the subject. She did no ethnographic fieldwork. After examining hundreds of textiles, Kent found that "Navajo weavers struck a balance between eclecticism and originality" (1985:115). Thus her research was synthetic, as it involved the reconstruction of a historical chronology developed through empirical research on the products of material culture (Hedlund 1989a:23).

Kent (1985:109, 111) perceived the "Navajo aesthetic" as "a set of formal stylistic principles, associated with characteristics of style and standards of taste." She did not deny that Navajo designs may be based on a set of unconscious, culturally defined principles. Like Reichard, she noted that weavers have proven particularly adept at incorporating diverse materials, techniques, and designs influenced by Pueblo, Spanish, and Anglo sources. Paradoxically, the changing nature of Navajo textile design appears to be one of the major characteristics that ties together three hundred years of Navajo weaving. Navajos are described as opportunists, because they adopted a wide array of cultural traits from indigenous and Euro-American sources. Because weaving was "borrowed" from the Pueblos and the materials (principally wool) from the Spaniards, there were no cultural constraints concerning the adoption of foreign designs. In contrast, Pueblo textiles remained conservative, as they were woven for ceremonial purposes.

In an anthology devoted to tourist arts, Kent remarked:

Navajo weaving has no deep historical roots in cultural tradition. Essentially, it has always been a commercial link with other Indians, Spanish, and Anglo-Americans. As such, it has thrived on innovation, change, and outside contacts. (1976:101)

Both economic necessity and the desire to create are seen as the driving forces behind the continued production by Navajo weavers. Cultural meaning in either color or design is denied, although a weaver may ascribe a personal meaning to her particular design. Weavers' aesthetic judgments rest on technical skills as much as design. The process of textile production using specific tools and techniques is of greater significance than a particular set of aesthetic standards. Technique, in particular, becomes the common denominator that links the diversity of Navajo textile production over several centuries:

Harmony in color and balance in design structure are consistently named by Navajo critics themselves as the most important aesthetic imperatives of textile design. In addition, Navajos judge the aesthetic value of a rug on the basis of the weaver's technical skill. Evaluating an art object in terms of the technical skill with which it was made, rather than as a personal expression, is a widespread practice in nonwestern societies. This is because technical skills are variable and can be objectively assessed and compared. (Kent 1985:114)

Kent notes that harmony and balance are related to the aesthetics of color and design in individual textiles. However, she fails to perceive that these factors are vital aspects of Navajo culture in general.

Contemporary Navajo Weaving as "Art"

It is evident that empirical description has dominated Southwest textile studies for nearly a century. Most research has focused on creating a taxonomy by categorizing and cataloging Navajo weaving according to type. Detailed measurements, yarn types, dyes, designs, styles, provenance, and pedigree constitute much of the available information on Navajo weaving (Amsden [1934] 1975; Berlant and Kahlenberg 1977; Blomberg 1988; James [1976] 1988; Kent 1985; Rodee 1981, 1987; Wheat 1976a, 1976b, 1977, 1989). In more recent exhibitions there has been a shift from descriptions of the "loom-centered" rug to the weaver herself. Her biography comes to the fore; weaving is no longer discussed as craft but as an art form. Indeed, an exhibition of contemporary Navajo weaving that recently toured several major galleries in the United States had several textiles mounted on walls behind glass so they will be seen, from a contemporary Western perspective, as "fine art." A transition that parallels the shift of historic weaving from craft to art is under way for a portion of contemporary Navajo weaving. This recent shift in perception emphasizes the weaver as an individual who may in fact be providing for her family through selling her work but wishes to be seen as an artist and not as a craftsperson (Hedlund 1992). Given the attitudes and perceptions concerning the creation of "fine art" and the status that artists hold in North American society, this appears a fruitful way to ensure an increased financial return to a select number of weavers.

The current discourse about the transformation of contemporary Navajo weaving from craft to art also denies cultural meaning in the weaving; rather, the weaver as artist selects and rejects designs much as any other artist. Influenced by numerous sources, weavers seek to produce compositions that are harmonious in color and design. The search for a Navajo aesthetic, or sense of style exhibited in visual traits, is sought in the rug. In an essay highlighting the exhibition "Reflections of the Weaver's World," the aesthetics of modernism informs the curator's perspective:

> The rugs and tapestries are personal statements in themselves, if we can only learn to view them as such, instead of as a collectively and anonymously produced native craft items. . . . [T]he exhibition draws from the past while looking to the future. . . . Navajo rugs are works of art, valuable to the weavers and other viewers for their visual impact. . . . [R]ecognizing and acknowledging the Navajo artists as any mainstream artists might be, becomes important in order to get beyond biases toward Navajo weaving as craft, as trader-driven, as economically imperative, rather than as art and as individual visual statements of self. (Hedlund 1994a:32, 35)

According to curator-anthropologist Hedlund (1988:86), a greater understanding of Navajo aesthetics "from the native point of view" can be gained by examining "the internal, culturally empowered processes of designing, executing and evaluating handwoven products." In the late 1980s, Hedlund initiated a pilot project as an extension of much of her own research, which she describes as "an empirically based characterization of modern textile production focused on sociocultural and technological factors" (1989a:26). She developed a series of structured questions designed to elicit information on aesthetic and technological values. Weavers were asked to compare and contrast specific image triads. Weavers admitted that sources for designs generally come from their minds, or thoughts. Whiteford (1989:32) noted that Hedlund's pilot study is a carefully designed attempt to gather empirical data that may help to define the nature of Navajo aesthetics. Wheat (1989:30) concurred, noting that the design and perspective adopted in this type of research should provide "a reasoned and secure answer to the problem."

"Reflections of the Weaver's World" includes a set of flash cards with various Navajo designs. The written material accompanying the display defines ethnoaesthetics as "how different societies decide what makes a design look good or bad." Each textile is perceived as an aesthetic product of an individual self-conscious artist, the weaver as cultural trendsetter. This current perspective tethers contemporary Navajo weaving to gallery aesthetics. The construction of the history, display, and preservation of textiles reveals the views, values, and assumptions of the caretakers. Vogt's (1961) acculturation model continues to influence museologists' publications (Hedlund 1983, 1989a, 1989b, 1990; Kent 1985; Rodee 1981; Tanner 1968; Wheat 1977, 1984).

There are clues in the literature on the Navajos that aid in explicating Navajo aesthetics. But few emerge from the publications by museologists (Kent 1985; Rodee 1981; Wheat 1984). The patterns that museologists privilege are the empirical designs woven into individual rugs. Most extant histories of Navajo textiles reflect the imposition of Euro-American ideas. With the exception of Witherspoon's, the perspective adopted by most ethnographers and museologists continues to emphasize those aspects of textiles associated with their marketability. Statements by weavers who spoke (sometimes through translators) to an audience attending the 1994 conference "Navajo Weaving since the Sixties" provide a marked contrast to the non-Navajo perspectives previously described. They support those made by weavers I interviewed in 1992. Both emphasize the importance of weaving in linking themselves and their relations. The quantified values that emerge from non-Navajo commentary are entirely absent from their statements.

"Navajo Weaving since the Sixties"

The four-day conference "Navajo Weaving since the Sixties," hosted by the Heard Museum in March 1994 and held in conjunction with an exhibition of contemporary Navajo weaving touring the United States, was attended by more than forty Navajo weavers and their families.[11]

Hedlund had prepared a series of questions for the Navajo weaver-presenters. Each weaver was asked to define the parts of her weaving that she considered "traditional": "Is it the techniques, colors, finished products or designs?" "Today [weaving] is simultaneously sacred and sold. . . . [D]oes the term 'authentic' apply?" Navajo weaver-respondents had diverse reactions to this question.

Weavers Respond

One young weaver, Gloria Begay, said tradition is the process of weaving and that "tradition comes from within": "There is a story behind every weaving tool, it's very emotional. The finished product itself is a traditional part of an artistic piece, and there's a traditional story behind it." She mentioned cosmology. Her grandmother passed it down, and she remarked that one cannot pick out one part and say only it is traditional.

In response to the organizer's question about who or what had the greatest influence on their design choices, weavers emphasized friends and families. Considerable emphasis was placed on providing for families. Annie Kahn, a longtime weaver, said:

Weavers weave sunlight, the rain—[they] weave all this together with their hands. . . . [You] express and restore yourself through weaving. . . . [One] walks in beauty when one finishes weaving a rug. . . . [The process] feeds our soul.

Another weaver remarked, "If one weaves a Yei, one should use commercial yarns so power is subdued." In other words, one should avoid using hand-spun wool. Irene Clark spoke eloquently:

Weaving goes with prayers, songs. Thank Mother Earth for plants, for sky, the air, good feeling to dye. . . . It's all in the weaving, . . . in your hands, tools, in your mind. Design and coloring, how you think of yourself is how you weave—good thoughts, prayers, songs. When you start to weave, design comes in your mind, in your hands. Can't leave work unfinished. . . . It will watch you. . . . The weaving will teach you. . . . If you let your loom stand too long it will have pain, just like you when you stand too long!

Barbara Jean Teller Ornelas, a weaver in her forties, said, "When you first set up your loom it is like giving birth to your child. . . . [W]atch it grow, find a good home for it." Barbara is a Christian. She does not know the stories or legends but feels she is "born to be a weaver." It is her life; it has centered her. The family lived from rug to rug (along with loans) as she put her husband through pharmacy school. If she sees a rug she wove years ago, it "talks for itself" and reminds her of what her life was like at the time. Barbara has to weave every day, otherwise there's no harmony in her home. Her two children tell her, "Get to weaving so you won't be grouchy."

One weaver said every time she finishes a rug "it is like gaining knowledge of life itself." "I never finish learning." Another weaver said for her weaving is equivalent "to a complex college education." Sadie Curtis commented that the "weaving circle is made up of makers and buyers." Grace Henderson Nez, in her eighties, remarked on how you "get graded [by traders] on your weaving." She wonders if rugs aren't selling as well as they used to "because weavers are using commercial yarns."

Elsie Wilson was born in 1924. Her presentation was translated by her daughter. Elsie said:

Navajo respect whites. Whites have the means to buy, therefore weavers strive to do their best. If I were white, I'd take this as a compliment.

Elsie looks on us as relatives and told organizers: "It must be hard to represent a culture that's not your own and do it well."

Nanaba Midge Aragon has made recordings of Navajo songs. She began weaving again as an adult after years away from her loom. She said, "It's like going home. . . . [W]eaving is beauty. . . . I learned my way back to my culture." Another weaver remarked that her mother told her, "Do both your weaving and your cooking with feeling." A young mother, she commented that "school is hard, because talk [in English] is from in the head. The feeling isn't there. . . . [I]t's all intellectual."

The women began weaving for a variety of reasons; one, because her grandmother was going blind. She imitated her at weaving: "It was a way for us to communicate." Another weaver learned at an early age. She was ordered by her mother: "Have to weave, cannot let loom be empty. . . . [W]eave to honor the elderlies."

A young man, Wesley Thomas, gave a long and eloquent presentation. He commented on how tradition and traditionalism are defined differently in "Navajo cultural space." His maternal grandmother saw he was fit after ten years to take over her weaving tools. He learned the weaving songs from his grandfather. After many years, he is just beginning to understand the importance of Navajo weaving:

Spider Man and Woman constructed the loom to the other world [as] metaphorical teaching tools. Through weaving . . . [I] learned a form of Navajo spirituality. Negative language is never used around the loom, or when someone is weaving. Nurturing tools—power of earth and sky embodied in the loom—there's ambiguity, esoteric knowledge, secretiveness. Navajo techniques of learning [are] song, stories, and prayers. In Western aesthetics, emphasis is on the finished product. Being a member of a family where weaving is important, you represent your family when you attend gatherings. . . . [E]xperience beauty in creating and expressing, not in preserving and possessing. The construction of Navajo culture is learned through interaction. The songs and prayers are metaphorical teaching tools. . . . Power and strength of Spider Woman is in the loom. Weaving while in college connects me to home. . . . [T]he beating of the batten is like a heartbeat of earth, that's my mother. . . . [R]ugs are an embodied part of me in the culture.

Another weaver remarked, "When I'm sitting at the loom, it's my mother, . . . she's talking to me." And still another hears the heart of her mother through the batten because "the sound makes a connection to the culture. . . . [W]eaving [was] given to us to use, [it's] very much a part of our lives." Another weaver said that it was "good that girls were learning to weave—keeping up with tradition by supporting family. . . . [T]hat's how they did it long ago."

Several songs were sung in celebration of weaving. One described a young weaver: "How beautifully you card wool, how beautifully you spin." Another song told about a Navajo woman weaving a rug for trade because her husband had run out of goods.

Ruth Roessel spoke eloquently:

The spindle represents the turning of the values . . . with the soft goods, with the jewels. You have five fingers. . . . [A]ll the values go through your fingers to your family. Family members are important. . . . [T]hey help each other. My mother always wove and raised her children through her weaving. . . . [I]t makes you a person, it makes you who you are. . . . [T]his is art, this is life. The warps are like a curtain of black clouds, . . . a hope for rain. . . . [W]eaving is to call the rain. . . . [A]ll tools have spiritual names, even the loom.

Ruth told the story related to me by Grace Joe and elaborated:

The tools cried out, "You must always love and care for us [and] have a beautiful buckskin bag to keep us. Without us, there is nothing, no life, no song in your heart." [You] can't weave while it's raining because of the lightning. . . . Mother Earth has designs. . . . [I]t's all out there, clouds, rainbows, sunrays, . . . the art, the four seasons. Our mother changes colors. She wears a beautiful colored dress. . . . In the spring it is green, in the fall it changes. Her skirts are beautiful. . . . Seasons change. This is how teaching takes place in our culture. . . . That's what is in the weaving.

Wendy Weston, a Navajo bead maker, remarked on how she takes designs from weaving and interprets them:

Art and my world are all one. . . . [T]here is no separation. There's no word for art, we call ourselves weavers. Then you move into the world and have terms put on you. Anglos categorize you. . . . Navajos must redefine who they are and "create tradition." I never had to define who I was at home. Here people ask me to "define" who I am. Concerning the question, "What is traditional?" . . . Institutions get hung up on these words, which are nice, neat categories. . . . [W]e are contemporary people, the art we do expresses who we are in this contemporary world.

Wendy spoke of the frustration she felt at meetings of the National Endowment for the Arts, where there are reviews of Hispanic arts, Western arts, and North American Indian crafts. She finds this upsetting:

> These people are artists, [they are] not given the recognition. . . . [S]ociety is too hung up on degrees. The art world has a lot to offer weavers, . . . lots of money, . . . [but] "famous" is not a becoming characteristic for Navajo women. There are many networks to be built. In the last ten years, doors are slowly opening in institutions. Why do we want to get in? Why do we have to validate ourselves this way? My husband, Joe, is a painter. . . . [I]t can be a damaging word. Navajo use the Western term, but the context is very different. The word can be applied to him, . . . but it is a mere reflection of your Western values and concerns.

Wendy's powerful and articulate presentation in English was translated into Navajo. Afterward, a bilingual Navajo told me that the translator spoke directly to the issues raised by Wendy and criticized the organizers at length for not addressing economic issues, as the market for makers' work is so poor.

Pearl Sunrise has been working on a book that will reveal her philosophy of weaving. She remarked:

> Writing is difficult. . . . [It is] an intimate part of you. . . . [I] do not want to reveal knowledge related to weaving, or put it on paper. It is like giving part of oneself away. . . . [It] causes conflicts, bothers us. It is important to start at the beginning; by spinning the wool, [one] becomes a person. Weaving mustn't be put behind glass—*it cuts off the energy. We touch the weaving.* . . . By touch we transfer blessings. Weavings bestow blessings. When you weave, you are creating yourself.

Pearl has spoken about her life as a Navajo weaver in other public presentations.[12] She commented that if the weaver is not in tune, "she cannot create anything." A weaver works with her material in a certain way. While spinning the yarn, then warping and setting up her loom, she always follows the movement of the sun. Pearl's parents told her many stories demonstrating how "everything is integrated," but younger Navajos do not want to impose on the elders to write down stories.

However, a number of weavers have recently written of its importance (Begay 1994, 1996; Keams 1996; Thomas 1996). For example, Mrs. Dorothy Begay, a grandmother from the Rough Rock area of the reservation, reminisced about her childhood:

> We were taught to weave all day and even at night, carding and spinning the wool for the next rug. Once the rug was completed and sold, you would be ready to begin another one. Young girls and women did this into the late hours of the night. Even then, we were able to get up before the sun rose, when it was still dark, and herd sheep. We were always told that herding sheep and weaving rugs were the ways we would survive in this world. (Cited in McCarty 1983:12)

Reflections on Contesting Presentations

The Navajo weavers' statements about their work and lives were the most detailed and eloquent ever presented in a public forum. However, the duality exhibited in the conference was striking. The comments and questions of many non-Navajo participants appeared to have little relevance to what Navajo weavers were saying. Yet several of these individuals have been involved in one way or another with Navajo weavers or their textiles for decades. Weavers' statements emphasized the importance of relationships perpetuated through weaving rather than weaving as a commodity, reflecting gallery aesthetics. The latter interpretation currently dominates the written literature on the subject (Baizerman 1989).

Presentations by textile scholars and traders at the conference also associated aesthetics with commodification. Three museologists gave slide presentations on the "history" of Navajo weaving. In one session three speakers showed four or five identical slides of "classic" historic textiles. Wheat remarked that the whole history of the Navajo is marked by adaptation and innovation:

> The Navajo have no fixed tradition. . . . They have a highly movable[,] . . . cumulative style. Each later style has incorporated elements of previous styles. The major element in Navajo weaving is its eclecticism. This is demonstrated by incorporation and integration [of outside influences].

Wheat referred to more complex designs as "fussiness." He had been asked to summarize and comment on the discussions. Instead, he reiterated the "history" of Navajo weaving (everything was borrowed) and said we are now beginning to recognize weavers' creative concerns and abilities whether we collect traditional or modern textiles.

Traders' and Dealers' Voices

Several traders and off-reservation dealers gave presentations about the types of rugs that would sell: "We want good, clean rugs." A dealer referred to rugs as units and products. A trader who does high-volume business because his purchasing is subsidized by the Park Service thinks the quality of weaving is at an all-time high: "I don't think they can become any better or more progressive."

In private conversation, weavers commented that traders try to "talk weavers down" and pay them less money. Traders and dealers criticize a rug if it has "too much of one color," or they comment, "Buyers don't like that" or "You're not there yet," or "There's a mistake in your rug. Don't get mad if I tell you." Ruth Roessel addressed this issue publicly. She commented that weavers sometimes cry when traders criticize their rugs because they try so hard. They resolve "to do better next time." It is evident that weavers continue to be pressured to produce higher-quality textiles, with more pattern, finer spinning and dyeing, and increased warp/weft counts. Competition is exacerbated by copy weaving imported from abroad.

While listening to the presentations, I had the impression that I was attending two conferences. One was composed of non-Navajo "experts" in various fields, the curators, collectors, dealers, and traders. The other was composed of weavers ages eighteen to eighty-five who spoke of the importance of weaving to them. Their testimonies were very moving but seemed to make little impression on the first group. In fact, the traders and dealers arrived late, gave their presentations, and left. Only one trader heard some of the weavers' presentations. He is married to a Navajo woman and he speaks the language.

Only one non-Navajo presentation, by Maureen Schwarz, dealt with cosmology in relation to weaving. Schwarz remarked on how the bi'il dress, the loom, the hogan, and the Navajo basket are microcosms of cosmology. "As Changing Woman restored order and life to the world[,] . . . thus the weaver restores order."

Response from the Navajo Audience

Gloria Emerson, director of the Center for Cultural Exchange at a New Mexico arts institution, had prepared a one-hour presentation. Because the conference ran overtime, she spoke for ten minutes. She cogently addressed the chasm that separates the textile experts and traders from the weavers:

> Every weaver who spoke is an educator. Many are in a transitional state, like myself. The whole time is an historic moment, as prominent weavers are heard and we celebrate who we are. . . . [T]hrough all the poetry there are some problems. . . . [W]hite scholars need to listen and understand us. There is a real clash between whites and tribal wisdom. Organizers need to ask how they can address this and pay attention to this. . . . [W]e heard words of wisdom. . . . [S]ome weavers can get their work into museums. What about weavers back home whose rugs aren't as beautiful, . . . what about them? The purpose of the conference wasn't clear. . . . [T]he questions "What is tradition?" and "What is contemporary?"—this is not an exciting debate. Let the weavers come up with the questions. [She is referring to the tiresome and repetitive refrain on the history of Navajo weaving—where Navajos acquired their patterns, etc.]

Conclusion

The usual museologists' perspective that continues to influence the subject of Navajo weaving emphasizes the empirical domain. What is measurable becomes real. What constitutes knowledge depends on an agreed-on methodology. Cut out of its context, a Navajo rug equals the sum of its parts. The isomorphic facts objectively collected according to museological practices confer their own kind of value. The typology of Navajo weaving developed by textile specialists and adhered to by many scholars has shaped perceptions and written commentary on the subject. In stark contrast to commentary orchestrated by most textile scholars and art historians, weavers' statements reveal a set of relations and values unacknowledged in most literature on Navajo weaving (Begay 1996; Keams 1996; Thomas 1996; Willink and Zolbrod 1996). To situate weaving in a more appropriate cultural framework, more in keeping with weavers' statements, it is necessary to move from analyses grounded in dualisms that advocate typologies to topology. To perceive the patterns, one must discard the dualisms. It is necessary to shift the emphasis from the textile as a marketable commodity with quantifiable value to the mapping of textiles as material manifestations of relationships, perpetuated through the production and exchange of weaving. The last chapter shifts the emphasis from typology to topology—the form that generates circulation of value that is both aesthetic and integrative.

Reconceptualizing Navajo Weaving

From Commodity to Cosmological Performance

To press non-economic values into the framework of the economic calculus ... is a procedure by which the higher is reduced to the level of the lower and the priceless is given a price. All it can do is lead to ... deception, for to undertake to measure the immeasurable is absurd. ... [T]he logical absurdity is not the greatest fault of the undertaking: what is worse and destructive of civilization is the pretence that everything has a price, or in other words, money is the highest of all values.

Schumacher 1974:37–38

Through the activities of traders, ethnographers, and museologists, Navajo textiles became isolated from their context. A new value system was created that was numerical and abstract—a logical system that substituted a radically different context for the original one. The rug initially became a commodity treated like a renewable resource and more recently an art form tethered to gallery aesthetics. The commodity system has imposed a value that is easily decontextualized. When an object is situated in such a physical field, other values are obliterated. When emphasis is placed on isomorphic objects divorced from their contexts, it is impossible to interpret relations between cultural phenomena (Roessel 1974:224). The patterns of relations that brought Navajo textiles into existence are fractured through adherence to this type of thinking. Yet it is clear from their statements that perpetuating relationships form the primary focus of weavers' concerns. These relationships are frequently linked to Navajo cosmology. Major discrepancies emerge when weavers' comments are compared to statements made by non-Navajo textile experts concerning the history, influences, and role of Navajo weaving. If textiles are just commodities, why do Navajos express reluctance to discuss sacred concerns in relation to weaving? Only a handful of texts link weaving to Navajo cosmology.

The following diagrams adapted from Wilden (1981) are two-dimensional topological illustrations depicting different contexts. Weavers' comments reveal that a Navajo rug evokes a set of relations:

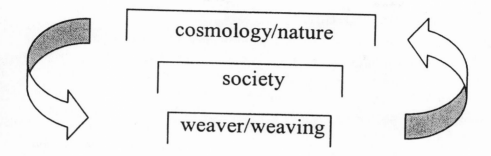

In ascending order, each level is dependent on the one above. The upper levels provide constraints. That is, weavers and their textiles cannot exist without Navajo society, and Navajo society in turn does not exist without the nonhuman world. These recursive relationships are also illustrated in figure 4. A recursive interpretation is nondualistic and nonlinear. In contrast, publications by many scholars and dealers evoke the hierarchy displayed in figure 3 and represented below:

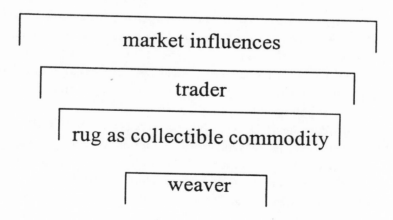

In the second diagram Anglos' unconscious epistemological frames are projected onto the relational. Patterns are doubly fractured when rugs become isolated from their context—the larger pattern of relations—and the focus is shifted to the rug as a commodity and isomorphic artwork. When objects become fetishized, the relationships that brought them into being vanish. Through adherence to the dualism sacred/profane it is impossible to perceive the complexities of the patterns.

Movement as the Basis of Life

There is a large volume of published information on Navajo language, religion, cosmology, kinship, and social organization.[1] Navajos tend to speak of the world in terms of process, event, and flux rather than parts and wholes or clearly distinguishable static entities. Continuous change is emphasized rather than atomistic structure. All aspects of reality in Navajo knowledge systems are processlike rather than thinglike. Thus Navajo culture differs from Euro-American cultures with regard to the emphasis on movement and motion. Witherspoon (1977:48–49) estimates there are several hundred thousand permutations of the verb "to go" in the Navajo language. If all the verbs relating "to move" as well as "to go" were included, the number of possible conjugations would be astronomical: "Movement is the basis of life. . . . [L]ife is exemplified by movement" (Witherspoon 1977:53). The universe is a place of motion and process; no state of being is permanently fixed. Beauty, balance, and orderliness are conditions that must be continuously re-created and maintained.

McAllester (1980:230) suggests that myth and ritual reiterate pervasive aspects of Navajo philosophy and worldview as pairing, alternation, reciprocation, progression, and sequence, "plentiful evidence of a universe ordered down to minute detail." From a communications perspective, McAllester's statement is just as easily applied to a Navajo rug. Weavings also express qualities of balance, rhythm, and harmony, key aspects of hózhǫ́. However, adherence to dualisms and concepts grounded in classical aesthetics makes it difficult for non-Navajos to perceive these similarities (see Kent 1985; Reichard [1934] 1974, [1936] 1968, [1939] 1971; Wheat 1989).

Worth and Adair's text, *Through Navajo Eyes* (1972), reveals the importance of active process. The authors describe a film on weaving made by Susie Benally, a Navajo, in which three-fourths of the footage is devoted to movement and preparations before weaving. Segments depict Susie's mother gathering plants for dyes and roots for yucca soap and shearing sheep. The creative process begins long before the physical act of weaving, with inspiration drawn from the environment. Weavers frequently emphasize the concentration that occurs when thinking their patterns (Hedlund 1994b). Thought is a vital aspect of any creative act. The quality of one's thoughts determines the quality of one's life. The *tsii yéél*, or thong made from white yarn, is used to tie up one's hair. It ties an individual's thoughts together and makes them strong (Roessel 1981:80).

Perceiving the Patterns

We can glean bits of information about the derivation of particular motifs from scholars' statements. Many ethnographers and textile experts note the perpetuation of specific motifs derived from Navajo ceremonial baskets (Dockstader 1978; Kent 1985; Reichard [1934] 1975; Wheat 1984). However, there are multiple forms of patterns to be perceived. To do so, it is necessary to shift the emphasis from the empirical to the relational (see fig. 4).

In using a perspective informed by communications, one searches for formal sequences recurring in various activities. Instead of separating weaving from the perceived sacred sphere, it is necessary to look for similarities in patterned activities. For example, both weavers and medicine men gather plants to be used in their respective activities. Similar images and outlining of images occur in textiles and in sand paintings. Weavers strive for harmony in color and balance in design. Faris summarizes it nicely:

> Navajo art in general—including poetry, prayers, songs, textiles, and silverwork, as well as sand paintings and other visual forms—are masterpieces of balance spatially, compositionally, and in terms of color use, sound play, contrast, rhythm, repetition, symmetry and sexual and directional symbolism. . . . Although balance requires control, aesthetic products need not be static—indeed visual art can be very dynamic, making it all the more compelling. (1986:139)

Reichard (1944, 1950) comments on how crucial it is for Navajo chanters to learn prayers as a whole. So also does a Navajo weaver perceive the whole pattern in her mind before weaving her rug. As weavers' commentary reveals, both prayers and weavings celebrate the beauty of the landscape and reverence for order and form. Values unfold; patterns emerge as weavers perpetuate order and harmony of the system. Thus textiles are far more than isomorphic objects; they become material manifestations of relationships. The activities, the rugs, the culture, and Navajo perceptions of nature—all are patterns in motion. But the motion is not linear, it is cyclical and recursive.

Collapsing the Dualisms

The West's rigid distinction between the daily round of work and play and religion is nonexistent for many Navajos (Kelley and Francis 1994; Mitchell and Frisbie 2001; Ortiz 1996). As the Navajo artist Conrad House said, his people do not separate art, religion, and life. For Navajos, order and continual regeneration inherent in the cosmos serve as a constant reminder of how to live one's life in balance, in a state of hózhǫ́. As we have seen, Navajos' interactions with the nonhuman world are characterized by a strong sense of connectedness to and respect for all living things. Through symbols, stories, and activities Navajos confirm that they exist within and function as part of a very large, complex world that includes other Navajos, the earth and the different landforms upon it, the heavens, the atmosphere, and the immortals who animate them (Begay and Maryboy 1996; Kelley and Francis 1994:46). Thus Navajos see themselves as part of a much larger living system (Witherspoon and Peterson 1995).

For Navajos to maintain harmonious relations with the universe, it is necessary to recognize and perpetuate their place in the web of life. Because there are no cosmological connections to textile making in the modernist West, most ethnographers, except for Witherspoon, have failed to perceive the extent to which weaving perpetuates hózhǫ́. Weavers' activities unite the two fields of ritual and work, as weaving is accompanied by songs, stories, and prayers. The importance of weaving in perpetuating Navajo culture becomes patently clear in weavers' statements. Their mapping of the domain of textile production includes a cosmological realm. Beauty, harmony, and order, hózhǫ́, are continually created by both chanters and weavers. This is in keeping with the Navajo Creation Story. Changing Woman restored order in the world, and weavers do the same. Weavers become Changing Woman when they weave. They are trying to tell us this, but because of our differing epistemologies, we hear their statements as poetic myth at best.

Several Navajo respondents commented that weaving is a prayer for rain. Depletion and regeneration are two halves of the hydrological cycle, as water, moisture, and clouds are essences of the immortals (Kelley and Francis 1994:209). Weaving plays a vital and integral role in perpetuating reciprocal relations between the Navajo people and their desert environment. But the environment is alive, since the outer forms of the Holy People are features that make up the landscape, animals, plants, the atmosphere, and even celestial bodies (Kelley and Francis 1994). The weaver begins at the bottom, close to the earth, and weaves up toward the sky. She uses living materials from Mother Earth, and Father Sky releases rain. Thus the loom is associated with emergence, growth, and ascendance.

Some Navajos refuse to weave on upright looms made from materials other than wood. Early authors criticized Navajo weavers' refusal to adopt mechanical floor looms. Their resistance was seen as stubborn refusal to modernize, as they chose to weave on the "primitive" upright loom that had not changed for centuries. Plausible explanations could be anticipated, given that the portable upright loom is more compatible with pastoralism. However, critics never understood that the rejection of floor looms was based on cosmology. Weavers may oppose the repair of old rugs because it interferes with the natural processes of growth and decay. These links become paramount when recontextualizing weaving within a framework more compatible to Navajo lifeways. Because harmony with kin, including nonhuman kin, is the ideal relationship for Navajos, it is perpetuated through acknowledgment and fulfillment of reciprocal responsibilities. These responsibilities are fulfilled by chanters and weavers who together, through their respective practices, perpetuate hózhǫ́. Grace McNeley writes:

> The Navajo term *ketl'ool*—derived from *k'e,* meaning "feet," and *tl'ool* meaning "root system"—expresses the concept of having a foundation for one's life in the earth, much as a plant is rooted in the earth. . . . Let us visualize the central root as extending all the way back to Asdzą́ą́n Nádleehi, "Changing Woman"—who is Earth Mother herself. Developing from this main root is the complex web of kinship relations extending back even to ancestors and including clan relations, the extended family and the immediate family. Tied to this system are material goods, familiar surroundings and livestock. This webbing of earth, of ancestors, of clan and familiar surroundings all constitute a Navajo home, enabling those within it to flourish, to thrive. (1987:163–64)

McNeley's statement reveals why many Navajos look on all the land as sacred. They see themselves as caretakers who, through the daily activities of stock raising and farming, turn the land into food, which becomes their flesh. Ceremonial performances bond Navajos by enveloping them in the diversity of the land's natural products. The social relations between mortals and immortals, between Navajos and the Holy People, are continually invoked through songs, stories, and prayers. Weaving is an integral part of this cycle as materials from the living environment are used to create the loom, weaving tools, and textiles. The importance of relationships was confirmed in a conversation I had in 1992 with Harry Walters, director of the Ned Hatathli Gallery at Diné Community College in Tsaile:

> What the women weave is part of the environment—it's in their hearts. If you take something from the environment, you must give something back. Navajo weaving is all about relationships. . . . [W]e are

like children in our relation to Mother Earth. . . . [T]hat's why shoes are important, and must be made right. . . . [T]he foot touches the ground, the Earth our Mother. The weaver has a relationship with the sheep . . . [S]he must respect them, and she uses the wool in her weaving[,] . . . and she must respect it too, because all are related.

An Empirical Quagmire

When individuals from one culture look at the patterns of another culture, they will often see what their own culture has trained them to see. When one complex culture comes into contact with another, the tendency is to oversimplify or dismiss. The themes of the other culture are actually complex patterns, yet they are simplified, or reified, and the mode of interaction tends to become quantitative (money, trade) (Berman 1989:196). This process aptly describes what has happened to Navajo weavers and their textiles in most of the literature. As this book attests, the most important aspects of Navajo textiles are seen to revolve around their function as a commodity. This is the case for the detailed descriptions Reichard provided on the role of weaving in Navajo society. Reichard frames the copious information she provides on all aspects of weaving much as it is framed in modernist Euro-American societies: that is, as women's activity associated with the domestic sphere engaged in for practical purposes.

The social relations and practices of Navajo weavers and chanters were labeled dualistically. Although the binary opposition of sacred and profane reflected in ethnographic works (Reichard [1934] 1975, [1936] 1968, [1939] 1971; Underhill [1956] 1983) appeared to "balance" activities of men and women in the religious and domestic spheres, it has had unfortunate consequences. The creation of textiles by Navajo women has suffered neglect by symbolic anthropologists as active ethnographers working with Navajo people. For example, they seldom discuss weaving in texts on Navajo religion. Except for Witherspoon and one of his colleagues, most publications before 1996 are closely associated with the perspective embraced by museologists.[2]

The perspective adopted by Anglo museologists typically provides an inadequate context for understanding Navajo weaving. This is because the views, values, and assumptions of the dominant society are reflected in the construction of its history. Museologists working with Navajo textiles are not concerned with ontology, either their own or that of Navajos. We might describe the museologists' model of what constitutes a Navajo rug as Cartesian. That is, one gains information about the rug by breaking it into its simplest measurable components and constructing a story about provenance based on the results of scientific analyses. The entire field privileges this empirical and quantifiable knowledge. Although described with mathematical precision in terms of measurements, textiles have been excised from their proper context. Thus practitioners of standard museological methods have fallen heir to Whitehead's "fallacy of misplaced concreteness." As empiricists, museologists are caught in a proverbial bind: the manner in which they structure their research determines the way they perceive the results. Their methodology becomes their epistemology.

Most information related to Navajo textile production is discursive. This digital information is verbal, rational, abstract, and incomplete. It is a way of thinking that posits the traders' influence as obliterating the wisdom of Navajo weavers. Navajo weaving is about relationships. These textiles are a primary form of meta-communication that impart information that cannot be transmitted discursively. Navajo society has its distinctive wisdom: it recognizes that the "unit of survival" is itself and the nonhuman world. The recursiveness, redundancy, and patterning that occur in weaving over the past century perpetuated Navajo relationships in the face of disruptions from government personnel, traders, and educators intruding on their world (Witherspoon 1987; Witherspoon and Peterson 1995).

Complex patterns of relations were occluded by the epistemological lens of the colonizers and later most ethnographers. The bifurcation of the sacred and the profane thrust Navajo weaving into an alien field. It became completely dissociated from what ethnographers have designated as Navajo religion. In a recent issue of *Cultural Survival Quarterly,* Alfonso Ortiz remarked:

> Native American religions embody a lot of practical knowledge, teachings which serve to put believers in rapport with their environments in a very deep and abiding way. This practical dimension of Native American religions has never been seriously studied, as the romantic tradition surrounding them in American scholarship has always drawn attention to their mystical and spiritual dimensions, and away from the practical tasks that they also perform. (1996:27–28)

Ortiz's remarks are most relevant to addressing the shortcomings of the perceived bifurcation between the male activities of sand painting created for curing ceremonies and female weaving tasks. Both activities are necessary complements to properly perpetuate Navajo lifeways. Both are recursive processes, sacred forms of reciprocation, that stress continual renewal and reanimation. Both sets of activities contribute to survival. Thus cyclical interdependence is continually expressed by both chanters and weavers.

Ortiz also remarks on how the term "traditions of spirituality" is more appropriate than the term "religion." Such traditions are embodied in the non-human world rather than occupy a transcendental realm:

> Native religious traditions also present a view of nature as a great mystery, and held all life to be sacred. They also extended kinship to all of nature, to all creation. To native peoples who still live their traditions, their sacred mountains and the whole earth are living breathing entities. . . . In regarding the earth as alive, they also think of her as mother. Earth and humans began a common consciousness together long ago, and they have a mutual responsibility to care for one another. (1996:29)

Reconstituting an Aesthetic Unity

Adopting a model grounded in communications provides an appropriate path to reorient our perceptions of Navajo weaving as cosmological performance. The real meaning of Navajo weaving is not about content or context per se; it lies in the relationship between context and content. Without context, no communication occurs. Until very recently, all the emphasis on the visible elements of specific textiles has produced no overall wisdom related to the subject. Rigidly focusing on any single set of relata destroys the more profound significance of the cultural aspect of the work. By shifting the emphasis from substance to form, broader patterns of relations come to the fore that set the context for verbal communication. These patterns of relations are expressed nonverbally. In fact, these analogic or nonverbal forms of communication create the environment that make thought and language possible (Wilden 1987:137). Bourdieu's (1977) notion of symbolic capital suggests a similar concept of communicative "field."

Learning the Context

Western philosophers differentiate between epistemology—origins, methods, and limits of knowledge—and ontology—the study of being and order in the world, that is, the nature of existence. However, epistemology and ontology should not be separated:

> His (commonly unconscious) beliefs about what sort of world it is will determine how he sees it and acts within it, and his ways of perceiving and acting will determine his beliefs about its nature. The living man

is thus bound within a net of epistemological and ontological premises which—regardless of ultimate truth or falsity—become partially self-validating for him. (Bateson 1972:314)

Thus it is inappropriate to separate "belief" as "mystery" from "truth" as "fact." Regardless of the society under scrutiny, belief becomes the metacontext for the message. The unconscious epistemological frames covertly influenced by dualisms and held by scholars and others provided a false context for analyzing Navajo weaving. Anglos perceive the rug as a craft commodity and more recently as an art form containing an aesthetic component. Museologists mapped the course of change primarily through visible and quantifiable elements and assumed the existence of a direct correspondence between material adoptions and value orientation, thus disallowing the existence of multiple ontologies. This is why such a remarkable discrepancy exists in statements made by traders, dealers, and most scholars in comparison to weavers.

In his work with the Balinese, Bateson found that stability required change and flexibility. The cultural emphasis in Bali is on balance, just as it is among Navajos (Faris 1993; Witherspoon 1977; Witherspoon and Peterson 1995). Learning is primarily an interpersonal process. Learning about cultural context is abstract rather than instrumental, but it is the abstract ideas of cultural context that tend to sink in and become less conscious and more habituated. As ideas become sunk to habit, they become more difficult to disrupt, and because these contexts indicate the nature of appropriate relationships, they become more difficult to change, because new information has been organized around habituated contexts. Shared understanding arises only when communicators have a common understanding of the premises of habituated contexts at several levels of significance. This suggests that learning is patterned in different levels. Moiré illustrates multiple patterning. A moiré pattern is a repetitive design. If another repetitive pattern is put against the tissuelike semiopaque fabric, a third pattern is created.

Patterns of redundancy of information (the external context) become overlaid with patterns formed in contexts of learning, and the whole yields a three-dimensional pattern. It is the interleaving of the two patterns of redundancy which yields a sense of creativity and beauty. (Harries-Jones 1995:202–3)[3]

This is a far more appropriate means to interpret weavers' statements. The aesthetics of Navajo weaving incorporate the aesthetics of systemic holism emphasizing relationships rather than the isomorphic aesthetic isolated in the individual textiles and favored by museologists.

When behaviorism was in its heyday, nearly all social science models were based on notions borrowed from physical systems: stimulus-response behavior was the most usual. Descriptions of learning were built around correspondence to stimulus-response and failed to consider patterns of learning in and for themselves. This perspective provides the basis for acculturation models reflecting others' understanding of changes in Navajo weaving patterns. Traders, tourists, and the market provided the stimulus, and weavers responded.

Mapping Differing Contexts

Language bears a relationship to the objects it denotes comparable to that which a map bears to a territory (Bateson 1972:180). There is a "field of relations" we construct between ourselves and the "territory," or the "objective world." What we map is that relationship in which we participate and not a direct representation of the things "out there." The values of any social network partly determine the network of perception. In other words, there is no such thing as unmediated perception or objectivity, because epistemology always shapes one's perception of the world. Thus if we think about the differing values a rug has for a young Navajo learning to weave and for a trader, for the Navajo the rug is a "message" about a relation. But the "message" is very different for the two parties when they meet.

Traders' relations to weavers involved a body of habituated assumptions or premises implicit in how they viewed weaving. The context for the trader lies in the sphere of economics. Until recently weavers may have known little of the commercial context. Thus the weavers' context overlaps very little with the traders'. However, when one reads the literature on the subject, there appears to be a great deal of overlap, as traders are seen to wield great influence on weavers' patterns. In chapters 4 and 5 I challenge the extent of their influence, given the magnitude of production. In any event, it is more appropriate to see weavers making multiple mappings of the context. The context has altered somewhat and varies for each weaver. For example, labels on flour sacks and canned goods may provide inspiration for a weaver, in addition to patterns she already knows. The maps or forms and patterns of relating created by non-Navajos in their descriptions of weaving are not complex enough for the territory. Weavers' mappings are not acknowledged by non-Navajos because they are not recognized for what they represent to the Navajo people. This is probably one of the reasons weavers enjoy looking at photographs of Navajo rugs but bilingual weavers seldom read texts on the subject (field notes 1992). The words have very little meaning for them, because weaving is not about words. It is about relationships.

The woven rug is the result of a long, complex process that entails inter-action among the sheep and the human herder, the shearer, the spinner of the yarn, and the weaver (Roessel 1983; Toelken 1976; Witherspoon 1987). In addi-tion, a number of plants are gathered during specific growing seasons. Hence there is interaction among the weaver, animals, plants, and the annual cycle of seasons that is repeated over the lifetime of the weaver herself. Thus repetition and redundancy of patterns occurs. A weaver is involved in ordered activity embedded in a context. The ordered activity is patterned, much of it grounded in habit. Patterns of relationships are maintained over time. These patterns con-tinue long after the rug is sold. In fact, weavers' patterns of relationships are perpetuated *because* the rug is sold. Thus aesthetic patterns cannot be objec-tively distinguished, isomorphic with individual textiles, and autonomous, as in museologists' models.

Concerning the Sacred

Navajos have expressed reluctance to speak openly on sacred matters (Kelley and Francis 1994; Ortiz 1999; Willink and Zolbrod 1996). Information can be easily exploited and misused. Stories must be told only at certain times in appro-priate settings. Stories are like verbal maps, and knowledge of them can only be gained with the consent of the teller. Researchers have encountered resist-ance to writing down narratives (Kelley and Francis 1994; Zolbrod 1984). Father Berard Haile discerned that

> [c]ertain subjects . . . are surrounded with more or less secrecy. To the singer this knowledge is his life or "breath"; part of his inner self or soul, which he carefully guards in the firm conviction that the moment he imparts it to others, his usefulness in life is spent. Pleading and tempt-ing offers are useless, the usual reply being that "when old age is upon me and death is approaching I will tell." (1968:31)

In the interviews I conducted in 1992 and at the Heard Museum conference in 1994, I learned that it was inappropriate to share stories related to weaving (see Tabaha 1999). If stories are shared at all, they must be told in the winter.

The indiscriminate dissemination of sacred knowledge lessens its power. Making the intimate public violates proper conduct. One is not to make mat-ters relating to the sacred explicit. Secrecy is the first line of defense. Several weavers have remarked to me on the inappropriateness of scholars identifying specific motifs as isomorphic symbols. Hedlund remarked on weavers denying any knowledge of specific symbols in textiles. But weavers may know more than they are willing to reveal. By not sharing stories with outsiders, it is possible that weavers may be choosing to maintain their integrity (Bateson and Bateson 1988:72). Perhaps if the world knew how sacred weaving was to Navajos, it could be "saved." But in revealing stories to save it, one compromises relationships that are not to be described.

Conclusion

At first glance, this book seems to center on a minor component of material culture, the textiles or "collectibles" created by Navajo weavers after the establishment of the reservation in 1868. On closer inspection, it concerns survival. Evidence in traders' archives revealed that the more Navajos wove, the poorer they became. However, the theme of cultural survival cannot be adequately appreciated using extant frameworks. The contexts developed by ethnographers and museologists to describe weavers' production privileges a particular history. Their interpretations have blocked a deeper understanding of the value of weaving to Navajo people. The recent escalation in the investment market for old textiles, coupled with emphasis on their economic value, ensures that the prodigious production of thousands of weavers historically threatens to bury contemporary producers.

When I began this research, I anticipated working only with the Hubbell archives to uncover hidden history related to weaving. But every box containing Hubbell records became a Pandora's box. I soon realized that the history that lay buried in this trading family's business records provided direct evidence of the origins and persistence of impoverishment among Navajo people. Downer (1990) and Russell (1999) discuss the systemic poverty that prevails on the reservation. Per capita income persists at one quarter the national average; unemployment and underemployment are the norm; more than half of the housing is substandard, lacking basic utilities (Satchell and Bowermaster 1994:61–64).

Using a perspective developed recently by feminist political economists provides a framework to address the marginalization of Navajo weavers' production. As Edholm, Harris, and Young (1977:126) remark, "Women are absent in many analyses especially in the domains of politics and economics, [but] women do not naturally disappear, their disappearance is socially created and constantly reaffirmed." Until very recently, women's domestic work was seen as "natural"; it was perceived as a constant throughout history—an unchanging set of necessities that did not require analysis. An adequate assessment of the economic contribution of Navajo weavers not only remained unanalyzed, it was airbrushed from the historical record. A newspaper article that I found in the archives epitomizes this neglect. On Friday, 16 December 1932, at the height of the depression, Roman Hubbell arrived in Kansas City with fifteen carloads of sheep. A journalist for the Kansas City *Times* described him as "Indian trader, farmer, freighter and mail contractor." Voicing his concern over the failing economy, Roman remarked:

> I have known the gusto of good times, but our present dilemma has resulted from the failure of congress to place minimum prices on the sale of wheat, wool, cotton, silver, copper and livestock. Those six staples form the backbone of the Southwest; our forebears traced their patterns of development on those basic commodities. Traders have driven producers to accept prices below the cost of production and depressed prices on those commodities have thrown our section out of gear. Others have toppled with us, of course, but these primary frameworks should be stabilized so that the farmer, miner and cattleman will be received with less frost by his banker. (HP Box 545)

Roman fails to mention weaving or weavers, although for decades a significant portion of his family's wealth accrued from textiles woven by thousands of Navajo women (see table 5). As my analysis reveals, the book credit received by Navajo weavers was well below the cost of production and predated the depression by decades.

Weavers were ignored by the very individuals who benefited most financially from their production. Coombe (1991) corroborates how such prolific output could be marginalized by social scientists. Critiquing cultural anthropology's formerly ensconced position within modernism, Coombe remarks:

> Hermeneutics and cultural interpretation can maintain . . . splendid isolation only insofar as they separate the symbolic from the political and construct cultural tradition as a monological realm of unified meanings and values. To do so is to evade the historically specific processes by which certain meanings become privileged, while others are delegitimated—the practices through which unity is forged from difference by the marginalization and silencing of oppositional voices and alternative understandings. (1991:191)

Coombe's statement describes the bifurcation evident in much of the literature on Navajos. To political economists, weaving was nonproductive, hence opaque to a sustained analysis (Weiss 1984). To cultural anthropologists, phenomena relating to political economy lay outside their purview (Reichard [1934] 1974, [1936] 1968, [1939] 1971; Underhill [1956] 1983). Prodigious production by thousands of women remained unanalyzed because the topic fell between the paradigmatic cleavages in the discipline. These cleavages, described in the introduction, were formed by a cluster of asymmetric dualisms that undergird Euro-American epistemology.

The first asymmetric dualism split the public world of waged labor from the "nonproductive" private sphere and sanctioned the "disappearance" of thousands of women toiling in the domestic domain. Chapters 2 through 5 examine the effects of newly imposed economic relations on Navajos after the formation of the reservation, with particular emphasis on weavers. Some of the literature asserts that the pernicious effects of merchant capital on weavers not only destroyed "tradition" but also substituted a bland product that was a shabby counterpart to its prereservation cousin (Rodee 1981; Weiss 1984). It is clear from information unearthed in the Hubbell archives on the relations of exchange that women's production was of primary importance: not only for their families' well-being but also for traders' profit margins. After the turn of the twentieth century, the production of Navajo weaving escalated dramatically. Although the population grew 50 percent, textile production increased more than 800 percent. This information has been available in the published literature for more than sixty years and was corroborated by documents in the Lorenzo Hubbell Papers over the same period. The scant documentation published in annual government reports indicates the value of textiles leaving the reservation, but information is ambiguous and fragmented and thus difficult to interpret. Because critical information was lacking, it was impossible to properly assess the magnitude and extent of production. The paucity of this information reflects the colonial attitude that sanctioned the marginalization of women's labor.

In a number of studies related to the Navajo economy, authors comment on how weaving was an alternative way to market wool (e.g., Bailey and Bailey 1986). My analysis reveals the effects of treating a fully finished product (a rug) as a renewable resource (marketed by weight) for decades as Navajo women labored millions of hours per year weaving wool from their flocks into rugs. Factors impinging on a fairer return to weavers were revealed, such as the appropriation of the niche for the Navajo blanket by trade blanket manufacturers and the stagnation in wool markets that led to pressures applied by traders to weavers to turn wool into marketable rugs. The gaps in the theoretical frameworks used by other investigators have resulted in the neglect of a realistic assessment of the exponential growth of textile production by indigenous housewives in tandem with increasing pauperization. My analysis provides support for Kelley (1976:247), who notes that low prices paid to producers generate increased production in the absence of alternative income sources. Increased production depletes resources, inducing greater production, which lowers prices further; the whole process constitutes a deviation-amplifying feedback loop. Evidence of this phenomenon is found in archival sources: although the cost of living quadrupled for Navajos between 1895 and 1928, the cash valuation of women's textile production stagnated at 1902 levels. As textiles were woven at home during weavers' "spare time," there was no wage scale. As the cost of production appeared minimal and impossible to quantify, it became invisible.

To summarize, the analysis of portions of the Hubbells' business records in tandem with pertinent evidence accessed from other sources demonstrates how subsistence insecurity began shortly after the reservation was established. My analysis of archival evidence challenges several assumptions that have dominated the literature on the Navajo for nearly a century:

1. Traders "saved" weaving by developing and expanding off-reservation markets.
2. Traders were primarily responsible for design changes in Navajo weaving.
3. "Pound" blankets were a short-lived phenomenon at the end of the nineteenth century.
4. Weavers benefited financially by trading their own blankets or rugs for machine-made trade blankets.
5. Rug weaving always decreased when wool prices were high and increased when wool prices dropped.
6. Traders' greatest profits lay in wool.

Abundant evidence in the Hubbells' business records renders these assumptions suspect. The Hubbells were not an anomaly. Corroborating information from other sources, such as the Fred Harvey Company ledgers and correspondence, reveals production of great magnitude, increasing competition, and additional pressures applied to weavers to improve their textiles in the face of decreasing returns.

The shift in emphasis from the mechanics of weaving in the past (e.g., Amsden [1934] 1975; Reichard [1934] 1975, [1936] 1968, [1939] 1971) to the ideational realm reflected in the recent application of theories grounded in classical aesthetics (e.g., Berlant and Kahlenberg 1977) replicates the bifurcation I discuss in the introduction. The historic textiles are currently redeemed in a particular manner, thereby benefiting specific groups.

The approach embraced by Witherspoon, that weaving is culturally inspired and not materially determined, and the museologists' emphasis on the empirical mirrors the idealist/materialist split in anthropology. Witherspoon emphasizes values, whereas the empiricists focus on the (noneconomic) facts. Postmodernist readings of pattern appropriation were perceived as stylistic hybridity and modeled on the notion of decorative art in previous interpretations.

In reconceptualizing weaving as cosmological performance, differences in perceptions of values are revealed. In the West, values are defined as "conceptions of the desirable" and are frequently quantified, whereas for Navajos, the value of weaving is integrative. As demonstrated previously, belief becomes the metacontext for the message. There are vast differences between the beliefs of Navajo weavers and those of museologists. The information I have unveiled and analyzed addresses significant issues that remain absent from current discussions on the subject of Navajo weaving. Using a communications perspective provides a means to understand why Navajo women would continue to weave under persistent, difficult conditions. Such a perspective provides a path to heal the division that splits cultural pattern from commodity.

The art historian Janet Berlo published a revealing statement in an article written two years after her comments embracing an "aesthetics of appropriation." The juxtaposition of these two statements reflects how deeply divided the discipline is about some fundamental issues. Berlo writes:

> To the Navajo, weaving is a sacred activity, as well as a paradigm for womanhood. In weaving a woman creates beauty and projects it into the world. In Navajo cosmology, the universe itself was woven on an enormous loom by the mythic female ancestor, Spider Woman, out of the sacred materials of the cosmos. . . . In many respects, Changing Woman provides the model for the Navajo aesthetic of transformation. She is, in essence, mother earth, clothing herself anew in vegetation each year. She follows an endless seasonal cycle of transformation: In spring she is young and beautiful, in summer, mature and beautiful, in fall she begins to fade. . . . When Changing Woman was discovered as an infant on a sacred mountain by First Man and First Woman, she was arrayed in the same cosmic materials with which Spider Woman wove the universe. (1993:37–38)

Then Berlo cites Witherspoon:

> Navajo women follow Changing Woman's patterns of transformation as they creatively synthesize the raw materials of diverse worlds[,] . . . plants, animals/humans, into handsome textiles. Navajo female artistic

identity comes from the transformative process of weaving, not the finished product. (1993:38)

Berlo essentially *describes* weaving as cosmological performance, but does she *perceive* it as such? The postmodernist argument that affirms the "aesthetics of appropriation" requires critique. To be aware that weavers value weaving in this manner and to sanction pattern appropriation is troubling.

I view weaving as material manifestations of relationships. Navajo textiles come into existence through these relationships; they do not exist outside of them, they would not exist without them. If we know nothing of these relationships, what do we really know about Navajo weaving? There are no rugs without weavers. We may continue to recycle stories our predecessors constructed based on empirical evidence and perceived trader influence. Yet recent stories emerging from weavers bear little resemblance to those previously published (Begay 1994, 1996; Keams 1996; Thomas 1994, 1996). In contemplating the recent flurry of weavers' statements, a friend remarked: "Information coming from the weavers themselves adds another stripe to the blanket." At first glance it appears an apropos statement—using the rug as an analogy. But in retrospect, it is inadequate. Weavers' stories are not just another stripe; they provide the foundation. A novice weaver quickly discovers the primary importance of having a strong, tightly spun warp. Only then can a proper foundation be built. The scaffold supporting the extant history of weaving is collapsing, and in the process the inadequacy of anthropological models used in its construction is revealed. Had weaving been adequately historicized by previous generations of scholars, the investment market may not have enjoyed the success it has. Had weaving been appropriately contextualized in Navajo culture, the multiple appropriations of Navajo patterns over the past century, first by trade blanket manufacturers and then by entrepreneurs wishing to cash in on "the Southwest look," would have met with critique.

In reconfiguring weaving as cosmological performance, one becomes aware that a way of life is being sold off to the highest bidder. Such activities are midwifed by the sacred/profane split and currently brokered by scholars who write for the investment market. Scholars who work with First Nations peoples and publish their findings have limited control over how their research is used. It may be misrepresented, misinterpreted, or quoted out of context. To support the dealers' and collectors' market for historic textiles by deliberately writing for that market at the expense of contemporary Navajo weavers threatens the maintenance of relationships vital to Navajo culture. Because the relationships are jeopardized, the culture is jeopardized. This is why scholars who are privileged to work with

Navajos need to acknowledge the inimical effects of such activity and subvert it. To divide pattern from commodity threatens Navajo lifeways:

> In perceiving pattern and quality [we] encounter the aesthetic. Our attention to quantity rather than pattern leads us to ignore aesthetic necessities: in child rearing and family, in architecture and diet, in philosophy and religion[,] . . . even in art—poetry. *In every one of these fields of human activity . . . there are problems of pattern about which very little formal thought has been done.* The result is a splitting of discourse between the pragmatic and the aesthetic, the structural and the functional, the eternal and the secular. . . . [T]he truth which is important is not a truth of preference, it is a truth of complexity[,] . . . of a total eco-interactive on-going web . . . in which we dance, which is the dance of Shiva[,] . . . which includes all cybernetic complementaries[:] . . . good/evil, health/pathology, aesthetics/pragmatics, family/individual. (Bateson, in Keeney 1983:123; original emphasis)

Can this understanding that Navajos demonstrate so well heal our own split aesthetics?

Appendix I

Navajo Cosmology

The first Diné were created by the acts of the Holy People, *diyin dine'e,* among them First Man and First Woman. These two prototypical beings ascended through a series of differently colored lower worlds, finally emerging into the present world. Each of the successive lower worlds was more ordered than the one before it. Each subsequent upward migration toward emergence onto earth's surface led to greater stability, order, and knowledge. First Man and First Woman discovered a female infant, later named Changing Woman, on top of Blanca Peak, a sacred mountain. Changing Woman became the progenitor of the Navajo (Diné, or Earth Surface People). Her name refers to her ability to age as time passes, and on reaching old age, she rejuvenates and becomes young again. During six months of summer the Earth is at work with the reproduction and growth of plants. In the winter months she rests and becomes old. There is a continuing cycle of senescence and rejuvenation. Corn, horses, sheep, and other life forms owe their origin to Changing Woman. She is considered to be in control of all reproduction, and she holds the answer to a long life (Witherspoon and Peterson 1995).

Changing Woman was impregnated by the Sun and gave birth to twins, Monster Slayer and Born for Water, who later killed monsters who roamed the earth making life unsafe for humans. Four sacred mountains delineate the sacred homeland of the Navajos.

Witherspoon reminds us,

Ritual knowledge is fixed and complete; it cannot be expanded. All there is to know about this world is already known because the world was organized according to this knowledge. Earth Surface people can expand their awareness or command of knowledge, but they cannot expand knowledge itself. (1977:33)

Trudy Griffin-Pierce summarizes Navajo philosophy:

In traditional Navajo thinking, spirituality, health, harmony, and beauty are inseparable. All the good things in life—health, prosperity, happiness, and peace—are a result of living life from a spiritual perspective that acknowledges all parts of the universe as alive and interdependent. (1992:29)

The Navajo ceremonial system, composed of two major parts, is transmitted orally from the medicine man, or "singer," to an apprentice. It sanctions and explains a large body of songs, prayers, and sand paintings and other practices designed to produce or restore the conditions implied by hózhǫ́. Thus hózhǫ́ carries a connotation of order and balance as achieved by beauty. It is inconceivable that beauty can exist without order, and vice versa (Faris 1986:138). Each ceremonial has special relations with certain groups of Holy People. Ceremonies vary greatly in elaboration and may last from two to nine nights. The ultimate purpose of the ceremonials is to restore hózhǫ́ if order and balance are disrupted because of violations of the order set down in the Creation Story. Navajos perceive order as based on the pairing of contrasting but complementary elements. Imbalance manifests itself in various ways, especially through illness. The universe contains evil as well as good. Evil and danger come from disturbance of the normal order. Disorder must be corrected through restructuring order. The singer learns appropriate songs, medicines, and practices necessary for curing a patient and restoring hózhǫ́. The source of the ritual is a story that relates how the ancestors of the Navajos acquired the ceremonial procedures from the supernaturals (Spencer 1957; Witherspoon and Peterson 1995). The singers create sand paintings specific to eliciting a cure for a particular illness. It is inappropriate to separate medicine from religion within the Navajo world, as the concepts of health and order are inseparable. Health stretches far beyond the individual. It concerns all Navajos and is based on a reciprocal relationship with the nonhuman world mediated through ritual.

The Holy People (Ye'ii) are thought to be irresistibly attracted to ceremonies by prayers and offerings and seeing their portraits beautifully painted in sand. The meaning and cultural significance of sand paintings are to reiterate and replicate the appropriate order. Thus the ceremonies re-create and restructure the Navajo universe, putting everything back in its proper place. Because humans are composed of the same elements as the mountains, plants, and stars, these beings are made in human form to remind participants they are related to them. Prayer offerings establish a kin relationship with the Holy People characterized by reciprocity (Griffin-Pierce 1992). It is an exchange, an invitation to the Holy People, and in return they restore the health of the patient, or "one sung over."

Such familial closeness is an essential part of reestablishing conditions of health and order. Individuals who help to create the sand paintings and participate in the ceremonies feel spiritual fulfillment because they contribute to restoring balance and order in the cosmos. Thus the principle of reciprocity governs human relations with many elements in the universe. Such relationships are still very real and maintain their importance among Navajos who continue to live the "Navajo way" (Begay and Maryboy 1996).

The Blessingway is considered the core of all Navajo ceremonies, and it is at the core of all Navajo culture, the "spinal column" of songs (Winter 1993:98). The stories provide the prototypes and sanctions for many of the acts and component rites of other ceremonies. The Blessingway has historical precedence over other chants because it originated just after Emergence. It describes the birth of Changing Woman and her Twins, the creation of corn, wild game, and domestic animals, the creation of the Navajo people, the origin of the loom and weaving tools, and the sacred Mountain Soil Bundle. This key ceremony consecrates the hogan, is central to Kinaaldá, and blesses a marriage and a mother and her newborn. It is intended to secure order and success in all phases of life. The Blessingway consecrates the Navajo family dwelling, which is seen as a model of the Navajo cosmos.

Through Changing Woman, the Holy People are tied genealogically through clan organization to the Diné (Reichard 1950:58–59). They experience human emotions, such as worry, jealousy, anger, sadness, and joy. Thus they have emotional and physical links to humans. With the conclusion of cosmic creation, the Holy People became invisible and retreated to the mountains, canyons, and sacred places of Navajoland. The responsibility for maintaining hózhǫ́ was passed on to Navajos.

Appendix II

The Hubbell Papers

The Hubbell Papers, weighing almost two tons, were processed by archivist Clint Colby over a seven-year period. The papers are stored in 573 Hollinger boxes.

Group I is composed of 125 boxes and contains all incoming, outgoing, and intra- and interpost correspondence and Indian letters. All correspondence is alphabetized to the initial of the middle name. Group II contains vendor files concerned with the exchange of goods or services between the Hubbells and individuals or companies and 114 boxes of orders, invoices, freight bills, and so on, from off-post vendors. Another 77 boxes (nos. 241–318) are intrapost vendor files containing orders, invoices, and receipts in alphabetical order. Group III is composed of business books and daily records (174 boxes), day books, cash books, individual accounts (ledgers, ledger sheets), journals, and daily sheets. The arrangement is alphabetical by post, with material for each location in chronological order. There are 29 boxes of summary records that cover a wide range of materials concerned with general accounting of the business on a monthly, quarterly, and yearly basis. Inventories, financial statements, accounts payable/receivable, and profit and loss records are arranged alphabetically by post. Five other boxes are labeled "Indian records." Several smaller groups of files contain all papers related to legal and banking matters, personal materials, post office materials, sales books and advertisements, price lists and catalogs. I reviewed information relevant to weaving in more than 200 boxes of papers and entered pertinent information into my notebook computer. Because much of the information was too detailed to assess and enter on site, the library staff photocopied nearly one thousand pages directly from the papers.

Hubbell maintained a double-entry bookkeeping system—devised in the fourteenth and fifteenth centuries in Venice, Italy (Turton 1991)—a sophisticated and unusual form of record keeping for a frontier trader. Some traders never kept formal records as so little cash changed hands (Adams 1968:135; Richardson 1986:11; Roberts 1987:45). They depended on wholesalers to notify them annually regarding their financial solvency. Records of individual transactions form the basis of an accounting system. Account records are kept in different types of record books, including books of prime entry (cash books and day books), journals, ledgers, accounts, and "other records." Often these types of records are kept in volume form, labeled and numbered by date.

Day book entries contain detailed information often summarized in either the journal or the ledger. Cash books contain debit and credit transactions. The debit columns represent transactions of moneys received, and the creditor trans-actions reflect sums paid. All transactions in the books of prime entry (cash books and day books) must be posted to the ledger. The journal stands between the books of prime entry and the ledger. In the journal, all transactions of the same kind are "arranged" sequentially in date order and gathered together, often alphabetically, under appropriate headings, with an indication of which sums are to be carried to the debtor side and which to the creditor side of the ledger.

The ledger is the central record in double-entry bookkeeping where all the transactions of an enterprise are classified by every activity in which it is engaged. The name of each account is written at the top of the page and the transactions entered below. Balance sheets show assets and liabilities; therefore, one can deduce net worth or value. Profit and loss accounts are subsidiary to the bal-ance sheets, detailing how the profit or loss figures have been arrived at. They bring together profits from the different activities of an enterprise and losses and other items that must be set against them.

Journals and ledgers contain the same information arranged in different ways. They are invaluable but by themselves can be frustrating. By using sales ledgers, researchers can work out monthly and yearly sales figures to show seasonal trends. (Hubbell's shipping records also revealed this type of information.)

Hubbell maintained a rudimentary bookkeeping system until 1895. His record keeping became more sophisticated after his former business partner, Clinton Cotton, left for Gallup to open a wholesale house. After 1900 Hubbell had hand-tooled leather-bound record books printed with column headings as follows: Wool (white/black), Goat Skins, Sheep Pelts, and Blankets. By 1905 more headings were added. His business records spanning the years 1895 to 1911 are quite complete. I was able to cross-check and verify a number of the figures and totals (see chapter 4). All of the information concerning post inven-tories, cash valuation of Navajo products, pawn accounts, and annual cumu-lative shipments was compiled after collecting and analyzing pertinent information. Hubbell served in the territorial legislature from 1912 to 1914 and left his younger son, Roman, in charge of Ganado. Record keeping deteriorated during that period.

Many of the rug entries in the ledgers and journals were coded. I discovered several codes deciphered in one of the earliest ledger books (HP Box 327 #2). Except for rug entries, no other entries were coded. Thus each rug entry had to be deciphered before figures could be tabulated. It was necessary to gather information on all other products the Navajo exchanged for goods to determine the importance of weaving relative to other primary products.

Appendix III

Terms and Description of the Weaving Process

Aniline Dye: coal-tar derivative or synthetic colorant developed in Europe in about 1850 and made available to Navajo weavers by traders after 1875.

Batten: a piece of smoothed hardwood from 18 inches to 3 feet long by 1 to 3 inches wide and one-half inch thick that is used to separate the warp threads before inserting the weft.

Bayeta or *baize:* a trade wool fabric unraveled by Navajo weavers, respun, and incorporated in pre-twentieth-century chief's blankets. Bayeta was available in various colors, but red was preferred.

Chief's Blanket *(hanoolchadi):* a nineteenth-century banded wearing blanket worn and traded by Navajos until 1885. These blankets were finely woven of home-spun wool and sometimes included bayeta. They have been classified into four different styles or phases, with increasingly complex patterns. Lorenzo Hubbell encouraged women to weave revival-style chief's blankets in about 1900.

Churro: the small, hardy breed of sheep introduced by the Spanish in the six-teenth century and adopted by the Navajos.

Germantown Yarns: 3- and 4-ply yarns produced from synthetic dyes and commercially spun. These yarns were originally manufactured in Pennsylvania.

Heddle: a continuous string looped around a long thin rod or dowel to which the weaver attaches every other warp thread after the loom is warped. This allows alternate warp strands to come forward simultaneously when the heddle rod is pulled.

Indigo: a dye extracted from a species of the pea family that produces a deep rich blue.

Saddle Blanket: a single saddle blanket measures thirty to thirty-six inches on a side; a double saddle blanket is twice the width and folded when placed under a saddle. These blankets may be used as small rugs.

Twill Weaves: called *iimaas* by Navajo weavers, these are produced when weft yarns pass over two or more warps. Usually each successive row moves one thread to the right, or left, producing a diagonal pattern. Frequently used for saddle blankets.

Vegetal Dye: a nonsynthetic colorant extracted from plants.

Warp: fine-spun wool yarn stretched tightly on the loom bars to form the foundation for the textile. When the loom is upright, the warp is vertical. It is covered by the weft. (See fig. 22.)

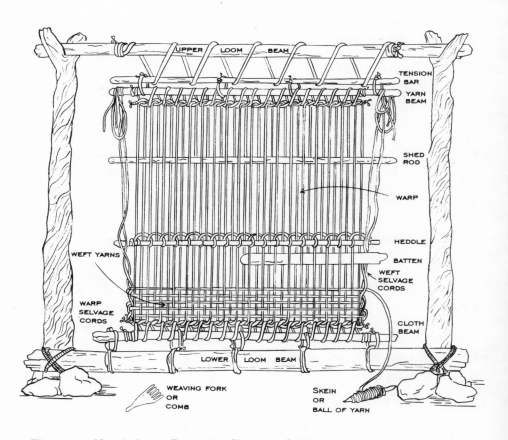

Figure 22. Navajo loom. Drawn by Christian Schnyder.

Weaver's Pathway: a thin line extending to the edge of a textile. Typically created for bordered rugs, as it allows the weaver's energy to escape, freeing her to begin another rug.

Weaving Fork or Comb: made of wood and containing from five to ten tines, the weaver uses the fork to pack down the weft yarns.

Weft: one-ply yarns, usually colored and not spun as fine as the warp yarn. They are woven over and under the warp yarns and make up the patterns seen in the textiles.

Yei weavings: Ye'ii are Holy People who are sometimes depicted in sand paintings created by medicine men during Navajo ceremonies. Some weavers, especially those from the Four Corners area, specialize in weaving sand painting blankets.

Process for Weaving a Navajo Rug

Fleece: From two to three sheep are needed to make a 3-x-5-foot rug. The best wool for weaving comes from the midbody area of the animal: the shoulders, back, and flanks. If the fleece is not too dirty, it can be shaken vigorously. Wool to be dyed should be washed, and washing may be done before or after carding and spinning. Fetching water to wash fleece in the past was time consuming as water sources such as wells and streams were not always convenient to reach from a weaver's home. Either pounded yucca root *(Yucca baccata* or *Yucca glauca)* or commercial detergent is used to wash the fleece. Several rinses are required before the wool is spread out to dry. It may take ten to fifteen hours to shear and wash the fleece before carding and spinning.

Carding: After the fleece has dried, the fibers must be straightened through carding, to remove tangles. Carding involves combing a handful of fleece between two metal boards with fine metal teeth. A single batt, or rolag, can be produced by an experienced carder in approximately one minute. However, hundreds of rolags are necessary to produce enough fleece to spin into yarn for an average rug. If the fleece has not been washed, it takes somewhat longer to produce the rolags, as the wool tends to be greasier and contain bits of dirt and debris.

Spinning: Navajo spinners create their yarn on a large spindle. Sitting on the ground, or on a chair, the spinner twirls the spindle against her thigh with one hand while twisting and pulling the rolag with the other. As the rolag becomes twisted into yarn of the desired thickness, the spinner pushes the spun yarn against the disk of the spindle. A new rolag is attached to the most recently spun yarn by twisting a few of the wool fibers. It is necessary to spin the wool in this manner at least twice and preferably three times to achieve the desired fineness for a smooth rug. To produce enough fine yarn for a 3-x-5-foot rug, at least three thousand yards of yarn are needed. Preparation may comprise as much as 70 percent of a weaver's time.

Dyeing: Many Navajo blankets and rugs are woven with commercially dyed yarn. The dyes are purchased in small packages and stirred into hot water before being added to the skeins of hand-spun yarn. However, if a weaver wishes to use vegetal dyed yarns, she must collect the plants that will provide the desired colors for her rug. Plants must be collected during the appropriate season, usually summer or fall. Most plants can be used fresh or dried for future use. Sometimes Navajo medicine men are consulted on the location of suitable plants, as they used them for ceremonial purposes.

Loom Preparation: The Navajo loom may be made from piñon trees, and logs six to eight inches in diameter are used for the uprights and crosspieces. The loom may be anchored to the ground or wooden legs added to serve as additional supports. Today weavers may use commercial lumber, metal pipes, old metal bed frames with the springs removed, or a combination of wood and metal to provide the necessary rigidity to keep the warp taut.

Winding the Warp: The loom becomes a temporary warping frame that holds the crossbars. The weaver winds tightly spun warp in a figure-eight motion around the bars held in place by ropes or nails to keep the warp perfectly even. If a large rug is planned, it usually takes two people to warp the loom, each sitting at either end of the loom frame, which is laid on the floor. The completed warp is laced to broom handles or dowels (this keeps the threads evenly spaced), then stretched tightly and anchored to additional dowels or heavy metal bars. It hangs vertically between the top and bottom bars.

Weaving: Nearly all Navajo weaving, with the exception of warp-faced belts, involves covering the warp completely with the weft yarns of various colors. Designs are created by introducing different colored wefts and weaving back and forth to build up the patterns. Adjoining colors may be hooked around each other to avoid gaps in the weaving. This is the technique typically known as tapestry. It is a time-consuming type of weave, as each row must be tightly packed to prevent the warp from showing. Since the weaver has wound the warp in a continuous, figure-eight motion, two sheds are created to facilitate construction of the patterns. A long flat stick or batten is inserted and turned on edge to hold the warp open temporarily while the weaver places the wefts in position. A weaving fork or comb is used to tightly pack the weft yarns.

Finishing: Because a Navajo textile has four selvedges, tension increases as the rug nears completion. The weaver uses a needle or umbrella rib to force the final few inches of yarns through the warp.

Clarification of Terms

The key difference between a blanket and a rug is size: wearing blankets varied in width from 5.5 to 6.5 feet, whereas rugs could vary between double saddle blanket size (2.5–3 × 5 ft) and room size. Textiles used as rugs were woven thicker and heavier to account for foot traffic, and many have borders. Sometimes the terms "small blankets" and "large blankets" are used in archival correspondence. It is difficult to determine how size is defined. Using the wearing blanket as an average, because it was the textile typically worn by Navajos before the reservation period, any textile less than 3 × 5 feet would be considered small; a textile 3 × 5 feet to 4 × 6 feet would be average; and textiles measuring more than 5 × 7 feet could be considered large. Don Lorenzo was known for his preference for large rugs.

Good Blanket/Common Blanket: "Common blanket" can be construed as a description of the typical saddle blanket, containing edge-to-edge stripes, a few colors, little if any pattern, and relatively "coarse" weave (fewer than ten wefts per inch). A good blanket could be a well-woven patterned saddle blanket or a rug with a highly patterned weave, woven on a wool warp, with a pleasing color combination, technically well executed, with at least twenty wefts per inch of weaving.

Modern Blanket/Historic Blanket: This designation refers to patterns in blankets and rugs. Historic blankets are those woven before 1880. They incorporate patterns found in wearing blankets, which have terraced diamonds and triangles, influenced by Navajo basketry patterns. Navajo weavers were also influenced by patterns produced by Hispanic weavers that had serrated diamonds, and so on. In his 1902 curio catalog, Lorenzo Hubbell depicts blankets and rugs woven with historic nineteenth-century motifs. These he termed revival-style textiles. The modern styles emerged during the transitional period beginning with Hwééldi, and many are bordered or include various combinations and permutations of patterns similar to or quite different from those found in earlier nineteenth-century Navajo textiles. In their correspondence, traders and wholesalers continued to refer to the rugs as "blankets." In his 1976 text, H. L. James highlights at least nine regional styles and several others, such as monogrammed and pictorial. Today many weavers have books and catalogs on the subject of Navajo weaving, and they may weave a pattern attributed to a particular region that is quite distant from their home. Non-Navajos generally refer to styles that are attributed to particular areas and posts, but Navajo weavers have their own names for styles and weaves that differ from descriptive terms designated in the published literature (Tabaha 1999).

Appendix IVa

The Fred Harvey Company's Earliest Shipment

The earliest Fred Harvey Company records date from 1901 in the Hubbell Papers. Yet several sources state that the trader and the company maintained a business relationship long before the turn of the century. Kaufman and Selser (1985) call Hubbell "the leading rug dealer in North America" and claim that in 1902 the Harvey Company purchased more than $20,000 worth of textiles from him; within ten years the amount had tripled. This is a typical statement on the sales of Navajo textiles. It cannot be substantiated, based on initial transactions noted in Hubbell's and Harvey's ledgers, and it was incorrectly quoted by James (1988:101). He quotes the authors: "In the year 1902 alone, Hubbell, negotiating through Harvey's representative buyer, Herman Schweizer, sold $60,000 worth of rugs." Errors are compounded when scholars neglect to work with primary data. The information quoted above should have alerted scholars researching the Navajo economy as to the economic importance of Navajo textiles.

Citing several of the earlier classic sources, Weiss (1984:50–51) states that Hubbell regularly resold about $25,000 worth of rugs each year to the Fred Harvey Company during the 1880s. Based on Hubbell's own records, this is impossible. I am unable to locate textiles being wholesaled by Hubbell for more than $0.35 per pound before 1900. Thus he would need to ship nearly seventy-five thousand pounds of textiles to the Fred Harvey Company alone. Even during the heyday of textile shipments, it appears that Hubbell never shipped more than fifty thousand pounds of weaving in a single year. Weiss (1984:74) also quotes McNitt on the high volume of textiles purchased by Harvey. McNitt claims the Harvey Company purchased between $20,000 and $25,000 worth of textiles from Hubbell annually "for many years." In analyzing Hubbell's shipping records in conjunction with the Harvey Company's blanket ledgers, if the amount just mentioned is correct, it must reflect the Harvey Company's retail price. Table 11 documents the earliest shipment from Lorenzo Hubbell to the Fred Harvey Company (March 1901). A variety of blankets were shipped, reflecting some of the styles categorized in table 6, above. Three of the blankets were actually located in Book 2 of the Fred Harvey Company ledgers housed at the Museum of International Folk Art in Santa Fe, New Mexico. Six of the old-style blankets were entered in the Hubbell's CASH PROFIT code, which allows the reader to decipher the amount of credit the weaver received in trade goods. According to information contained in Hubbell's 1902 curio publication, the old-style blankets ranged in size from 4 x 5 feet to 5 x 6¹/₂ feet. The sizes were estimated according to the retail cost listed in Hubbell's catalog.

Table 11. Fred Harvey Company Shipment, 1901 (Box 333, HP).

Type of Textile	Credit Received by Weaver [$]	Price to Harvey Co.
Old Style	11.00 [cctt]+	17.50
"	11.00	20.00
"	16.50 [crpt]	25.00
"	15.00 [cptt]	30.00 [7#]/$50*
"	16.50 [crpt]	25.00
"	15.50 [cppt]	25.00
Portieres	35.50 [sppt]	65.00
Total	121.00	207.50
Old Style		25.00
"		25.00
O.S. Zuni red,blk & blue		12.50 [4-7/8#]**
Indian Dye Blanket		25.00
"		25.00
"		15.00
"		20.00
O.S. Native Wool		10.00/30.00***
"		20.00
5 Bed Blkts choice 50# @ .41/#		20.50
7 saddle blkts @ 2.50-5.00/ea.		25.50

* Fred Harvey Company Ledger Books 4/27/01
** #3349 FHCo.
*** #3341 FHCo., p 20 Ledger Book #2
+ Code: CASH PROFIT
              1234 567890

Appendix IVb

The Fred Harvey Company and Indian Demonstrators on Display

A fair proportion of the Hubbell-Harvey correspondence concerns Navajo and Hopi demonstrators Hubbell supplied to the Harvey Company. Tourists traveling by railroad were treated to a visual ethnographic feast as baskets, pottery, rugs, and jewelry adorned the walls, floors, and tables of the impressive Indian Rooms located in many of the hotels. To augment the attraction the Harvey Company arranged for Hubbell to send reliable demonstrators who would weave and make jewelry at railroad stations and larger hotels at the Grand Canyon, Santa Fe, Albuquerque, and so on. Their unique position enabled them to acquire valuable ethnological material, including many items sacred to Hopi religious ceremonies. Byron Harvey notes:

> Serving as a source of supply for the East, in the early years the company had a virtually insured profit in their sales of Indian craft. Freight rates, moreover were by contract extremely advantageous; empty boxcars or their equivalent could easily be loaded with collection material. The company's agents, present the year round, frequently were able to purchase items never offered to summer visitors. Winter brings hard times to the Indian or Spanish American farmer and consequently whole wagon loads of irreplaceable Santos and Indian arts were brought in for sale. (1963:35–36)

In this way the Harvey Houses were stocked with artifacts and the company's valuable collection continually increased in size. Herman Schweizer culled the best and most unusual items that crossed his path. Major museums in the United States, including the Chicago Natural History Museum, Columbia University, and the Carnegie Museum, owe the nucleus of their ethnographic collections from the Southwest to Schweizer and the Harvey family. The Berlin Museum also benefited, and the kachina collection at the Heye Foundation was originally compiled by Schweizer (Harvey 1963:37).

In a letter dated 6 July 1903, Hubbell asked the company not to pay the demonstrators all their money because they owed him on accounts. Elle of Ganado and her husband, Tom, worked at the Indian House for years. The company wanted the demonstration rooms to look as authentic (exotic) as possible. Schweizer wrote to Hubbell on 17 November 1904 (HP Box 36) requesting that the Navajos use handmade forges and bellows while demonstrating silversmithing and that they bring their own homemade cooking pots "as he would not want them to use a stove there." The U.S. Indian Service sanctioned the Harvey Company's policy of hiring demonstrators because they "[were] paid good wages" (HP Box 43, 4/06/06, R. Perry to Lorenzo Hubbell). However, it appears that the Harvey Company and Hubbell served as "each other's bill collectors when it came to Indian accounts" (Blue 2000:154).

Much of the correspondence over the years concerned the Indian families supplied by Hubbell to the various Harvey Houses. The company placed implicit trust in Hubbell's judgment regarding appropriate individuals. Often families were away from the reservation for months at a time. The Harvey Company was reluctant to release any demonstrators until their replacements arrived. If one of the women was about to deliver her baby, or if one of the men proved extremely troublesome, only then would an individual be sent home without an immediate replacement. Evidence of resistance on the part of demonstrators recurs over the years in the correspondence. In a one-week period in April 1905 Huckel wrote to Hubbell twice with complaints about Taos the silversmith:

> [W]e cannot control Taos. He is making silver for other Indians and they are selling it, he is going over town and selling it and also selling it to our guests on the quiet, no matter how closely we watch him. I find he has been doing this ever since he has been at Albuquerque. It is a bad precedent for our other Indians and is spoiling them. . . . Taos has been spoiled by his experience at St. Louis. . . . [H]e is spoiling *Megil-li-to* also. (HP Box 36)

In 1905 the Hopi potter Nampeyo demonstrated at the Grand Canyon along with four men, two women, and five children. According to the correspondence, the Indians at Hopi House were creating a good market for their goods. In a letter dated 30 September 1905, Huckel wrote to Hubbell stating that Nampeyo's party was "pretty independent and pretty much spoiled when they were at the Canyon last spring."

They did not want to do anything unless they were paid for it. . . .
[O]n the other hand, Nampeyo and her daughter are excellent pottery
makers. . . . [T]he Indian children are the greatest attraction at the Canyon.

Today Nampeyo is acknowledged as the "matriarch" of Pueblo potters and
her pieces sell for thousands of dollars each. Sometimes Hubbell had to make
arrangements to ship entire families on short notice, and on a number of occasions he would receive a telegram canceling the request. On 4 April 1907
Schweizer requested more Indians "as soon as possible" because one thousand
Shriners were expected at the Grand Canyon by the end of April. In a letter
dated 19 May 1910, from the Grand Canyon, Huckel noted his displeasure
with Navajo silversmith Charley, who attempted to sell jewelry directly to
tourists. Another Navajo smith had been retained as a demonstrator for over a
year. Huckel notes: "These Indians seem to think they can come and go as they
please and the only way to handle them is to be firm with them" (HP Box 36).

Appendix IVc

The Fred Harvey Company as Broker of Historic Navajo Textiles

Before 1900 Navajo weavers had to compete with textiles woven by their ancestors. Evidence of an active market for historic weavings appears in texts (Amsden [1934] 1975; James [1914] 1974), magazine articles, and advertisements (Spiegelberg 1904; Young 1914). For decades, Don Lorenzo corresponded with and provisioned collectors, traders, museum curators, and dealers, such as the Fred Harvey Company. The investment market for historic Navajo textiles has been active for more than a century, and individuals such as Herman Schweizer played a pivotal role in maintaining it.[1] Schweizer's ledgers show that the purchase of historic textiles made up a large portion of his entire annual inventory, particularly from 1900 to 1920. Sometimes these historic pieces remained unsold for decades because of huge markups and fluctuating demand. Thus has the collectors' market in historic Navajo weaving plagued the contemporary market for a century.

Schweizer was relentless in his desire to own the best, and over a forty-year period he acquired more than six thousand choice objects of Indian and Spanish origin for the Harvey Company collection alone (Dutton 1983:95).[2] Amsden sanctioned the Harvey Company's farsightedness in purchasing old blankets:

> [I]t is no exaggeration to say that Fred Harvey has saved from destruction thousands of worthy old specimens of Navajo weaving. The vision and initiative of Mr. J. F. Huckel, Vice President of the company, and Mr. H. Schweizer, veteran manager of the Indian Department, have brought to the Fred Harvey Company the honor of being a staunch and enlightened protagonist of Navajo weaving, old as well as new. ([1934] 1975:192)

Although Schweizer lacked unlimited funds with which to purchase textiles, he tied up thousands of dollars per year in old collections. For example,

Blomberg (1988:20) notes that Schweizer paid retired merchant Abe Spiegelberg $7,000 for his collection in 1901.[3] This equals the *entire* amount of credit extended to 272 Ganado area weavers in 1900 (Weavers' journals Boxes 344 #1, 523). Schweizer did not purchase $7,000 worth of textiles (482 blankets and rugs) from Hubbell until 1906 (Blanket Book #3, Museum of International Folk Art).

Spiegelberg was one of the early New Mexico merchants, described as individuals who had the opportunity and foresight to amass fine collections for pleasure and/or profits. Spiegelberg opened a curio shop in Santa Fe and "assembled one of the finest collections of Navajo and other Indian and native blankets and rugs in the Southwest, which was sold to the Fred Harvey company. . . . He became recognized as the premier expert authority on such fabrics" (Blomberg 1988:20). In his article in *Out West*, Spiegelberg (1904:447–49) advised collectors to purchase blankets from reputable dealers. He contrasts the beauty and quality of the historic blankets woven with pride for Navajo use with the more coarsely woven counterparts being produced for the burgeoning external market.[4]

Today textile collectors contact the Heard Museum, whose library houses a significant portion of Herman Schweizer's ledger books. As Schweizer purchased and sold thousands of Navajo textiles for the Fred Harvey Company for nearly fifty years, many old textiles retain the company's tag with stock number and wholesale price in code. Verification of the date and cost immediately increases its value.

Appendix V

Weavers' Ledger Accounts

Although many authors state that Hubbell standardized the trade, women wove rugs in many different sizes. If Hubbell wished a weaver to make a particular size, he probably provided two pieces of string to give her an idea of the length and width of the piece. Hubbell's weavers' account books (Box 344 #1, #2) provide evidence of how he dealt with women exchanging textiles for household necessities. Although a number of entries are illegible, many are quite straightforward. I perused hundreds of pages of rug inventory sheets covering several decades and discovered that the Hubbells noted the width, length, and weight of each blanket or rug. "Standardization" is a misnomer, as it appears that no two textiles are exactly alike in dimension or pattern. I have noted the approximate size (small, medium, or large) adjacent to a particular description (appendix III).

Nearly three hundred women's names are entered in the 1900–1902 Ganado ledger book. Hubbell wrote down every item he gave each weaver and debited it to her account. The debit was not discharged until she returned with a blanket. At times he may have provided the fleece (unspun wool) and/or yarn and dyes. It is important to distinguish between fleece (unspun wool), "rough" yarn or roving, and yarn, the commercial product that is always prespun by machine. Whether or not Hubbell supplied the fleece, the weaver had to spin it before weaving, a time-consuming activity that adds considerably to production time. In a finely woven textile it may take twice as long to prepare the fibers as it does to weave the piece, especially if the pattern is not too complex. Warp yarns must be spun more tightly and several more times because they are subjected to constant tension and friction from packing of the weft.

Hubbell may have issued wool to weavers for several reasons. At the turn of the century, wool production had plummeted (see fig. 6). Navajo flocks were decimated by a series of storms and droughts in the 1890s (see chapter 2). It is estimated they lost 75 percent of their stock by that date. Some Navajos had no stock at all (Bailey and Bailey 1986:100–105). In any event, issuing fleece to weavers appears to decline over time.

I copied 48 of 308 pages from the 1900–1902 ledger book (Box 344). Each page contains the names of two women, and a number of weavers' accounts were transferred to pages toward the back of the ledger when the first page was filled. For example, on page 44, the account of Atzi-di Biteshi' No. 2 is listed. She was credited with $6.00 in two increments to "make wool blanket." On 11 July 1902 she was given 5.25 pounds of warp ($1.75), a total of 37 pounds of wool to spin (entered at $0.16 per pound), doled out over several months. As fleece was averaging $0.08 per pound, this could be scoured wool. The total cost of supplies provided by Hubbell was $7.97 and included three packages of dye. The final transaction is dated the following February. This weaver appeared at Ganado on three occasions (and notations were made on her account) while weaving this blanket. The textile she eventually produced likely weighed 20 pounds. She received approximately $0.30 per pound to spin and weave it, which Hubbell advertised in his catalog as selling for $0.75 to $2.50 per pound. Therefore, this type of blanket retailed for $18.75 to $62.50. Weavers had to return any unused wool or warp to Hubbell. If they had spun all the wool, he granted them credit (which varied between $0.20 and $0.30 per pound). When Hubbell issued prepared warp to weavers, he entered it at $0.60 per pound at the turn of the century. This woman's account shows another entry for 13 March 1905. She was issued more warp, 20 pounds of wool, and four packages of dye. But the word "died" is written over the final entry for her account. Several other weavers died during this period, and on at least two occasions family members had to complete the blankets.

"Weaver" is the name of another women who wove continuously and traded at Ganado. Her account (1900–1907) is listed on pages 87, 155, 188, and 273. She wove several kinds of textiles, including portieres and bayeta and common blankets. On 24 October 1902 Hubbell advanced her $28.50 for a pair of portieres. (Portieres are two identically woven rectangular textiles that served as room dividers between the parlor and dining room in Victorian homes.) On 11 March 1903 "Weaver" was advanced another $12.00, issued 9 yards of bayeta (valued at $1.75 per yard) and 10 skeins of rough yarn or roving (r.y.) for $0.70 to weave a bayeta blanket. Red bayeta blankets in particular were important in nineteenth-century trade, and Hubbell was keen to see them revived (see Amsden [1934] 1975; James [1914] 1974). On 11 May she was issued another $9.50 in credit and given 6 yards of bayeta. On 2 January 1904 another 2.5 yards of bayeta were issued, and the following note is inscribed in Hubbell's hand: "Do not give her any more to weave. Let her make our portieres that she owes." The word "settled" is also written diagonally across this transaction, indicating she eventually finished the portieres. On 1 February 1904 "Weaver" was given $6.00 in cash and issued $7.50 in "tickets." On 6 July she was advanced another $40.00 to make two portieres. The following February (1905) she was issued eight pounds of wool to make five small blankets for a total of $5.00 in credit. On 21 April the following is noted: "to make a bayeta blanket to be paid $8.00." Six yards of bayeta were issued between 21 April and September. On 14 February 1906 she was issued 60 skeins of yarn. Her account continues on page 273, noting that a pair of portieres was owing. On 4 March 1907 she was issued more bayeta and given $3.00 "paid in advance" and $6.00 worth of "tickets." Hubbell notes: "To receive $8.00. If well done, $2.00 more." On 7 May and 17 August she received more bayeta. The last transaction entered for "Weaver" is dated 30 November. She was issued more bayeta, advanced $8.00 in credit, and given a "gift" worth $2.00. On one of the earlier transactions, the word "Wanton" was gracefully inscribed and underlined over one of her account entries.

Numerous entries note the amount a weaver was "to be paid" based on the type of blanket she produced. It appears that a weaver received $5.00 in credit to weave two small gray blankets. Yet a number of these entries reveal that women were given more than twenty pounds of wool to spin before weaving. Box 344 #5 contains a list of sixteen spinners who provided yarn for Hubbell. Two entries note the amount of wool charged out, the weight of the yarn returned, and the credit the spinner received. It appears that spinners received between $0.09 and $0.14 per pound of spun yarn, and approximately 40 percent by weight was lost during the process. (Commercially scoured wool reduces the weight of raw fleece by 40 to 60 percent.)

The account of Hastin Bitzi At?? No. 5 is listed on page 108, Box 344 #2. On 11 September 1903 she was advanced $6.00 in credit and given a total of $9.10 worth of yarns (13.75 pounds) in navy blue, black, white, and scarlet. She wove a *hanoolchadi* (chief's blanket), which Hubbell probably retailed for $35.00. Given the amount of yarn, it may have measured at least 5.5 x 6 feet. The commercial yarn that Hubbell issued to weavers was priced at $0.65 per pound. Yet a weaver received at most $0.30 per pound for her hand-spun warp. In 1905 this weaver wove a wool blanket for which she furnished the wool. She received $10.00 in credit for her efforts.

Weavers appeared to be averaging $6.00 in credit for weaving gray blankets and hanoolchadis when Hubbell supplied the wool. According to the 1902 catalog, Hubbell retailed grays for $0.75 to $2.50 per pound, and he sold hanoolchadis for $17.50 to $35.00, depending on the size. There are a number of entries in which weavers received $0.75 for weaving a small saddle blanket and $1.50 for two pillow covers. Capitan's Daughter (p. 158) received $2.50 for making a wool blanket, but she had to spin twenty-five pounds of wool before weaving the textile. All of these accounts have "Settled" scrawled across them, so it appears that weavers were not being paid extra chits or credit—the entries are complete. Several weavers earned $30.00 in credit making blankets that measured 9 feet square when they spun and wove their own wool. A blanket this size would be considered a large blanket. Page 217 contains a notation: "to make blanket 6.5 feet square, she to furnish wool . . . $10.00." This size would probably be classified as a medium blanket.

Chi Bita Wife is listed on page 166. On 25 May 190? she was allowed $2.50 in credit and issued twenty pounds of wool (at $0.16 per pound, or $3.20) to weave one small gray blanket. (Note that the value of the wool issued to her was worth more than her labor.) The following February she was issued thirteen pounds of wool and advanced $5.00 to weave five small blankets. Both of these entries were marked "Settled." However, an entry dated 16 February was transferred to page 237. She was issued $16.00 worth of credit in increments between 16 February and 25 May 1905. There are four more notations including one "due on next . . . $6.50." The words "Dead Beat" are scrawled across the entire entry, and that is the last notation on her account. This phrase was written across at least six women's accounts in this ledger.

On 22 July 1903 Dichadi Biquii Bitzi (p. 170) was advanced $21.00 to make a large blanket, but she died, so her sister was charged with finishing it, and Hubbell gave her $15.00 in credit. Another weaver was issued 8.5 pounds of yarn to weave a small hanoolchadi. She received $2.50 on 11 September, and the following March she was given another $2.50. "Dead Beat" was scrawled across her account as she never returned with the blanket. Tzepi Bicha Bitzi (p. 185) also wove portieres for Hubbell. Between 18 December and 3 February, she received a total of $27.20 in advances and chits to weave the pair of portieres. In March she received a cash advance and was issued more chits to make another pair of portieres for which she received a total of $29.00. Hubbell advertised portieres in his 1902 catalog as follows: ". . . sold only in pairs. Made only by the best weavers, of whom there are but few living with skill to make two blankets nearly alike. In bright and old style colors and patterns, size about 5 x 12 feet. Price varies according to fineness of weave . . . $200 to $300 per pair." Several weavers received up to $75 in credit for weaving a pair, but the few women who wove them generally averaged between $25.00 and $50.00 in credit.

Weavers appeared to receive approximately $5.00 in credit for weaving a 4-x-6-foot textile if Hubbell supplied the wool. A textile this size was in the "small" range. In some cases he issued more than fifteen pounds of wool for such a blanket or rug and the weaver had to spin all the warp and weft. On average, several months elapsed between such entries. In addition to the two rug weaving experiments previously described, Roessel (1983a:20) provides another example in which it took a weaver 388 hours to spin and weave a 3-x-5-foot vegetal dye rug. Given the time needed to produce a textile, it is not too difficult to account for weavers' infrequent visits to Ganado.

One of the textiles Hubbell advertised in his 1902 catalog is described as a "native wool Navajo blanket, grey ground." There are numerous entries in his ledgers dating from 1900–1907 in which weavers are issued more than twenty pounds of wool to weave such blankets for $2.50 in credit. Hubbell retailed these textiles for $0.75 to $2.50 per pound, depending on the fineness of the weave. When women wove large blankets and furnished the wool themselves they received $10.00 in credit.

Page 208 lists the account of Paji Bilshaad, who appears to have woven only gray blankets for Hubbell. Within a seven-month period she was given a $4.00 advance on each of three blankets. He supplied her with twenty-five to thirty-eight pounds of wool to spin for each blanket, some dyes, and some warp. Each entry is marked "Settled."

Hastin Bitzi Atini Baad received $8.00 on 9 January by promising to make a blanket 6 feet square. The following July she received $10.00 for making one gray blanket 6.5 feet square (p. 220). On page 229, the 1905 account of "Tonto's wife" shows that on 11 March she was issued 5 pounds of wool for warp to make a wool blanket. She was issued dyes and a total of 20 pounds of wool between 29 March and 20 July, and she received a $4.00 credit for her efforts. The following 24 February she received 4 pounds of wool to make the warp for another wool blanket. She was issued a total of 26 pounds of wool and some dye and received another $4.00 in credit.

Occasionally Hubbell gave a blanket to a weaver to copy. Tagalichi Bitzoi No. 2's account is listed on page 270. This weaver produced several blankets for Hubbell, and under the last entry he noted that blanket was not returned yet. The final notation states: "brought blanket 3-9-10. Did not give her another." "Burt's Wife" is listed on page 273. She was given yarn and advanced a total of $10.00 in credit to make a "squaw dress."

The latter part of this ledger book (Box 344 #2) contains forty pages similar to pawn notations, but the word "borrowed" appears at the top of the page. Some entries indicate Hubbell gave fleece to spinners to be spun into wool. Other entries appear to be more like pawn; that is, bracelets, beads, baskets, and one saddle blanket (at $0.55) are listed as "borrowed" from Hubbell.

Box 523 #6 contains lists of weavers' accounts from 1902 to 1905. Each list, dated 1 January, is six to seven pages long. Although the number of weavers is unknown for 1902, $2,769.89 was recorded adjacent to the notation "blankets being made and merchandise advanced." This phrase indicates that Hubbell is indeed paying for anticipated blanket production via extension of credit. The "accounts owing" totaled $3,203.62, with 263 names listed for 1903. There are 237 names for 1904, with $1,555.55 posted in the "cash advanced" column and $1,069.98 in the merchandise column (total $2,625.53). In 1905, 227 weavers' accounts add up to $1,038.42 in cash advance and $1,564.75 in merchandise (total $2,603.17). For the latter years, Hubbell separated the cash advance from the merchandise and entered the dollar value in two adjacent columns. However, he lumps the weaving materials he issued to weavers with the chits for merchandise, because, in effect, it was all his "merchandise." "Cash" (i.e., credit) advances range from $1.00 to $21.00, but most entries cluster between $2.00 and $6.00. For 1904, there are twenty-four entries for more than $10.00—about 10 percent of all weavers were currently weaving a textile worth more than $10.00 in credit. If a weaver was not working on a blanket when inventory was taken (1 January of each year) or if she did not owe Hubbell on her account, she was not included in the weavers' accounts inventory list for that year. Box 523 #6 also contains a list of nonweaver Indian accounts for 1 January 1905. Eighty-three names are recorded that total $1,924.18 outstanding. Both Tom Ganado and his wife, Elle, are listed, as is Maria Antonia. These three Navajos were demonstrating for the Fred Harvey Company. Their wages were sent to Hubbell rather than paid directly to them; their families lived on the reservation and maintained accounts with Hubbell. Sometime during 1909 "Capitan's Wife" was allowed $5.00 in credit to weave a blanket, to be paid $5.00 more if it was a one-of-a-kind blanket (p. 290). Of the thousands of Navajos who dealt with the Hubbells for many decades, these individuals represent the handful whose names are recognizable.

Most of the entries from Box 344 #2 and #3 mention the type of textile woven, but the size is not noted. Several entries from Box 344 #5 indicate not only the materials issued to the weaver but also the size produced. However, it is unclear whether these records are for the year 1907 or 1910. "Many Sheep's Girl" is listed on page 22. She wove a blue blanket measuring 9 x 9 feet. She must have provided the wool because no wool was entered on her account. She received sixteen packages of dye and $9.55 worth of goods, including calico, flour, baking powder, syrup, coffee, crackers, and axle grease. The total amount came to $12.45, which included the dyes. Just underneath that amount is listed "Chips," $12.55. Therefore, she may have received an additional $12.55 in seco, especially since she probably used her own wool. Hubbell's curio catalog issued in 1902 reveals that he charged a minimum of $40.00 for an 8-x-9-foot rug.

Pages 18 and 23 of this ledger contain the account of "Stout Girl," who wove an 8-x-9-foot blue blanket for Hubbell (listed at $40 in his catalog). He issued her 10 pounds of spun wool valued at $3.00, 10 pounds of unspun wool for $1.00, 4 skeins of yarn, and 13 packages of dye. She was given $6.00 worth of "chips" and another $2.00 was added to the total. The next blanket she wove for Hubbell was a hanoolchadi pattern. Hubbell gave her $8.55 in "chips." She also purchased a sash at $1.25, and $0.20 worth of sugar went to her mother. Stout Girl also wove a large 12-x-12-foot gray blanket for Hubbell. He issued her 60 pounds of fleece, 48 skeins of yarn, 12 pounds of spun wool, and 11 packages of dye to create the rug. She received $14.05 worth of "chips," $9.20 worth of food, and $.50 worth of calico. Total credit and food received was $23.75. "Settled" is written diagonally across this entry, which indicates it is complete. Hubbell advertised textiles this size for $150.00 in his 1902 Indian curio catalog.

Page 17 lists the account of "Lame Girl," who was to weave a blue blanket for Hubbell. Her husband was also charging on her account ("Goods to buck"). Although the size is not noted, Lame Girl received $19.10 in "chips" and goods. She also wove a gray blanket for Hubbell (p. 20). She probably used her own wool, as none was issued to her. Lame Girl received goods valued at $4.50, beads valued at $8.00, and 18 packages of dye. She also wove for Hubbell in 1902–3 (Box 344 #2, p. 105). In December 1902 she received some roving yarn and was advanced $11.00 in credit to weave one gray blanket. She supplied the warp. On 16 March 1903 she was advanced $6.00 and given thirty-five pounds of yarn and 12 packages of dye to weave another blanket. Another weaver entered on this page whose name is illegible wove two "common" blankets for Hubbell. Both are marked "paid." Hubbell supplied her with dyes and warp but no wool. Food and goods valued at $4.00 are listed on her account.

Page 19 (Box 344 #5) contains an interesting notation for "My Girl" written in Hubbell's hand. (Hubbell is known to have fathered a number of children by Navajo women [Blue 2000:112–15].) She was obviously a weaver as the words "grey blanket" are written sideways beside the following entry. She was given $6.25 worth of merchandise, $2.25 "cash," $2.50 worth of "chips," beads valued at $28.00, and credit for $4.00 for a bracelet that she returned. Written across the entry are the words "Transferred to my acct." The account of "Stout Girl's Sister" is listed just below "My Girl." She wove both blue and gray blankets for Hubbell. She received $8.20 in food, calico and chits and was issued twenty-two pounds of wool, ten packages of dye, and four skeins of yarn to weave a grey blanket. "Paid" is written sideways across the entry. She also wove two blue blankets.

Page 21 lists the account of "Mushkelly's wife No. 2." She was issued $12.00 in chips and received a headband and flour ($2.00) to weave a blue blanket. Another entry for "Mushkelly woman" (p. 24) lists $3.50 in "chips," $4.45 in food, and $0.80 for goods. She was issued $1.20 in dyes and wool, so for both entries this woman (or these two women) used their own wool as Hubbell issued very little. Although several years elapsed between the earliest weavers' journal entries (1900–1901) and the entries listed in Box 523 #5, which cover 1907 or 1910, it appears credit allotted to weavers in return for blankets increased very little, whereas the cost of living according to post inventory records continually rose.

The data analyzed in this "weavers' ledger" reveal women bartering blankets and rugs from three to ten times a year. They also correspond to statements made by elderly Navajos in interviews at Ganado in 1971. Several remarked on how in earlier times women had to work much harder. Investigation of archival records reveals the real beneficiaries of the rapid escalation in textile production by hundreds of anonymous weavers.

Notes

Chapter One

1. I complied with the government of the Navajo Nation regarding their policy on ethnographic research on the reservation. The Historic Preservation Office issued Permit A9213-E to me, and in October–November 1992 I paid interviewees $10 per hour and my interpreter (when needed) $15 per hour.
2. Two recent exhibits, *Woven by the Grandmothers* (Bonar 1996) and *Weaving a World* (Willink and Zolbrod 1996), are provocative exceptions.
3. See Witherspoon and Peterson (1995:78–79) for a powerful critique of the intellectual provincialism and cultural imperialism endemic to anthropology's reliance on Western epistemologies anchored in binary oppositions.
4. According to Witherspoon (1975:23), kinship solidarity is framed and focused in the concepts of sharing and giving, whereas non-kin, or affinal solidarity, is framed in systems of exchange and reciprocity. There is an effort by Navajos to think of and relate to everyone in terms of kinship. Navajos are more likely to use terms of relationship than personal names. Everyone is addressed as kin: it is offensive to speak anyone's personal name in his or her presence. Kinship is so important that the worst thing that can be said of someone is "he acts as if he didn't have any relatives" (Witherspoon 1975:64).

Chapter Two

1. As New Mexicans acquired more weapons, Navajos became a major target of the suppliers of captives for the slave trade. By the mid-nineteenth century, thousands of Navajos were enslaved, working in Spanish haciendas and workshops. The attempt by Navajos to regain captive relatives resulted in warfare (Roessel 1983b:507). Navajos also took captives, but they did not make them slaves; instead, they formed the basis for new clans. However, ricos (Navajos with large numbers of stock) kept slaves to serve as herders (Bailey and Bailey 1986:99).
2. During prereservation trade, the Utes and Yavapais typically traded two buckskins for a large blanket. In their trade with the Pueblos, Navajos exchanged a large blanket for a string of turquoise. The northeastern Yavapais traded a Navajo blanket for six or seven undressed deer hides; three blankets for one buckskin; one large blanket for two buckskins; and one small blanket for one small buckskin (Hill 1948:380).
3. Federal control over Indians was first established by the Continental Congress in 1775. In 1784 Indian affairs were placed under the War Department (USFTC 1973:35). Indian trade, officially regulated by Congress, began in 1796. The government sought

to control abuses of the fur traders. Regulation was difficult if not impossible because of distance and communication problems on "the frontier" (Roberts 1987:15). In 1834 the Office of Indian Affairs was created, and in 1876 the Commissioner of Indian Affairs became the sole authority to appoint traders (USFTC 1973:35). Indian agents reported to the commissioner, who reported to the secretary of the interior and the president. High turnover, poor communication, inadequate or rejected appropriations, and graft exacerbated the situation.

4. In 1890 the Riordan Mercantile Company of Flagstaff (operated by the former Indian agent) advertised the largest and most complete stock of goods in northern Arizona. It was a wholesale and retail dealer in groceries, clothing, furniture, drugs, grain, feed, saddles, hardware, wagons, mill supplies, wool, pelts, skins, and Indian curios. The Babbitt Brothers purchased the company in 1893, thereby neutralizing a very strong competitor by absorbing it (Akbarzadeh 1992:334–35).

5. Table 10 in Parish (1961:156) contains information related to the value of Ilfeld's wool (both partido and open) between 1894 and 1904. The rate of return to Ilfeld averaged 5.3 to 15.8 percent in the years from 1894 to 1904, which compares to the 12 percent simple interest that was charged to delinquent accounts. This is not a bad return, taking into consideration that these partidos were still customers of the company and Ilfeld made a more than reasonable profit on all goods sold to clients, as evidenced by the growth of his company over the years.

6. During the period of free wool (1894–97), prices were more than one-third lower than during the years 1885–90, when the new lower price level occurred. The Dingly tariff was reinstated from 1897 to 1912, and prices gradually rose until 1905, when the average price per pound was the same as in 1890. After 1901 the general level of prices was from 17 to 25 percent below that maintained in the period 1870–89 and still further below that for the years 1840–59 (Wright 1910:276).

7. Several major studies examine the development of trading posts on the Navajo Reservation after Hwééldi. McNitt (1962), the ethnohistorians Bailey and Bailey (1986), and the anthropologist William Adams (1963) published texts that have become classics on the subject. The Federal Trade Commission investigated trader abuses during a series of hearings in 1972 (USFTC 1973). Weiss (1984) analyzed the development of capitalism on the reservation. Thus he incorporates much useful information on the subsequent expansion of the trading system.

   The earliest and most comprehensive study of southwestern traders and trading in general was published by McNitt (1962). He draws on archival collections, interviews, correspondence, books, articles, pamphlets, reports, diaries, and government documents. He provides a backdrop of early trading history beginning with the Spaniards, followed by the appearance of mercantile houses, sutlers, and Anglo traders. He profiles several traders' influence on the development of Navajo weaving (see chapters 3–5).

8. Elizabeth Hegemann traded with her husband at Shonto. They paid the Babbitts $5,000 for the post in 1929 and sold it to Mildred Carson Heflin and her husband, Reuben, in 1945 for $45,000. In 1957 the Heflins sold it for $80,000.

9. Several attempts were mounted by the government to get Navajo weavers "off the ground" (Weiss 1984:80). Floor looms and spinning wheels had met a frosty reception from weavers incarcerated at Hwééldi. Two more attempts failed in 1871 and 1875, when weavers were hired to teach the Navajo women how to use the unfamiliar equipment (Bailey and Bailey 1986:51).

10. Although Bureau of Indian Affairs regulations prohibited government employees from having an interest in trading with the Indians, many traders were also postmasters; thus they "worked" for the U.S. Postal Service (USFTC 1973:40). Some reservation traders have been charged with mail tampering (USFTC 1973:14).

11. According to the trader Tony Richardson (1986:6), Hubbell's seco looked so much like real American coins that the government made him stop issuing them. I have been unable to corroborate this in the government correspondence contained in the Hubbell Papers.

12. The Pajarito Land Grant was not a Spanish Crown grant but was acquired through purchase, occupancy, and continual use (Blue 2000:6).

13. This report was prepared for the Southwest Parks and Monuments Association to assess the importance of Hubbell's farm, which outlasted him by thirty-five years. An abridged version appeared as "Big House at Ganado: New Mexican Influence in Northern Arizona" (1989).

14. It is possible that a major portion of the trading the Hubbell family transacted with the Navajos for eighty years was never entered into government records such as the annual USRCIA reports. Hubbell's post was surrounded by the reservation, but he had "homesteaded" his 160 acres before the reservation was enlarged in 1880 and owned it outright. Legally he was not "on the reservation"; thus he was not required by law to be licensed. Only licensed traders were required to submit annual reports. I have failed to locate copies of such reports in the Hubbell Papers to date. However, Roman was issued a license in 1912, when his father left Ganado to serve as the first Republican senator of Arizona. There is a copy of a license issued to Lorenzo Jr. at Oraibi during the 1920s (Box 529). Blue (2000:82–85) provides detailed information concerning the convoluted events surrounding ownership of Ganado by Cotton and Hubbell before 1900.

15. In an exchange of letters filed in the intrapost correspondence, the Hubbells reveal their tactics for acquiring Navajo wool. As Lorenzo Sr. was away serving in the state legislature in 1913, Roman was in charge. On 21 March (HP Box 97 #1), just before the wool season, Lorenzo wrote his son, "[A]t the beginning of the trade it is always necessary to have the I[ndians] go out with the report that you pay a good price." But Roman, barely out of his teens, already knew that, because on 19 February (HP Box 97 #19) he wrote to John Owens, the trader at Cedar Springs, on the fine points of acquiring Navajo wool, especially if there was another trader "nearby":

> [S]tart by paying Indians around Indian Wells .28 per pound for wool[,] . . . then pay .22, then .20 per pound, then .12–.20 per pound. . . . [T]alk wool. . . . Pay only tin money. Sell sugar for $10 a sack. . . . Let them kick all they want. . . . Skin them every chance you get.

By 12 March he wrote to another trader, "[W]ill pay .15 now and lower later—not more than .13.5 all around." In April Charles Hubbell ran into trouble buying wool: "[W]hat will I do without cash? I will have to pay tin money and Crane [the Indian agent] will get after me because I have strict orders from him to pay strictly cash."

16. Kinaaldá was created by First Man and First Woman so women would be able to have children and the human race could multiply (Frisbie 1967). Changing Woman had the first Kinaaldá, which is considered the richest gift provided by the Holy People. It is the rock on which Navajo life and culture are built (Roessel 1981:38). For many Navajos, the knowledge and stories given in Kinaaldá by the Holy People form the foundation and basis for current Navajo family life. The knowledge and stories provide a charter on how to live in general. The stories concern subsistence, responsibility and marriage, behavior toward family and kin, respect for Holy People, and the importance of hospitality and self-sufficiency tempered with support for family members. Poverty is to be avoided, but overaccumulation of goods is frowned on. Respect is due all things as all things are alive and interrelated (Roessel 1981:39–40).

A dramatic four-night ceremony, Kinaaldá is a celebration that ushers a girl into society, invokes positive blessings on her, ensures her health, prosperity, and well-being, and protects her from potential misfortune. Sand paintings, masks, prayer sticks, rattles, and drums are not used during Kinaaldá, because it is prophylactic rather than curative (Frisbie 1967:8–9). According to Schwarz (1994), nearly 50 percent of Navajo girls still have Kinaaldá (Heard Museum Notes). The young girl receives instructions and knowledge to assume her adult role. It is thought to have a lasting effect on her life. She is considered to be soft and capable of being reshaped through molding by an ideal woman, one who has physical strength, perfect health, beauty, energy, and ambition. The girl is molded on a pile of blankets and other articles contributed by participants, who believe that in doing so these goods will soon be replaced by new ones. Beautiful fabrics, blankets, and deerskins are "soft goods" that collectively symbolize life (Frisbie 1967). Sometimes a weaving batten is pressed on the girl during the molding process. Reichard (1950:584) has noted that *pressing* is a common procedure that promotes "identification by absorption." Because Changing Woman was molded during the first Kinaaldá, repetition of this process will make the young woman resemble Changing Woman.

17. In 1924 Leo Crane, superintendent of the Colorado River Indian Agency, requested information from the Hubbells for a book on Indians he was writing. He asked for the *highest* price the Hubbells had paid for Navajo wool during the war ($.45 per pound) and in subsequent years. The prices were as follows: 1919, $.55; 1920, $.40; 1921, $.10; 1922, $.30; 1923 and 1924, $.37 (HP Box 44, 12/16/24). (Note the differences between these amounts and figures entered in Bailey and Bailey, appendix B.) In 1924 a sugar embargo drove up the price of canned fruit and vegetables 5 to 40 percent. Such wild fluctuations jeopardized Navajo well-being and placed additional pressure on women to provide for their families.

Chapter Three

1. Weiss (1984:54) quotes from Berlant and Kahlenberg (1977), who do not cite their source, that "in the early 1890s . . . traders brought into the territory inexpensive machine-made blankets. . . . Pendleton blankets were cheaper than native blankets, and the technical skill and energy consumed by blanket-making could now be utilized more profitably by weaving for trade." This statement cannot be supported in light of the information contained in traders' business records. Table 3 lists wholesale or retail costs of trade blankets extrapolated from Hubbell's post inventories. A comparison with data in figure 7 or table 1 provides a more realistic assessment.

2. Weiss (1984:81) reports on the tremendous drop in textile production at the end of World War I, because of increased prices for wool and mutton. Such a decrease is clearly not evident in Hubbell's records (see chapter 4). He quotes Kate Peck Kent concerning the nadir in Navajo textile production that occurred around 1920 (Weiss 1984:84). This is certainly not borne out in the Hubbell Papers. In fact, there is evidence to the contrary. A letter from Carl Steckel to Superintendent Daniel, Keams Canyon, lends additional support. Steckel wrote, "We do not find any marked improvement in quality of wool. We do note a very marked improvement in quality of rugs such as to fineness of weave and design" (Zimmerman n.d.:62, letter of 6/10/22). It appears the ghost of the superb-quality chief's blanket continually haunts the narrative of the post-Hwééldi "cheapened product." Such unreflective criticism, coming from economists, textile experts, and anthropologists, does a deep disservice to countless Navajo weavers.

3. Weiss (1984:173) states, "It is important to emphasize, however, from the perspective of the author of this study, that the fact of increasing wage payment is the crucial

element. The family or clan relations of those involved in the wage relationship and the cultural aspects surrounding the wage relation are of secondary importance." See O'Neill (1999) for a culturally sensitive interpretation of Navajo values and the wage economy.

4. McNitt collected far more information on weaving than he incorporated in his book. In addition to the traders listed in table 4, between 1 July 1910 and 30 June 1911 another fourteen traders acquired $77,186 worth of rugs from weavers and $5,767 worth of silver from smiths. Kelley and Whiteley (1989:210) report 116 trading posts on the reservation in 1910. Trader Ohlin of Thoreau reported paying weavers an average of $.83 per pound for their rugs (McNitt Papers Box 8). In their reports nearly all traders commented on the economic importance of blanket weaving, the use of aniline dyes and the rarity of vegetal dyes, and the infrequent use of cotton warp and Germantown yarns. Trader Frank Noel of Sa-nostee quipped, "The squaws are the grub getters" (McNitt Papers Box 8). Trader Olin Walker from Red Rock purchased $10,417 worth of weaving between 1 July 1910 and 30 June 1911. McNitt sketched a rug design reminiscent of a Two Grey Hills pattern that appeared in Walker's brochure. The trader included the value of the rugs: "a 3 x 5 is worth from $4 to $10, but averages $5 or $6.00. A 4 x 6 from $8 to $20, average price $10 to $14," and so forth. The rug pictured contains multiple borders and no aniline dyes, and the pattern is quite detailed. Walker is not generally considered to have been influential in rug design, yet the complexity of the pattern and the low values corroborate information in the Hubbell Papers. It becomes obvious from reading these reports that there was an enormous glut of weaving on the market that pressured weavers to perfect their textiles if they were to realize any returns at all. For comparison, a Pendleton robe cost $12.50 in 1911.

5. Although Francisconi (1998) also uses a materialist framework, more than one-third of his book contains interviews with Navajos who share their life histories and frequently mention the importance of the Creation Story, ceremonies, prayers, and kin relations.

Chapter Four

1. As wool was usually bagged in 250-pound lots, Cotton probably held an estimated 1.5 million pounds that year. Ilfeld (chapter 2) typically purchased that amount of wool annually before 1900 (Parish 1961).

2. Box 44 (8/01/16) contains a letter from Superintendent Leo Crane concerning the 1904 government edict requiring licensed traders to pay cash for Indian products.

3. My breakdown (table 6) reveals $16,000 worth of textiles shipped, but it is incomplete. Hubbell made several large sales to the Hyde Exploration Company that year, but they are not noted in this day book. Perhaps Hyde sent its own teams to pick up its large orders, as the company was also purchasing from other reservation suppliers. Certainly "old style patterns" make up by far the largest category of the number listed.

4. Nearly forty years later a similar tone is reflected in a letter sent by J. T. Cactus Rogers, of the Santa Fe Trail Trading Post, Raton, New Mexico. Mr. Rogers had ordered fifty-two rugs, and he complained about the wholesale prices of several, including a 6-x-11-foot for $75.00. He claimed to have purchased 7-x-13-foot rugs "for $45.00 delivered, as good in weaving and better patterns." "I just wanted to call your attention to the numbers and the prices, as they are so different from other houses" (HP Box 73, 5/16/40).

5. Hubbell wrote to E. A. Burbank that 1909 was a record year in blanket sales (HP Box 95 #13, 3/27/09). He told retailer J. B. Field of Atlantic City, New Jersey, that

he anticipated sales of between $50,000 and $60,000 on blankets alone (Box 96, 6/01). Box 349 reveals the following blanket shipments from other Hubbell posts: 13,698 pounds from Keams, 4,042 pounds from Oraibi, and nearly 2,000 pounds from Cedar Springs. He shipped a total of 10,263 pounds to the Fred Harvey Company that year. The ledger book in Box 348 reveals that Hubbell shipped at least 40,460 pounds of Indian "curios," mostly textiles. His profit for the year totaled $27,558.42 in curio sales (Box 347)and $1,945.37 in wool.

6. When I first encountered these entries, I thought the numbers were for wool and had been noted erroneously in the "Blanket" column in Hubbell's ledger. However, wool is never shipped in August as the wool season ends in June. In the corresponding day book for the year (HP Box 353, p. 28), I found the breakdown of the shipment. At first it appeared to be an alfalfa shipment, but the numbers added up to the exact weight of the blanket shipment. This enormous shipment totaled more than the entire weight of sheep pelts freighted from Ganado that year.

7. Parker wrote to Lorenzo Jr. on 9 September 1921 that he had contacted J. W. Robinson (the most exclusive department store in southern California). The manager told him the company had sold more than $50,000 worth of Chinese rugs during a big promotion in August. He thought if merchandised properly and if the Hubbells could keep up the supply, the same thing could be done with Navajo weaving (HP Box 102, September–December 1921 folder).

8. The Hubbells sought other ways to cope with the post-World War I recession. Box 103 #8 contains a letter from Roman to his brother dated 29 July 1924, saying that J. J. Gould wanted the Hubbells to supply the Indian labor: "[W]e can get so much a head for them and have half their wages delivered to us. . . . [R]emember Cotton and Hubbard made their money start by furnishing Indian labor. If we can get $25,000 in Indian money in December it would help."

9. Lorenzo Jr. wrote to his father, who was running his curio outlet in Hollywood, California: "Turn all the blankets you can Dad, it's the one thing that keeps our business going and its just where you shine, I fail to give it the attention it needs" (HP Box 104, 6/18/26). Sales for June 1927 totaled $1,278.12. Navajo rugs were the biggest seller at $734.35. Jewelry placed second at $251.57, and baskets were a distant third, $88.01 (NPS Group VIII Box 65). April 1927 receipts show sixty-five sales of which forty-six were rugs (NPS Group VIII Box 65).

10. In the fall Lorenzo's correspondence indicates that he wholesaled 3-x-5-foot rugs for $10.00 to $17.50, 6-x-9-foot rugs for $70 to $100, and 4-x-7-ft sand painting rugs for $65 to $80. Common black, white, and gray saddle blankets were wholesaled for $0.90 per pound, and "fancies" containing red cost $1.10 to $1.25 per pound (HP Box 104, 10/24/25, 11/19/25, 11/24/25).

11. The calculations to be made are very similar to those in a study mounted by the Office of Navajo Women and Families in 1987. More than four hundred weavers were asked a series of questions, including the time it takes to weave a double saddle blanket and a 3-x-5-foot rug.

12. Box 340 contains information related to sales and profits on blankets in 1906. With $6,597.22 worth of blankets in stock, Hubbell sold $31,249.19 and had "purchased" $26,152.21. Thus his profit appears to be $5,096.98, although I am unable to corroborate that amount. He made $1,384.86 profit on wool sales of $15,702.42. At the time the inventory was taken, he had advanced $1,264.32 to weavers (HP Box 253 #6). Hubbell shipped more than 7,500 pounds of textiles to the Fred Harvey Company that year. Cotton wrote to Hubbell (Box 19) noting that he was having trouble purchasing trade blankets and robes from mills because they had so much other work to do. On 19 May 1906, Cotton shipped Hubbell fifty-seven robes—"all we had"—and mentioned, "can't seem to sell wool."

13. After 1900 the reservation was divided into five jurisdictions, each with an agent who was required to submit an annual report to the CIA in Washington (Iverson 1981:17).
14. Two posts were excluded for different reasons: Bert Foutz's post and his business records burned; the amount and value of wool reported by C. Newcomb at Crystal were ambiguous and could not be used (RCIA 1925 NACoo1, 1682–3, in Parman Papers).
15. Hubbell's "Weavers' Inventory List" on 1 January 1904 (HP Box 523 #6) contains six and a half pages with 237 women's names. The credit advanced on textiles owed to Hubbell was $2,625.53.
16. In his assessment of the operation of posts and the costs involved, Youngblood noted that some traders kept incomplete records or that traders kept no records of their withdrawals of cash and goods from their posts. In some cases, significant withdrawals were made for personal use (i.e., automobile) even when the activity was unrelated to post business. Youngblood (1935:90–91) suggested segregation of record keeping as practiced by urban businessmen (HP Box 527).
17. Reinhart (1999) confirms the importance of food. Hegemann (1963:271) notes that women typically purchased 2.5 yards of velveteen for a blouse and 7 to 9 yards of sateen or cotton for their skirts.
18. If one calculates an average of forty hours' preparation and weaving time per pound of yarn produced, weavers expended more than twenty million hours from shearing to finished product in 1911. This averages out to six hours per weaver per day, if nine thousand women were weaving (the population was estimated at twenty-two thousand that year). This may not be an unrealistic estimate, as other female household members and children frequently were involved in carding and cleaning wool. Photographs in the Navajo File at the University of Arizona Special Collections Library show girls of preschool age carding wool. The Fred Harvey Company featured six-year-old "Tuli" weaving her own patterns while demonstrating at the Indian House in Albuquerque (James [1914] 1974:fig. 142). Navajo families were very reluctant to send their daughters away to school, as weaving was so important to the household. See Mitchell and Frisbie (2001) for evidence of continued production by Mitchell family members for decades.
19. Lorenzo Jr. submitted a report that was included in Youngblood's statistics. His operation at Oraibi had nearly four times the volume of business of the average reservation trading posts, and his reported gross profits ranged from 30 to 55 percent between 1929 and 1934, the depression years. He acquired 2,725 textiles averaging $3.60 apiece in 1934.
20. Appropriation was not unique to Navajo makers. In 1935 Reverend Raley of Canada wrote that the Japanese were manufacturing Canadian Indian curios for souvenir markets. He suggested high tariffs might alleviate the problem (McMaster 1989:230).
21. In his 1902 catalog, Hubbell advertised 3-x-5-foot weaving for $10.00 to $17.50. In 1931 this size sold for between $7.00 and $11.00. In 1936 Macy's Department Store requested such weavings priced from $5.00 to $8.00 for a promotion. Prices stagnated during the 1940s, yet the cost of flour, coffee, and canned vegetables had doubled and trade blankets and tow cards had quadrupled in price between 1902 and 1940 (table 3).
22. Reichard ([1936] 1968) confirmed the variation in Navajo wool.
23. The following year, the 76-page Winslow warehouse inventory revealed more than 3,500 rugs (HP Box 482 #8A). By 1943 the inventory was 100 pages long (HP Box 482 #7). In November 1947 Roman had the Winslow warehouse inventoried, with 71 pages of figures on rugs alone. The inventory amounted to $36,295.90, less than usual.

Chapter Five

1. A special issue of *Masterkey* was devoted to James (Parezo 1986). Whittaker (1998:62–63) has a provocative discussion of James's personal and professional clashes with his contemporaries. James claimed that to ignore the importance of Hubbell's influence on Navajo weaving would be equivalent to describing the history of the phonograph and leaving out Edison's name.

2. In her article, "Navajo Rugs: A Marketing Success," in *Designers West*, Laura Graves Allen, curator at the Museum of Northern Arizona, describes the long-term popularity of Navajo textiles. Geometric elements incorporated over time into the earliest textiles were part of the Navajo "design repertoire" on early baskets. The "Transitional Period" led to a "wild period of experimentation" as weavers began to use brightly colored Germantown yarns. Allen depicts the trader J. B. Moore as developing a "production line." She notes that the Storm pattern is the only one that contains symbolism. She describes Hubbell as "flooding the market," as he had more than three hundred weavers "employed" at Ganado. The quality of weaving from Ganado was "unsurpassed." Weavers are described as accepting and mixing the "oddly matched ingredients," such as Oriental design influences, into their weaving. Thus Navajo weaving is a "continually evolving textile tradition steeped in heritage."

3. Publications devoted to Oriental rugs have featured articles on how weavers ultimately incorporated these "foreign" influences. In the December 1990 issue of the *Oriental Rug Review* (pp. 14–17), Rodee notes the dramatic changes that occurred in the textiles woven by weavers "working" for J. B. Moore between the publication of his first (1903) and second (1911) catalogs. Patterns with multiple borders, airplanelike motifs, and simple "guls" contrast with previous patterns and represent a "complete break" with previous "styles." Although there is no *direct* evidence of influence, Oriental carpets were popular, and paper rug hooking and other domestic craft patterns were made available to housewives through companies such as E. S. Frost. In another publication, Rodee (1981:56) illustrates five of Frost's Turkish hooked rug stencils. Both types of textiles exhibit multiple borders, but the patterns are quite dissimilar. With the exception of a "latch hook" motif and two rug patterns that have "airplanelike" motifs, the comparison seems overdrawn.

4. Moore's wife may have instigated the scandal. An interesting letter written by Gil Maxwell (11/10/58) surfaced in McNitt's Papers (Box 8). Maxwell, claiming Charlie Newcum [*sic*] as his source, said Moore's wife had been an English barmaid and was "tough as a pig's nose." She convinced Moore to run a mission for Navajos. A letter-writing campaign ensued and gifts were sent, including food and money. The merchandise was sold to Navajos, and the money went into her "sock." Postal authorities deemed it fraud, and the Moores departed for Texas.

5. According to Brody (1976:footnote 17), Hubbell had copies of Ruskin's texts in his library at Ganado. Brody (1976:12) claims that Hubbell and Moore "applied the canons of good taste of the arts and crafts movement to Navajo weaving." Yet most patterns are variations of nineteenth-century Navajo patterns. McNitt (1962:217) also mentions Ruskin.

6. Rodee's (1981) text provides a corollary to Amsden's. In reproducing eighteen patterns from Moore's 1911 catalog, she neglects to include the names of the weavers-designers identified by Moore (1981:36–53). Rodee (1990:17) credits the traders with "working hard to achieve a high degree of perfection in weaving." She also notes:

> Ganado . . . had developed its own style under the management of Lorenzo Hubbell. . . . [T]oday weavers buy the latest books on their art. . . . So common are the Oriental styles that Navajo weavers believe

they are completely traditional since their mothers and grandmothers wove in this way. They are surprised and often incredulous of the great change which took place in Navajo weaving as a result of the taste of the dominant American society for Caucasian rugs. (1990:17)

7. The McNitt Papers (Box 8) contain extensive notes extracted from Moore's report to Abbott (1911). Moore provides great detail concerning the importance of using clean fleece to improve rug quality, whether dyed or undyed wool.

8. The concept of standardization becomes troublesome given the magnitude of contrary evidence unearthed in archival sources. What if one were to apply this concept to paintings hanging in art galleries? It appears ludicrous, yet if one were to calculate size, framing, brands of paints, types of canvas, and subject matter it is quite plausible one could make a greater case for "standardization" in the latter example. After all, many artists train professionally in groups for years, network with their peers, and attend each other's openings. Do gallery owners create an environment for "standardization" when they reject the purchase of a painting? Had traders continually rejected weavings, their goods would have stayed on the posts' shelves. One could argue that applying the concept to "crafts" produced by native women and not to "art" (frequently) produced by men smacks of sexism and racism.

9. Boles (1977:17) also notes that a Miss Bonsell, an associate of the anthropologist Stewart Culin, was paid $30 by Hubbell to paint two of the rug studies in 1902. In one day this woman earned more in cash than a Navajo weaver would receive in credit for weaving three 9-x-9-foot "blue" blankets or a pair of portieres—requiring up to six months' labor (HP Box 344).

10. This statement is probably the source of Weiss's comment and James's ([1914] 1974:203). A number of other authors (e.g., Hogg 1930) also quote it.

11. On 19 May 1902 Hubbell shipped Maratta a pair of portieres to pay for his brochure (HP Box 54).

12. The senior Hubbell lobbied vigorously in Washington, D.C., to be reimbursed for this project, which began in about 1902 and took many years to complete. The dam and reservoirs diverted water from the Pueblo Colorado Creek. In 1912 the House of Representatives passed a bill to reimburse him for $25,000, ultimately allocating $75,000 for the project. Hubbell held the majority rights to the water that irrigated his farm. According to Arthur Hubbard, an elderly Navajo interviewed in 1971, Navajos had no right to the water, as Hubbell held two-thirds rights and the Presbyterian Mission the other one-third. In 1931 Navajos were told that the government could not lend any money to construct earthen dams and reservoirs in the southern sector of the reservation (Kelley and Whiteley 1989:92).

13. Incoming inter- and intrapost correspondence makes up the first 125 of 573 Hollinger boxes of the Hubbell Papers. Thus there are a minuscule number of requests relative to the correspondence.

14. Yet an overemphasis on traders' influence persists. Coe (1986:210) comments on his visit with the master weaver Mae Jim while she was weaving an enormous rug. He describes the rug as "a superbly controlled Ganado design [that continues] the Don Lorenzo Hubbell tradition. . . . Hubbell worked out the general concept of a locally woven rug that would compete with Oriental carpets." Scholars who have perused Hubbell correspondence have not recorded evidence that he worked to develop similar designs to capture that market. The only correspondence related to competition from "Persian" carpets that I have discovered thus far is a letter from Karl Schlatter (HP Box 73, 1902), who remarked that his son was unable to sell Navajo rugs in Europe because people preferred the less expensive Turkish rugs.

15. Correspondence concerning Misrepresentation of Native American Arts & Crafts

1932–80 (CMNAAC). My thanks to Cory Silverstein of McMaster University for calling this letter to my attention.

16. Watson (1957:25) provides an illustration of an "ordinary stock" rug placed in the doorway of the New Mexico exhibit at the 1933 Chicago World's Fair. Nearly 2.8 million fairgoers walked on the rug; it sustained no damage.

Chapter Six

1. The differentiation and treatment of indigenous expressive forms by museums reflects the extension of the mind/body dualism so prevalent in Western thought into the realm of art. The institutional separation of art from craft occurred during the Renaissance when painting and sculpture became intellectual activities, differentiated from utilitarian crafts that emphasized technical excellence. Only objects released from formal considerations of function could be truly expressive. Thus the production of crafts, including weaving, was considered equivalent to manual labor, primarily attractive because a wage was involved (Kant 1951). The elevation of aesthetics to philosophy during the eighteenth century further undermined attitudes toward "crafts." The Western concept of beauty, central to classical aesthetics, was expressed only in the fine arts of painting and sculpture, providing the justification for the exclusion of indigenous creations globally (M'Closkey 1985).

2. While admiring a traveling exhibition of historic Navajo textiles in 1982, the director of a Canadian gallery remarked to me, "All sorts of things about modernism fell into place when I hung this show."

3. See MacCannell (1994:164–65) for a scorching critique that he terms "hysterical metaphorical appropriation."

4. Numerous individuals have benefited from Wheat's scrupulous documentation, including dealers and collectors anxious to establish either the provenance or pedigree of their holdings. In the proceedings of a conference on southwestern textiles, Ann Hedlund, curator, anthropologist, and Wheat's former student, notes:

> An intriguing by-product of Wheat's scholarly work has been the interest shown in the research results by private collectors, gallery owners and others who buy and sell historic textiles. The complex mechanisms of proving authenticity through dating, sourcing and otherwise identifying have attracted a wide and supportive audience. (1989b:134)

5. Founded in 1744, Sotheby's is the oldest and largest auction firm in the world. The company maintains centers in Europe, Asia, and North America and recently held auctions in China and Russia. The company surpassed $1 billion in annual sales more than a decade ago (Sotheby's 1989).

6. Intrigued as to the thirty-five-fold increase in value in fifteen years (between 1974 and 1989), I contacted Sotheby's for an explanation. The curator of Indian art informed me that the blanket was originally appraised by Harmer Johnson, their acknowledged expert, at $100,000 to $150,000. The auction house requested that Wheat write a one-page description of the blanket. Wheat wrote that it had been owned by Herman Schweizer of the Fred Harvey Company, who later sold it to John Collier in the 1930s. Evidently only three other blankets of this type remain in private hands. One is owned by Tony Berlant, and another is owned by Jack Silverman. The Janss blanket was auctioned for a record-breaking $522,000, and Sotheby's made more than $50,000 on the sale. Silverman owns art galleries in Santa

Fe, New Mexico, and Aspen, Colorado. During the 1970s, he began to market large serigraphs of historic blankets that he owns in limited editions of one hundred, netting several hundred thousand dollars on each edition. Based on recent auctions of comparable pieces, the original textiles are now worth several hundred thousand dollars each. He titles the serigraphs "'Navajo Chief's Blanket' by Jack Silverman." One wonders if the exact translation of an article from a "craft" medium into an "art" medium negates the notion of plagiarism. Distinctly uneasy about this appropriation, a well-known Canadian art dealer refused to act as his Canadian representative when Silverman contacted him in the 1970s. In 1993, when I queried the dealer about the remarkable similarities between color field painting and Navajo blankets, he retorted: "Where do you think those guys got their ideas?!"

7. During the 1980–81 auction season, a number of nineteenth-century Navajo textiles reached record prices. A man's sarape was auctioned by Sotheby's for $54,000, and a Third Phase chief's blanket sold for $11,500. Six years later, another chief's blanket sold for $33,000, and a Germantown measuring 2½ by nearly 6 feet was auctioned for $27,000. In 1989 a classic man's weaving blanket sold through Sotheby's for $93,000, and an eye dazzler went for $35,200. This buying frenzy affected textiles auctioned from Andy Warhol's collection; some weaves sold for more than $10,000.

Sotheby's auctioned the collection of George Horace Lorimer, editor in chief of the *Saturday Evening Post*, on 26 November 1991. According to the catalog, Lorimer and his family toured pueblos and Indian reservations collecting Indian "art," favoring textiles. Twenty pieces were acquired directly from the Fred Harvey Company. In the preface to the presales catalog, the Lorimers are praised for "their rare collecting acumen[,] . . . insightful awareness[,] . . . and . . . avant-garde appreciation for a largely unknown 'art' form." A conservative appraisal of forty textiles from their collection was $750,000. One of the First Phase chief's blankets ($125,000–$175,000) had been given to Lorimer by a grateful "Navajo Chief." Sotheby's gratefully acknowledged Wheat for his "generous and insightful comments" and Wheat's chemist associate for making dye analyses.

8. The one-day sale in November 1989 realized $2,364,560 for four hundred individual Indian articles, half a million dollars more than their appraised value.

9. During the 1980s, Noland designed a series of commissioned tapestries for a select number of Navajo weavers. This "collaboration" is celebrated as contributing to "the evolution of Navajo weaving" (Hedlund 1986). A major exhibition containing several Noland-designed pieces toured the United States for several years. Hedlund described the genesis of this collaboration in *The Weaver's Journal* (1986). She noted how Noland's geometric paintings are perfectly suited to the Navajo nonsymbolic notions of design. According to Hedlund, Noland remarked that "traditional [Navajo] textiles led him to discover that the history of abstraction went back further in the decorative arts than it did in the fine arts" (1986:33). Hedlund concludes: "This New York–Navajo connection has forged bonds that transcend the distinctions between fine arts and fine craft, between East and West, between primitive and sophisticated" (1986:34).

10. In 1995 Joshua Baer ran a full-page ad in *American Indian Art Magazine*. He was interested in buying fine examples of nineteenth-century Navajo wearing blankets, as he had clients who were willing to pay premiums: Classic Bayeta Poncho, circa 1820–1850: $250,000–$350,000; Classic First Phase, circa 1800–1850: $250,000; Second Phase, circa 1830–1855: $100,000–$150,000. There were a total of twenty-one "categories." The final entry read: "Pictorial Blankets & Early Pictorial Rugs, circa 1890–1930: $5,000–25,000." He remarked: "We will pay these prices for fine examples of each type of Navajo blanket. 'Fine' in this case means that the blanket

is a satisfying, compelling work of art with unique qualities which distinguish it from more typical examples of its type."

The child's blanket is another type of Navajo textile that has received attention recently. Long ignored by textile aficionados, a new breed of collector has turned its attention to the child's blanket. In 1986 Baer mounted a "retrospective" of forty child's blankets that are slightly larger than single saddle blankets. In the exhibition catalog, Baer entices speculators, noting that the man's sarape that brought $115,000 in 1984 had "come to look more and more like the bargain of the decade." Several months later an article titled "An Investment in Beauty" appeared in *Southwest Profile* (fall 1988). In it the author revealed that a collector purchased a child's blanket for $30,000. On 26 May 1999 Sotheby's sold a child's blanket for $76,750, triple its appraised value (Hannon 1999:152)

11. While on a reservation field trip in fall 1993, I was stunned to find a large pile of "coarsely woven" pound blankets stacked in the stockroom at Ganado with price tags ranging from $1000 to $15,000. They had been placed on consignment by owners anxious to cash in on the craze for historic weaving. The trading post, now a National Historic Site, continues to purchase rugs from reservation weavers that are displayed in the "rug room." I asked the clerk working in the rug room why Ganado was handling historic textiles. He replied that some people much preferred the old pieces; the post complied by taking old rugs on consignment as they earned a percentage on every sale, whether new or old.

12. In 1997 a federal grand jury found the Indian arts dealer Rodney Tidwell guilty of purchasing eighteenth-century vestments from a resident of Acoma Pueblo. Tidwell had been indicted in March 1995 for trafficking in stolen artifacts (*Indian Trader* 4/95:28).

13. Within the past two decades, numerous texts and articles have explicated the "salvage" mentality associated with the collection practices of museums and other institutions over the last century (e.g., Handler 1992, 1993). Dominguez (1986) reviews some of the literature on the subject.

14. I attended an auction of historic Indian art held at this post in October 1992. More than three hundred people came by bus and automobile, crowding into a large "circus tent" erected for the occasion. Many bidders were draped in sterling silver and turquoise squash blossom necklaces or heavy concho belts. Trading post employees, auctioneers, and their children were dressed in period costumes: cowboys and cowgirls, "ladies of the evening," outlaws, and sheriffs.

15. A Navajo weaver active at the Crownpoint auction related a story that describes a disturbing trend. A cluster of experienced bidders (possibly dealers) previews the textiles and each decides *in advance* what she or he will bid on to avoid competitive bidding.

16. An Arizona acquaintance who had stopped at a trading post on the reservation in summer 1991 told me that a young Navajo woman came into the post carrying her infant and a saddle blanket she had just completed. The trader offered her $10, commenting that he disliked the "yellow" in it. She had hand spun the background yarn, and it had taken her more than two weeks to weave the single saddle blanket, given her new responsibilities. Dejected, she turned to leave, and the "acquaintance" inquired what she would accept for the rug. The two-pound blanket was purchased for $20, and the "distasteful yellow" turned out to be a lovely gold.

17. The first exhibition curated by Berlant and Kahlenberg that toured for several years was exhibited on the Navajo Reservation in September 1972. The National Museum of the American Indian (NMAI) in New York City toured a collection of historic Navajo textiles in 1995. According to an anthropologist who frequently works in the Southwest, the NMAI was reluctant to display the textiles on the reservation because the physical plant was simply not sophisticated enough to handle such a

valuable collection. Twenty-four blankets were placed on display under heavy security for five days in June 1995 at Diné Community College in Tsaile, Arizona, Navajo Nation. Navajos continued to travel to the college for several weeks after the exhibit was returned to the museum (Bonar, Begay, and Ash-Milby 1996).

Chapter Seven

1. In 1909 Alfred Kroeber published an article on Pomo basketry that was reprinted in Matthews and Jonaitis (1982). Typical for a publication on "craft," the author describes the materials, techniques, and manufacturing processes of Pomo basket making. In one paragraph Kroeber summarizes how anthropologists have viewed the "meaning" of functional objects. He continually juxtaposes the religious (non-functional) to the conventional, artistry to pragmatism, and states, "There is no evidence that any decorative figure originated directly from a creative symbolic impulse. Symbolism can only interpret what is already given" (Kroeber 1982:165). In other words, when an article is commodified or produced for utilitarian purposes, it has no sacred associations. He concludes that there is a complete absence of religious or symbolic significance in decorative designs in Pomo basketry. This is essentially the explanation that is offered for the lack of symbolism in Navajo weaving. One of Kroeber's contemporaries, Ruth Bunzel, worked extensively with Pueblo potters. Bunzel ([1929] 1982:185) claimed that "the great source of decorative ideas is, of course, tradition. . . . [T]he artistic impulse is only expressed in articles which depart from tradition."

2. Reichard also commented that because of the varied nature of women's domestic activities combined with frequent interruptions, it would be a mistake to attempt to calculate how long it takes to weave a rug.

3. Tanner (1968) remarks that the essentially decorative nature of Indian art contributes heavily to its formal style. She echoes Reichard when she declares that "Southwest Indian secular arts are not symbolic. Sometimes the same design element or motif may be found in sacred and secular context; in the former it is symbolic, in the latter it is not, for here it is design and no more" (1968:195). The Indian used decoration on objects he used. Although it did not improve utility value, it satisfied an ancient feeling.

4. With regard to sand painting blankets, Reichard ([1936] 1968:161) notes, "Money . . . dangling at the end of a string pulled ever shorter, has the same effect on the Navajo as upon ourselves. It supersedes all other values, be they social, moral or spiritual." This is an unfortunate assumption, as her friend Roman Hubbell pressured women into weaving them because the market for mohair vanished during the depression.

5. Although Wheat was an archaeologist, he is considered the dean of Navajo textile studies.

6. Witherspoon (1974) examines approaches to determining "worldview." He notes that Reichard (1950) made an exhaustive study of Navajo religious beliefs, but the study is like a dictionary and hardly provides a unified picture of the world as seen by Navajos. Witherspoon also criticized Kluckhohn's "eight keystones" of Navajos' view of the world for having little connection between them or coherence. Witherspoon subscribes to a symbolic approach influenced by Durkheim. Following Geertz, he perceives meanings as stored in symbols, dramatized in rituals, and related in stories. He claims that the translations of Reichard and Kluckhohn provide a general notion of hózhǫ́ but are inadequate because they deal with only one of the two morphological components of the word.

7. Witherspoon's analysis is not atypical. Anthropologists acknowledge the existence

of both verbal and nonverbal forms of communication. However, the nonverbal dimensions of culture are frequently organized in patterned sets so as to incorporate "coded information" in a manner analogous to the sounds, words, and sentences in language. Thus many anthropologists look to linguists for a model according to which they can analyze nonverbal modes of communication (Leach 1976:93). Compositions are perceived as containing a "visual grammar" that may be "read." Art forms are treated as if they had features comparable to the rules of syntax in language. Modes of communication such as dance and dress are seen as interchangeable units, subject to analyses suited to and developed for linguistic models (Turner 1967, 1975; Leach 1976; Lévi-Strauss 1963).

8. The Anglo weaver and textile restoration specialist Noel Bennett discusses Navajo meaning and weaving in her *Halo of the Sun* (1987). The folklorist Barry Toelken (1976) has also written eloquently on Navajo crafts and beliefs.

9. Roessel's associate, the Native American author Anna Lee Walters, enlarges on the interconnections among native peoples and their lifeways. For example, corn pollen is considered sacred and is used in prayers and ceremonies. Pollen is needed for all vegetation:

> One plant communicates with another by pollination. . . . [T]hinking and praying are collective mindfulness. [In] native American communities, survival means to seek life. . . . [S]eeking life is a community matter. . . . [A] knowledgeable human being was one who was sensitive to his/her surroundings. Thus one could have mystical learning experiences. In order that knowledge did not get separated from experience, wisdom from divinity, the elders stressed listening and waiting, not asking why. . . . [Y]ou don't ask questions when you grow up. . . . [Y]ou watch, listen and wait. (1992:40)

10. Toelken (1976) contrasts Euro-American notions of linear order with "sacred reciprocation" evident in the interactions of many indigenous peoples. He lived with a Navajo family for several years and found that to be healthy by Navajo standards, one must participate properly in all the cycles of nature. For weavers, it is interaction with the nonhuman world that is the important part of making a rug. "Something which for us is a secular craft or a technique is for the Navajo a part of the extension of the reciprocation embodied in religion" (1976:20).

11. To my knowledge, this event was the first time a group of Navajo weavers appeared before an audience and spoke about their work. Additional information is derived from a series of interviews the curator Clarenda Begay held with Ganado area weavers sponsored by the National Park Service in 1985–86.

12. Pearl was the only Navajo weaver present at a conference on the topic hosted by Kate Peck Kent at the University of Denver in 1983. Kent quotes a portion of Pearl's presentation:

> The custom of spinning at every odd moment exemplifies the Navajo ideal of keeping busy, while carding, spinning and weaving itself express the value placed on patience and determination. It is important to work steadily at one's own rate and to keep at a task until finished. The Navajo believe that beauty lies within the individual, and in visualizing a pattern and then projecting it onto her loom, the weaver is expressing this beauty. Her designs will be judged good if they meet the Navajo ideals of harmony and balance. (1985:113–14)

Chapter Eight

1. The principal works cited are Farella 1984; Faris 1986, 1990; Frisbie 1967, 1982, 1987; Griffin-Pierce 1992; Kluckhohn and Leighton 1974; McAllester 1980; O'Bryan 1956; Reichard [1934] 1974, [1936] 1968, [1939] 1971, 1950; Spencer 1947, 1957; Witherspoon 1974, 1975, 1977, 1983, 1987; Wyman 1970, 1983; Zolbrod 1984.
2. Recent exceptions to this statement are evident in *Woven By the Grandmothers* (Bonar 1996) and *Weaving a World* (Willink and Zolbrod 1996), in which weavers' voices are heard extensively.
3. Redundancy is a vital clue to patterning; it involves convention, habit, and practice. Rather than a universe of symbols (Victor Turner), redundancy implies an ordering process. The structure of society expresses order in practice, not as a matrix of symbols that then reads a culture as "text." Although Washburn (2000) does not use communications models, she addresses a number of similar issues.

Appendix IVc

1. For example, in Blanket Book #2, pages 136–37 (1902), Schweizer purchased sixteen historic textiles from Hubbell for $177.50. He retailed them for $1148.50, an increase of 650 percent.
2. Schweizer bought a portion of the Richard Weatherill collection from his widow who was left with five children to support. Weatherill was killed in 1910 by a Navajo while trading at Chaco in northwestern New Mexico. On 22 August 1910 Schweizer purchased thirty-two textiles, including several bayeta squaw dresses (Blanket Book #4, p. 55, Museum of International Folk Art). He paid Mrs. Weatherill $692.75 and marked up the historic pieces to $3,562, a 500 percent increase.
3. The Spiegelberg collection was not the only collection purchased by Schweizer that year. Blomberg (1988) states that the newspaper magnate William Randolph Hearst acquired most of his nineteenth-century collection of Navajo textiles from Schweizer. Working with Schweizer's blanket journals, Blomberg replicates the huge markups (from 100 to 1000 percent) between the amounts Schweizer paid for a textile (usually purchased from Hubbell or other traders, collectors, or peddlers) and his retail price. She shows that Schweizer not only had a difficult time collecting money from Hearst, but Hearst insisted on receiving a large discount (1988:13).
4. On 16 August 1903 Schweizer purchased more of the Spiegelberg collection, which included eight Acoma and Moqui textiles. This portion of the collection wholesaled at $615 and retailed at $2,775 (Book #4, #6053–6065, Heard Museum). On 20 January 1903 the company purchased twenty-five textiles from the Seligman collection, which wholesaled for $2,257.50 and retailed at $8775. Seligman had been a major competitor of the Spiegelbergs, and Schweizer had purchased a major portion of this collection in 1902.

Bibliography

Abbott, F. H. 1911. Traders' Reports to Assistant Commissioner. Classified Files 71406/11.910. Copy in McNitt Papers, Box 8.

Aberle, David F. 1983. "Navajo Economic Development." In *Handbook of North American Indians*, vol. 10, *Southwest*. Alfonso Ortiz, ed., 641–58. Washington, D.C.: Smithsonian Institution Press.

———. 1966. *Peyote Religion among the Navajo*. Chicago: Aldine.

———. 1962. "Navajo." *Matrilineal Kinship*. David Schneider and Kathleen Gough, eds., 96–201. Berkeley: University of California Press.

Adair, John. 1944. *Navajo and Pueblo Silversmiths*. Norman: University of Oklahoma Press.

Adams, William Y. 1990. "The Agent, the Trader, the Missionary and the Anthropologist: Rival 'Godfathers' of the Colonial Era." *Diné Be'iina'* 2(1):67–80. Shiprock, N.Mex.

———. 1968. "The Role of the Navajo Trader in a Changing Economy." *Markets and Marketing in Developing Economies*. R. Moyer and S. Hollander, eds., 133–52. Homewood, Ill.: R. D. Irwin.

———. 1963. *Shonto: A Study of the Role of the Trader in a Modern Navajo Community*. Bureau of American Ethnology, Bulletin 188. Washington, D.C.: Government Printing Office.

Adams, William Y. and Lorraine Ruffing. 1977. "Shonto Revisited: Measures of Social and Economic Change in a Navajo Community, 1955–1971." *American Anthropology* 79(1):58–83.

Akbarzadeh, Abdorrahim. 1992. "The House of Babbitt: A Business History of the Babbitt Brothers Trading Company, 1886–1926." Ph.D. dissertation, Northern Arizona University.

Albers, Patricia and Bea Medicine. 1983. *The Hidden Half*. Lanham, Md.: University Press of America.

Allen, Laura Graves. 1983. "Navajo Rugs: A Marketing Success." *Designers West* (April):133–38.

Ames, Michael. 1994. "The Politics of Difference: Other Voices in a Not Yet Post-Colonial World. *Museum Anthropology* 18(3):9–17.

———. 1991." Biculturalism in Exhibitions." *Museum Anthropology* 15(2):7–15.

Amsden, Charles Avery. [1934] 1975. *Navajo Weaving, Its Technique and History*. Salt Lake City: Peregrine Smith.

———. 1932. "Reviving the Navajo Blanket." *Masterkey* 4:136–47, 149.

Anderson, Lowell E. 1951. "Factors Influencing Design in Navajo Weaving." M.A. thesis, University of California, Berkeley.

Anderson, Richard. 1989. *Art in Small Scale Societies*. Atlantic Highlands, N.J.: Prentice Hall.

Anonymous. 1998. "Huge Rug Goes Unsold, Leaving Navajo Clinic in a Bind." *Arizona Star*, May 20.

Appadurai, Arjun. 1986. *The Social Life of Things*. New York: Cambridge University Press.
Arizona Highways. 1974. Special Issue on Southwest Indian Weaving. July 50(7).
Arnold, Judith. 1988. "An Investment in Beauty." *Southwest Profile* (fall):38–41.
Art-Talk. 1998. "Who Owns the $370,000 Navajo Rug?" June–July: 13.
Atherton, Lewis E. 1982. "The Santa Fe Trader as Mercantile Capitalist." *Missouri Historical Review* (October):1–12.
Babbitt Brothers Trading Company Papers, 1886–1926, and additional archives, 1886–. Special Collections Library, Northern Arizona University, Flagstaff.
Babcock, Barbara. 1990. "'A New Mexican Rebecca': Imaging Pueblo Women." *Journal of the Southwest* 32:400–437.
Baer, Joshua. 2001. Advertisement. *American Indian Art Magazine* 26(2): n.p.
———. 1991. "Garments of Brightness: The Art and History of Navajo Eyedazzlers." *Antiques* 140(4): 580–91.
———. 1989. "Space and Design: A Brief History of the Navajo Chief's Blanket." *Antiques* 138(3): 528–41.
———. 1986. "Collecting the Navajo Child's Blanket." Santa Fe, N.Mex.: Morning Star Gallery.
Bahr, Howard M. 1999. *Diné Bibliography to the 1990s*. Lanham, Md.: Scarecrow Press.
Bailey, Garrick and Roberta Bailey. 1986. *A History of the Navajo: The Reservation Years*. Santa Fe, N.Mex.: School of American Research Press.
Bailey, Lynn R. 1980. *If You Take My Sheep: Evolution and Conflicts of Navajo Pastoralism 1630–1868*. Pasadena, Calif.: Westernlore Publications.
———. 1970. *Bosque Redondo: An American Concentration Camp*. Pasadena, Calif.: Socio-Technical Books.
Baizerman, Susan. 1989. "The Study of Material Culture: The Case of Southwest Textiles." The Legacy of Kate Peck Kent. *Museum Anthropology* 13(2):14–18.
Barton, Marcia L. 1989. "Zapotec Weaving of Teotitlan del Valle, Oaxaca, Mexico." *Masterkey* 62(4):16–24.
Bateson, Gregory. 1972. *Steps to an Ecology of Mind*. San Francisco: Chandler.
Bateson, Gregory and Mary Catherine Bateson. 1988. *Angels Fear*. Toronto: Bantam Books.
Batkin, Jonathan. 1999. "Tourism Is Overrated: Pueblo Pottery and the Early Curio Trade, 1880–1910." In *Unpacking Culture: Art and Commodity in Colonial and Postcolonial Worlds*. Berkeley: University of California Press.
Bauer, Liz. 1987. Research for a Catalogue of the Navajo Textiles of Hubbell Trading Post. National Endowment for the Humanities.
Baxter, John. 1987. *Los Carneradas: Sheep Trade in New Mexico, 1700–1860*. Albuquerque: University of New Mexico Press.
———. 1983. "Restocking the Navajo Reservation after Bosque Redondo. *New Mexico Historical Review* 58(4):325–45.
Bedinger, Margery. 1973. *Indian Silver: Navajo and Pueblo Jewelers*. Albuquerque: University of New Mexico Press.
Begay, D. Y. 1996. "Shi'Sha'Hane'" (My Story). In *Woven by the Grandmothers*. Eulalie Bonar, ed., 13–27. Washington, D.C.: Smithsonian Institution Press.
———. 1994. "A Weaver's Point of View." In *All Roads Are Good*, 80–89. Washington, D.C.: Smithsonian Institution Press.
Begay, David and Nancy Maryboy. 1996. "Nahookos Bika, Nahookos Bi'aad Doo Biko Binanitin: Gender Construction in Accordance with Diné Holarchical Cosmology." In *The Construction of Gender and the Experience of Women in American Indian Societies*, 180–218. Occasional Papers. Chicago: Newberry Library, Center for the History of the American Indian.
Bennett, Noel. 1987. *Halo of the Sun: Stories Told and Retold*. Flagstaff, Ariz.: Northland Press.
———. 1979. *Designing with the Wool: Advanced Navajo Weaving Techniques*. Flagstaff, Ariz.: Northland Press.

———. 1974. *The Weaver's Pathway: A Clarification of the "Spirit Trail" in Navajo Weaving.* Flagstaff, Ariz.: Northland Press.

———. 1973. *Genuine Navajo Rug—Are You Sure?* Santa Fe, N.Mex.: Museum of Navajo Ceremonial Art and the Navajo Tribe.

Bennett, Noel and Tiana Bighorse. 1997. *Navajo Weaving Way.* Loveland, Colo.: Interweave Press.

Bennholdt-Thomsen, Veronika. 1988. "Subsistence Production and Extended Reproduction." *Of Marriage and the Market.* Kate Young, et al., ed., 41–54. London: Routledge.

Berlant, Tony. 1973. "Navajo Blankets from the Private Collections of Contemporary Artists." New York: Andre Emmerich Gallery.

Berlant, Tony and Mary H. Kahlenberg. 1977. *Walk in Beauty.* New York: Little, Brown.

———. 1972a. "Blanket Statements." *ARTnews* 71(4):42–45, 69–71.

———. 1972b. "The Navajo Blanket." *Art in America* 60(4):78–82.

Berlo, Janet C. 1993. "Dreaming of Double Woman: The Ambivalent Role of the Female Artist in North American Indian Myth." *American Indian Quarterly* 17(1):31–43.

———. 1991. "Beyond Bricolage: Women and Aesthetic Strategies in Latin American Textiles." In *Textile Traditions of Mesoamerica and the Andes: An Anthology.* Margot B. Schevill, Janet C. Berlo and Edward Dwyer, eds., 437–75. New York: Garland.

Berman, Morris. 1989. *The Re-Enchantment of the World.* New York: Bantam Books.

Blomberg, Nancy. 1988. *Art from the Navajo Loom: The William Randolph Hearst Collection.* Tucson: University of Arizona Press.

Blue, Martha. 2000. *Indian Trader: The Life and Times of Juan Lorenzo Hubbell.* Walnut, Calif.: Kiva Press.

———. 1988. "Money Made of Tin." *Coins* (October): 66–68.

Boles, Joann. 1981. "The Navajo Rug at the Hubbell Trading Post, 1880–1920." *American Indian Culture and Research Journal* 5(1): 47–63.

———. 1977. "The Development of the Navajo Rug, 1890–1920, as Influenced by Trader J. L. Hubbell." Ph.D. dissertation, Ohio State University.

Bonar, E. 1996. *Woven by the Grandmothers.* Washington, D.C.: Smithsonian Institution Press.

Bonar, E., D. Y. Begay, and K. Ash-Milby. 1996. "Woven by the Grandmothers." *Native Peoples Magazine* 9(4): 36–42.

Bourdieu, Pierre. 1977. *Outline of a Theory of Practice.* New York: Cambridge University Press.

Bowers, Kendra. 1988. "Current Trends in the Navajo Weaving Market." *Oriental Rug Review* 8(6): 38–40.

Boyce, George. 1942. "Sales and Profits of Navajo Traders." *A Primer of Navajo Economic Problems,* fig. 22. USDI, Office of Indian Affairs, Navajo Service, Window Rock.

Boyd, Dennis. 1979. "Trading and Weaving: An American/Navajo Symbiosis." M.A. thesis, Northwestern University.

Brody, J. J. 1976. *Between Traditions: Navajo Weaving toward the End of the Nineteenth Century.* Iowa City: University of Iowa Museum of Art.

Brugge, David. 1996. Telephone conversation, December.

———. 1993. *Hubbell Trading Post National Historic Site.* Tucson: Southwest Parks and Monuments Association.

———. 1985. *Navajo in the Catholic Church Records of New Mexico, 1694–1875.* Tsaile, Ariz.: Navajo Community College Press.

———. 1983. "Navajo Prehistory and History to 1850." *Handbook of North American Indians,* vol. 10, *Southwest.* Alfonso Ortiz, ed., 489–501. Washington, D.C.: Smithsonian Institution Press.

———. 1971. "The Call of the Plateau." *Plateau Sciences Society* 10: 3. Window Rock.

Brugge, David and Charlotte Frisbie. 1982. *Navajo Religion and Culture: Selected Views.* Museum of New Mexico Papers in Anthropology, no. 17. Santa Fe: Museum of New Mexico Press.

Bunzel, Ruth. [1929] 1982. "The Personal Element in Design (Pueblo)." Reprinted in *Native North American Art History: Selected Readings*. Zena Pearlstone Matthews and Aldona Jonaitis, eds., 179–206. Palo Alto, Calif.: Peek Publications.

Burden, John. 1972. Letter to Senator Barry Goldwater 3/7/72. RG 435, CMNAAC general correspondence, 1936–1975. National Archives.

Chronis, P. 1990. "Pagosa Art Dealer Arrested." Denver *Post,* April 7:1A, 18A.

Clark, Jackson. 1993. *The Owl in Monument Canyon.* Salt Lake City: University of Utah Press.

Clifford, James. 1997. *Routes: Travel and Translation in the Late Twentieth Century.* Cambridge, Mass.: Harvard University Press.

———. 1988. *The Predicament of Culture.* Cambridge, Mass.: Harvard University Press.

———. 1986. Writing Culture. The Poetics and Politics of Ethnography. Berkeley: University of California Press.

Coe, Ralph T. 1986. *Lost and Found Traditions.* Seattle: University of Washington Press.

Cohen, Jeffrey. 1998. "Craft Production and the Challenge of the Global Market: An Artisans' Cooperative in Oaxaca, Mexico." *Human Organization* 57(1): 74–82.

———. 1990. "Markets, Museums and Modes of Production: Economic Strategies in Two Zapotec Weaving Communities of Oaxaca, Mexico." *Society for Economic Anthropology Newsletter* 9(2): 12–27.

Collier, John. 1962. *On the Gleaming Way: Navajos, Eastern Pueblos, Zunis, Hopis, Apaches, and Their Land; and Their Meanings to the World.* Denver: Sage Books.

Colton, Mary Russell F. 1932. "Wool for Our Weavers: What Shall It Be?" *Museum Notes* 4(12): 1–5.

Conner, Debbie. 1991. "An Ethnography of the Crownpoint Navajo Rug Auction." M.A. thesis, New Mexico State University, Las Cruces.

Coolidge, Dane and Mary R. Coolidge. 1930. *The Navajo Indians.* Boston: Houghton Mifflin.

———. 1924. *Lorenzo the Magnificent.* Los Angeles: Southwest Press.

Coombe, Rosemary. 1991. "Encountering the Postmodern: New Directions in Cultural Anthropology." *Canadian Review of Sociology and Anthropology* 28(2): 188–205.

Cotton, Clinton. 1926. "The Use of Blankets as Home Decoration." Gallup. Copy at Special Collections Library, University of Arizona.

———. 1896. *Indian Traders' Supplies and Navajo Blankets.* Denver: Williamson Haffner.

Crane, Leo. [1925] 1972. *Indians of the Enchanted Desert: An Account of the Navajo and Hopi Indians and the Keams Canyon Agency.* Glorieta, N.Mex.: Rio Grande Press.

Dary, David. 1986. *Entrepreneurs of the Old West.* New York: Alfred A. Knopf.

Day, Sam. Papers. Cline Library, Northern Arizona University, Flagstaff.

Dedera, Don. [1975] 1990. *Navajo Rugs: How to Find, Evaluate, Buy and Care for Them.* Flagstaff, Ariz.: Northland Press.

Dilworth, Leah. 1996. *Imagining Indians in the Southwest: Persistent Visions of a Primitive Past.* Washington, D.C.: Smithsonian Institution Press.

Dockstader, Frederick J. 1987a. *Song of the Loom.* New York: Hudson Hills Press.

———. 1987b. "Tradition Updated." *American Craft* 47(4): 39–44.

———. 1978. *Weaving Arts of the North American Indian.* New York: Thomas Y. Crowell.

———. 1976. "The Marketing of Southwestern Indian textiles." In *Ethnographic Textiles of the Western Hemisphere: Irene Emery Roundtable on Museum Textiles, 1976 Proceedings.* Irene Emery and Patricia Fiske, 467–76. Washington, D.C.: Textile Museum.

Doerfler, Susan. 1987. "Navajo Weavers Are Tailoring Tradition." *Indian Trader* 18(1): 6–7.

———. 1986. "Contemporary Navajo Weaving." *Arizona Republic.* 10/26: S-35.

Dominguez, Virginia. 1986. "The Marketing of Heritage." *American Ethnologist* 3(3): 546–55.

Downer, Alan. 1990. "Life on the Reservation and Historic Preservation." In *Preservation* on the Reservation. A. L. Klesert and Alan S. Downer, eds. Papers in Anthropology No. 26, 201–6. Window Rock: Navajo Nation.

Downs, James F. 1964. *Animal Husbandry in Navajo Society and Culture*. University of California Publications in Anthropology, vol. 1. Berkeley: University of California Press.

Drooker, Penelope. 1998. *Makers and Markets: The Wright Collection of Twentieth-Century Native Art*. Cambridge, Mass.: Peabody Museum at Harvard.

Duclos, A. F. 1925. Report to the Commissioner of Indian Affairs. Copy in McNitt Papers, Box 8.

Durham, Jimmie. 1992. "Geronimo!" In *Partial Recall*. Lucy Lippard, ed., 54–58. New York: New Press.

Dutton, Bertha. 1983. "Commerce on a New Frontier: The Fred Harvey Company and the Fred Harvey Fine Arts Collection." In *Colonial Frontiers: Art and Life in Spanish New Mexico, the Fred Harvey Company Collection*. Christine Mather, ed., 91–109. Museum of International Folk Art. Santa Fe: Ancient City Press.

———. 1975. *Navajo Weaving Today*. Santa Fe: Museum of New Mexico Press.

Duus, Gloria. 1987. "Navajo Weavers' and Wool Growers' Market Study." Window Rock, Ariz.: Office of Navajo Women and Families. Copy in author's possession.

Dyk, Walter, ed. [1938] 1967. *Son of Old Man Hat: A Navajo Autobiography*. Lincoln: University of Nebraska Press.

Edholm, Felicity, O. Harris, and K. Young. 1977. "Conceptualizing Women." *Critique of Anthropology* 9–10: 101–30.

Ehlers, Tracy Bachrach. 1990. *Silent Looms: Women and Production in a Guatemalan Town*. Boulder, Colo.: Westview Press.

Elder, Jane and David Weber. 1996. *Trading in Santa Fe*. Dallas: De Golyer Library.

Ellis, Florence H. 1974. "An Anthropological Study of the Navajo Indians." In *Navajo Indians I*. David Horr, ed., 27–571. American Indian Ethnohistory Series, Indians of the Southwest. New York: Garland Press.

Emmanuel, Lita. 1980. "Santa Fe Seminar Celebrates Navajo Weaving." *Indian Trader* (June): 32–33.

Etienne, Mona. 1980. "Women and Men, Cloth and Colonization: The Transformation of Production-Distribution Relations among the Baule (Ivory Coast)." In *Women and Colonization*. M. Etienne and E. Leacock, eds., 214–38. New York: Praeger.

Fairbank, Nathaniel. 1934. "Handcraft." Federal Emergency Relief Administration, Division of Self-Help Cooperatives. Mimeo. RG 435 Miscellaneous Files 1930–1935. National Archives, Washington, D.C.

Fane, Diane. 1991. *Objects of Myth and Memory: American Indian Art at the Brooklyn Museum*. Seattle: University of Washington Press.

Farella, John. 1984. *The Main Stalk: A Synthesis of Navajo Philosophy*. Tucson: University of Arizona Press.

Faris, James. 1996. *Navajo and Photography: A Critical History of the Representation of an American People*. Albuquerque: University of New Mexico Press.

———. 1993. "Taking Navajo Truths Seriously: Consequences of the Accretion of Disbelief." *Papers from the Third, Fourth, and Sixth Navajo Studies Conferences*, 181–86. Window Rock: Navajo Nation Historic Preservation Department.

———. 1990. *The Nightway: A History, and a History of Documentation of a Navajo Ceremonial*. Albuquerque: University of New Mexico Press.

———. 1988. "ART/artifact": On the Museum and Anthropology." *Current Anthropology* 29(5): 775–79.

———. 1986. "Visual Rhetoric: Navajo Art & Curing." *Medical Heritage* (spring): 136–47.

Faunce, Hilda. [1928] 1981. *Desert Wife*. Lincoln: University of Nebraska Press

Ford, Richard. 1983. "Inter-Indian Exchange in the Southwest." *Handbook of North American Indians*, vol. 10, *Southwest*. Alfonso Ortiz, ed., 711–22. Washington, D.C.: Smithsonian Institution Press.

Foster, Hal. 1985. "The Primitive Unconscious in Modern Art." *October* 34: 45–70.

Franciscan Fathers. 1910. *An Ethnologic Dictionary of the Navajo Language*. St. Michaels, Ariz.

Franciscan Missionary Fathers. 1935. *The Franciscans Present Navajo Crafts*. St. Michaels, Ariz.

Francisconi, Michael. 1998. *Kinship, Capitalism, Change: The Informal Economy of the Navajo, 1868–1995*. New York: Garland.

Frazier, Lessie Jo. 1993. "Genre, Methodology and Feminist Practice. Gladys Reichard's Ethnographic Voice." *Critique of Anthropology* 13(4): 363–78.

Frisbie, Charlotte. 1987. *Navajo Medicine Bundles or Jish: Acquisition, Transmission and Disposition in the Past and Present*. Albuquerque: University of New Mexico Press.

———. 1982. "Traditional Navajo Women: Ethnographic and Life History Portrayals." *American Indian Quarterly* 6(1–2): 11–33.

———. 1967. *Kinaaldá: A Study of the Navajo Girl's Puberty Ceremony*. Middletown, Conn.: Wesleyan University Press.

Fryer, E. R. 1939. "The Navajo Agency Report of 1939–1940." Copy in Hubbell Papers, Box 527.

Gallagher, Marsha. 1981. "The Weaver and the Wool: The Process of Navajo Weaving." *Plateau* 52(4): 22–27.

Garaway, Philip. 1991. "Collecting Native Southwestern Antiques." *Indian Trader* 22(10): 10.

Garland, Hamlin. 1976. *Hamlin Garland's Observations on the American Indian, 1895–1905*. L. E. Underhill and Daniel Littlefield Jr., eds. Tucson: University of Arizona Press.

Gilbreath, Kent. 1973. *Red Capitalism: An Analysis of the Navajo Economy*. Norman: University of Oklahoma Press.

Gill, Sam. 1981. *Sacred Words: A Study of Navajo Religion and Prayer*. Westport, Conn.: Greenwood Press.

———. 1979. *Songs of Life: An Introduction to Navajo Religious Culture*. Leiden: E. J. Brill.

Gillmor, Francis and Louisa Wade Wetherill. 1953. *Traders to the Navajo*. Albuquerque: University of New Mexico Press.

Goin, Chelsea Miller. 1994. "Design Origins: The Influence of Oriental Rugs on Navajo Weaving." *Fibrearts* 20(4): 43–49.

Goodman, James. 1982. *The Navajo Atlas*. Norman: University of Oklahoma Press.

Goody, Jack. 1977. *The Domestication of the Savage Mind*. Cambridge: Cambridge University Press.

Gordon, Deborah. 1993. "Among Women: Gender and Ethnographic Authority of the Southwest, 1930–1980. *Hidden Scholars: Women Anthropologists and Native American Southwest*. Nancy Parezo, ed., 129–45. Albuquerque: University of New Mexico Press.

Gregg, Josiah. [1844] 1954. *Commerce of the Prairies: or, the Journal of a Santa Fe Trader, During Eight Expeditions Across the Great Western Prairies, and a Residence of Nearly Nine Years in Northern Mexico*. 2 vols. Norman: University of Oklahoma Press.

Griffin-Pierce, Trudi. 1992. *Earth Is My Mother, Sky Is My Father: Space, Time, and Astronomy in Navajo Sandpainting*. Albuquerque: University of New Mexico Press.

Grimes, Kimberly and B. Lynne Milgram. 2000. *Artisans and Cooperatives: Developing Alternative Trade for the Global Economy*. Tucson: University of Arizona Press.

Haile, Father Berard. 1968. *Property Concepts of the Navajo Indians*. Anthropological Series 17. Washington, D.C.: Catholic University of America.

Hall, Ed. 1994. *West of the Thirties*. New York: Doubleday.

Hall, Thomas D. 1989. *Social Change in the Southwest, 1350–1880*. Lawrence: University Press of Kansas.

Hamamsy, Laila S. 1957. "The Role of Women in a Changing Navajo Society." *American Anthropologist* 59(1): 101–11.

Handler, Richard. 1993. "An Anthropological Definition of the Museum and Its Purpose." *Museum Anthropology* 17(1): 33–36.

———. 1992. "On the Valuing of Museum Objects." *Museum Anthropology* 16(1): 21–28.

Hannon, Kerry. 1999. "A Bull Market in Navajo Rugs." *Business Week Investor*, July 12, 1999: 152–53.

Harries-Jones, Peter. 1995. *Gregory Bateson: A Recursive Vision and Ecological Understanding*. Toronto: University of Toronto Press.

———. 1993. "Affirmative Theory: Reflections on the ASA Decennial—The Oxford Conference." Report to Graduate Students, Dept. of Social Anthropology, York University. Paper in author's files.

Harris, Olivia. 1981. "Households as Natural Units." In *Of Marriage and the Market: Women's Subordination Internationally and Its Lessons*. Kate Young et al., eds., 136–56. London: Routledge.

Hartsock, Nancy C. 1983. "The Feminist Standpoint: Developing the Ground for a Specifically Feminist Historical Materialism." In *Discovering Reality*. Sandra Harding and M. Hintikka, eds., 283–310. Boston: D. Reidel.

Harvey, Byron. 1963. "The Fred Harvey Collection, 1889–1963." *Plateau* 35(2): 33–53.

Fred Harvey Company Rug Ledgers, 1900–1946. Heard Museum, Phoenix, and the Museum of International Folk Art, Santa Fe.

Fred Harvey Fine Arts Collection. 1976. Exhibition catalog. Heard Museum, Phoenix.

Harvey Papers. Business documents and personal correspondence (1896–1945). Special Collections Library, University of Arizona, Tucson.

Hastings, Julia. 1994. "Specialist Weaves New Life into Navajo Rugs, Blankets." *Arizona Daily Sun*, December 27: 1, 12.

Hedlund, Ann Lane. 1997. *Navajo Weavings from the Andy Williams Collection*. St. Louis: St. Louis Art Museum.

———. 1994a. "Speaking *For* or *About* Others: Evolving Ethnological Perspectives." *Museum Anthropology* 18(3): 32–43.

———. 1994b. "Thoughts That Count: Contemporary Navajo Weaving." *Plateau* 65(1). Flagstaff: Museum of Northern Arizona.

———. 1992. *Reflections of the Weaver's World: The Gloria F. Ross Collection*. Denver: Denver Art Museum.

———. 1990. *Beyond the Loom: Keys to Understanding Early Southwestern Weaving*. Boulder, Colo.: Johnson Books.

———. 1989a. "In Pursuit of Style: Kate Peck Kent and Navajo Aesthetics. The Legacy of Kate Peck Kent." *Museum Anthropology* 13(2): 23–28.

———. 1989b. "The Study of Nineteenth-Century Southwestern Textiles." In *Perspectives on Anthropological Collections from the American Southwest*. Proceedings of a Symposium Anthropology Research Papers, no. 40., 121–38. Phoenix: Arizona State University.

———. 1988. "Designing among the Navajo: Ethnoaesthetics in Weaving." In *Textiles as Primary Sources*. Proceedings of the First Symposium of the Textile Society of America, 86–93. St. Paul, Minn.: Minneapolis Institute of Art.

———. 1986. "Contemporary Navajo Weaving." *Weaver's Journal* 11(1)41: 30–34.

———. 1983. "Navajo Weaving: The Ethnography of a Craft." Ph.D. dissertation, University of Colorado.

Hegemann, Elizabeth C. 1963. *Navajo Trading Days*. Albuquerque: University of New Mexico Press.

Hill, W. W. 1948. "Navajo Trading and Trading Ritual: A Study of Cultural Dynamics." *Southwestern Journal of Anthropology* 4(4): 371–96.

Hogan, Linda. 1992. "The Columbus Debate." *Elle* (October): 90–94.

Hogg, John Edwin. 1930. "Fifty Years an Indian Trader." [Biography of Lorenzo Hubbell.] In *Touring Topics*, 24–29, 51.

Hooker, Kathy. 1991. *Time among the Navajo*. Santa Fe: Museum of New Mexico Press.

Houlihan, Patrick. 1987. "Where Lifeways Endure." In *Harmony by Hand: Art of the Southwest Indians*, 9–20. San Francisco: Chronicle Books.

Howard, Kathy. 1999. "Weaving a Legend: Elle of Ganado Promotes the Indian Southwest." *New Mexico Historical Review* (April): 127–53.

Hudson, Kenneth. 1991. "How Misleading Does an Ethnographical Museum Have to Be?" In *Exhibiting Cultures: the Poetics and Politics of Museum Display*. Ivan Karp and Steven Lavine, eds., 457–64. Washington, D.C.: Smithsonian Institution Press.

Lorenzo Hubbell Papers. Documents, personal correspondence, journals, ledgers, and day books, 1865–1965. Special Collections Library, University of Arizona.

Hurtado, Albert and Peter Iverson. 1994. *Major Problems in American Indian History*. Lexington, Mass.: D. C. Heath.

Indian Arts and Crafts Board. 1956. "Navajo Indian Rugs: An Information Pamphlet." Copy at Museum of Northern Arizona Library.

Indian Print Shop. 1907. *Navajo Blankets; Other Indian Handiwork*. Chilocco, Okla.: Indian Print Shop.

Indian Trader. 1980–2001. Monthly newspaper. Martin Link, ed. Gallup, N.Mex.

Iverson, Peter. 1987. "Continuity and Change in Navajo Culture: A Review Essay." *New Mexico Historical Review* 62(2): 191–200.

———. 1981. *The Navajo Nation*. Westport, Conn.: Greenwood Press.

Jacobs, Margaret. 1998. "Shaping a New Way: White Women and the Movement to Promote Pueblo Indian Arts and Crafts, 1900–1935." *Journal of the Southwest* 40(2): 187–215.

James, George Wharton. [1914] 1974. *Indian Blankets and Their Makers*. New York: Dover.

———. 1917. *Arizona, the Wonderland*. Boston: Page Company.

James, H. L. [1976] 1988. *Rugs and Posts: The Story of Navajo Rugs and Their Homes*. Tucson: Southwest Parks and Monuments Association.

Janus, Stephen. 1916. Report to Commissioner of Indian Affairs from Leupp Jurisdiction. Copy in D. Parman Papers, Newberry Library, Chicago.

———. 1915. Report to Commissioner of Indian Affairs from Leupp Jurisdiction. Copy in D. Parman Papers, Newberry Library, Chicago.

Jensen, Joan. 1994. "Native American Women and Agriculture: A Seneca Case Study." In *Unequal Sisters: A Multicultural Reader in U.S. Women's History*. V. Ruiz and E. C. DuBois, eds., 70–84. 2d ed. New York: Routledge.

Jett, Stephen. 1993. "Oriental Carpets and the 'Storm Pattern' Navajo Rug Designs." In *Why Museums Collect: Papers in Honor of Joe Ben Wheat*. Meliha Duran and D. Kirkpatrick, eds., 103–25. Albuquerque: Archaeological Society of New Mexico.

———. 1990. "Culture and Tourism in Navajo Country." *Journal of Cultural Geography* 11(1): 85–107.

Johnson, Harmer. 2000. "Auction Block." *American Indian Art Magazine* 26(1): 20–25.

———. 1984. "Auction Block." *American Indian Art Magazine* 9(2): 17–18.

Johnston, Denis. 1966. *An Analysis of the Sources of Information on the Population of the Navajo*. Smithsonian Institution Bulletin, no. 197. Washington, D.C.

Jones, Marianne. 1994. "Guud San Glans:." In *Robert Davidson: Eagle of the Dawn*. Ian Thom, ed., 125–30. Vancouver: Vancouver Art Gallery in association with Douglas MacIntyre, Vancouver.

Jones, Marilyn. 1994. "Making a Difference: We Each Have Our Part to Play." *Taos Magazine* (August): 20–22.

Jorgensen, Joseph A. 1978. "A Century of the Political-Economic Effects on American Indian Society." *Journal of Ethnic Studies* 6(3): 1–82.

Kahlenberg, Mary Hunt and Tony Berlant. 1972. *The Navajo Blanket*. New York: Praeger.

Kant, Immanuel. 1951. *The Critique of Judgement*. New York: Hafner.

Kapoun, Robert. 1992. *The Language of the Robe*. Salt Lake City: Peregrine Smith.

Kaufman, Alice and Christopher Selser. 1985. *The Navajo Weaving Tradition 1650 to the Present*. New York: E. P. Dutton.

Keams, Kally. 1996. "Beeldléí Bäh Häné (The Blanket Story)". In *Woven by the Grandmothers*. Eulalie Bonar, ed., 43–46. Washington, D.C.: Smithsonian Institution Press.

Keeney, Bradford. 1983. *Aesthetics of Change*. New York: Guilford Press.

Kehoe, Alice. 1983. "The Shackles of Tradition." In *The Hidden Half*, 53–76. Lanham, Md.: University Press of America.

Kelley, Klara B. 1986. *Navajo Land Use: an Ethnoarchaeological Study*. Orlando, Fla.: Academic Press.

———. 1985. "Ethnoarchaeology of Navajo Trading Posts." *Kiva* 51(1): 19–37.

———. 1980. "Navajo Political Economy before Fort Sumner." In *The Versatility of Kinship*. Linda Cordell and Stephen Beckerman, eds., 307–32. New York: Academic Press.

———. 1976. "Dendritic Central Place Systems and the Regional Organization of Navajo Trading Posts. In *Regional Analysis I. Economic Systems*. Carol Smith, ed., 219–54. New York: Academic Press.

Kelley, Klara B. and Harris Francis. 1994. *Navajo Sacred Places*. Bloomington: Indiana University Press.

Kelley, Klara B. and Peter Whiteley. 1989. *Navajoland: Family, Settlement and Land Use*. Tsaile, Ariz.: Navajo Community College Press.

Kelly, Dan. 1972. *The Buffalo Head: A Century of Mercantile Pioneering in the Southwest*. Santa Fe, N.Mex.: Vegara Press.

Kelly, Lawrence C. 1968. *The Navajo Indians and Federal Indian Policy, 1900–1935*. Tucson: University of Arizona Press.

Kent, Kate Peck. 1985. *Navajo Weaving: Three Centuries of Change*. Santa Fe, N.Mex.: School of American Research Press.

———. 1981. "From Blanket to Rug: The Evolution of Navajo Weaving After 1880." *Plateau* 52(4): 10–21.

———. 1976. "Pueblo and Navajo Weaving Traditions and the Western World." In *Ethnic and Tourist Arts*. Nelson H. Graburn, ed., 85–101. Berkeley: University of California Press.

Klein, Kathryn. 1997. *The Unbroken Thread: Conserving the Textile Traditions of Oaxaca*. Los Angeles: Getty Conservation Institute.

Kluckhohn, Clyde, W. W. Hill, and Lucy W. Kluckhohn. 1971. *Navajo Material Culture*. Cambridge, Mass.: Harvard University Press.

Kluckhohn, Clyde and Dorothea Leighton. 1974. *The Navajo*. Cambridge, Mass.: Harvard University Press.

Kramer, Hilton. 1972. "How 'Primitive' Is the Folk Art of the Navajos?" *New York Times*, October 8: 27.

Krech, Shepard. 1994. "Museums, Voices, Representations." *Museum Anthropology* 18(3): 3–8.

Kroeber, Alfred. [1909] 1982. "California Basketry and the Pomo." In *Native North American Art History, Selected Readings*. Zena Pearlstone Matthews and Aldona Jonaitis, eds., 157–66. Palo Alto, Calif.: Peek.

Krug, J. A. 1948. "Report on the Navajo; Long Range Program of Navajo Rehabilitation." U.S. Department of the Interior. Mimeo.

Kwok, Abraham. 1989. "Efforts Planned to Promote Navajo Rugs." *Indian Trader* 20(12): 23–24.

Ladd, John. 1957. *The Structure of a Moral Code: A Philosophical Analysis of Ethical Discourse Applied to the Ethics of the Navajo Indians*. Cambridge, Mass.: Harvard University Press.

LaFarge, Oliver. 1936. Letter to John Collier, 4/20/36. RG 435 Correspondence re: misrepresentation of Native American arts and Crafts 1932–80. CMNAAC. National Archives, Washington, D.C.

Lamphere, Louise. 1992a. "Gladys Reichard among the Navajo." *Frontiers* 12(3): 79–116.
———. 1992b. "Women, Anthropology, Tourism and the Southwest." *Frontiers* 12(3): 5–12.
———. 1989. "Historical and Regional Variability of Navajo Women's Roles." *Journal of Anthropological Research* 45(4): 431–56.
———. 1977. *To Run after Them: Cultural and Social Bases of Cooperation in a Navajo Community.* Tucson: University of Arizona Press.
———. 1976. "The Internal Colonization of the Navajo People." *Southwest Economy and Society* 1(1): 6–14.
Laut, Agnes. 1915. *Through Our Unknown Southwest.* New York: McBride, Nast & Co.
Leach, Edmund. 1976. *Culture and Communication: The Logic by Which Symbols Are Connected.* Cambridge: Cambridge University Press.
Leacock, Eleanor and Mona Etienne, eds. 1980. *Women and Colonization.* New York: Praeger.
Leafdale, Keith. 1974. "Weaving . . . Alive and Well." *Arizona Highways* 50(7): 29.
Lears, T. Jackson. 1981. *No Place of Grace: Antimodernism and the Transformation of American Culture, 1880–1920.* New York: Pantheon Books.
Leighton, Alexander H. and Dorothea Cross Leighton. 1944. *The Navajo Door: An Introduction to Navajo Life.* Cambridge, Mass.: Harvard University Press.
Leighton, Willard. 1958. Interview with Frank McNitt, Box 10, June 25. McNitt Papers, New Mexico State Archives, Santa Fe.
Leupp, Francis E. 1925. *The Indian and His Problem.* New York: Charles Scribner and Sons.
Lévi-Strauss, Claude. 1963. *Structural Anthropology.* New York: Basic Books.
Levy, Jerrold. 1998. *In the Beginning: The Navajo Genesis.* Berkeley: University of California Press.
Limerick, Patricia. 1987. *The Legacy of Conquest: The Unbroken Past of the American West.* New York: Norton.
Lippard, Lucy. 1984. *Get the Message? Activist Essays on Art and Politics.* New York: Dutton.
Lipps, Oscar. 1906. "The Evolution of the Navajo and His Blanket." *Southern Workman* 35(1): 14–24.
Littlefield, Alice and Martha Knack, eds. 1996. *Native Americans and Wage Labor.* Norman: University of Oklahoma Press.
Lockwood, Frank. 1929. *The Life of Edward Ayer.* Chicago: McClurg.
Lummis, Charles. 1925. *Mesa, Canon and Pueblo: Our Wonderland of the Southwest.* New York: Century Co.
Lundburg, Lea. 1981. "Threads of Tradition." *Arizona Living* 12(19): 16–18.
Luomala, Katharine. 1938. "Navajo Life of Yesterday and Today." U.S. Department of Interior, National Park Service, Berkeley, Calif.
Lyon, William H. 1989. "Gladys Reichard at the Frontiers of Navajo Culture." *American Indian Quarterly* 13(2): 137–63.
MacCannell, Dean. 1994. "Traditions' Next Step." In *Discovered Country.* Scott Norris, ed., 161–79. Albuquerque: Stone Ladder Press.
M'Closkey, Kathleen A. 1996a. "Art or Craft? The Paradox of the Pangnirtung Weave Shop." In *Women of the First Nations: Power, Wisdom and Strength.* Christine Miller and Patricia Chuchryk, eds., 113–26. Winnipeg: University of Manitoba Press.
———. 1996b. "Myths, Markets and Metaphors: Navajo Weaving as Commodity and Communicative Form." Ph.D. dissertation, York University, Toronto.
———. 1994. "Marketing Multiple Myths: The Hidden History of Navajo Weaving." *Journal of the Southwest* 36(3): 185–220.
———. 1985. "The Institutionalization of Art within Two Internal Colonies: A Comparative Study of the Inuit and the Navajo." M.A. thesis, University of Windsor.
Malone, Bill. 1997. Telephone conversation.
Matthews, Washington [1884] 1968. *Navajo Weavers.* Palmer Lake, Colo.: Filter Press.

Maxwell, Gilbert S. [1963] 1984. *Navajo Rugs: Past, Present and Future*. Palm Desert, Calif.: Desert Southwest Publications.

McAllester, David. 1980. "Shootingway, an Epic Drama of the Navajos." *Southwestern Indian Ritual Drama*. Charlotte Frisbie, ed., 199–237. Albuquerque: University of New Mexico Press.

McCarty, T. L. 1983. *Of Mother Earth, Father Sky*. Chinle, Ariz.: Rough Rock Press.

McCloskey, Joanne. 1999. "Family Dynamics in Three Generations of Navajo Women." *Diné Baa Hané Bi Naaltsoos*. Collected Papers from the Seventh thorough Tenth Navajo Studies Conferences. June-el Piper, ed., 139–46. Window Rock, Ariz.: Navajo Nation Historic Preservation Department.

McCoy, Ron. 1995. "Legal Briefs." *American Indian Art Magazine* (spring): 33.

———. 1989. "Legal Briefs." *Indian Trader* (September): 5–6.

McMaster, Gerald. 1989. "Tenuous Lines of Descent: Indian Arts and Crafts of the Reservation Period." *Canadian Journal of Native Studies* 9(2): 205–36.

McNeley, Grace. 1987. "Home: A Family of Land and People." *Diné Be'iina': A Journal of Navajo Life* 1(1): 161–64. Shiprock: Navajo Community College Press.

McNitt, Frank. 1972. *Navajo Wars: Military Campaigns, Slave Raids, and Reprisals*. Albuquerque: University of New Mexico Press.

———. 1962. *The Indian Traders*. Norman: University of Oklahoma Press.

McNitt Papers. New Mexico State Archives, Santa Fe.

McPherson, Robert. 1992a. "*Naalyéhé Bá Hooghan*—House of Merchandise": The Navajo Trading Post as an Institution of Culture Change, 1900 to 1930." *American Indian Culture and Research Journal* 16:(1): 23–43.

———. 1992b. *Sacred Land, Sacred View*. Salt Lake City: Brigham Young University Press.

Means, Russell. 1988. "On Mother Earth: an Interview." Annette Jaimes, ed. *Bloomsbury Review* (September–October): 25–26.

Meriam Report. 1971. *The Problem of Indian Administration*. New York: Johnson Reprint Corp.

Meyer, Karl. 1973. *The Plundered Past*. New York: Atheneum.

Miele, Frank. 1989. *Eye Dazzlers: Navajo Weaving and Contemporary Counterparts*. New York: Hirschl and Adler Folk Gallery.

Mies, Maria. 1988. *Women: The Last Colony*. London: Zed Books.

———. 1982. *The Lace Makers of Narsapur: Indian Housewives Produce for the World Market*. London: Zed Press.

Miller, Daniel. 1987. *Material Culture and Mass Consumption*. Oxford: Blackwell.

Miller, Layne. 2001. "Visiting the Medicine Man Gallery website." *Indian Trader* 32(3): 5–7.

Mitchell, Daniel H. 1972. "An Indian Trader's Plea for Justice, 1906." *New Mexico Historical Review* 47: 238–48.

Mitchell, Rose and Charlotte Frisbie, eds. 2001. *Tall Woman: The Life Story of Rose Mitchell a Navajo Woman, 1874–1977*. Albuquerque: University of New Mexico Press.

Montgomery, Beverly. 1982. "Navajo Blankets and Rugs." *Collector-Investor* (March): 22–27.

Moore, Edgar. 1979. "The Hubbell Trading Post at Ganado, Arizona, 1878–1900: Foundation of a Frontier Enterprise." Great Lakes Historical Conference.

Moore, Henrietta. 1988. *Feminism and Anthropology*. London: Polity.

Moore, J. B. [1911] 1987. *Collection of Catalogues Published at Crystal Trading Post, 1903 and 1911*. Albuquerque: Avanyu Press.

———. 1910. "Navajo Indian Industries and Art." *Red Man* 2: 99–103.

———. 1909. "How Shall We Aid the Navajo?" *Indian Craftsman* 1(4): 29–38.

Mott, Dorothy. 1931. "Don Lorenzo Hubbell of Ganado." *Arizona Historical Review* 4(1): 45–51.

Muhlert, Jan K. 1976. "Foreword." *In Between Traditions: Navajo Weaving toward the End of the Nineteenth Century*. Iowa City: University of Iowa Museum of Art.

Mullin, Molly. 2001. Culture in the Marketplace. Durham, N.C.: Duke University Press.

Nash, June. 1993. *Crafts in the World Market: the Impact of Global Exchange on Middle American Artisans*. New York: State University of New York Press.

Nestor, Sarah. 1987. "The Woven Spirit." In *Harmony by Hand: Art of the Southwest Indians*. Patrick Houlihan, ed., 51–58. San Francisco: Chronicle Books.

Newcomb, Franc. 1966. *Navajo Neighbors*. Norman: University of Oklahoma Press.

———. 1957. Interview with Frank McNitt. McNitt Papers, Box 10.

O'Bryan, Aileen. 1956. "The Diné Origin Myths of the Navajo Indians." *Bureau of American Ethnology Bulletin 163*. Washington, D.C.

O'Neill, Colleen. 1999. "The 'Making' of the Navajo Worker: Navajo Households, the Bureau of Indian Affairs, and Off-Reservation Wage Work, 1948–1960." *New Mexico Historical Review* 74(4): 375–405.

Oriental Rug Review. 1988. Vol. 8(6). Special Issue on Navajo Weaving.

Ortiz, Alfonso. 1996. "American Indian Religious Freedom." *Cultural Survival* 19(4): 26–29.

Ortiz, David. 1999. "Road Project Ethnography: The Role of the Anthropologist and the Cultural Specialist." In *Diné Baa Hané Bi Naaltsoos*, 51–62. Window Rock, Ariz.: Navajo Nation Historic Preservation Department.

Parezo, Nancy. 1990. "A Multitude of Markets." *Journal of the Southwest* 32(4): 563–75.

———. 1986. "Now Is the Time to Collect." *Masterkey* 59(4): 11–18.

Parish, William J. 1961. *The Charles Ilfeld Company: A Study of the Rise and Decline of Mercantile Capitalism in New Mexico*. Cambridge, Mass.: Harvard University Press.

Parker, Rozika and Griselda Pollock. 1981. *Old Mistresses: Women, Art and Ideology*. New York: Pantheon Books.

Parman, Donald L. 1976. *The Navajo and the New Deal*. Yale Western American Series 27. New Haven: Yale University Press.

———. 1998. Papers deposited at the Newberry Library, Chicago.

Pearson, Bill. 1997. "A Personal Introduction." In *Navajo Weavings from the Andy Williams Collection*, 6–7. St. Louis: St. Louis Art Museum.

Penney, David. 1988. "Reflections on the Task Force." *Museum Anthropology* 16(2): 6–11.

Peterson, Charles S. 1993. "Headgates and Conquest: The Limits of Irrigation on the Navajo Reservation, 1880–1950." *New Mexico Historical Review* 68(3): 269–90.

———. 1989. "Big House at Ganado." *Journal of Arizona History* 30(1): 51–72.

———. 1986. "Homestead and Farm: A History of Farming at the Hubbell Trading Post National Historic Site." Tucson: Southwest Parks and Monuments Association.

Phillips, Ruth. 1998. *Trading Identities: The Souvenir in Native North American Art from the Northeast, 1700–1900*. Montreal: McGill-Queens University Press.

———. 1994. "Fielding Culture: Dialogues between Art History and Anthropology." *Museum Anthropology* 18(1): 39–46.

Phillips, Ruth and Christopher Steiner, eds. 1999. *Unpacking Culture: Art and Commodity in Colonial and Postcolonial Worlds*. Berkeley: University of California Press.

Pomeroy, Ralph. 1974. "Navajo Abstraction." *Art and Artist Magazine*: 9(7) 30–35.

Price, Sally. 1989. *Primitive Art in Civilized Places*. Chicago: University of Chicago Press.

Pyne, Lynn. 1987. "Weavers Art Is Never Stronger." *Indian Trader* 18(4): 14–16, 20.

Rappaport, Roy. 1999. *Ritual and Religion in the Making of Humanity*. Cambridge: Cambridge University Press.

Record Group 435. CMNAAC. General Correspondence, 1936–75. National Archives, Washington, D.C.

Redfield, Robert. 1971. "Art and Icon." In *Anthropology and Art*. Charlotte Otten, ed., 39–65. Austin: University of Texas Press.

Reeve, Frank D. 1964. "The Sheep Industry, 1906." *New Mexico Historical Review* 39(2): 111–56.

Reichard, Gladys. [1934] 1974. *Spider Woman*. New York: Macmillan.

———. [1939] 1971. *Dezba, Woman of the Desert*. Glorieta, N.Mex.: Rio Grande Press.

———. [1928] 1969. *Social Life of the Navajo Indians*. New York: AMS Press.

————. [1936] 1968. *Navajo Shepherd and Weaver*. Glorieta, N.Mex.: Rio Grande Press.

————. 1944. *Prayer, the Compulsive Word*. Seattle: University of Washington Press.

————. 1950. *Navajo Religion: A Study in Symbolism*. Bollingen Series, no. 18. New York: Pantheon.

Reif, Rita. 1983. "Navajo Weavings Are Choice Collectors' Items." *New York Times*, October 9: H35.

Reinhart, Theodore. 1999. "The Trader and Navajo Culture Change." In *Diné Baa Hané Bi Naaltsoos*. Collected Papers from the Seventh thorough Tenth Navajo Studies Conferences. June-el Piper, ed., 97–104. Window Rock: Navajo Nation Historic Preservation Department.

Reno, Dawn. 1988. *American Indian Collectibles: Official Identification and Price Guide*. New York: House of Collectibles, Division of Random House.

Richardson, Gladwell. 1986. *Navajo Traders*. Philip R. Rulon, ed. Tucson: University of Arizona Press.

Roberts, Willow. 1987. *Stokes Carson: Twentieth-Century Trading on the Navajo Reservation*. Albuquerque: University of New Mexico Press.

Rodee, Marian. 1990. "The Oriental Connection: Caucasian Rug Influence on Navajo Weaving." *Oriental Rug Review* 10(2): 15–17.

————. 1987. *Weaving of the Southwest*. West Chester, Pa.: Schiffer.

————. 1981. *Old Navajo Rugs: Their Development from 1900 to 1940*. Albuquerque: University of New Mexico Press.

Roessel, Robert. 1983a. *Navajo Arts and Crafts*. Rough Rock, Navajo Nation, Ariz.: Navajo Curriculum Center, Rough Rock Demonstration School.

————. 1983b. "Navajo History, 1850–1923." In *Handbook of North American Indians*, vol. 10, *Southwest*. Alfonso Ortiz, ed., 506–23. Washington, D.C.: Smithsonian Institution Press.

————. 1980. *Pictorial History of the Navajo from 1860 to 1910*. Rough Rock, Navajo Nation, Ariz.: Navajo Curriculum Center, Rough Rock Demonstration School.

Roessel, Ruth. 1994. "Navajo Weaving since the Sixties." Conference presentation. Heard Museum, Phoenix. March.

————. 1983. "Navajo Arts and Crafts." In *Handbook of North American Indians*, vol. 10, *Southwest*. Alfonso Ortiz, ed., 592–604. Washington, D.C.: Smithsonian Institution Press.

————. 1981. *Women in Navajo Society*. Rough Rock, Navajo Nation, Ariz.: Navajo Resource Center, Rough Rock Demonstration School.

————. 1974. *Navajo Livestock Reduction: A National Disgrace*. Tsaile, Ariz.: Navajo Community College.

Rogers, Susan C. 1978. "Women's Place: A Critical Review of Anthropological Theory." *Comparative Studies in Society and History* 20(1): 123–62.

Rosaldo, Michele Z. 1983. "Moral/Analytical Dilemmas Posed by the Intersection of Feminism and Social Science." In *Social Science as Moral Inquiry*. N. Haan, R. Bellah, P. Rabinow, and W. Sullivan, eds., 76–95. New York: Columbia University Press.

————. 1980. "The Use and Abuse of Anthropology: Reflections on Feminism and Cross-Cultural Understanding." *Signs* 5(3): 389–417.

Rosaldo, Michele Z. and Louise Lamphere. 1974. *Women, Culture and Society*. Stanford: Stanford University Press.

Ruffing, Lorraine Turner. 1979. "Dependence and Underdevelopment." In *Economic Development in American Indian Reservations*. Roxanne D. Ortiz, ed., 91–113. Native American Studies, no. 1. Albuquerque: University of New Mexico Press.

Rug Study Interviews. 1985–86. Hubbell Trading Post, National Historic Site. U.S. National Park Service. Ganado, Ariz.

Russell, Scott. 1999. "Contemporary Navajo Wage Labor and Income Patterns." In *Diné Baa Hané Bi Naaltsoos*. Collected Papers from the Seventh thorough Tenth Navajo Studies Conferences. June-el Piper, ed., 147–56. Window Rock, Ariz.: Navajo Nation Historic Preservation Department.

Sacks, Karen. 1982. *Sisters and Wives: The Past and Future of Sexual Equality*. Urbana: University of Illinois Press.

Satchell, Michael and David Bowermaster. 1994. "The Worst Federal Agency." *U.S. News and World Report*, November 28: 61–64.

Schevill, Margot, Janet Berlo, and Edward Dwyer, eds. 1991. *Textile Traditions of Mesoamerica and the Andes: An Anthology*. New York: Garland.

———. 1986. *Costume as Communication: Studies in Anthropology and Material Culture*. Vol. 4. Bristol, R.I.: Haffenreffer Museum of Anthropology, Brown University.

Schmedding, Joseph. [1951] 1974. *Cowboy and Indian Trader*. Albuquerque: University of New Mexico Press.

Schoepfle, G. Mark, K. Nabahe, A. Johnson, and L. Upshaw. 1988. "The Effects of the Great Stock Reduction on the Navajos." *Diné Be'iina* 1(2): 58–83.

Schrader, Robert F. 1983. *The Indian Arts and Crafts Board*. Albuquerque: University of New Mexico Press.

Schumacher, E. F. 1974. *Small Is Beautiful*. London: Sphere Books.

Schwarz, Maureen. 1997. *Molded in the Image of Changing Woman*. Tucson: University of Arizona Press.

———. 1993. "Traditional Navajo Female Attire." In *Papers from the Third, Fourth and Sixth Navajo Studies Conferences*, 355–78. Window Rock: Navajo Nation Historic Preservation Department.

Sells, Cato. 1913. Annual Report of the Commissioner of Indian Affairs. Washington, D.C.

Sheridan, Tom. 1994. "The Other Arizona." *Journal of the Southwest* 36(3): 255–86.

Shiffman, John. 1998. "Indian Art: Buyer Beware, Artisans Pay Price of Counterfeiting." *USA Today* (April 8, 1998): 1–2A.

Simmons, Katina and Carol Stout. 1976. "East Meets West." *New Mexico Magazine* 54(February): 50–52.

Smith, Dean. 1989. *Brothers Five: The Babbitts of Arizona*. Tempe: Arizona Historical Foundation.

Smith, Laurence. 1989. *Artlist: North American Indian Arts, an Index of Prices and Auctions, 1985, 1986, 1987*. Albuquerque: Artlist.

Sotheby's Great Sales, 1987–1988. 1989. London: Barrie and Jenkins.

Southwest Indian Foundation. 2000. Sales catalog.

Spencer, Ann. 1989. "A Museum Curator's View: The Legacy of Kate Peck Kent." *Museum Anthropology* 13(2): 7–8.

Spencer, Katherine. 1957. *Mythology and Values: An Analysis of Navajo Chantway Myths*. Philadelphia: American Folklore Society.

———. 1947. *Reflections of Social Life in Navajo Origin Myth*. University of New Mexico Publications in Anthropology 3. Albuquerque: University of New Mexico Press.

Spicer, Edward H. 1962. *Cycles of Conquest: The Impact of Spain, Mexico, and the United States on the Indians of the Southwest, 1533–1960*. Tucson: University of Arizona Press.

———. 1952. "Sheepmen and Technicians." In *Human Problems in Technological Change, a Casebook*, 185–207. New York: Russell Sage Foundation.

Spiegelberg, Abe. 1904. "Navajo Blankets." *Out West Magazine* 20(5): 447–49.

Stamp, Patricia. 1989. *Technology, Gender and Power in Africa*. Technical Study 63e. Ottawa: International Development Research Centre.

Stanton, Andra. 1999. "Woven by History." *Native Peoples* 13(1):38–42.

Steadman, William E. 1974. "Navajo Blankets from the Collection of Anthony Berlant." Tucson: University of Arizona Museum of Art.

Steere, Peter. 1992. Personal conversation, August.

Stephen, Lynn. 1993. "Weaving in the Fast Lane: Class, Ethnicity and Gender in Zapotec Craft Commercialization." In *Crafts in the World Market*. June Nash, ed., 25–57. New York: State University of New York Press.

———. 1991a. "Export Markets and Their Effects on Indigenous Craft Production: The Case of the Weavers of Teotitlan del Valle, Mexico." In *Textile Traditions in*

Mesoamerica and the Andes. Margot Blum Schevill, Janet Berlo, and Edward Dwyer, eds., 381–99. New York: Garland.
———. 1991b. *Zapotec Women.* Austin: University of Texas Press.
———. 1991c. "Culture as a Resource: Four Cases of Self-Managed Indigenous Craft Producers in Latin America." *Economic Development and Culture Change* 40(1): 101–30.
———. 1989. "Anthropology and the Politics of Facts, Knowledge and History." *Dialectical Anthropology* 14: 259–69.
Stewart, Irene. 1980. *A Voice in Her Tribe: A Navajo Woman's Own Story.* Socorro, N.Mex.: Ballena Press.
Swagerty, J. 1988. "Indian Trade in the Trans-Mississippi West to 1870." In *Handbook of North American Indians,* vol. 4, *History of Indian-White Relations.* Alfonso Ortiz, ed., 351–57. Washington, D.C.: Smithsonian Institution Press.
The Systems Thinker. 1994. Vol. 5(10). Cambridge, Mass.: Pegasus Communications.
Tabaha, Kathleen. 1999. "Diné Interpretations of Navajo Rug Styles." In *Diné Baa Hané Bi Naaltsoos.* Collected Papers from the Seventh through Tenth Navajo Studies Conferences. June-el Piper, ed., 11–19. Window Rock, Ariz.: Navajo Nation Historic Preservation Department.
Tanner, Clara Lee. 1968. *Southwest Indian Craft Arts.* Tucson: University of Arizona Press.
Terrell, John U. 1967. *Traders of the Western Morning: Aboriginal Commerce in Pre-Columbian North America.* Los Angeles: Southwest Museum.
Thomas, Diane. 1978. *The Southwestern Indian Detours: The Story of the Fred Harvey/Santa Fe Railway Experiment in "Detourism."* Phoenix: Hunter.
Thomas, Wesley. 1996. "Shił Yóól T'ool: Personification of Navajo Weaving." In *Woven by the Grandmothers.* Eulalie Bonar, ed., 33–42. Washington, D.C.: Smithsonian Institution Press.
———. 1994. Conference presentation. "Navajo Weaving since the Sixties." Heard Museum, Phoenix.
Thompson, Gerald. 1976. *The Army and the Navajo: The Bosque Redondo Reservation Experiment, 1863–1868.* Tucson: University of Arizona Press.
Tice, Karin. 1995. *Kuna Crafts: Gender and Global Economy.* Austin: University of Texas Press.
Todd, Loretta. 1990. "Notes on Appropriation." *Parallellogramme* 16(1): 24–32.
Toelken, Barry. 1976. "A Circular World: The Vision of Navajo Crafts." *Parabola* 1: 30–37.
Trafzer, Clifford. 1973. "Anglos among the Navajo: The Day Family." In *The Changing Ways of Southwest Indians.* A. H. Schroeder, ed., 259–74. Glorieta, N.Mex.: Rio Grande Press.
Trevathan, Buzz. 1997. "Contemporary Navajo Weaving: A Collector's Guide." *Indian Artist* (fall): 32–37.
Turner, Victor. 1975. "Symbolic Studies." *Annual Review of Anthropology* 4: 145–61.
———. 1967. *The Forest of Symbols.* Ithaca: Cornell University Press.
Turton, Alison, ed. 1991. *Managing Business Archives.* Oxford: Butterworth.
Underhill, Ruth. [1956] 1983. *The Navajo.* Norman: University of Oklahoma Press.
U.S. Federal Trade Commission. 1973. *The Trading Post System on the Navajo Reservation: Staff Report to the Federal Trade Commission.* June. Washington, D.C.: Government Printing Office.
U.S. Government. Annual Reports from the Commissioner of Indian Affairs [RCIA]. National Archives, Washington, D.C.
———. Superintendents' Annual Narrative and Statistical Reports. [Eight Navajo Agencies], 1910–35. National Archives, Washington, D.C.
Utley, Robert M. 1961. "The Reservation Trader in Navajo History." *El Palacio* 68: 10–35.
———. 1959. "Special Report on Hubbell Papers/Trading Post. Ganado, Arizona." U.S. Department of the Interior. National Park Service, Santa Fe, N.Mex.

Van Valkenburgh, Richard F. and John McPhee. 1974. *A Short History of the Navajo People*. New York: Garland.

Vastokas, Joan. 1992. *Beyond the Artifact: Native Art as Performance*. Robarts Centre for Canadian Studies. Peterborough, Ont.: Porcupine's Quill.

Vogt, Evon. 1961. "The Navajo." In *Perspectives in American Indian Culture Change*. E. H. Spicer, ed. 278–336. Chicago: University of Chicago Press.

Volk, Robert W. 1988. "Barter, Blankets and Bracelets: The Role of the Trader in the Navajo Textile and Silverwork Industries, 1868–1930." *American Indian Culture and Research Journal* 12(4): 39–63.

Wade, Edwin L. 1985. "The Ethnic Art Market in the American Southwest 1880–1980." In *Objects and Others: Essay on Museums and Material Culture*. George Stocking, ed., 167–91. Madison: University of Wisconsin Press.

Walters, Anna Lee. 1993. "Introduction." In *Women of the Native Struggle*. Ronnie Farley, ed. New York: Orion Books.

———. 1992. *The Sacred: Ways of Knowledge, Sources of Life*. Peggy V. Beck, Anna Lee Walters, and Nia Francisco, eds. Tsaile, Ariz.: Navajo Community College Press.

———. 1989. *The Spirit of Native America*. Del Mar, Calif.: McQuiston and Partners.

Washburn, Dorothy. 2000. "Perceptual Anthropology: The Cultural Salience of Symmetry." *American Anthropologist* 101(3): 547–62.

———. 1993. "Structural Analysis of Design on Navajo Sarapes from the Nineteenth Century." In *Why Museums Collect: Papers in Honor of Joe Ben Wheat*. Meliha Duran and D. Kirkpatrick, eds., 225–38. Albuquerque: Archaeological Society of New Mexico.

Watson, Editha. 1957. "Navajo Rugs." *Arizona Highways* (August): 16–25.

Weigle, Marta. 1989. "From Desert to Disney World: The Santa Fe Railway and the Fred Harvey Company Display the Indian Southwest." *Journal of Anthropological Research* 45(1): 115–37.

Weigle, Marta and Barbara Babcock, eds. 1996. *The Great Southwest of the Fred Harvey Company and the Santa Fe Railway*. Tucson: University of Arizona Press.

Weiner, Annette and Jane Schneider. 1991. *Cloth and the Human Experience*. Washington, D.C.: Smithsonian Institution Press.

Weiss, Lawrence. 1984. *The Development of Capitalism in the Navajo Nation: a Political Economy History*. Studies in Marxism, vol. 15. Minneapolis: MEP Publications.

Wheat, Joe Ben. 1996. "Navajo Blankets." In *Woven by the Grandmothers*. Eulalie Bonar, ed., 69–85. Washington, D.C.: Smithsonian Institution Press.

———. 1990. "Introduction." In *Beyond the Loom: Keys to Understanding Early Southwestern Weaving*. Ann Lane Hedlund, ed. Boulder, Colo.: Johnson Books.

———. 1989. "Discussion." The Legacy of Kate Peck Kent. *Museum Anthropology* 13(2): 29–30.

———. 1988. "Early Trade and Commerce in Southwestern Textiles Before the Curio Shop." *Reflections: Papers of the Archaeological Society of New Mexico* 14: 57–72. Santa Fe, N.Mex.: Ancient City Press.

———. 1984. *The Gift of Spiderwoman: Southwestern Textiles, the Navajo Tradition*. Philadelphia: University Museum, University of Pennsylvania.

———. 1981. "Early Navajo Weaving." *Plateau* 52(4): 2–9.

———. 1977. "Documentary Basis for Material Changes and Design Styles in Navajo Blanket Weaving." In *Ethnographic Textiles of the Western Hemisphere: Irene Emery Roundtable on Museum Textiles, 1976 Proceedings*. Irene Emery and Patricia Fiske, 420–40. Washington, D.C.: Textile Museum.

———. 1976a. "The Navajo Chief Blankets." *American Indian Art* 1(3): 44–56.

———. 1976b. "Spanish-American and Navajo Weaving, 1600 to Now." In *Collected Papers in Honor of Marjorie F. Lambert*. Papers of the Archaeological Society of New Mexico 3:199–223.

———. 1974. *"Navajo Blankets" from the Collection of Anthony Berlant*. Tucson: University of Arizona Museum of Art.

Wheeler, Marilyn. 1990. "Pendleton Has Indian Blanket Trade All Sewn Up." *Indian Trader* 21(3): 27–28.

White, Richard. 1991. *"It's Your Misfortune and None of My Own": A New History of the American West*. Norman: University of Oklahoma Press.

———. 1983. *The Roots of Dependency: Subsistence, Environment, and Social Change among the Choctaws, Pawnees, and Navajos*. Lincoln: University of Nebraska Press.

White, Richard and William Cronon. 1983. "Ecological Change and Indian and White Relations." In *Handbook of North American Indians*, vol. 10, *Southwest*. Alfonso Ortiz, ed., 417–29. Washington, D.C.: Smithsonian Institution Press.

Whiteford, Andrew H. 1989. "Discussion." The Legacy of Kate Peck Kent. *Museum Anthropology* 13(2): 31–33.

Whittaker, Kathleen. 1998. *Common Threads: Pueblo and Navajo Textiles in the Southwest Museum*. Los Angeles: Southwest Museum.

Wilden, Anthony. 1987. *Rules Are No Game: The Strategy of Communications*. London: Routledge.

———. 1982. "Postscript to 'Semiotics as Praxis: Strategy and Tactics.'" *Semiotic Inquiry* 2: 166–70.

———. 1981. "Semiotics and Praxis: Strategy and Tactics." *Semiotic Inquiry* 1: 1–34.

———. 1980. *System and Structure: Essays in Communication and Exchange*. London: Tavistock.

Wilkins, Teresa. 1999. "The Creation of a Useable Past." In *Diné Baa Hané Bi Naaltsoos. Collected Papers from the Seventh thorough Tenth Navajo Studies Conferences*. June-el Piper, ed., 203–10. Window Rock, Ariz.: Navajo Nation Historic Preservation Department.

Williams, Lester L. 1989. *C. N. Cotton and His Navajo Blankets*. Albuquerque: Avanyu.

Willink, Roseanne and Paul Zolbrod. 1996. *Weaving a World: Textiles and the Navajo Way of Seeing*. Santa Fe, N.Mex.: Museum of New Mexico Press.

Winter, Joseph. 1993. "Navajo Sacred Sites and the Transwestern Pipeline Expansion Project." In *Papers from the Third, Fourth, and Sixth Navajo Studies Conferences*, 65–109. Window Rock, Ariz.: Navajo Nation Historic Preservation Department.

Wistisen, M. And Annette Larsen. 1975. *A Study to Identify Potentially Feasible Small Businesses for the Navajo Nation: Phase II*. Provo: Center for Business and Economic Research, Brigham Young University. 11 vols.

Witherspoon, Gary. 1987. "Navajo Weaving: Art in Its Cultural Context." MNA Research Paper, no. 36. Flagstaff: Museum of Northern Arizona.

———. 1983a. "Language and Reality in the Navajo World View." In *Handbook of North American Indians*, vol. 10, *Southwest*. Alfonso Ortiz, ed., 570–78. Washington, D.C.: Smithsonian Institution Press.

———. 1983b. "Navajo Social Organization." In *Handbook of North American Indians*, vol. 10, *Southwest*. Alfonso Ortiz, ed., 524–35. Washington, D.C.: Smithsonian Institution Press.

———. 1981. "Self-Esteem and Self-Expression in Navajo Weaving." *Plateau* 52(4): 28–32.

———. 1977. *Language and Art in the Navajo Universe*. Ann Arbor: University of Michigan Press.

———. 1975. *Navajo Kinship and Marriage*. Midway Reprint. Chicago: University of Chicago Press.

———. 1974. "The Central Concepts of Navajo World View. (I)." *Linguistics* 119(January): 41–59.

Witherspoon, Gary and Glen Peterson. 1995. *Dynamic Symmetry and Holistic Asymmetry*. New York: Peter Lang.

Woodman, Nancy. [1954] 1980. "The Story of an Orphan." In *The South Corner of Time*, 77–88. Tucson: Sun Tracks.

Worth, Sol and John Adair. 1972. *Through Navajo Eyes: An Exploration in Films Communication and Anthropology*. Bloomington: Indiana University Press.

Wright, Chester. 1910. *Wool Growing and the Tariff: A Study in the Economic History of the United States.* Cambridge, Mass.: Harvard Economic Studies.

Wyman, Leland. 1983. "Navajo Ceremonial System." In *Handbook of North American Indians,* vol. 10, *Southwest.* Alfonso Ortiz, ed., 536–57. Washington, D.C.: Smithsonian Institution Press.

———. 1970. *Blessingway.* Tucson: University of Arizona Press.

Young, Etta Gifford. 1914. "The Weavers." *Arizona Magazine,* pp. 4, 15.

Youngblood, B. 1935. "Navajo Trading." A Report to the Office of Experiment Stations, U.S. Department of Agriculture. Mimeo. HP Box 527 #4.

Zimmerman, Chanda, ed. N.d. "Carl Steckel, Early Day Trader to the Navajo." MS Copy at Cline Library Special Collections, Northern Arizona University, Flagstaff.

Zolbrod, Paul. 1997. "Benally Women, Three Generations of Navajo Weavers." *Indian Artist* (fall): 42–45.

———. 1984. *Diné Bahané: The Navajo Creation Story.* Albuquerque: University of New Mexico Press.

Index